NEVER COME TO PEACE AGAIN

Campaigns and Commanders

CAMPAIGNS AND COMMANDERS

GENERAL EDITOR

Gregory J. W. Urwin, *Temple University, Philadelphia, Pennsylvania*

ADVISORY BOARD

Lawrence E. Babits, *East Carolina University, Greenville*
James C. Bradford, *Texas A&M University, College Station*
Robert M. Epstein, *U.S. Army School of Advanced Military Studies, Fort Leavenworth, Kansas*
David M. Glantz, *Carlisle, Pennsylvania*
Jerome A. Greene, *National Park Service*
Victor Davis Hanson, *California State University, Fresno*
Herman Hattaway, *University of Missouri, Kansas City*
Eugenia C. Kiesling, *U.S. Military Academy, West Point, New York*
Timothy K. Nenninger, *National Archives, Washington, D.C.*
Bruce Vandervort, *Virginia Military Institute, Lexington*

NEVER COME TO PEACE AGAIN

Pontiac's Uprising and the Fate of the British Empire in North America

David Dixon

UNIVERSITY OF OKLAHOMA PRESS : NORMAN

ALSO BY DAVID DIXON

Hero of Beecher Island: The Life and Military Career of George A. Forsyth
(Lincoln, 1994)

Never Come to Peace Again: Pontiac's Uprising and the Fate of the British Empire in North America is Volume 7 in the Campaigns and Commanders series.

Library of Congress Cataloging-in-Publication Data

Dixon, David, 1954–
    Never come to peace again : Pontiac's uprising and the fate of the British empire in North America / David Dixon.
        p.   cm. — (Campaigns and commanders; v. 7)
    Includes bibliographical references and index.
    ISBN 0-8061-3656-1 (alk. paper)
    1. Pontiac's Conspiracy, 1763–1765. I. Title. II. Series.

    E83.76.D595 2005
    973.2'7—dc22
                                                            2004057999

1   2   3   4   5   6   7   8   9   10

CONTENTS

ILLUSTRATIONS

PREFACE

The idea for this book evolved over the years while I was teaching the Pennsylvania history course at Slippery Rock University. Students began this class with many preconceived notions about the commonwealth's contribution to early America. They knew, of course, about William Penn's "holy experiment" and that our founding fathers gathered in Philadelphia to sign the Declaration of Independence and the Constitution of the United States. They had great difficulty, however, in conceptualizing Pennsylvania's pervasive role in the coming of the American Revolution. For them, revolutionary origins could be found only in Massachusetts. After all, they argued, this is what they had been taught throughout elementary and high school. They were all familiar with the Boston Massacre, the Boston Tea Party, Paul Revere's ride, and the battles of Lexington and Concord. Yet none of them were aware of revolutionary agitation deep in the backcountry of Pennsylvania.

I was quick to point out to the students that New England was not the only region where revolutionary sentiment percolated. Many were surprised to learn that the first shots fired in anger against British soldiers took place at Fort Loudon, on the Pennsylvania frontier, in 1765—not at Lexington Green in 1775. They were equally shocked to learn that, like Boston, Pittsburgh had its own tea party and that the Westmoreland County committee, meeting in a log courthouse, adopted resolutions remarkably similar to language used in the Declaration of Independence, a full year before that document was adopted by the Second Continental Congress. Many of these same men were among the first to join George Washington's Continental Army that assembled near Boston in 1775.

What motivations, the students asked, possessed their frontier ancestors to take up the cause of independence? Surely these rough-hewn frontier folk could not have been prompted by issues related to trade and taxation? They lived far removed from the bustling commercial centers of the American seaboard in communities where the price of paint and tea meant nothing. My student's bewilderment set me on the path to uncover these motivations.

It became apparent from the beginning that, as my students suspected, backcountry residents gave little concern to issues that affected the distant eastern seaboard communities. Their agricultural produce and livestock was, for the most part, consumed by a domestic market. They were, however, stirred to agitation by questions over land acquisition and Indian policy. During the French and Indian War, their farms and families had been ravaged by roving war parties that laid waste most of the interior of the colony. When the French threat was finally removed, these pioneers believed it was safe to return to their homes and start to rebuild their lives. Then, in 1763, another terrible Indian war erupted that once again took its toll in lives and property. This conflict, later known as Pontiac's Uprising, convinced the frontier settlers that their government could not manage Indian affairs and cared little for their welfare. This line of inquiry led me to take a closer look at Pontiac's War.

A cursory investigation of the historical literature concerning this Indian conflict proved unsatisfactory. Most of the earliest accounts mimicked the narrative written by the great romantic historian Francis Parkman, entitled *The Conspiracy of Pontiac and the Indian War after the Conquest of Canada* (1851). Despite its biased and racist approach, this book remained the standard reference on the subject for nearly a century.[1] In 1946 Howard Peckham published *Pontiac and the Indian Uprising*, which offered a strong corrective to Parkman's earlier views. While Peckham's account provided a great deal of new information and was far more balanced in its perspective, his decision to once again emphasize the role of Pontiac and events at Detroit produced a monograph that cast little new light on the broad causes, conduct, and consequences of the war.[2]

In the past forty years, many other historians have taken up the challenge of exploring the relationship between Europeans and native peoples in early America and, in doing so, have continually exposed Francis Parkman's flawed research and racist approach.[3] Many of these insightful studies are largely interpretive, however, and examine broad themes in which the 1763 conflict plays only a small role. In addition, each of these works is more concerned with viewing events from the much needed Indian perspective than with shedding light on British and American military, political, and social experiences.[4] Other recent studies that do probe English and American perspectives are once again interpretive in scope and do not focus on Pontiac's War in any great detail.[5]

After a thorough review of the topical literature dealing with this period, I became convinced that it was time to reexamine Pontiac's Uprising, drawing on interpretations of Indian cultural history and the mountain of primary source material that have surfaced since both Parkman and Peckham wrote their histories. In recounting the narrative of this horrific confrontation that erupted on the frontiers of North America following the Seven Years' War, I hope to offer readers new insight into the causes and important consequences of that war.

To gain a clear understanding of the events that brought on Pontiac's Indian uprising, one must look beyond Detroit to the inflamed Upper Ohio River Valley. For several generations this volatile region had been the center of a complex web of competing interests between tribes, colonies, and empires. This cauldron of adverse interests in the Ohio Country produced the French and Indian War, a conflict that assumed global proportions. The war's aftermath did little to eliminate the region's intense rivalries, and native inhabitants soon discovered that they had simply replaced one master for another. In addition, Indian experiences during the Seven Years' War had given birth to new and invigorated spiritual movements that hinged on recognition of their distinctiveness from the Europeans, particularly the English. Within this framework can be found the roots of Pontiac's War.

The conflict itself reveals the special social, political, and economic problems that Great Britain faced in administering its new, expanded empire. In the aftermath of their attempts to conquer France's overseas empire, the English quickly discovered that they could not even defeat a handful of what they considered inferior people living in that empire's far reaches. This should have provided British officials with a valuable lesson.

Instead of restoring peace to the frontier, Britain's policies and actions served only to propel its colonial subjects to revolutionary agitation. Frustrated by their government's inability to contend with the Indians, backcountry settlers concluded that the best way to insure security was to rely on their own devices. No longer were they willing to depend on an insensitive government in Philadelphia or a monarch three thousand miles away in England. While their urban neighbors along the seaboard fumed over taxation measures such as the Stamp Act and Townshend Duties, frontier folk were more exasperated over land issues and Indian affairs. In the end, the backwoodsman joined with the laborer to form the nucleus of George Washington's Continental Army. Pontiac's Uprising helped forge this crucible of interests between urban and frontier patriots. The conflict should thus be viewed as far more than a bloody interlude situated between Great Britain's two great global wars in the eighteenth century. It was, in fact, the bridge that linked these two bitter encounters.

At this point I should explain some nomenclature. Despite the debate over Pontiac's individual role, I have chosen to call this conflict Pontiac's War or Pontiac's Uprising. While it is quite certain that the war was too complex to be ascribed to any one individual, for better or worse, this is how it is recognized by most people. I suppose this underscores Francis Parkman's lasting impact on history. In regard to identifying Native American peoples, I use the terms "tribe" and "nation" interchangeably. I trust we have moved beyond construing the word "tribe" as pejorative, just as we have learned that the word "Indian" need not bear a negative connotation. I have also chosen to use the words "frontier," "backcountry," "wilderness," and "hinterland" to define the same geographical space. In a strict, technical sense the land beyond European settlement cannot be accurately construed as a frontier because it was already inhabited by large native populations.

Again, my use of the word "frontier" should not be construed as an attempt in any way to denigrate Indian inhabitants. The term is simply used in a traditional fashion to designate a region that is distinct from the areas of early America more densely settled by Europeans.

I have intentionally made no attempt to edit material quoted from primary sources. While readers will often find the language of the eighteenth century both strange and vexing, it adds a rich texture to the narrative. Occasionally, I have inserted clarifying words in brackets.

Lastly, I beg the reader to be indulgent through the relation of numerous horrific atrocities perpetrated by both sides during the conflict. It was not my intention to sensationalize such events. By all accounts, Pontiac's War was unprecedented for its awful violence, as both sides seemed intoxicated with genocidal fanaticism. There can be little doubt that the English and their Indian adversaries both indulged in unspeakable deeds as forms of terror and vengeance. Therefore, I hope that the discussion of these events will be viewed as an attempt to communicate the growing sense of desperation and hatred that both sides manifested.

Acknowledgments

I began my research on Pontiac's Uprising in typical fashion by reading both classic accounts and the most recent monographs concerning the period. In doing so I found a group of scholars who continue to push the boundaries of our understanding of the Native peoples of early North America. I am grateful, therefore, for the efforts of historians such as Richard White, Daniel Richter, Francis Jennings, Michael McConnell, and Gregory Dowd. In addition, Colin Calloway provided special encouragement at a time when I considered abandoning the project.

I conducted a considerable amount of research at the William L. Clements Library at the University of Michigan and the David Library of the American Revolution in Washington Crossing, Pennsylvania. At the David Library, Director David Fowler demonstrated his mastery of the voluminous Amherst Papers, and Gregory Knouff, who was serving a stint as a research assistant at the time, offered his insight into the American Revolution in the Pennsylvania backcountry. When I arrived at the Clements Library for the first time, I was interviewed by the director, John Dann. In order to judge my competence to conduct serious research at the library, John asked me only one question: how did Slippery Rock get its name?

Fortunately, I responded with the correct answer. Thereafter, John provided me with many helpful suggestions to guide my research. I also benefited from the extensive knowledge of Brian Dunnigan. I doubt that anyone knows more about the French and Indian War and its aftermath than Brian. His advice and counsel will always be greatly appreciated. Lastly, research at the Clements would have been impossible without the assistance of John Harriman. He knows the collections inside out and directed me to many important sources.

I also visited many regional archives, museums, and libraries. At the Western Pennsylvania Historical Society, research assistant Doug MacGregor helped me locate a number of useful files relating to Fort Pitt and the Battle of Bushy Run. Louis Waddell, who edited the final volume of *The Papers of Henry Bouquet*, guided me through typescripts of the unpublished Bouquet Papers, which are housed at the state archives in Harrisburg. Martin West, executive director of Fort Ligonier and a leading authority on eighteenth-century frontier fortifications, spent many hours with me discussing events and personalities related to Pontiac's War. Shirley Iscrupe, the librarian at Fort Ligonier, also helped me to resolve many vexing questions. Throughout the course of my research, I made frequent trips to Bushy Run Battlefield, where I discussed and debated aspects of the engagement with Jack Giblin, the former director, and David Miller, the education specialist. The Pennsylvania Historical and Museum Commission is truly blessed to have both of these talented individuals in its employ. I am also indebted to the staffs of the Darlington Memorial Library at the University of Pittsburgh and the Cumberland County Historical Society, two repositories containing information that cannot be found elsewhere.

I am also grateful to many individual historians who offered insight and suggestions to improve this study. Scott Stephenson led me to an important letter proving that Henry Bouquet was responsible for the brilliant tactics employed at Bushy Run. Wes Andrews, director of research and archives for the Little Traverse Odawa Nation, shared with me his extensive knowledge about Pontiac. Likewise, I learned a great deal about the Seneca leader Kiasutha from Tom Abler, professor of history at the University of Ontario. Ray Schwick, historian at Blennerhasset Island, provided me with a manuscript copy of Alexander Fraser's journal. Also, I am grateful to

Steve Brumwell who supplied me with the necessary information to locate a copy of Robert Kirk's valuable memoir. In all, it would have been a daunting task for me to complete this work without the gracious assistance of these dedicated professionals.

At the University of Oklahoma Press, I am indebted to Greg Urwin, editor for the *Campaigns and Commanders* series, for his patience and encouragement. He enthusiastically supported this project from its inception and provided invaluable guidance throughout the process. Greg's thorough reading of an earlier draft has made this a much better book. I am also grateful to Chuck Rankin for his suggestions and counsel. I'm sure Chuck thought at times that he would never see the final manuscript.

Closer to home, I would like to thank the administration of Slippery Rock University for providing me with a sabbatical leave to complete the research for this book. My gratitude must also be extended to Kathy Manning at the university library, who patiently allowed me to monopolize the entire collection of books relating to early America.

My wife, Amy, received a crash course in Pontiac's Uprising shortly after we were married. Three days after we returned from our honeymoon, we set out for Ann Arbor on one of my many research trips to the Clements Library. When we arrived, I asked her to go to the Graduate Library and attempt to find a few obscure journal articles while I poured over the Gage Papers. When I emerged from the Clements, Amy was patiently waiting with a huge stack of photocopied material. To my surprise she had easily located the information I requested and a multitude of other rare and valuable sources. It was only then that she demurely informed me that she had served as a research assistant while in graduate school! Throughout this long process, Amy's support, care, and love have never wavered. I owe her everything.

Never Come to Peace Again

1

"Why Do You Come to Fight on Our Land?"

C hristian Frederick Post rode slowly through a torrent of showers to reach his destination at Fort Allen, located along the Lehigh River. He carried with him instructions from William Denny, provincial governor of the colony of Pennsylvania, to meet with the various Indian nations in the Ohio Country and convince them of the English government's desire for peace. It was July 19, 1758, the fourth year of the Great War for Empire between Britain and France, a conflict that had led many of the Native peoples living in the trans-Appalachian frontier to ally themselves with the forces of Louis XV, France's Bourbon ruler. The wilderness struggle had desolated the interior of North America, and Post was resolved to do his part "to restore peace and prosperity to the distressed."[1]

As Post rode on through the downpour, far to the west loomed the dark and imposing slopes of the Appalachian Mountains. Beyond the crest of that seemingly impenetrable barrier lay the Ohio Country, a cauldron of unrest and awful violence.[2] For more than a hundred years the region had been a scene of instability. As early as 1656 the Iroquois had swooped down on the Erie Indians living in this area and all but annihilated them. In an attempt to replenish their dwindling population and establish barriers against encroaching Europeans

Pontiac's

Map 1

90°0'0"W

85°0'0"W

Lake Huron

Fort Michilimackinac

45°0'0"N

Fort Edward
Augustus

Lake Michigan

Bloody Bridge

Fort
St. Joseph

Fort Detroit

Cuyler
Defe.

Fort Sandusky

Maumee

Fort Miami

Wabash

Fort Ouiatenon

Great Miami

Scioto

Pickawillany

40°0'0"N

St. Louis

Cahokia

Fort
De Chartres

Extent of
Map 2

Extent of
Map 1

90°0'0"W

85°0'0"W

Cartographer: Erin Heffron, 2004

Uprising

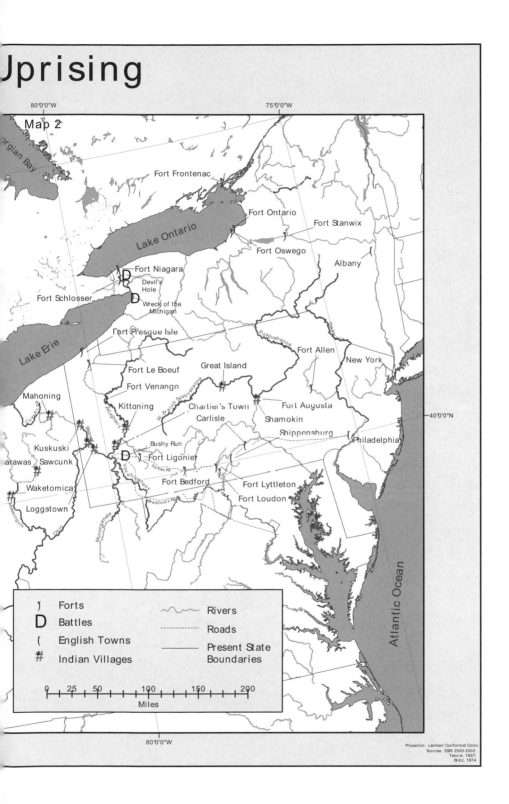

Map 2

80°0'0"W · 75°0'0"W

Fort Frontenac

Fort Ontario

Fort Stanwix

Lake Ontario

Fort Oswego

Albany

Georgian Bay

Fort Niagara

Devil's
Hole

Fort Schlosser

Wreck of the
Michigan

Fort Presque Isle

Lake Erie

Fort Le Boeuf

Great Island

Susquehanna

Fort Allen

New York

Fort Venango

W. Branch Susquehanna

Mahoning

Kittaning

Charlier's Town

Fort Augusta

Allegheny

Carlisle

Shamokin

Shippensburg

40°0'0"N

Kuskuski

Bushy Run

Philadelphia

Sawcunk

Fort Ligonier

Tarawas

Forbes Rd.

Waketomica

Youghiogheny

Fort Bedford

Fort Lyttleton

Braddock's Road

Fort Loudon

Loggstown

Muskingum

Ohio

Monongahela

Atlantic Ocean

)	Forts	～～～	Rivers
D	Battles	- - - -	Roads
(	English Towns	——	Present State
#	Indian Villages		Boundaries

0   25   50   100   150   200
| | | | | | | | | |
Miles

80°0'0"W

Projection: Lambert Conformal Conic
Sources: ESRI 2000-2002;
Tanner, 1987;
Stotz, 1974

and other Indians, the League of Five Nations, as the five tribes of the Iroquois Confederacy were sometimes called, devastated and displaced yet other Indian peoples. Afterward, the Iroquois claimed the Ohio Country as part of their domain, and some members of the confederacy, such as the Senecas, chose to stay in the region. Many Iroquois who decided to remain in the Ohio Country eventually lost the connection with their own tribes and clans and became known as the Mingoes.[3]

Later, as the Europeans became more numerous and began occupying the Delaware River valley in Eastern Pennsylvania, more Indian people moved to the Ohio Country. The Lenapes, known to the English as the Delawares, had vacated most of their land in the East and settled into a new environment in the Susquehanna River valley. From there, small bands and entire villages began to leave the valley and trek across the mountains to join the "people on the other side" in the Allegheny River valley region.[4] This resulted in an effective split between the Susquehanna Delawares and those who had decided to immigrate to the Ohio Country.[5]

Perhaps one of the biggest blows to the Delawares who remained east of the mountains came with the 1737 "Walking Purchase." This land transaction occurred as a result of the Penn family's desire to obtain more property along the upper Delaware River valley. The practice of purchasing land from the Indians had begun with the founder, William Penn, who would then sell the land to prospective European immigrants. When the area around Philadelphia became too congested, the Penn heirs decided to acquire the remaining Delaware land along the river, north of the City of Brotherly Love. To accomplish this task, Thomas Penn instructed his provincial secretary, James Logan, to arrange yet another land purchase from the Delawares. When the Indians refused to sell, Logan requested that the Iroquois intercede and force the remaining Delawares to relocate. The League of Five Nations, interested in furthering its growing ties with the English in Pennsylvania, agreed to assist Logan and sent a delegation to the Delaware villages to compel their removal. Eventually, the land transaction was completed when Englishmen marked off the boundaries by walking along the bank of the Delaware River for a day and a half. This so-called Walking Purchase served to terminate all Indian claims to land in the Delaware River valley. The dispossessed tribespeople, filled with bitterness and resentment toward the English, begrudgingly moved west into the Susquehanna River valley, and some went even further, across the mountains into the Ohio Country.[6]

The Senecas, Mingoes, and Delawares were not the only tribes that occupied the land beyond the Appalachians. Other refugee Indians migrated into the region in the early years of the eighteenth century. The Shawnees, whom other tribes often called "wanderers," once resided in small villages east of the mountains. Like their Delaware neighbors, they moved to the Ohio Country. There they were joined by other Shawnees who came from the south and west. One particular band aligned itself with a mixed-blood French trader named Peter Chartier, who established a trading community along the Allegheny River in 1734. Other Shawnees assembled at villages such as Sewickley Town, near the winding river that the Indians called Youghiogheny, and Keckenepaulin's Town, which was located west of Laurel Ridge at the mouth of what would later be known as Loyalhanna Creek.[7]

Soon other Indian people entered the region. Mahicans came in small numbers from the Hudson River valley, where they had been pushed out by the Dutch and English. Wyandots came from the west and settled near the Delaware village of Kuskuski, along the river, lined with bull thistles, that the Indians called Shenango. Miamis (also known as Twightwees), Neutral Hurons, Piankashaws, Ottawas, and others could be found from time to time in the Ohio Country as they all participated in a lively intertribal trade network. While animosity and suspicion often accompanied the relations between these various peoples, more and more, as Indians entered the region, they learned to coexist. Before long, multitribal communities sprang up along the Ohio, Allegheny, and Monongahela river valleys. In 1748, when the Pennsylvania Indian agent and interpreter Conrad Weiser visited the village of Loggstown, an important trading community along the Ohio River, he found 789 warriors assembled there. These Indians included representatives from the Delawares, Wyandots, Shawnees, Hurons, and Mahicans and from each of the five tribes of the Iroquois Confederacy. During his negotiations with the many nations of Indians present, Weiser noted that they identified themselves as "all one People." In particular,

the Iroquois representatives insisted that they spoke "in behalf of all
the Indians on Ohio."[8]

The Native peoples of the Ohio Country could well manage this
cohabitation as a result of shared experiences, common political
agendas, and similarity in dress, appearance, and material culture.
Peter Williamson, who spent time with the Ohio tribes as a captive,
described their common dress:

> That they in general, wear a white blanket. . . . Their mog-
> ganes [moccasins] are made of Deer Skins, and the best Sort
> have them bound round the Edges with little Beads and Rib-
> bands. On their Legs they wear Pieces of blue Cloth for
> Stockings. . . . Breeches they never wear, but instead thereof,
> two Pieces of Linen, one before and another behind. The bet-
> ter Sort have Shirts of finest Linen they can get, and to those
> some wear Ruffles; but these they never put on till they
> have painted them various Colours, which they get from the
> Pecone Root, and Bark of Trees, and they never pull them off
> to wash, but wear them, till they fall in pieces. They are
> very proud, and take great delight in wearing Trinkets; such
> as Silver Plates round their Wrists and Necks . . . from their
> Ears and Noses they have Rings and Beads, which hang dan-
> gling an Inch or Two. The Men have no Beards, to prevent
> which, they use certain Instruments and Tricks as soon as it
> begins to grow. The Hair of their Heads is managed differ-
> ently, some pluck out and destroy all, except a Lock hanging
> from the Crown of the Head, which they interweave with
> Wampum and Feathers of various Colours.[9]

Similarly, another white captive, John McCullough, described
an Ohio warrior as having an appearance "very terrifying to us."
McCullough later wrote about his encounter with the Indian:

> He had a brown coat on him, no shirt, his breast bare, a
> breech-clout, a pair of leggins and moccasons—his face and
> breast painted rudely with vermillion and verdigrease—a bunch
> of artificial hair, dyed of a crimson color, fixed on the top
> crown of his head, a large triangle piece of silver hanging
> below his nose, that covered almost the whole of his upper
> lip; his ears (which had been cut according to their particular

This late-eighteenth-century image of a Great Lakes warrior adorns a map of the Ohio Country prepared by an unknown French cartographer. Note the scalps dangling from the trade musket that he carries. The original map is in the Bibliotheque Nationale de France, Paris. Courtesy the Rock Foundation, New York.

custom) were stretched out with fine brass wire, made in the form (but much larger) of what is commonly fixed in suspenders, so that, perhaps he appeared something like what you might apprehend to be the likeness of the devil.[10]

Most observers also noted that the Indians of the Ohio Country were adorned with tattoos. Williamson remembered that one "old Indian had his body covered over, from head to foot, with certain hieroglyphics—which they perform by inserting gunpowder, or charcoal, into the skin with the point of a turkey quill, sharpened in the form of a pen, or some other instrument they have for that purpose; which always denotes valor."[11]

Indeed, the various tribes' residence in the Ohio Country—where they shared common land, resources, experiences, and material culture—allowed the various tribes to begin the process of forging a collective identity. They had all arrived on the Allegheny Plateau as refugees of sorts, escaping the press of European colonization or taking advantage of a new land rich in resources. They chiefly desired to recapture their traditional and familiar ways of life and preserve their cultural integrity, which had been threatened by their close proximity to the whites east of the mountains. While the Ohio Indians certainly did not deter the presence of European traders among them, they had no intention of sharing the land with white inhabitants. It is perhaps ironic that their very presence along the waters of the Ohio Country would eventually result in a struggle between France and Great Britain for control and occupation of this coveted region.[12]

It was only natural that when the people of the Northeastern Woodlands began to migrate into the Ohio Valley region, European traders would soon follow. The intercourse that developed between the various Indian nations of the Ohio Country and the British and French traders who converged on them transcended purely economic concerns. The commercial exchange that they conducted helped to open diplomatic discourse, cement alliances, conclude land transactions, and eventually, conduct war. The dynamics that governed the trade supported the Indians' belief that whichever European trading partners offered the finest and least expensive goods represented the nation that was the most attractive friend and ally. Consequently, perceptive Indians frequently attempted to manipulate both European rivals by using trade as a precondition for a positive diplomatic relationship. While Indians commanded some leverage in their trade relationships with whites, their increasing dependence on European goods made it impossible for them to remain neutral in the face of a growing rivalry between England and France.

The merchandise that the English carried across the mountains and the French transported along the lakes and rivers included woolen blankets, linen shirts, looking glasses, beads, copper and tin kettles, combs, bars of lead, hatchets, firearms, and gunpowder. For the most part, early relationships between the traders and Indians were cordial. James Adair, who began to transact business with the various tribes in 1735, commented on this relationship:

> Before the Indians were corrupted by mercenary empirics, their good sense led them to esteem the Traders among them as their second Sun, warming their backs with the British fleeces, and keeping in their candle of life, both by plentiful support and continual protection and safety, from the arms and ammunition which they annually brought them. While the Indians were simple in manner and uncorrupt in morals, the Traders could not be reckoned unhappy, for they were

kindly treated and watchfully guarded by a society of friendly and sagacious people, and possessed all the needful things to make a reasonable life easy. Through all the Indian countries every person lives at his own choice, not being forced in the least degree to anything contrary to his own inclination.[13]

The introduction of rum and other spirits by unscrupulous traders profoundly altered the idyllic nature of the exchange. In a meeting with Pennsylvania officials in 1753, one Iroquois leader complained, "Your Traders now bring scarce anything but Rum and Flour; they bring little Powder and Lead, or other valuable goods. The Rum Ruins us. We beg you would prevent its coming in such quantities by regulating the Traders. . . . These Whiskey Sellers, when they have once got the Indians in Liquor, make them sell their very clothes from their backs. In short, if this practice be continued, we must be inevitably ruined."[14]

Both England and France claimed the prerogative to trade and settle the land beyond the Appalachians. The French "claimed the River Ohio, otherwise called the Beautiful River, and its tributaries . . . by virtue of its discovery by Sieur de la Salle; of the trading posts the French have had there since; and of possession; which is so much the more unquestionable, as it constitutes the most frequent communication from Canada to Louisiana."[15] While La Salle had indeed touched upon the lower Ohio River during his 1682 journey, he certainly had never explored the upper valley region. In La Salle's wake, the French began to establish trading posts in the vicinity of the Great Lakes. In 1691 they constructed Fort Saint Joseph, situated near the southern end of Lake Michigan. A decade later the French soldier Antoine de la Mothe Cadillac established another military post, called Fort Pontchartrain, located along what is now known as the Detroit River. In this area resided the Ottawa, Potawatomie, Chippewa, and Wyandot nations. In 1715 another post, Fort Michilimackinac, helped secure the vital Straits of Mackinac between lakes Michigan and Huron. Two years later the French erected Fort La Baye along the Green Bay in present-day Wisconsin. Like other such establishments, La Baye was occupied by a small militia, fur traders, and Jesuit missionaries intent on converting the Indians. With the Great Lakes in seemingly firm control, the French began to establish other military posts to protect

the access route from Quebec to New Orleans. In 1719 work commenced on Fort Ouiatenon along the banks of the Wabash, a river that
wound its way to the lower Ohio, giving access to the Mississippi.[16]
With the construction of all these posts, France was able to secure
its claims to the Great Lakes, protect the line of communication
between Canada and New Orleans, and establish a viable trade relationship with the Indian inhabitants of the region. As more and more
Indians relocated to the Ohio Country after 1720, the Canadians cast
their eyes toward the possibility of the lucrative trade that might be
fostered there.

In the meantime, the British were also looking across the mountains to the Ohio Country. The Indians of the Great Lakes, attracted
by the higher prices the English paid, had for years smuggled their
furs to Albany traders. One of the provisions of the Treaty of Utrecht,
which ended the European conflict known as the War for the Spanish
Succession in 1713, gave the British and French belligerents equal
access to the American fur trade. From that time on, an intense
rivalry ensued for domination in the industry. By the end of the
1720s, Pennsylvania traders were firmly established in the various
Indian villages along the Allegheny, Monongahela, and Ohio rivers.
Records from the Pennsylvania Assembly indicate that enterprising
men such as James Le Tort, Edmund Cartlidge, and Henry Bailey
were trading among the Delawares, Shawnees, and Mingoes at Loggstown, Kuskuski, and Kittaning in 1727.[17]

Within a few years, the English made serious inroads in breaking
the French monopoly of the fur trade along the trans-Appalachian
frontier. Indians in the Ohio Country and along the Great Lakes
quickly learned that British trade goods were generally better in
quality and cheaper in price. A major turning point in the rivalry
between Britain and France for dominance in the fur trade came
when war once again broke out between the two European powers
in 1744. While fighting in the War for the Austrian Succession was
confined to the European continent and the New England frontier,
the British traders attempted to take advantage of the conflict by
expanding their influence among the western tribes.

That year a recent Irish immigrant named George Croghan purchased £700 in trade goods from Philadelphia merchants and headed
into the frontier. Although generally viewed as a cunning rogue by

many of his business associates, Croghan learned how to conduct himself in the trade, and Ohio Country Indians came to trust and respect him. Croghan's trading activities took him as far west as the Cuyahoga River just south of Lake Erie in the autumn of 1744. Here he exchanged his assortment of trade goods for furs gathered by Seneca tribesmen living in the area. The French commandant at Fort Pontchartrain along the Detroit River, Céloron de Blainville, was greatly alarmed over the presence of English traders on the Cuyahoga. The French urged the Ottawas, Shawnees, and Miamis to drive Croghan and any other Englishmen in the region back across the mountains. Several French envoys arrived at the Seneca village where Croghan operated to claim the Irishman as their prisoner. The Indians, however, refused to give up their new trading partner. Nonetheless, a band of Shawnees managed in the spring of 1745 to confiscate a load of valuable furs that some of Croghan's associates were transporting back east. This incident made it abundantly clear that the French and some of their Indian allies along the Great Lakes were intent on contesting the English presence in the region.[18]

Friction between the French and English traders continued to escalate in 1747, when George Croghan wrote to Pennsylvania's provincial secretary, Richard Peters, insisting that the colony had a "fair Opertunity," with assistance from Iroquois tribesmen living along the Cuyahoga, to "have all the French Cutt off in them parts." The Irishman was certain that "allmost all the Ingans in the Woods, have Declared against ye French" and that presents of powder and lead would help to seal the bond between Pennsylvania and the Ohio Country Indians.[19] To make the point more explicit, Croghan's communication was accompanied by a French scalp lifted by a Seneca warrior near the "fortt which is Called Detroat." In response Peters opened a diplomatic initiative with the Ohio Country people in hopes of encouraging them to push the French out of the coveted lands to the west.

Peters' initiative was fraught with a great deal of uncertainty and danger, however, for it tended to represent a breach in long-standing protocol customary to Indian affairs. In the past, officials from the Quaker colony preferred to treat solely with the League of Five Nations Iroquois from their council fire at Onondaga in New York. The Pennsylvanians had discovered that it was considerably more problematic to deal with local tribes, which often resisted ceding land to the whites. By negotiating with the Onondaga council, the Pennsylvania officials added weight to Iroquois claims of dominance over other tribes and simplified the diplomatic process. This arrangement had been beneficial when Pennsylvania enlisted the aid of the Iroquois to force the Delawares to give up their land during the Walking Purchase of 1737. In the ten years since, however, much had changed. The League of Five Nations now assumed a stance of neutrality in the conflict between the French and British. Consequently, in their efforts to extricate the French from western lands, the Pennsylvanians could not expect support from the New York Iroquois. Peters therefore reasoned that perhaps the Mingoes in the West would assist the English in this task.

In November the Oneida leader Monacatootha, along with a delegation of other Indians from across the mountains, arrived outside Philadelphia to discuss such an alliance against the French. Monacatootha was recognized as a "half-king," or vice regent, sent by the League of Five Nations to supervise the Shawnees living in the Ohio Country. An imposing figure despite his advanced age, the Oneida boasted of having participated in thirty battles, killed seven men, and taken eleven captives during his tenure as a warrior. He had a hatchet symbol engraved on his chest and bows and arrows were tattooed on each side of his face. Monacatootha believed his role was to serve the interests of the Ohio people, despite the fact that those interests could be at odds with the wishes of New York Iroquois. He informed Peters that the Ohio Indians were no longer bound to the dictates of the league council. The Oneida chief said, "The old men at the Fire at Onondaga are unwilling to come into the War so the Young Indians, the Warriors, and Captains consulted together and resolved to take up the English Hatchet against the will of their old People, and to lay their old People aside as of no use but in time of Peace."[20] Clearly, Monacatootha and the other Ohio tribesmen were initiating a new Ohio council, autonomous from the fire at Onondaga. The shared interests and experiences of the Indians who lived in the land beyond the mountains had facilitated the growth of this new alliance. For too long the Indians living along the Ohio and its tributaries had allowed others to dictate their fate. Now they seemed determined to make their own arrangements with the

English. The chiefs asked for powder, lead, and other material support. Richard Peters warmly embraced this Ohio delegation and loaded the Indians down with presents to take back to their villages.[21]

At least one Pennsylvania official was uncomfortable with Peters's new diplomatic initiative with the Mingoes and their allies. Conrad Weiser, a German Palatine who had long served as an interpreter and agent for the colony, was deeply concerned over the possible reaction from the League of Five Nations. Fearful that the council at Onondaga would feel slighted by Pennsylvania's decision to bypass them and negotiate directly with the Ohio Indians, the old interpreter cautioned Peters that they should "move with sure steps." Making his position regarding this new diplomatic practice clear, he flatly stated in his letter to the provincial secretary, "I don't think it proper our Government should Countenance such doings, and I hope the Counsel will not look upon it worthy of their approbation."[22]

On the other hand, George Croghan continued to apply for material support for the Ohio Indians. Undoubtedly, the Irishman realized that with the French removed from Lake Erie, his own trading enterprise would flourish. In September 1747 Croghan sent a letter to Philadelphia merchant Thomas Lawrence that was later read before the governor's council:

> The Ingans att this side of Lake Eary is Makeing warr very Briskly Against the French, Butt is very impatiant To hear from there Brothers, ye English, Expecting a Present of powder & Lead, which if they Don't gett, I am of Opinion, By the Best Accounts I Can gett, That they will Turn to the French, which will be very willing to make up with them again.[23]

Croghan's blandishments outweighed Conrad Weiser's dire warnings, and Secretary Peters decided to continue his diplomatic overtures to the western tribes.

In the meantime the alliance among Ohio Country Indians continued to grow. The Shawnees asked Monacatootha to intercede on their behalf in order to join in the "Chain of Friendship" with Pennsylvania. In addition, an important Piankashaw (Twightwee) chief, Memeskia, whom the French called La Demoiselle, moved his village away from French influence along the Maumee River to a new site at the headwaters of the Miami River called Pickawillany. From here he

urged other tribes south of Lake Erie to join with the English.[24] By
the end of 1747 it appeared that French influence in the West was
waning. The Pennsylvanians had made strong diplomatic overtures to
the Ohio Country Mingoes and their allies. For their part, the Indians
hoped that the English would give them arms and ammunition to
fight the French and drive them from their lands. George Croghan
and other English traders were engaged in lively and profitable commerce with these Indians as far west as the gates of the French fort at
Detroit, and there seemed little that their French rivals could do to
prevent such an exchange. Events were taking shape in the refined
plantations of Virginia, however, that would eventually cause many of
the Native peoples of the Ohio country to rethink their position and
transform the region into a flashpoint that would lead to world war.

Citing their original charter from King James I, Virginians had
always considered the lands drained by the Ohio to be part of their
colony. In November 1747 a group of tidewater land speculators that
included Thomas Lee and Lawrence Washington formed a partnership
called the Ohio Company and petitioned King George II to grant them
title to a half million acres of land "on the branches of the Allagany."
The partners placed their petition in the hands of prominent London
merchant John Hanbury, who had favor with the king. British officials
viewed the Ohio Company project as a way to counteract growing
French influence in the area, and on March 16, 1749, King George
granted the company's petition on condition that one hundred families be settled on the land and a strong fort be built to protect them.
Needless to say, when the Virginians sent the frontiersman Christopher
Gist to explore the territory, he neglected to inform the Indians that
the company intended to settle whites on their land.[25] When Gist
arrived at Loggstown, he recorded in his journal, "The People in this
Town began to enquire my Business, and because I did not readily
inform them, they began to suspect me, and said, I was come to settle
the Indian's Land, and they knew I should never go Home again safe;
I found this Discourse was like to be of ill Consequence to me."[26]
It is clear that the Ohio Country Indians no more wanted the English to settle on their lands than they did the French. Most of them
had come to the region having been driven from their traditional
homelands in the East by the English. Still others moved into the Ohio
River Valley from the West in order to escape French influence. They

had all found refuge in the lush valleys and rolling hills. It was now becoming increasingly evident that this last sanctuary was about to be violated by whites from both European nations.

The activities of the Ohio Company and the increasing encroachment of the English traders in the trans-Appalachian frontier finally prompted the French to take decisive action. In 1749 the Marquis de la Galissonnière, governor of New France, ordered Captain Pierre Joseph Céloron de Blainville to mount an expedition to the Ohio to eject any English traders found in the region and counsel the Indians to reject British presence throughout the Ohio Country. Céloron had considerable frontier experience, having served as the commandant at the remote wilderness posts of Michilimackinac and Detroit. While Céloron had been at Detroit, Ottawa chiefs had been satisfied with his administration. He would not find the same warm reception, however, among the Indians of the Ohio Country.[27]

The captain organized an impressive force of nearly 250 men, including several companies of French marines, 180 Canadian provincials, and thirty Abenaki and Caughnawaga Iroquois warriors. He was also accompanied by the able interpreter Philippe-Thomas Chabert de Joncaire. Joncaire's father had been post commander at Niagara and had operated a trading post near Geneva, New York. The young Joncaire grew up among the Senecas who resided in the region, and he eventually became an adopted son of the tribe. The French hoped that Joncaire's presence on the expedition would dispel fear among the Ohio Indians that Céloron's intentions were anything but peaceful.[28] Nonetheless, as the expedition traveled down from Montreal in a large flotilla of canoes, Indians abandoned their villages "with such precipitation that they . . . left a part of their utensils, their canoes, and even their provisions, to gain the woods." The captain dispatched Joncaire down the Allegheny in an attempt to "reassure the natives of these countries . . . that they should be desired to keep themselves tranquil in their tents, and assure them that [he had] only come to treat with them of good things." Céloron's message to the Indians, however, served only to further convince many of them that the French intended to occupy their land. When the captain finally managed to gain an audience with a group of Senecas along the Allegheny, he addressed them on behalf of the French governor:

My Children, since I have been at war with the English, I
have learned that that nation has deceived you; and not content
with breaking your heart, they have profited by my absence
from this country to invade the land which does not belong
to them and which is mine. . . . I will not suffer the English
on my land; and I invite you, if you are my true children, to
not receive them any more in your villages. I forbid . . . the
commerce which they have established lately in this part of
the land, and announce to you that I will no longer suffer it.

To reinforce the French claims to the region, Céloron buried lead
plates at the confluence of major streams "as a monument of the
renewal of possession which we have taken of the said river Ohio,
and of all those that therein empty; and of all the land on both sides to
the source of said river." In addition, he nailed iron plaques engraved
with the French coat of arms to the trees. Referring to these symbols,
Céloron informed the Indians, "You see the marks to be respected
which I have attached along la Belle Rivière, which will prove to the
English that this land belongs to me and they cannot come here without exposing themselves to be chased away." The Senecas must have
been truly mystified by these bold assertions since they had always
considered the land to be theirs, belonging neither to the French nor
to the British. Nonetheless, their response to Céloron was polite and
evasive. They told the haughty French commander, "We are not a
party capable of deciding entirely of the general sentiments of the
Five Nations who inhabit this river; we wait for the decision of the
chiefs of our villages lower down." With that reply, Céloron continued downstream.[29]

Several days later the expedition came upon a small Delaware
village. Again, the captain delivered his stern warning, to which the
Indians replied, "Examine, my Father, the situation in which we
are. If thou makest the English retire, who give us necessaries, and
especially the smith who mends our guns and hatchets, we would
be without help and exposed to die of hunger—of misery in the Belle
Rivière." Afterward, Céloron confided in his journal that "this representation embarrassed me very much," since he realized that his
countrymen had indeed failed to keep the Indians of the region supplied with trade goods and gunsmiths.[30]

On August 8, after nearly two months of traveling, the French column reached the village of Loggstown on the Ohio. Here Captain Céloron encountered Mingoes, Delawares, Shawnees, and representatives of many other tribes, including the Nippissings, Abenakis, and Ottawas. He also noticed that flying above the village were three French flags and an English banner. Sensing the suspicious and seeming hostility among the assembled warriors, the interpreter Joncaire warned the French commander to be vigilant. At a grand council held several days later, Céloron delivered his by now tired speech to the Indian leaders, adding that the English "hide from you their intentions, which are to establish themselves in such a manner that they will drive you away." The Indians' response was similar to that given by the Delawares upstream. The French had neglected them and their interests, and the English had moved in to supply them with those commodities that were so necessary to their survival. The Indians requested that the French send traders to replace the British they intended to evict. The Loggstown inhabitants concluded by saying that the village contained only young men, incapable of making important decisions and that they would relay Céloron's message to their chiefs when they returned. Again, the disgruntled captain had met with evasion. Having concluded business along the Ohio, the expedition continued on toward Lake Erie. Céloron paused at Pickawillany to confer with the Piankashaw leader Memeskia, who had abandoned French influence to trade with the English. Despite his attempts to cajole the old chief back to the French fold, Memeskia promised only to visit the French villages sometime in the spring. Frustrated and tired, Captain Céloron turned north to return to Montreal. At the end of his journal, the commander reflected on the situation in the Ohio Country: "All that I can say is, that the nations of these places are very ill-disposed against the French and entirely devoted to the English. I do not know by what means they can be reclaimed." He admitted that the Indians could not be won over by increased trade, since the British could undercut French prices. His only suggestion was to make "a strong defence" of the territory.[31]

While Céloron floated down the Allegheny River in his attempt to cajole and intimidate the Indians into expelling the English, Pennsylvania authorities were informed of the French presence. In June 1749 the newly appointed colonial governor, James Hamilton,

informed the provincial council that "an Army of One thousand
French [was] ready to go on some Expedition . . . to prevent any Settlements being made by the English on Belle Riviere, i.e. Ohio."[32]
Instead of taking aggressive and determined action to counter the
French transgression, Governor Hamilton was content to simply
monitor Céloron's intrusion. In fact, the governor seemed more concerned with the activities of the rival Virginians of the Ohio Company. Thomas Lee, one of the company's principal partners, wrote to
Hamilton in the fall of 1749 complaining that Pennsylvania traders
were attempting to turn the Indians against the firm. Lee made the
company's position clear: "His Majesty has been graciously pleased
to grant to some Gentlemen and Merchants of London and some of
both sorts Inhabitants of this Colony, a large Quantity of Land West
of the Mountains, the design of this Grant and one condition of it is
to Erect and Garrison a Fort to protect our trade [from the French]."[33]
Warming to his main point, the aspiring speculator wrote, "Your
Traders have prevailed with the Indians on the Ohio to believe that
the Fort is to be a bridle on them. . . . I need not say any more to prevail with you to take the necessary means to put a stop to these mis-
chievous Practices of those Traders." Hamilton was quick to respond,
politely informing Lee that he would "endeavor by all possible methods
to put an end to so vile a Practice." The governor also suggested,
however, "that the Western Bounds of this Province be run by Commissioners to be appointed by both [the Pennsylvania and Virginia]
Governments, in order to insure that none of the Lands contained in
the [Ohio Company] Grant are within the Limits of this Province."[34]

   The correspondence between Governor Hamilton and Thomas
Lee underscores the complex and conflicting aspects of British colonialism that left the Ohio Indians befuddled and helped to eventually
transform their homeland into a bloody battleground. Thomas Lee
was undoubtedly correct in asserting that Pennsylvania traders such
as George Croghan were cautioning the Indians to be suspicious of
Virginia agents. After all, Ohio Company forts and trading posts represented competition. Not only the Virginians but apparently Maryland traders also had designs on the Ohio Country. From his trading
center at Pickawillany Croghan informed Provincial Secretary
Richard Peters that the Indians had been invited "to go down to see
the Governor of Marryland which perhaps may be a determent to the

tread of Pensilvanie as the[y] want to enter into the Indian tread. I can put a stop to thire going down if you think itt convenent."[35]

Alarmed over the aggressive plans of the Virginians and Marylanders, the Machiavellian Peters wrote to Pennsylvania proprietor Thomas Penn, complaining that the Ohio Company's efforts would "undoubtedly rob this province of great advantages." In an attempt to thwart the Virginians, Peters began putting together a new trading firm that included George Croghan and former militia captain William Trent, whose father had founded Trenton, New Jersey. This new trading enterprise was partly funded by none other than the proprietor himself, Thomas Penn. With such vast resources at their disposal, the Pennsylvanians could monopolize the fur trade and prevent the Ohio Company from gaining a foothold in the land beyond the mountains. Penn agreed to contribute £400 to build a fort on the Ohio or Allegheny to protect the colony's traders and their merchandise. This offer may have prompted Croghan to convince the Ohio Country chiefs to convey to him two hundred thousand acres of land near the forks of the Ohio.[36]

At a time when the two colonies should have been working together to confront the French threat, they instead continued to compete against one another in the worst possible way. Although every colony had, from the beginning of British expansion in North America, jealously safeguarded its sovereignty, the competition between Pennsylvania, Virginia, and Maryland was a matter of simple greed and unrelenting ambition among speculators, Indian traders, merchants, and provincial officials.

While Thomas Lee called for Pennsylvania and Virginia "to unite and not divide the Interest of the King's Subjects on the Continent," the actions of his Ohio Company tended to preclude such unification. In the fall of 1751 the company once again sent frontiersman Christopher Gist into the wilderness to scout locations for a storehouse on the Ohio and to take note of good land for establishing settlements. On his return home Gist encountered a Delaware warrior who "desired to know where the Indians Land lay, for the French claimed all the Land on one Side the River Ohio & the English on the other Side." Gist simply recorded in his journal, "I was at a loss to answer him."[37]

The following spring Gist returned to the frontier to hold a conference with the Indians at Loggstown to inform them of the Ohio

Company's intention to settle the land along the river. Gist was instructed to tell the Indians that the New York Iroquois council had sold the land to the king of England in a treaty held in Lancaster, Pennsylvania, in 1744. Since the proposed settlements might tend to drive away the game in the region, the company was willing to provide the Indians living in the vicinity with additional compensation.[38]

When Gist and other commissioners from Virginia arrived at Loggstown, the Indians insisted that no negotiations could be conducted until their principal spokesman, Tanacharison, arrived. Like Monacatootha, Tanacharison was a Seneca vice-regent, or half king, sent by the New York Iroquois council to "preside" over the Delawares living along the Ohio and its tributaries. Also like his fellow vice-regent, Tanacharison was committed to his charges, not to Iroquois league dictates.[39]

When the formal conference finally got under way, the Virginia commissioners displayed a copy of the Lancaster Treaty to Tanacharison and pointed out that the League of Five Nations had ceded all the land as far as "the setting sun." To this assertion the half king diplomatically replied, "We are willing to confirm anything our council has done in regard to the lands but we never understood before you told us . . . that the lands then sold were to extend further to the sunsetting than the hill on the other side of Allagany hill so we cannot give you a further answer."[40] Tanacharison's reply made perfect sense, for the Indians considered the boundary to extend only to where the sun set—behind the crest of the mountains. In the end, the Half King relented to endorsing the Lancaster agreement and providing the Virginians with enough "ground upon which to construct a stronghouse at the fork of Monongahela [Ohio] to keep such goods [as] powder, lead and necessaries as shall be wanting."[41] Tanacharison's consent to a fort at the confluence of the Allegheny and Monongahela was in response to the growing threat posed by the French in the region. Some historians would later contend that by confirming the Lancaster Treaty, Tanacharison had sold out to the Virginians. On the contrary, the half king was only confirming what the council at Onondaga had already agreed on, and the actual boundary was still disputed and open to interpretation.[42]

Tanacharison's suspicions of French aggression were soon confirmed when, on June 21, 1752, a war party of 250 Ottawas, Chippewas, and

Potawatomies, led by a mixed-blood French colonial officer named Charles Langlade, swooped down on the Miami trading village of Picka-willany. The motive for the raid stemmed from French concerns over the growing influence of the Piankashaw leader Memeskia, who had abandoned the French in favor of an alliance with the British and their Iroquois allies. George Croghan and other English traders had been making tremendous profits at Pickawillany since courting the favor of Memeskia. French colonial authorities feared that if some action was not taken, their link between Canada and Louisiana might be severed. A small group of British traders were captured during the attack and carried off to the French outpost at Detroit. Memeskia was also captured, and while his followers looked on, the Ottawas killed him, boiled his body, and ate it. The new governor in Canada, the Marquis Duquesne, praised Charles Langlade for his zeal and bravery. In a letter to a French minister, Duquesne asserted, "I hope that this blow, taken with the total pillage that the English have sustained on this occa-sion, will deter them from coming to carry on trade in our lands."[43]

The destruction of Pickawillany convinced the French that the only way to secure the Ohio Country was through force of arms. In the early spring of 1753, two thousand French soldiers descended on the region and began building forts to protect their water route to the Ohio River. The first outpost was constructed on the southern shore of Lake Erie just east of a fine peninsula that the French called Presque Isle. From there the expedition cut a portage road overland to the headwaters of a stream known as LeBoeuf Creek. After con-structing a small, square fort with four bastions at the corners, the French advance moved downstream to where the creek emptied into the Allegheny at a Delaware village called Venango. The French invasion drove off the trader and gunsmith John Fraser, who had established a trading post among the Delawares some twelve years earlier. Fraser's cabin and storehouses became the headquarters for the French commandant, Philippe-Thomas Joncaire, the noted interpreter.[44]

John Fraser retreated down the Allegheny to spread the alarm to other English traders. At Loggstown Tanacharison departed for the new fort at Presque Isle to deliver the first of three warnings to the French not to advance any farther into Indian land. When the Seneca vice-regent arrived along the shore of Lake Erie, he declared to the French commander the Sieur de Marin:

My father, evil tidings are innumerable in the lands where
we live. The river where we are belongs to us warriors. The
chiefs who look after affairs [the council at Onondaga] are
not its masters. It is a road for warriors and not for these
chiefs. . . . I am speaking my father, in the name of all the
warriors who inhabit the Belle Rivière. With this belt we
detain you and ask you to have them cease setting up the
establishments you want to make. All the tribes have always
called upon us not to allow it. We have told our brothers the
English to withdraw. They have done so, too. We shall be on
the side of those who take pity on us and who listen to us.
Although I am small, the Master of Life has not given me
less courage to oppose these establishments. This is the first
and last demand we shall make of you, and I shall strike at
whoever does not listen to us. . . . We ask you only to send
there what we need, but not to build any forts there.[45]

Tanacharison's speech underscores the growing autonomy of the Ohio
tribes. They intended to conduct their own diplomatic affairs from
this point on, and they disavowed the Iroquois Confederacy's ownership of the land. The half king was adamant in his contention that
the various nations wished neither the French nor the English to
build forts and settle the land.

Marin scoffed at Tanacharison's assertions and responded in a
haughty and belligerent manner rare in Native American diplomacy.
Refusing the wampum belt offered by the Seneca leader, Marin replied:

The establishments which I am setting up and which I shall
continue along the Belle Rivière are founded on the fact that
it belongs incontestably to the King. . . . I despise all the
stupid things you said. I know that they come only from you,
and that all the warriors and chiefs of the Belle Rivière think
better than you, and take pity on their women and children. I
am obliged to tell you that I shall continue on my way, and if
there are any persons bold enough to set up barriers to hinder
my march, I shall knock them over so vigorously that they
may crush those who made them.[46]

Marin's claim that Tanacharison was speaking only for himself may have been closer to the truth than the Seneca leader would have cared to admit. Already some of the Delawares had made overtures to the French forces and were assisting the invaders to construct their portage road between Fort LeBoeuf and Venango. With the English traders expelled, the Delawares and Shawnees now depended on the French for arms, powder, lead, and other necessities. Winter was approaching, and the hunters had to give thought to taking in a supply of meat.[47]

While Tanacharison sought to halt the French invasion, Monacatootha and a delegation of Ohio Country chiefs struck out for Winchester, Virginia, and Carlisle, Pennsylvania, to seek assistance from the English. If the Indian leaders from the West expected arms, ammunition, and other material support from Pennsylvania, however, they were sorely disappointed. Over the years the power of the assembly had increased its power by assuming sole control over appropriations. Furthermore, the assembly had also borne the expense of Indian affairs, paying for presents given to the tribes and hiring negotiators such as Conrad Weiser and George Croghan. When the colonial legislators requested that the proprietors, the Penn family, also contribute to the cause of Indian affairs, they flatly refused. This astonished the assembly since the Penns paid no tax on their vast property holdings and reaped all the benefits when land was obtained from the Indians and then sold to settlers.[48]

To confound the situation even more, the Pennsylvania assembly was dominated by Quakers whose pacifist inclinations made it extremely difficult for them to appropriate funds for colonial defense. They were willing to provide the Indians with presents of powder and lead and have them serve as buffers between the French threat and the settled province; and they were not even wholly opposed to raising a colonial militia, provided that recruits were volunteers whose conscience did not forbid their participation in the military. The Quakers, however, feared a standing army under the authority of the Penn family, which might attempt to conscript soldiers despite their conscientious objections. In addition, the assembly was adamant that the proprietors should share in the cost of defending the colony. The Penn family again refused to bear such expense. Consequently, the French invasion led to inertia in Pennsylvania.[49]

In Virginia Monacatootha's appeals for assistance fared only somewhat better. The delegation of Ohio tribes met with Commissioner William Fairfax and requested arms and ammunition to deal with the French. Instead, Fairfax informed the Indians that his colony intended to build a fort at the forks of the Ohio. Monacatootha responded, "You told Us, You wou'd build a Strong House at the Forks after bidding us take Care of Our Lands; We now request You may not build that Strong House, for we intend to keep Our Country clear of Settlements during these troublesome Times."[50] Again, the message from the Ohio Indians was clear and consistent: they wanted neither the French nor the British in their lands. Yet, despite these protestations, the Virginians, under the strong influence of the Ohio Company, were intent on constructing an outpost along the river. With no military support forthcoming, the dejected Monacatootha returned to Loggstown with his delegation. The Indians were utterly bewildered by their failed diplomatic mission. The English had continuously encouraged the Indians to resist the French, promising them aid if it became necessary. Instead, the Indians were forced to stand by helplessly as two great European powers propelled themselves headlong into conflict in the middle of the Ohio Country.

By the fall of 1753, the Virginians were ready to act. Governor Robert Dinwiddie ordered the twenty-one-year-old provincial major George Washington to deliver a message to the French commander in the Upper Ohio River Valley. Washington was to inform the French that they were trespassing on land claimed by the king of England and the colony of Virginia and that they should depart at once. With Tanacharison as a guide young Washington made his way to Fort LeBoeuf, where he recited his fateful message. The new French commander, Captain Jacques Legardeur de Saint-Pierre, politely refused to depart. Washington returned to Virginia to prepare for war.

In the spring of 1754, Washington—recently promoted to lieutenant colonel—returned to the frontier at the head of a small provincial army of ill-trained Virginians. Governor Dinwiddie ordered the colonel to advance on the forks of the Ohio and garrison the long anticipated fort that was being constructed at the site. En route, Washington discovered that a French force of more than a thousand men had surrounded the tiny English outpost and forced its surrender. Afterward, the French had begun to build their own post at the confluence, which they named Fort Duquesne, in honor of the Canadian governor. Undaunted, Colonel Washington continued on and encamped at a small clearing in the wilderness called the Great Meadows, located about fifty miles northwest of Wills Creek (present-day Cumberland, Maryland). Here Washington hoped to receive supplies and reinforcements from South Carolina. He also expected to be reinforced by the Indians of the Ohio Country. The young militia commander was disappointed when Tanacharison arrived at his camp with only a small war party. When the half king informed Washington that a French scouting party was advancing on the Great Meadows, the intrepid colonel sallied out from his encampment with about forty men to locate and engage the enemy. At daybreak on May 28 the mixed English-Indian force crept up on about thirty French soldiers cooking breakfast at their camp in a small ravine. Washington deployed his forces to surround the camp and then ordered his men to open fire. When the powder smoke cleared, ten French marines lay dead, including their commander, Ensign Coulon de Jumonville. Twenty-one others were captured. Later, when news of the skirmish reached London, the noted British statesman Horace Walpole remarked, "The volley fired by a young Virginian in the backwoods of America has just set the world on fire."[51]

Following the brief engagement in the ravine that would forever be known as Jumonville Glen, Washington returned to the Great Meadows to await the French counterattack that he knew would come. Meanwhile, Tanacharison and Monacatootha attempted to rally the Ohio tribes to join the English and repel the French. To entice the Delawares and Shawnees, Monacatootha carried four French scalps with him on his recruiting mission.[52] Despite these efforts, the tribes of the Ohio failed to reinforce Washington's meager army. The Delawares and others had for some time beseeched the English to supply them with arms and ammunition to repel the French invaders. They had watched as Marin's forces drove through the heart of their land and seized the forks of the Ohio. They had also noted the Indian allies the French had brought with them from the Great Lakes country. Ottawas, Caughnawagas, Hurons, Abenakis, and others had set up camps around Fort Duquesne. All the while, the English had provided no assistance. When Washington and his militia finally arrived, it was too late. The Indians were not interested in being pawns in a struggle between the two European powers. Consequently, the Delawares turned their backs on Tanacharison and proclaimed their neutrality. With all support gone, Monacatootha burned the village at Loggstown and fled eastward with Tanacharison and a few Mingo followers. Washington and his soldiers ended up alone at the Great Meadows.[53]

As expected, an army of six hundred French marines and Canadian militiamen, along with one hundred Indian allies, surrounded Colonel Washington's position and, on July 4, 1754, forced his surrender. Washington and his men were allowed to return to Virginia, leaving the Ohio River Valley in undisputed control of the French.

Even before George Washington surrendered his makeshift barricade called "Fort Necessity" at the Great Meadows, delegates from eight of the thirteen British colonies met in Albany, New York, in an attempt to draw up a concerted plan to deal with the French invasion. Also in attendance at this Albany Congress were representatives from the Iroquois Confederacy. Although historians have often pointed to the conference as the first significant display of intercolonial unity, little was accomplished to bring about a union of the disparate English provinces. In fact, the commissioners at Albany devoted more effort attempting to further their respective colonies' political and economic aims. In summoning the Iroquois, the delegates hoped to obtain the confederacy's commitment to join in a war against the French. Instead, the Mohawk chief Hendrick chastised the English for their reckless Indian policy of bypassing the league and negotiating directly with the Ohio Indians. "The Governor of Virginia and the Governor of Canada," Hendrick said,

> are both quarreling about lands which belong to us: and such a quarrel may end in our destruction. They fight who shall have the land. The Governors of Virginia and Pennsylvania have made paths through our country to trade, and build houses, without acquainting us with it. They should first have asked our consent to build there."[54]

Iroquois resentment may have played an important role in the confederation's decision to adopt an official stance of neutrality. Only the Mohawks proclaimed their loyalty to the English, due in large part to the influence of, Sir William Johnson, who had been living among the tribe for more than fifteen years.

As it relates to later developments, perhaps the most significant event to take place at the Albany Congress was the Iroquois agreement to sell to Pennsylvania all the land lying between the Susquehanna and Ohio rivers.[55] This astonishingly large transaction was negotiated by the Pennsylvanians for a variety of reasons. To begin with, officials from the Quaker colony had real fear that the Iroquois might sell the Ohio Country to the French, thereby reinforcing their claims to the territory. The 1713 Treaty of Utrecht, which ended the War for the Spanish Succession, recognized the Iroquois as subjects of Great Britain. In the minds of the Pennsylvanians, if British subjects sold land to the French, they would be acknowledging French claims to the Ohio, or so the act might, at the very least, be construed in the court of world opinion. The Pennsylvania commissioners at Albany were wary of officials from Connecticut who believed that land in the Susquehanna valley belonged to their colony and were eager to persuade the Iroquois to sell this land to them. Therefore, Pennsylvania was not simply concerned with the French but also with rivals from another British province. Needless to say, some of the commissioners from the Quaker colony were also interested in seeing proprietary lands increased for the profit of the Penn family. With these motivations at the forefront, the Pennsylvania authorities worked diligently through their negotiator, Conrad Weiser, to secure the deed.

No one at Albany, neither the English nor the Iroquois, thought to consult the people who lived in the Ohio Country—the Delawares, Shawnees, Mingoes, and others. As with the Walking Purchase of 1737, the Delawares would come to realize that the land they claimed had been sold out from under them. Interestingly, after first selling the land to Pennsylvania, these same Iroquois chiefs then sold a portion of the same land to the Connecticut commissioners, thereby opening the way for an intense rivalry between the two colonies that would not entirely be settled until after the American Revolution. Neither the Pennsylvania deed nor Connecticut purchase was approved by the entire Iroquois council. The colonial diplomats had met with several more pliable Iroquois leaders and conducted the land sales "in the bushes." It was not until a year later that the Onondaga council was made fully aware of the land transactions, and then they wholly denounced them.[56]

Meanwhile in London, British officials had already concluded that the provincials were incapable of dealing with the French on a concerted level. The emergency required a response greater than any single colony could muster, and to encourage cooperation between the various provinces might lead to a usurpation of royal authority that would be dangerous to imperial interests. Indeed, many English administrators lamented the power that the colonial assemblies already enjoyed. Therefore, they determined that his majesty's forces would have to cross the ocean to the provinces and expel the enemy from the Ohio River Valley. For the first time in the 150-year history of the British colonies, large numbers of English soldiers began to arrive in America.

In the early part of April 1755, an army of over two thousand troops began the march from Alexandria, Virginia, toward the land beyond the mountains. Their military objective was to seize Fort Duquesne at the forks of the Ohio. The expedition commander, Major General Edward Braddock, had spent over forty years as an officer in his majesty's Coldstream Guards and was regarded as an "officer of rank and capacity." George Washington, who served as a volunteer aide to the general, believed Braddock to be "brave even to a fault . . . generous and disinterested, but plain and blunt in manner, even to rudeness."[57] The general's force consisted of two British regular regiments; seven hundred provincials, mostly from Virginia; and fifty sailors employed to rig the supply wagons in order to pull them over the rugged mountains. Braddock also enlisted the services of experienced frontiersmen such as George Croghan, Christopher Gist, and Andrew Montour to act as guides. Montour, a mixed blood who had lived all his life in the Ohio Country, was described by an early missionary: "like another European but around his whole face an Indian-ish broad ring of bear fat and paint, [he] had on a sky-colored coat of fine cloth, black cordovan neckband with silver bugles, a red damask lapelled waistcoat, breeches over which his shirt hung, shoes and stockings, a hat, and both ears braided with brass and other wire like a handle on a basket."[58]

Conspicuously absent from Braddock's command were Indian allies from the Ohio Country. Recalling George Washington's debacle at Fort Necessity the previous year, the warriors hesitated to join in the fray. In addition, with all the English traders forced back across the mountains, the Indians grew increasingly dependent on French trade goods. The Delawares, Mingoes, and Shawnees were content to simply stand back and see which of these European powers would best the other in their homeland. General Braddock did secure the services of a band of Cherokees from the South; but tiring quickly from the campaign's slow progress, the warriors decided to return home, leaving the British with only a handful of Iroquois under the vice-regent, Monacatootha. Braddock managed to alienate even this small contingent of Indian allies. Monacatootha recalled, "He looked upon us as dogs, and would never hear anything what was said to him. We often endeavored to advise him and to tell him of the danger he was in with his soldiers, but he never appeared pleased with us."[59]

Indeed, Braddock's arrogance and overconfidence would not permit him to accept the notion that potential Indian foes could be a match for well-trained and disciplined British regulars. When the Pennsylvania politician Benjamin Franklin warned the general that "the only danger I apprehend of obstruction to your march is from ambuscades of Indians," Braddock responded, "The savages may indeed be a formidable enemy to your raw American militia, but upon the King's regulars and disciplined troops, Sir, it is impossible they should make any impression."[60]

Impatient over the slow movement of his army across the mountains, Braddock divided his force. Leaving behind a third of his command at a supply camp near the Great Meadows, the general forged ahead with a flying column of thirteen hundred–odd troops to quickly seize Fort Duquesne. After crossing the Monongahela, the British were only a few miles from their objective when suddenly their vanguard ran directly into a mixed force of the enemy, comprised of only some seventy French marines, nearly 150 Canadian militia, and more than six hundred Great Lakes Indians.[61]

The fate of General Braddock's column was sealed almost from the beginning. After the British infantrymen fired their first volley into the oncoming enemy, the French and Indians spilled around either side of the invading column. The vanguard of Braddock's army began to retreat at the same time that the general rushed forward support from the main column. The two excited units ran into each other, throwing the Redcoats into panic and confusion. As the officers tried to regain control of their jumbled companies, the Indians poured deadly fire from the cover of trees on both sides of the road. George Washington, General Braddock's aide, remembered the melee and proclaimed that the British soldiers "were immediately struck with such a deadly panic that nothing but confusion and disobedience of orders prevailed amongst them."[62] The young Virginian urged Braddock to allow him to direct the men to the cover of the trees and fight like the enemy. Enraged, the general exclaimed, "I've a mind to run you through the body. We'll sup today in Fort Duquesne or else in hell!" The war cries of the Indians intensified the state of fear and panic among the regular troops. As one British officer later recalled, "The yell of the Indians is fresh on my ear, and the terrific sound will haunt me until the hour of my dissolution. I cannot describe the horrors of that scene."[63]

After three hours of appalling slaughter, the British managed to retreat across the Monongahela, leaving behind over half of their force in killed, wounded, and missing. Among the casualties was the proud General Braddock, who had been mortally wounded by a musket ball that lodged in his lung. George Washington helped load the general into a cart as the remnants of the British army, seized by the horror and confusion that enveloped them, fled in wild panic. As the surviving Redcoats and camp followers waded across the river, the Indians gave chase. "The enemy pursued us butchering as they came as farr as the other side of ye River; during our crossing," remembered one soldier. "They Shot many in ye Water both Men & Women, & dyed ye stream with their blood, scalping & cutting them in a most barbarous manner."[64]

The Indians chose not to follow the shattered army beyond the river, returning instead to the battlefield to dispatch the wounded, collect prisoners, and gather up the spoils of war. General Braddock lingered in agony for nearly five days as the stunned British force made its long retreat back to the base camp near the Great Meadows. Even while he lay dying, the old soldier could not believe what had happened. "Who would have thought it," he was heard to mutter. Before he died, Braddock delivered one statement that proved to be prophetic: "We shall know better how to deal with them another time."[65]

Braddock's defeat at the Battle of the Monongahela convinced many of the wavering Ohio Country Indians that the French held the upper hand in the land beyond the mountains. Consequently, the Delawares, Senecas, and Shawnees increasingly moved to the French sphere of influence, where they could expect to receive gifts of powder, lead, guns, and even food in exchange for taking up the hatchet against the English. For the next three years, the frontier settlements in Pennsylvania and Virginia were constantly exposed to Indian raids. The woodland warriors torched isolated farms and killed or captured thousands of Scots-Irish and German pioneers. With no British soldiers to defend them, the petrified frontier inhabitants appealed to Pennsylvania's new governor, Robert Morris, for assistance. In October 1755 seventeen men living on the west bank of the Susquehanna petitioned Morris for aid, claiming, "The terror . . . has drove away almost all these back inhabitants except us, the Subscribers, with a few more who are willing to stay and endeavor to defend the land; but as we are not able to defend it for want of Guns and Ammunition, and but few in number, so that, without assistance we must fly and leave the Country at the mercy of the Enemy."[66]

The Quaker colony, however, was still gripped by inertia as the feud between the provincial assembly and the proprietor continued. The Penn family finally broke the deadlock when it agreed to grant £5,000 for defense in lieu of a proposed tax on proprietary lands. The assembly quickly requisitioned another £60,000 and authorized the recruitment of a Pennsylvania regiment comprising thirteen hundred men. In addition, Governor Morris authorized the construction of a chain of forts that extended in an uneven arc to protect the more settled areas of the colony. These efforts did little to stem the tide of depredations as more Indians, from both the Ohio and Susquehanna, joined the French cause.[67]

Out of seeming desperation, Governor Morris took drastic action by formally declaring war on all the Delawares and Shawnees. On April 8, 1756, the governor signed the Scalp Act, which provided bounties of $130 "for the Scalp of every male Indian of above Twelve Years old" and $50 for the scalp of every Indian woman.[68] Somewhat ironically, whereas Pennsylvania declared war against its Indian inhabitants in April 1756, Great Britain did not officially declare war against France until one month later.

The war between Europe's two great powers quickly engulfed much of the world. British and French forces battled in India, Africa, and the Caribbean and on the continent of Europe. In America Native peoples, who had once found themselves factors in the sphere of international trade, now discovered that they had become players in a global military conflagration. Slowly, under the aggressive ministry of Secretary of State William Pitt, English force of arms began to overcome the power of the Bourbon monarchy. British sea power seemed to make the deciding difference in the conflict. The royal navy blockaded French colonial ports, transported troops around the world to fight the enemy, and more important, prevented the French from reinforcing or supplying their far-flung colonial possessions. Not surprisingly, the Indians of the Great Lakes and the Ohio River Valley inevitably began to feel the shift in power, although they most certainly could not fathom the cause. All they knew was that the presents from the French father, which sustained them during the war, began to dry up. The Indians also noticed that the French were finding it difficult to reinforce their own garrisons on the remote frontier. Perhaps most distressing was the realization that a large English army was marching across Pennsylvania headed for the heart of the Ohio Country.

The troops that the Indians observed traversing the Quaker colony's frontier during the spring and summer of 1758 were part of what one historian has called a "hydra-headed" initiative orchestrated by the British government to destroy French power in North America once and for all. The plan involved sending a fleet to seize the fortress at Louisbourg, an ice-free port located on Cape Breton Island. This strategic French post provided protection for the Saint Lawrence River and the Canadian capital at Quebec. Another expedition was to proceed up the Lake George–Lake Champlain corridor, which cut northward from New York into the heart of New France. British success in these two campaigns would lead to a two-pronged assault on Quebec and Montreal. Yet another advance was planned on Fort Frontenac, located at the eastern end of Lake Ontario. This French outpost served as the main supply base for the garrisons along the Great Lakes and Ohio River Valley.[69]

The final prong of the British offensive consisted of another large-scale expedition against Fort Duquesne. Since the decimation of Braddock's forces back in 1755, Duquesne had been a staging area for innumerable French and Indian raids against the frontier settlements—or as one British officer described it, "a nest of corsairs." Once the British seized Fort Duquesne, they could march northward and take the other French forts at Venango, LeBoeuf, Presque Isle, and Niagara. Brigadier General John Forbes, a Scotsman noted for being "ambitious of the military character," commanded the expedition.[70] The forty-eight-year-old Forbes arrived in Philadelphia in mid-April and immediately set about the task of organizing his campaign. While the general found that dealing with provincial authorities could be vexing, the Pennsylvanians were, after nearly three years of unceasing warfare, more willing to support the military effort than they had been before Braddock's defeat. Forbes's plan involved cutting a road over the mountains that would lead to Fort Duquesne. Unlike Braddock, General Forbes proposed to pause at intervals along the march and construct forts that could be used for defensive purposes should his army be overwhelmed. These forts could also serve as supply depots and help keep open the line of communication from the frontier to Philadelphia. To execute his plans, the general assembled a mixed force of regular and provincial soldiers including a detachment of the 77th Regiment of Foot, better known as Montgomery's Highlanders, recruited from Scotland to serve in the North American campaigns. The colonial troops came from Pennsylvania, Virginia, Delaware, Maryland, and North Carolina. Forbes had little regard for the provincial soldiers, remarking "that a few of their principle Officers excepted, all the rest are an extream bad Collection of broken Innkeepers, Horse Jockeys, & Indian traders, and that the Men under them, are a direct copy of their Officers . . . they are a gathering from the scum of the worst people, in every Country."[71] Nonetheless, the general realized that he desperately needed these "scum" to achieve his goal, and he worked diligently to keep colonial officials satisfied.

While General Forbes supervised the thousand and one tasks necessary to organize a major military campaign, he became deeply concerned about the disposition of France's Indian allies. In June the general wrote a brother officer that he had "just now fixed with the Governor to send a solemn message among the Delawares and Shawanese to beg a meeting with them where they choose to appoint, when I hope to persuade many of them at least to remain neutrals for this Campaign."[72] In attempting to reconcile the Ohio people to the British interest, Forbes confronted several problems. The general needed first to uncover the source of Indian alienation and then seek remedies to placate the disaffected tribes. Afterward, he had to find a trustworthy person to deliver this message.

Entering the complex web of Indian affairs, the general grappled with a host of intrigues that had plagued relations with the Ohio tribes from the beginning. He applied to Sir William Johnson, the superintendent of Indian affairs, for assistance in arranging a meeting with the Delawares. From Sir William, however, the general received only silence. The superintendent believed that any attempt to deal directly with Pennsylvania's Indians would be an affront to his main charge, the Iroquois Confederacy. What Johnson either failed to appreciate or chose to ignore was the fact that the Delawares, Shawnees, and others were no longer willing to mindlessly abide by dictates from the New York Iroquois.[73]

Forbes's attempts to induce the provincial authorities of Pennsylvania to deal with the Delawares were equally exasperating. Pennsylvania's new governor, William Denny, realized that any attempt to arrange peace with the Indians would require the province to address the fraudulent land transactions that had taken place over the years. Delawares living along the Susquehanna bitterly complained about the deceit of both the Walking Purchase of 1737 and the Albany deed given to Pennsylvania by the Iroquois in 1754. To achieve a lasting peace would, in all likelihood, require Pennsylvania to make just compensation for those lands or return them to the Indians.

General Forbes soon discovered that the best chance to reconcile the Indians to the English lay in relying on a council of the Society of Friends and one of its principal leaders, Israel Pemberton. For some time the Quakers had endeavored to make peace with the Delawares. Under Pemberton's leadership a number of influential Quakers had formed the Friendly Association, an organization devoted to restoring tranquility among the warring Indian tribes of Pennsylvania. The association had been instrumental in 1757 in arranging a peace conference at Easton with the Susquehanna Delawares and their principal spokesman, Teedyuscung, whose name the Quakers understood to mean "he who makes the earth tremble." At this meeting

Teedyuscung demanded that provincial authorities guarantee his people a homeland in the Susquehanna valley and address the issue of previous land frauds. Hoping to gain the support of dominant New York Iroquois, Governor Denny insisted that the earlier land deals had been sanctioned by the Onondaga council and that any attempt to alter these transactions would require their approval. Teedyuscung refused to be pushed aside by the Iroquois and responded to Denny's assertion by claiming that the Delawares were no longer "women," obligated to accept Iroquois decisions without themselves having a voice. The conference ended when the governor gave vague assurances that the Delawares would have a homeland along the Susquehanna and that past land purchases would be reviewed by royal officials and adjusted accordingly.[74] While the Easton council produced no lasting peace, it did somewhat strengthen Delaware claims of independence from the Iroquois to conduct their own negotiations. Pennsylvania officials were also obligated to guarantee a homeland for Teedyuscung's people and to form a tribunal to evaluate the colony's previous land purchases.

When General Forbes learned of the Quaker initiative, he wrote Governor Denny, "I realy think Teedyuscung's Demands ought to be agreed with as he has the Publick Faith for making such a Settlement."[75] With the Susquehanna Indians placated to some degree, there still remained the task of neutralizing the Ohio Delawares and other confederated tribes in the West. To effect this end, it was instrumental to reassure the Indians that they retained ownership to their lands beyond the mountains. George Croghan, then employed as a deputy Indian agent, wrote to his superior, Sir William Johnson, that the chief cause of the defection of the western tribes stemmed from the Albany purchase of 1754. Johnson agreed and informed the English Board of Trade that "the Indians are disgusted and dissatisfied with the extensive purchases of land, and do think themselves injured thereby."[76] With the backing of the superintendent of Indian affairs, the powerful Board of Trade, and General Forbes himself, the Pennsylvania proprietors had no recourse but to relinquish their claims to the Ohio Country. The only thing left to do was to inform the Indians living there.

The foregoing series of events stretching back to the Delawares' first penetration of the Ohio Country put the Moravian missionary

Christian Frederick Post on his perilous mission to the frontier, where he was resolved to "restore peace and prosperity to the distressed." Post was the perfect candidate for this dangerous assignment. Born in Germany, he came to America in 1742 to take up missionary work among the Indians on behalf of the United Brethren, an enthusiastic religious sect that had originated in Moravia and Bohemia. Post first worked among the Mahicans and Wampanoags in New York and Connecticut before coming to Pennsylvania to preach to the Delawares. He had been married successively to two Delaware women and understood their language. In addition, he was familiar with many Delaware leaders from beyond the mountains. A contemporary Quaker named Charles Thomason remembered Post as "a plain, honest, religiously disposed Man." Fellow missionary John Heckewelder called Post a "man of undaunted courage and enterprising spirit."[77]

The forty-eight-year-old Post set off on his journey in July 1758, just as General Forbes's army began to ascend the Allegheny Mountains. He was accompanied by a small party of Ohio Delawares that included an influential headman called Pisquetomen and a noted warrior named Essoweywallund, known to the English as Shamokin Daniel. Along the way, Post beheld the shattered frontier. "It gave me great pain," he recalled, "to observe many plantations deserted and laid waste; and I could not but reflect on the distress, the poor owners must be drove to, who once lived in plenty." The intrepid missionary also noticed three scalps that had been stretched on hoops and tied to trees along the trail as a warning to interlopers. Nonetheless, he refused to be deterred and in early August arrived at the Delaware village of Kuskuski, located along the Shenango River. There Post met Tamaqua, called King Beaver by the British, who was already disposed toward peace. He also found in the village a party of fifteen French soldiers who were engaged in building cabins for the Delawares. The Indians informed Post "that they get a great deal of goods from the French; and that the French cloath the Indians every year, men women and children, and give them as much powder and lead as they want." "Turn thy eyes once more upon the road, by which I came," Post told Tamaqua and his followers. "I blind the French, that they may not see me, and stop their ears, that they may not hear the great news I bring you." After Post read excerpts from the treaty held at Easton the previous year, where Pennsylvania agreed to relinquish its claim to the Ohio Country, Tamaqua replied, "Now brother, we have but one great fire . . . we alone cannot make peace; it would be of no significance; for, as all the Indians from the sunrise to the sunset, are united in a body, it is necessary that the whole should join in the peace, or it can be no peace." After assuring Post that "all the Indians, a great way from this, even beyond the lakes," were interested in reaching an agreement with the British, Tamaqua insisted that the missionary visit the other important Indian towns in the region to deliver his message.[78]

When Post arrived at Sawcunk, along the Beaver River, a group of Shawnees and Mingoes informed him that "there are eight different nations there [at Fort Duquesne] who want to hear your message." The diplomat objected to going to Fort Duquesne, where the French might take him captive, but the Indians assured Post that they would protect him. Here was an opportunity to meet with the combined Indian tribes that were supporting the French and perhaps persuade them to abandon the warpath. When Post arrived at the villages scattered about Fort Duquesne, the French entered his camp and demanded that the Indians turn the missionary over to them. Tamaqua and the others refused and instead ordered the French "to send them one hundred loaves of bread; for they were hungry." In rebuffing the French demand, the Ohio Indians indicated they were well aware of just how much the French depended upon their continued alliance. Nonetheless, Post knew not to wander too far from the Indian village: "Some of my party desired me not to stir from the fire; for that the French had offered a great reward for my scalp." While the Moravian delivered his message to the assembled tribes, his traveling companion, Shamokin Daniel, visited the French at the fort. He returned with "a laced coat and hat, a blanket, shirts, ribbons, a new gun, powder, lead & c." The Delaware warrior, easily swayed by the presents the French had given him, told Post, "The English are fools, and so are you." Daniel later rebuked the missionary further, exclaiming, "Damn you, why do not you and the French fight on the sea? You come here only to cheat the poor Indians, and take their land from them."[79]

Returning to Kuskuski, Post had yet another conference with Tamaqua and his brothers, Pisquetomen and Shingas. One of the frontier's most formidable warriors, Shingas must have presented a frightful appearance with his ears distended and wrapped with wire and a portion of his nose bitten off, the reminder of a drunken brawl. Sometimes he wore a silver cone over his disfigured nose that was tied around his head with a ribbon. Colonial officials in Pennsylvania had offered a £100 reward for his head.[80] During the conference, the Indians made clear their deep concern over the large British army under General Forbes that was moving ominously toward them. They told Post, "We have great reason to believe you intend to drive us away, and settle the country; or else why do you come to fight in the land that God has given us?" Post insisted that the British offer of peace was sincere and that Forbes's only purpose was to drive off the French. With that the Delaware leaders asked the Moravian to return to the settlements and bring back "the great belt of peace to them, and then the day will begin to shine clear over us. When we hear once more from you, and we join together, then the day will be still, and no wind, or storm, will come over us, to disturb us.[81]

As he had promised, Christian Frederick Post returned to the Ohio Country carrying the peace belts in October 1758, just as General Forbes prepared for his final push on Fort Duquesne. By this time, Forbes's army had constructed a crude road across the mountains and erected a chain of forts along the trail. The general's largest outpost, Fort Ligonier, was built along Loyalhanna Creek less than fifty miles from the French stronghold at Duquesne. From this point Forbes hoped to advance in one bold stroke and seize the enemy outpost. He was still greatly concerned over the disposition of the Ohio Country Indians. Perhaps he imagined himself approaching the French fort and, like his predecessor Braddock, being routed by hundreds of Native warriors. When Forbes finally received intelligence that the French garrison was reduced in number and that most of the Indians had departed, he decided to forge ahead.[82]

When the Delaware people at Kuskuski learned that General Forbes's army was only fifteen miles from Fort Duquesne and that the French were preparing to abandon the forks of the Ohio, they "danced round the fire till midnight, for joy of their brethren the English, coming." Christian Frederick Post was in the village and heard Cayugas tell the Delawares "to do their best endeavors to send the French off from this country; and when that was done they would go and tell the general [Forbes] to go back over the mountains." Post produced large white wampum belts and proclaimed that these tokens "signify our union and friendship for each other; with them we jointly take the tomahawks out of your hands, and bury them in the ground."[83]

The same day, November 25, 1758, John Forbes looked down from a prominent rise to view the smoldering ruins of Fort Duquesne. With their Indian allies gone, supplies depleted, and manpower low, the French had no option but to destroy their fort and retreat up the Allegheny River to the sanctuary of Venango. After four years of unceasing frontier warfare, the prized strategic objective of the forks of the Ohio was at last in British hands.

Several days later Christian Frederick Post prepared to depart from Kuskuski with a party of Indians to meet with General Forbes at the ruins of Fort Duquesne. Tamaqua, Shingas, and other Delaware leaders called the Moravian diplomat into council yet again. During the meeting, Keekyuscung, a noted "chief counsellor," reminded Post of the promises that had been made to restore peace. The missionary later recorded Keekyuscung's ominous warning:

> All the nations had jointly agreed to defend their hunting place at Allegheny, and suffer nobody to settle there; and as these Indians are much inclined to the English interest, so he begged us very much to tell the Governor, General, and all other people not to settle there. And if the English would draw back over the mountain, they would get all other nations into their interest; but if they staid and settled there, all the nations would be against them; and he was afraid it would be a great war, and never come to peace again.[84]

Within five years Keekyuscung's words would ring out like a prophecy.

2

"A Colony Sprung from Hell"

Standing amid the charred ruins of Fort Duquesne, Lieutenant Colonel Henry Bouquet shivered in the cold December air. The mercury had dipped to a bone-chilling sixteen degrees, and many of the soldiers from General Forbes's army lacked adequate clothing. Nonetheless, it was a satisfying moment for Bouquet. A Swiss-born officer who had served as the general's second in command throughout the grueling campaign, no man in the army could better appreciate the sacrifice it had taken to seize the French fort at the forks of the Ohio. Much of the success of the expedition could be credited to Bouquet's tireless efforts. Throughout the summer and fall of 1758, as the British army inched its way toward the French stronghold, General Forbes suffered unbearably from a severe intestinal malady that one military surgeon called "the flux." This ailment was accompanied by "a most violent constipation attended with inflamation in the Rectum, violent pain & total suppression of the Urine." The illness left the general incapable of carrying out the day-to-day command of the army, and Bouquet took over, seeing to almost every detail.[1] It was Bouquet who oversaw the construction of the roadway over the mountains and supervised the erection of military outposts along the trail. He was also the person responsible for the disposition of troops along the line of march, for it was important to keep the six-thousand-man force dispersed so as not to exhaust any one area of supplies. In addition, the colonel had to provision the army, arrange for transports to carry those supplies, and attend to other endless details. Perhaps no soldier in Forbes's mixed force of provincials and British regulars was better suited for command of the expedition than Henry Bouquet.

Born in 1719 in the small Swiss town of Rolle along the shores of Lake Geneva, Bouquet had zealously pursued a military career. At seventeen he enlisted as a cadet in a Swiss regiment recruited to fight for Holland. During the War for the Austrian Succession, he served as a lieutenant in another Swiss unit pledged to the king of Sardinia. Following the war, he reentered Dutch service, where he was commissioned lieutenant colonel in a regiment of Swiss Guards. The young officer's capabilities apparently caught the eye of some of Europe's most accomplished military figures, and he eventually settled into the Hague to study "matters pertaining to military art and tactics, especially of the higher mathematics which forms their basis."[2]

When war between England and France once again loomed in 1755, the English Parliament decided to recruit among the Protestant Germans and other European settlers in America. This move would help offset the tremendous cost of sending even more regulars to the colonies. British military officials, including the Duke of Cumberland, favored granting commissions to non-British-born Protestants with military experience to help recruit, train, and lead these troops in North America. At the urging of Sir Joseph Yorke, the British ambassador to the Hague, Bouquet accepted a commission as lieutenant colonel in what became the 60th Regiment of Foot, also known as the Royal American Regiment. The young officer, along with his personal groomsman, Abraham Traxell, sailed for America in May 1756.[3]

Almost from the beginning of his service in America, Bouquet proved himself a competent and indefatigable officer. While assigned to British forces in New York, he advised General John Campbell on defensive structures. He carefully detailed plans for conducting extensive campaigns in the wilderness and, in 1757, actually drew up a plan of operations that would form the strategic formula for Forbes's advance on Fort Duquesne a year later. He represented himself as a cultured soldier-gentleman, and his wardrobe boasted several scarlet coats with broad gold lace, a silk night gown, and thirty-three shirts.[4]

Colonel Henry Bouquet, painting by John Wollaston (active 1736–1767), c. 1759. Wollaston painted many eighteenth-century American notables, including Sir William Johnson and Martha Custis. The accuracy of his portraits, however, is somewhat suspect. All of his subjects look remarkably similar, with the same almond-shaped eyes and cleft double chin. Courtesy the Historical Society of Pennsylvania Collection, Atwater Kent Museum of Philadelphia.

He was fluent in both French and English. In fact, his correspondence reveals his understanding of the English language to have been superior to most of his British-born contemporaries, especially those living in America. While stationed in Philadelphia before the Forbes campaign, Bouquet cultivated the friendship of many society notables, such as Benjamin Franklin; Dr. William Smith, who taught at the College of Philadelphia, and Charles Willing, a prominent merchant. Willing's charming daughter, Anne, became Bouquet's sweetheart.[5] The only existing portrait of Colonel Bouquet reveals a rather portly figure with a double chin, soft features, and dark hair, although this image is quite likely more the result of artistic license than an authentic likeness.[6]

Regardless of any genteel appearance, Henry Bouquet developed into a rugged frontier soldier. He was a keen observer of wilderness warfare and advocated the use of tactics conducive to fighting an irregular war against Indians. Reflecting on Braddock's debacle at the Monongahela, Bouquet suggested that the lead elements of an army on the march "must detach Small Parties a Mile forward, who Shall march in great Silence, and visit carefully all Suspected Places, as Copses, Ditches, and Hallows, where ambuscades may be concealed." The colonel further recommended that "there must be 3 flancking Parties upon each Flanck at an half mile distance from each other." During the advance on Fort Duquesne, General Forbes agreed with Bouquet's advice that "in this Country, wee must comply and learn the Art of Warr, from Enemy Indians, or any thing else who have seen the Country and Warr carried on inn itt."[7] Joseph Shippen, an officer with the Pennsylvania militia, observed Bouquet drilling troops during the campaign and wrote, "Every afternoon he exercises his men in the woods and bushes in a particular manner of his own invention, which will be of great service in an engagement with the Indians."[8] Colonel Bouquet also advocated that soldiers be equipped with muskets with browned barrels and wear short coats made from green or brown material.[9]

While Bouquet's contempt for the provincial soldier was similar to that of other British officers, he recognized those among the provincials who, despite their alleged lack of discipline and dedication, had considerable experience in fighting an irregular war against Indians. In a letter to a fellow officer Bouquet shared his impressions of the Pennsylvanians: "Everything most abominable that nature has produced, and everything most detestable that corruption can add to it, such are the honest inhabitants of this province." Yet, Bouquet noted, when it came to wilderness campaigning, "the provincials seem to have done well, and their good men are more suitable for this warfare than the regular troops."[10]

Colonel Bouquet's writings regarding the military profession reveal a dedicated man filled with a sense of duty who never questioned the necessity of armed conflict. While the Swiss soldier recognized warfare's destructiveness, he believed that this destruction brought renewal. In a letter to Anne Willing, Bouquet wrote:

> You are very right to hate war—it is an odious thing, tho' if considered in a proper light we could discover many advantages arising from that very calamity. Is it not a fact that a long and uninterrupted peace corrupts the manners, and breeds all sorts of vices? Like a stagnated air we require then the agitation of winds, and even storms to prevent a general infection, and to destroy a multitude of insects equally troublesome and dangerous to society. The necessity of action gives a new spring to our souls, real merits and virtues are no longer trampled upon by the arrogant pride of wealth and Place."[11]

It is doubtful that the colonel's defense of war was enough to alter Anne's opinion.

The laborious campaign to seize Fort Duquesne would add luster to Henry Bouquet's growing reputation as a dependable and competent officer in the British army. Almost single-handedly, he engineered the remarkable feat of hacking a military highway across the rugged Allegheny Mountains. Seeing to every detail, the colonel moved a massive army of six thousand men across the frontier, building a string of forts to protect his line of support and communication. He endeavored to understand the nature of frontier warfare and advocated important changes to deal with a cunning and resourceful enemy who lurked behind every tree, rock, and ditch. In addition, Bouquet carefully managed the complexities of a mixed force of provincials and British regulars to achieve relative harmony in the ranks.

Despite all of his efforts, success did not come without a heavy price. When the vanguard of Forbes's army reached the advanced outpost of Fort Ligonier, scouts informed Colonel Bouquet that the

French forces at the forks of the Ohio were in a weakened condition. Major James Grant, an officer in the 77th Highland Regiment, proposed a reconnaissance in force against Fort Duquesne. Although Colonel Bouquet may have been reluctant to acquiesce to Grant's request before the rest of the army came up, he could see the advantages to such a enterprise. While gathering valuable intelligence for the final thrust toward the enemy position, Grant's soldiers could also give the French and Indians a taste of their own medicine. Throughout the long summer, enemy skirmishing parties had harassed the British army. Work crews and hunting parties at Fort Ligonier had exercised constant vigilance against these guerrilla sorties. Grant could conceivably strike the same kind of terror into the enemy. Consequently, Bouquet gave his consent to the reconnaissance.[12]

Bouquet instructed Major Grant to reconnoiter Fort Duquesne with a mixed force of eight hundred Highlanders and provincials, attempt to destroy any Indian camps in the vicinity, and then retire in such manner as to entice any pursuers into an ambush posted along either side of the trail. The plan reveals that Bouquet had learned a great deal about frontier warfare and his Native American foes. The colonel reasoned that the Indians, enraged over an attack on their villages, would view the retreating troops as a sign of panic rout and charge headlong into the ambush that awaited them along Grant's return route.[13]

Grant and his junior officers, however, did not follow through on the proposed ruse. After setting fire to a few blockhouses that served as sentinel posts, Grant remained on a rise overlooking the fort. Perceiving the enemy too weak to sally out of their bastions and fight him, the major dispatched one hundred Highlanders down the hill, straight toward the fort. The French and their Indian allies, numbering perhaps six hundred to eight hundred, poured out of the compound and quickly encircled these Scottish soldiers. Grant and his reserve force rushed into the fray to rescue their beleaguered comrades and found themselves hemmed in on all sides. Hearing the firing coming from the direction of Fort Duquesne, the troops Grant had held in ambush along the trail also rushed forward and joined the fight. Confusion reigned as Grant attempted to rally his men. It was like Braddock's defeat all over again. Eventually, the remnants of Major Grant's force broke and retreated, leaving behind nearly three hundred casualties—

including Grant, who was captured.[14] When Bouquet and the rest of
the army finally occupied the ruins of Fort Duquesne in late November, they were shocked to see the heads and kilts of the brave Highlanders who had fought with Grant impaled on poles along the trail.[15]

Despite the setback of Grant's defeat, the conquest of Fort Duquesne
was indeed a satisfying moment to Henry Bouquet. Yet the modest
colonel gave most of the credit to the ailing General Forbes for his
efforts to draw the Ohio Indians away from their French allies. In a
letter to Anne Willing, Bouquet wrote:

> The glory of our success must after God be allowed to our
> General who from the beginning took those wise measures
> which deprived the French of their chief strength, and by the
> treaty of Easton kept such a number of Indians idle during the
> whole campaign, and procured a peace with those inveterate
> enemies, more necessary and beneficial to the safety and
> welfare of the Provinces than the driving the French from
> the Ohio.[16]

Without doubt, the treaty negotiated at Easton in October 1758
had gone far to assuage the various tribes and seduce them away from
French influence. The accord reached at the conference formalized
many prior agreements that Pennsylvania officials had made to the
Indians. The Albany purchase of 1754, which gave the Quaker colony
all the land west of the mountains, was rescinded and the land returned
to the Iroquois for use as hunting grounds by the other Ohio tribes.
The Delawares living along the Susquehanna were, for the time being,
guaranteed a homeland in the Wyoming Valley, and the Indians agreed
to return all of the English prisoners that had been kidnapped during
the war. Throughout the treaty conference, the Iroquois confederation
had taken a leading role. This well suited the Pennsylvania representatives. Previously, these same colonial officials had found it convenient to bypass Iroquois hegemony and deal directly with the Ohio
Indians. That diplomatic faux pas had given the Delawares a new
sense of leadership among the western tribes, and they had asserted
their new-found power to claim that the Pennsylvanians had stolen
their land in the Walking Purchase of 1737. By once again dealing
directly with the Iroquois league at Easton, the Pennsylvanians could
ignore Delaware complaints. This also enabled the Iroquois Confederacy

to reassert dominance over the Delawares, Shawnees, and other tribes living in the Ohio Country. The Ohio Indians' struggle for independence from the New York Iroquois had, for the time being, been tempered. Nonetheless, the very presence of Teedyuscung at Easton underscored the fact that the Delawares and other tribes were no longer willing to remain silent while the Iroquois negotiated on their behalf.[17]

Although peace had been reestablished with the Indians, John Forbes and Henry Bouquet still feared that their success was in jeopardy. It was the dead of winter, and the British army was more than three hundred miles from Philadelphia. It would be impossible to transport supplies over the mountains to sustain such a large force. The only recourse was to withdraw the army from the forks of the Ohio and leave behind a skeleton garrison of two hundred men to occupy the hard-won triangle of territory, which Forbes dubbed Pittsburgh, in honor of William Pitt. On December 4 the general, carried in a litter between two horses, led the vanguard of his army on the trail back to Fort Ligonier.[18]

Later that same day, a group of Delawares including Tamaqua, Shingas, and Keekyuscung crossed the river to confer with Colonel Bouquet at Fort Pitt. The Indians arrived at the forks accompanied by the missionary Christian Frederick Post, who had recently convinced them that the British promise to withdraw from the Ohio Valley was genuine. As it happened, Post could not secure a raft to cross the Allegheny River. Instead, George Croghan and Andrew Montour served as interpreters at the conference. Bouquet welcomed the chiefs and informed them that General Forbes's illness had compelled him to leave before speaking with them. Bouquet then told the assembled Indians, "We are not come here to take Possession of your hunting Country in a hostile Manner, as the French did when they came amongst you, but to open a large and extensive Trade with you and all other Nations of Indians to the Westward who chuse to live in friendship with us." Referring to the soldiers who were about to be left behind at the fort, he asked the Delawares to assist them until provisions arrived. And he further promised the Indians that trade would resume as soon as the French had been driven from the area.[19]

By the time Christian Frederick Post finally managed to cross the river, the conference had adjourned. The Delaware leaders informed the Moravian that they had told Bouquet "to leave this place and go back; but they insist upon staying here." Post also asked Croghan about the conference, and the Irishman replied that the Indians had agreed to allow the small garrison to remain at the forks. When Post insisted that the Indians had not altered their desire for the British to withdraw, Croghan indignantly replied that "it was a damned lie."[20]

After his conference with the Delaware headmen adjourned, Bouquet departed from Pittsburgh and headed east to join General Forbes at Philadelphia. The colonel left behind a force of less than 250 provincial soldiers to hold the strategic point until supplies and reinforcements could be brought west in the spring. General Forbes gave command of the coveted triangle to a most unlikely soldier, Colonel Hugh Mercer. Born in 1726 in Scotland, Mercer graduated from medical college in Aberdeen. He served as a surgeon for the forces of Bonnie Prince Charlie as the Stuart heir attempted to rally support among the Scottish clans for his bid to capture the English throne. Mercer was present at the Battle of Culloden when Stuart's Highland troops were overwhelmed by the Hanoverian prince the Duke of Cumberland. As British soldiers scoured the moors and farms in search of Scottish rebels, Mercer went into hiding. Believing that he would never be safe in his homeland again, the young doctor eventually fled to America in 1747 and settled in with Scottish kinsmen on the Pennsylvania frontier. He served as a physician to his pioneer neighbors, who soon recognized him as a natural leader.

In the aftermath of Braddock's defeat, Mercer was commissioned captain in the Pennsylvania militia. Perhaps the most harrowing experience in Mercer's life came in the fall of 1756, when he and his company of colonial troops joined Colonel John Armstrong's punitive expedition against the Delaware village of Kittanning, located along the Allegheny River. After burning the village and killing a number of Indians, including a noted warrior named Captain Jacobs, Armstrong's force retreated in a disorderly fashion. Mercer, who had been shot through the wrist during the engagement, became separated from his command and suddenly found himself alone and unarmed in the merciless wilderness. Hiding during the day and traveling at night, Mercer utilized all his pioneer skills to elude Indian pursuers and survive in the harsh forest environment. He ate berries, freshwater clams, and rattlesnake flesh as he slowly made his way back to Fort

Lyttleton, located along the eastern edge of the Allegheny ridge, one hundred miles from Kittanning. It took the tough Scotsman fourteen days to make this perilous trek. By the time of the Forbes's campaign, Mercer had become a seasoned veteran who could be relied on to hold the strategic forks of the Ohio during the dead of winter, even with the enemy still lurking in the vicinity.[21]

Mercer's immediate concerns involved building adequate shelter for the troops and keeping tabs on the disposition of the French. Beginning construction of a new military post around the ruins of Fort Duquesne, he was able by mid-January to send Colonel Bouquet a satisfactory report on his progress. Although nothing had been completed at this time, Mercer had begun to build barracks, storehouses, and a stockade that enclosed everything. He was also engaged in constructing five flat-bottomed boats to transport goods on the three rivers.[22]

Mercer did not neglect Indian affairs, holding periodic conferences with Iroquois, Delaware, Shawnee, and Mingo leaders. The Ohio Country Indians selected representatives from the Iroquois council to speak on their behalf and attempt to pressure the British to abandon the forks. Prior to one such conference, a group of five Iroquois chiefs came to Mercer's tent to speak in private about the Delaware and Shawnee desire to see the troops depart. The Iroquois proposed a ruse whereby they would request, on behalf of their Delaware cousins, that the English retire across the mountains. One of the Indian chiefs then instructed Mercer "to tell me at the Same time, that you are Resolved to Stay here, and fight the French till they are drove off from this Country." Accordingly, the next day, the Iroquois leader told Mercer that they should "Return Back to their Own Country." As instructed, Mercer responded, "The French are not gone from this Country, they are just at Our door, and give Out that they will Soon Return to this place. Our Great Man's words are true, as soon as the French are gone, he will make a Treaty with all the Indians and then go home, but the French are still here."[23] From this exchange it seems apparent that the British and their Iroquois allies from New York were once again in league to undermine the autonomy of the Ohio tribes.

Throughout the long winter, Mercer worked to shelter his troops, pacify the local Indians, and guard against a French counteroffensive to regain the forks of the Ohio. He received numerous reports that the enemy was wintering at Venango along the Allegheny River and was planning to attack his position. As it turned out, Mercer's concerns were ill founded. The French were in no condition just then to mount a campaign against even the small garrison at the forks. The British campaigns of the previous year had finally put the forces of Louis XV on the defensive. In July 1758 British generals Jeffrey Amherst and James Wolfe seized the strategic fortress of Louisbourg on Cape Breton Island. This fortified city had denied the British access to the Saint Lawrence. The English had also succeeded at the southern end of the river in seizing Fort Frontenac, which had served as the principal supply base for the other French forts in the Ohio Valley and Great Lakes region. The loss of Louisbourg and Frontenac came as a severe blow to the French, but not a decisive one. The resourceful French commander the Marquis de Montcalm, had successfully repulsed a British invasion force under General James Abercromby at Fort Carillon, along the Lake George–Lake Champlain corridor in New York. In a foolhardy assault against Montcalm's entrenchments, Abercromby sacrificed more than two thousand men, including nearly 650 Scots from the 42nd Regiment of Foot, later known as the Royal Highland Regiment. One British officer who watched the doomed "Black Watch" soldiers storm the enemy breastworks was prompted to remark, "I have seen men behave with courage and resolution before now, but such determined bravery can hardly have been equaled in any part of the history of ancient Rome."[24] Five years later, Colonel Henry Bouquet would make an almost identical remark regarding the courage of this Scottish regiment.

As the cold winter months of 1759 passed away, Mercer's position at Pittsburgh improved significantly. The entrenchments around the fort had been completed and the garrison reinforced with troops from the Royal American Regiment. A large quantity of Indian trade goods, including nearly five hundred blankets, 161 hunting shirts, twenty muskets, and eighteen silver gorgets arrived to satisfy the growing conglomeration of Ohio Indians camped around the fort. On a more melancholy note, Mercer received word that General Forbes, who had suffered excruciating pain as a result of his mysterious intestinal illness, had died in Philadelphia on March 11. Major General Jeffrey Amherst, the British commander in North America, selected Brigadier General John Stanwix to replace Forbes and ordered him to oversee the construction of a much stronger outpost at the forks of the Ohio. Even from his distant headquarters in New York, Amherst could see the strategic importance of the triangle. He told Colonel Bouquet that the point "is a Post of the greatest Consequence, great Care must be taken to Keep it in Respectable Condition, and all means must be used to protect & Defend it."[25]

Clearly, General Amherst intended the new post at Pittsburgh to serve as the main staging point for a British offensive northward to seize and occupy all the French forts in the Ohio Country and beyond to the Great Lakes. The campaigns of the previous year had succeeded in chipping away at France's outer defensives, and the British intended to continue the initiative in 1759 by striking the enemy's heartland at Niagara, Quebec, and Montreal. To achieve this goal, France's remaining frontier bastions must be reduced.[26]

Any plans to resume the offensive into enemy territory depended of course upon the continued neutrality of the Ohio Country tribes and their ability to convince other Indians from the Great Lakes to abandon the French. At Pittsburgh Colonel Mercer received assurances from Tamaqua and Shingas that the Ottawas, Chippewas, and their western neighbors were all determined to "bury the French Hatchet." To insure this development, the British had to offer continuous reassurances that they did not intend to remain in the land beyond the mountains. At a conference in Philadelphia with Iroquois and Delaware chiefs in the spring of 1759, Governor William Denny instructed an interpreter to inform them that "the French have told the Indians that the English intend to cheat them of the Land on the Ohio, and settle it for themselves, but this he assures you is false." Again at Pittsburgh that summer, George Croghan, speaking as an agent for the Indian superintendent, Sir William Johnson, assured a large assembly of Ohio and Great Lakes tribes that once the French were finally driven away, "the General will depart your Country after securing our Trade with you and our Brethren to the Westward."[27] Despite these promises the Delawares, Shawnees, and others looked on with suspicion as a royal engineer, Captain Harry Gordon, arrived at the forks of the Ohio at the end of July with more than three hundred artificers to begin construction on Fort Pitt.[28]

Another issue that required attention in order to placate the Ohio Indians concerned the resumption of trade. As Forbes's soldiers had returned from the ruins of Fort Duquesne in the winter, they had passed traders en route to the forks anxious to be the first to resume the lucrative commerce with the Indians. By February 1759 Lieutenant Caleb Graydon, a Pennsylvania provincial officer stationed at Fort Lyttleton, counted forty-five sutlers and Indian traders headed west with nearly 250 pack horses laden with goods for soldiers and Indians alike. The following month, another forty-two enterprising souls carried merchandise such as rum, flour, molasses, shoes, and tobacco past the post. Surprisingly, one of these merchants was a woman, Catherine Winepilt, who guided a packhorse bearing apples and eggs to sell to the garrison and neighboring Indians.[29] Despite this seemingly steady stream of commerce flowing into the new fort at Pittsburgh, there was still an insufficient quantity of merchandise for the Indians, who had again become eager consumers. The problem stemmed partly from the army's commandeering vast amounts of trade items for its own purposes due to its inability to contract enough horses and wagons to transport its own goods from the east. Consequently, Colonel Mercer and other commanders on the frontier seized the merchandise of private traders in return for a receipt. Finally, at the end of May, Colonel Bouquet was able to contract one hundred wagons and a thousand horses to transport military supplies across the mountains.[30]

Another problem that plagued the steady flow of trade goods to the West was the constant threat of attack along the road. On April 16 a party of Indians preyed on a convoy herding cattle to feed the inhabitants at Pittsburgh. Two days later, another war party ambushed a detail escorting sick soldiers from Fort Ligonier to Bedford. The corporal in charge of this escort fled, leaving the "Sick to the Mercy of the Enemy. Eleven are killd or missing in this Affair." As summer approached, the Indians, mostly Great Lakes tribesmen who still supported the French, grew bolder. On May 14 a group of Chippewas and Caughnawaga Iroquois skirmished with a small detachment of provincial troops just beyond Fort Pitt. Nine days later Captain Thomas Bullitt and one hundred Virginia soldiers were attacked by a large war party that succeeded in destroying four wagons loaded with pork to feed the Pittsburgh garrison. This attack took place within three miles of Fort Ligonier and prompted the post commandant to complain to General Stanwix, "I beg Leave to observe to you Sir that this Garrison is harrassed to Death with continual Escorts and within a very short Time prove utterly incapable of that severe Duty."[31] This almost constant harassment of the convoys along the trail and the pinprick attacks by roving Indian war parties paralyzed the frontier outposts and threatened British efforts to maintain the good will of the Ohio Country Indians. When the Indian agent, George Croghan, arrived at Fort Pitt in mid-June, he found the assembled Delawares and Shawnees destitute and "bear of Cloathing." He later reminded them "that while the Enemy are in Possession of your Country, we cannot Trade safely with you."[32]

For Colonel Hugh Mercer it must have seemed as if everything was beginning to unravel. Tamaqua and other Delaware leaders had failed to bring the majority of the Great Lakes tribes into the league of peace signed at Easton. The uncertainty of a stable trade and the growing presence of English troops threatened the fragile peace with the Ohio Indians as well. At any moment these volatile people might go back over to the French, who were still menacingly close by at Venango. Mercer was a long way out on the proverbial limb, with reinforcements and provisions unreliable and the best hope for assistance three hundred miles away at Philadelphia. As the earth began to warm in the spring of 1759, Colonel Mercer and other British officers became increasingly concerned over the possibility of a French counteroffensive to retake the forks of the Ohio.

Mercer's fears were well founded, for the French at Presque Isle and Venango were simply waiting for reinforcements from Detroit and Niagara in order to launch a campaign against the British frontier outposts. On June 1 a detachment of French troops under Captain Jean-Baptiste Testard de Montigny left Niagara with supplies of flour, muskets, and ammunition to reinforce the garrison at Presque Isle in preparation for an attack against Fort Pitt. Back in Philadelphia, Colonel Bouquet received "Intelligence that the french had 300 men & 200 Indians at Venango, & expected more with an Intention to act offensively." By July 1 Indian informants told George Croghan at Fort Pitt that "the French had called all the Militia of that part of the Country [Detroit], [and] told the Indians they were going to Preskisle where they expected to meet a Party from Niagara with Cannon that they were going to fortifie Venango, and that they should have three Hundred Indians with them."[33] However, as the garrison at Pittsburgh braced for an attack, fate, which so often takes a hand in armed conflict, stepped in to alter the course of the war.

On July 12, 1759, Captain Francois Le Marchand de Lignery, commandant at Venango, assembled his campaign force of over seven hundred French and four hundred western Indian allies to attack Fort Pitt. While Lignery was exhorting the warriors to annihilate the English on the Belle Rivière, several Indian runners approached with a packet of dispatches for the French officer. After reading the letters, Captain Lignery turned to the assembled chiefs and said, "Children I have bad news to tell you, there is a great Army of the English coming against Niagara with Sir William Johnson who has with him all the Six Nations [Iroquois], with a great Number of other Indians who live that way." Further, the captain said, "I have Orders to go directly to Niagara and take you with me, we must give over the thoughts of going down this river till we have drove the English away from Niagara, you know the Consequence that place is of, both to you and us, if the English take it you must be poor, as it is stopping the Road to your Country."[34] Indeed, as Lignery had reported, a British army of twenty-five hundred men led by Brigadier General John Prideaux had invested Fort Niagara on July 6. Prideaux's forces included nearly one thousand Iroquois warriors commanded by Sir William Johnson.

Two weeks later, while the British laid siege to Fort Niagara, Johnson received word from his Iroquois scouts that French reinforcements were approaching along the portage road. The Iroquois advanced to meet Captain Lignery and his command and counsel them not to attempt to relieve their beleaguered comrades in the fort. While many of Lignery's Indian allies heeded this ominous warning and turned back, the French commander pushed on toward Fort Niagara. When Lignery's force struck the British front lines guarding the path to the fort, the Redcoats rose up from both of their flanks and fired into the French line. Captain Lignery was wounded and his relief force cut to pieces. The remaining French soldiers retreated up the portage road toward Niagara Falls. With no hope of receiving further reinforcements, the French surrendered Fort Niagara to Sir William Johnson on July 26, 1759. The British victory doomed all French forces in the Ohio River Valley. Caught between English forces at Pittsburgh and

Niagara, the French had no recourse but to abandon their forts at Presque Isle, LeBoeuf, and Venango. After five years of awful violence, the French presence in the Ohio Country finally was at an end.[35]

The defeat of the French at Fort Niagara marked the beginning of the final phase of the Seven Years' War in North America. By the fall of 1759, General Amherst was able to conquer the Lake George–Lake Champlain corridor and seize Fort Carillon. At the same time, France suffered a bigger blow as Wolfe's forces assaulted Montcalm's on the Plains of Abraham outside the city of Quebec. The fall of the capital of New France left only Montreal and the remote outposts that dotted the Great Lakes region to be conquered.

Throughout the bitter contest, Indians in the Ohio Country and along the shores of the Great Lakes had participated not as pawns of either European power but in an effort to control their own destinies. For decades the English had used their relationship with the Iroquois in the Covenant Chain to wring land concessions from the Delawares, Shawnees, and others. These tribesmen had fought to gain independence from Iroquois hegemony and preserve their final homeland in the Ohio River Valley. While the Easton Treaty had brought them back into the Iroquois sphere of influence, it also provided them with guarantees from the English that their lands across the mountains would remain free from white infestation. With the power of the French broken, the Indians began to wonder when the British were going to fulfill their promises.

In 1760 the British army's objectives were to consolidate and reinforce the hard-won gains of the previous year. To that end Brigadier General Robert Monckton, who replaced John Stanwix as the regional commander, ordered Colonel Bouquet to advance northward from Fort Pitt and occupy the abandoned French outposts at Venango, LeBoeuf, and Presque Isle. Monckton instructed the Swiss commander to take along an engineer, artificers, and tools to construct a blockhouse at Lake Erie. Bouquet was also accompanied by George Croghan and a small delegation of Indian guides, who were directed to make contact with any Indians that might be encountered and reassure them of the British government's peaceful intentions.[36]

As Bouquet marched out of Pittsburgh on July 7, he became acutely aware of how ignorant the British were of the lands beyond the confines of the fort. His five hundred men marched only six miles when they discovered they had taken the wrong path! Bouquet blamed his Indian guides and complained, "No Body in this detachment without Exception knows any thing of the Country or distances except the Indians, who are almost always drunk." When the colonel arrived at the ruins of Fort Presque Isle on the southern shore of Lake Erie, he set about constructing redoubts and a blockhouse while Croghan and the Indians scoured the region for French and Indian skirmish parties from the West. On July 19 one of the Irishman's guides returned to report that he had encountered four Huron and Chippewa warriors lurking in the area who "informed him that there was Twenty of their Party, that they were employed by the French at D'Troit to come there as Spies, and to take an English Prisoner; but that their Nations had determined not to commit any Hostilities against the English and desired he might assure me that they would Return without doing any mischief." Despite these professions of peace this same war party later ambushed a small group of Bouquet's men near the neck of the peninsula, killing and scalping two men. This attack made it clear that, while the Ohio Country Delawares and Shawnees may have been sincere in their intentions to remain at peace, many of the Great Lakes tribes were still closely allied with the French.[37] Despite the attack, Colonel Bouquet continued the task of building a small post at Presque Isle. By the first week of November, Bouquet could report that the forts at Lake Erie, LeBoeuf, and Venango were secure and in no danger of assault. With his mission accomplished, he returned south to assume command of Fort Pitt.

With the Ohio-Niagara corridor firmly in the hands of the British, General Amherst could turn his attention to the French fortifications remaining to the west at Detroit and throughout what was called the Illinois country. In September 1760 Amherst finally seized Montreal and obtained a formal surrender from the governor of Canada, the Marquis de Vaudreuil. In the terms of the capitulation, Vaudreuil agreed to surrender his western outposts, and General Amherst ordered the famous ranger Robert Rogers to mount an expedition to Detroit to formally take possession of the region. Perhaps no one had achieved a greater reputation during the war with France than the fearless Major Rogers. Having organized a corps of New England rangers early in the war, Rogers and his men quickly became the eyes and ears for the British army in the long struggle to conquer the Lake George–Lake

Champlain corridor. Rogers himself was somewhat of an enigma, variously described as a rogue, opportunist, and braggart, as well as a courageous, cunning, and indefatigable warrior. On numerous occasions Rogers and his rangers found themselves outnumbered and surrounded by hordes of French and Indians; yet somehow the resourceful commander always managed to escape. In one daring episode the major and his men drove deep into the heart of enemy territory in a punitive strike against an Abenaki Indian village at Saint Francis. After burning the village to the ground, Rogers and his desperate battalion were vigorously pursued by the French and vengeful Indians. Facing torture, death, and starvation, the rangers scattered throughout the trackless mountains and forests of New England. By the time his command reunited at the relative safety of Fort Number Four on the Connecticut River, Rogers had lost nearly a third of his men.[38]

On September 13, 1760, Rogers and two hundred of his celebrated rangers embarked from Montreal in fifteen whaleboats. Arriving at Presque Isle on October 8, Rogers left his men at the fort and traveled by canoe down to Pittsburgh to consult with General Monckton. The general instructed the major to proceed to Detroit with his rangers and a company of one hundred Royal Americans under the command of Captain Donald Campbell. Once there, Rogers was to demand formal capitulation of the post from the French officer in charge and administer the oath of allegiance to the local inhabitants. After completing this task, Rogers was to return to New York, leaving Campbell and his company behind to garrison Fort Detroit.[39] General Monckton also ordered George Croghan, Andrew Montour, and a small party of Indians to accompany the expedition in order to make contact with the various western tribes and inform them of the British government's peaceful intentions.[40]

Rogers returned to Presque Isle and on November 4 departed with his command for Detroit by sailing along the southern shore of Lake Erie. A master of irregular warfare, Rogers gave explicit orders regarding the voyage and line of march to insure that the men would not be surprised by hostile Indians still aligned with the French. No soldier was permitted to discharge his musket or travel beyond the sentry posts that would be established at every campsite. In addition, the officers were directed to inspect all firearms daily.[41]

Major Robert Rogers and an Indian chief, from the *Hibernian Magazine* (September 1776). This engraving is a strange amalgamation of a 1776 mezzotint likeness of Rogers published by Thomas Hart and several characters found in Benjamin West's 1771 painting, *Death of Wolfe*. There is no known authenticated portrait of Rogers. Courtesy the William L. Clements Library, University of Michigan.

On November 7 the whaleboats approached the mouth of the Cuyahoga River and were met by a party of thirty Ottawas who "Saluted . . . with a discharge of their Guns and an English flagg Flying." Later Croghan informed the Indians that Montreal had fallen and that the English had come to take over the French forts. Croghan also promised the Ottawas that they "should enjoy a Free Trade with their Brethren the English, and be protected in Peaceable Possession of their Hunting Country as long as they wou'd adhere to His Majesty's Interest." Continuing on the journey, Rogers's command finally reached the entrance to the Detroit River on November 20 and found a body of four hundred warriors gathered to block their advance. Major Rogers parlayed with a delegation of Huron, Ottawa, and Potawatomie chiefs, telling them of his mission. The Indians permitted Rogers to continue, and he arrived at Fort Detroit nine days later. As the French garrison laid down its arms, the Union Jack was hoisted as an assemblage of seven hundred Indians looked on. Rogers then administered the oath of allegiance to the seven hundred French settlers, or habitants, who lived near the fort.[42]

On December 3 Croghan opened a grand council with the Hurons, Ottawas, and Potawatomies by informing them that he was there to "brighten the Ancient Chain of Friendship between his Majesty's Subjects, The Six United Nations and our Brethren of the several Western Nations to the Sun setting." He assured them that Captain Campbell, as the new commandant at Detroit, would see to it that they were treated fairly in regard to trade. Croghan recognized, he said, that the "Warriors have all a Martial Sperit & must be imployed at War" and that to fulfill that desire they should go south and fight the Cherokees, who were presently engaged in an uprising against the English. He reminded them of previous promises to return any captives they still had in their possession and admonished them not to steal from the English soldiers or inhabitants of the community. Responding to Croghan's address, a Huron chief, speaking on behalf of the other tribes, said, "All the indians in this Country are Allies to each other and as one People." The Indians agreed to release those captives willing to be repatriated and promised to take hold of the "Ancient Chain of Friendship." The chief warned Croghan, however, that "if ever it be broak it will be on your side, and it is in your Power, as you are an Able People to prevent it for while this Friendship is

preserved we shall be a Strong Body of People." The council concluded
with the Indians asking that trade prices be reduced from the rates
they had been forced to accept from the French. When the conference
adjourned, the Indians gave up forty-two captives. While the tribes
seemed sincere in their desire to maintain peace with their new neighbors, there was at least one Ottawa leader, perhaps standing aside
during the negotiations, who vowed never to bury the hatchet with
the English. His name was Pontiac.[43]

Born along the Detroit River, Pontiac was probably in his early
forties when the English raised their flag in his country. The meaning
of his name seems to be lost in antiquity. He had spent his entire life
in close proximity to the French and had even defended them against
other neighboring tribes over the years. It is entirely possible that
Pontiac had participated in the annihilation of General Braddock's
troops near Fort Duquesne in 1755. He was certainly fighting for the
French in the Ohio Valley two years later and may have been one of
the last Indians to abandon his allies when John Forbes seized the
forks in 1758. It is also quite possible that Pontiac attended one of
the numerous conferences that George Croghan held with the western
tribes at Fort Pitt during the spring and summer of 1760. No contemporary portrait of the Ottawa leader exists, but he was described
as being tall and "not handsome" with "a proud, vindictive, war-like
and easily offended" countenance.[44]

Having secured the important fort at Detroit, Rogers and his
ranger detachment returned east, leaving behind Captain Campbell
and the Royal Americans to garrison the post. Rogers's departure from
the Great Lakes marked the beginning of a new phase of imperial
policy in North America. Amherst's soldiers had won a vast new
territory for the new British monarch, George III. All of this land was
beyond the traditional boundaries of the thirteen colonies and, therefore, required royal authority to administer and control. To facilitate
this administration, Amherst had to continue reinforcing and aug-
menting the former French outposts that stretched from the Ohio
River Valley to the Illinois country. Throughout 1760–1761, work
progressed on enlarging and strengthening Fort Pitt. As the bricks
and mortar continued to pile up, forming part of the outer works of
the fort, a substantial community of traders, merchants, tavern keepers,
prostitutes, speculators, and laborers sprung up outside the walls.

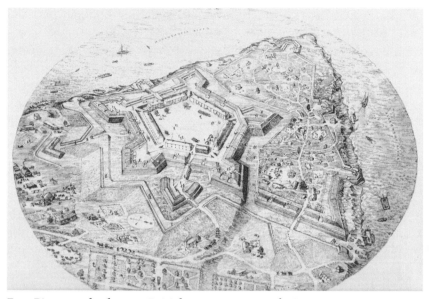

Fort Pitt was the largest British outpost in North America, encompassing seventeen acres. By the time of Pontiac's Uprising, a sizable community existed outside the compound. The Lower Town, as it was called, stood within the shadows of the fort and crowded the land existing at the extreme point of the triangle. The Upper Town was situated to the southeast, as shown in the left corner of the drawing. This sketch by historical architect Charles Stotz was executed after consulting fifteen separate plans of the fort made in the eighteenth century. Courtesy Library and Archives Division, Historical Society of Western Pennsylvania.

Colonel Bouquet took a census of Pittsburgh in April 1761 and discovered the town contained a total of 160 structures with a population of 219 men, 75 women, and 38 children. Most of the structures Bouquet surveyed were log cabins, storehouses, grog shops, or ramshackle huts. One notable exception was Croghan Hall, a rambling edifice with new furniture and pewter chamber pots that stood downriver from the fort. Croghan claimed a great deal of land around the forks that had been sold to him by the Indians before the war. Consequently, the shrewd Irish Indian agent was poised to become extremely wealthy parceling out property to prospective settlers. One of the earliest pioneers to purchase land from Croghan was William Clapham, a former colonel in the Pennsylvania militia.[45]

As for the rest of the settlement's inhabitants, Bouquet regarded most of them as a useless and indolent lot. The raw frontier community served as a depository for opportunists of every description. In a letter to General Monckton Bouquet complained that "this Place is Particularly infested with a number of Inhabitants the Scum of the neighboring Provinces, who have no visible means to live, except a License, & think it bad Consequence for the garrison, and I could wish the number of Traders was limited & obliged to give security for their Behaviour." One evening while Bouquet was at supper, thieves broke into his quarters within the walls of the fort and stole his entire bureau containing £1,687.10, intended for personal use and military subsistence. The money was never recovered, and the chagrined colonel was forced to repay the missing funds. All of this prompted Bouquet to label Pittsburgh "a Colony sprung from Hell for the Scourge of mankind."[46]

Economic opportunity was the magnet that drew English frontiersmen and their families into the land beyond the mountains. Christopher Gist once described the vast resources that abounded in the region:

> This Place . . . is fine, level Land, well timbered with large Walnut, Ash Sugar Trees Cherry Trees &c, it is well watered with a great Number of little Streams or Rivulets, and full of beautiful natural Meadows, covered with Wild Rye, blue Grass and Clover, and abounds with Turkeys, Deer, Elks and most Sorts of Game particularly Buffaloes, thirty or forty of which are frequently seen feeding in one Meadow: In short it wants Nothing but Cultivation to make it a most delightfull Country—The Ohio and all the large Branches are said to be full of fine Fish of several Kinds, particularly a Sort of Cat Fish of a prodigious Size.[47]

Descriptions such as this fueled the speculative efforts of individuals such as Croghan, as well as those of large investment groups such as the Ohio Company, which still pressed its claims despite agreements made with the Indians at Easton.

While the fanciful descriptions of a land of milk and honey inspired an increasing wave of immigration over the mountains, life at the remote frontier community of Pittsburgh proved for many to be a bitter disappointment. A Quaker trader named James Kenny arrived at the forks in the wake of John Forbes's army. He provided a far more realistic picture of conditions at Fort Pitt. Keeping a daily journal of activities at the post, Kenny's entries reveal that the residents were constantly plagued by a variety of illnesses, including measles, smallpox, dysentery, and a deadly intestinal disorder called the flux. Sanitary conditions within the squalid dwellings left much to be desired, and Kenny complained of the biting fleas that infested his trading post and kept him awake at night. He also lamented that the frontier seemed to attract a violent breed of men to whom the slightest insult could result in death. In September 1761 he recorded in his journal that a man had brutally murdered a teamster for striking his dog. In another incident Kenny recorded, the post physician seduced the blacksmith's daughter and had to fight a duel with an officer in the Royal American Regiment over the girl's honor. The Quaker trader witnessed wickedness at every turn and was especially shocked to discover that the local preacher lived with a prostitute.[48]

Alcohol usually lay at the root of most of the detestable and violent acts perpetrated on the frontier. This was especially true among the scores of Indian inhabitants who frequented the trading posts. Kenny reported that "ye Indians frequently get Drunk pawning their Clothss Wampum & all they have for it; that two Mohaks Indians got Drunk . . . & ye one kill'd ye other in fighting, him self being much wounded." The rum trade among the Indians became such a problem that Colonel Bouquet issued orders to all traders "to Sell no Rum or Strong Liquor nor give to Indians on Pain of having their Houses pull'd Down, & ye Transgressors being banished [from] the place." Disease and drunken violence claimed so many lives in and around Fort Pitt that, Kenny observed, "burying a dead man is thought but a light matter at garrisons."[49]

The wilderness environment also posed deadly problems for the frontier settlers. While traveling along the old Braddock Road between the Great Meadows and Fort Pitt, Kenny discovered "a man's skull with ye teeth in ye upper jaw, lying in a swamp," which inspired him to label the place "Golgotha." Presumably this unfortunate pilgrim became lost in the forest and died from starvation. In the winter of 1761, the Quaker merchant noted in his journal that three traders had set out on foot to visit the Indian camps along Beaver Creek.

Two of the men became separated from their partner and "perished in the snow." Later the same winter, a great flood nearly swept Pittsburgh away, forcing poor Kenny and other residents to seek refuge in Fort Pitt. The water rose to the top of one of the fort's ramparts before subsiding.[50]

Like Colonel Bouquet, James Kenny believed himself to be in the midst of hell, with robbery, murder, drunkenness, and environmental disaster all around him. Soldiers, traders, laborers, harlots, Indians, and African slaves had all come together at the edge of the world and seemed to struggle for life. Walking to the top of Grant's Hill, overlooking the fort, Kenny was shocked to discover that everyone seemed to be so engaged in his or her own pursuits that no one had bothered to bury some of the dead Highlanders who had been killed four years earlier. All of this compelled Kenny to confide in his diary that Pittsburgh seemed under the influence of "Satan's Government." Certainly, the odious environs of Fort Pitt were a far cry from the pristine wilderness that Christopher Gist and others had discovered less than a decade before. This despoilment greatly alarmed the Ohio Country Indians, who grew increasingly resentful over the pestilence that accompanied the English presence. One Delaware who came to Kenny's store told of a rat that had been found in one of the Indian villages up the Allegheny River. To the Delawares, the rat was an omen foretelling that the British would remain in their country. Old Indians in the village remembered that rats had also invaded their homes along the Delaware River years before when the English came to claim those lands. In a futile attempt to forestall the coming of the white man, the Delawares scoured their village in search of the rat.[51]

While frontier civilians suffered greatly in the remote wilderness environment, it was perhaps worse for the soldiers who garrisoned the far-flung outposts of the backcountry. Generally, the common soldier, both regular and provincial, was recruited from the lower classes and considered little more than a tool by the officers who commanded him. Due to rigorous training and discipline, the regular British soldier considered himself superior to his colonial counterpart. Provincials, on the other hand, had little regard for such training and considered themselves adapted for wilderness warfare. Despite these differences both groups shared the misery that accompanied the frontier military. Rations were of poor quality, the pay was meager, quarters were cramped and filthy, and punishment for even minor infractions was severe. A soldier could expect to receive a thousand lashes for as small an offense as stealing a keg of beer. In addition, the troops were frequently at the mercy of unscrupulous traders who cheated the men and kept them well supplied with alcohol. Colonel Bouquet finally issued orders forbidding Pittsburgh's inhabitants from allowing soldiers in their homes after dark. Soldiers who were not broken by alcoholism could succumb from the same diseases that plagued the civilians. James Kenny was present at Fort Cumberland, Maryland, when Lieutenant James Riley, an officer who had distinguished himself at Grant's defeat, died from smallpox. The dreaded disease moved west with the army and plagued Fort Pitt for months.[52]

Given the many hardships the troops had to endure, it is not surprising that Colonel Bouquet and all his officers complained about desertion from posts along Forbes Road. Apprehended deserters could expect to face a firing squad. Thomas Barton, who served as a physician during Forbes's campaign, witnessed one such execution, that of Private John Doyle, an Irishman from a Pennsylvania regiment. Barton recalled the scene in his journal: "He would suffer no Handkerchief to be ty'd over his Face, but looked at his Executioners to the last, who advanced so near him that the Muzzles of their Guns were within a Foot of his Body. Upon a Signal from the Serjeant Major they fir'd, but shot so low that his Bowels fell out, his Shirt & Breeches were all on Fire, & he tumbled upon his Side." Barton called it "a shocking Spectakle to all around him, & a striking Example to his Fellow Soldiers."[53]

Like the men in the ranks, officers also experienced the deprivation of frontier garrison life. Most of General Amherst's army was scattered throughout the wilderness at small, isolated posts such as Venango and Presque Isle. These forts were usually garrisoned by a lieutenant with fewer than twenty enlisted men. The officers at these remote bastions frequently complained about a lack of supplies, including general hardware, forage for livestock, powder, lead, rations, and even writing paper. Discipline and morale were difficult to maintain. Captain Lewis Ourry, a Swiss national and officer in the Royal American Regiment stationed at Fort Bedford along Forbes Road, complained to Colonel Bouquet that "the Men of this Garrison are lost to all discipline and continually guilty of drunkenness and Theft.

. . . And tho' I have confined some of the Persons concerned in the roguery, the Two principal Thieves . . . have escaped me being deserted last Night."[54] Ourry chafed at having to deal with "the drunks, the cuckolds, the whores, the loafers, the thieves, and the bitchers" that gravitated to the post.[55]

Life was little better for officers stationed at the larger forts on the frontier. In September 1760 Colonel Bouquet sadly reported the suicide of Dr. James Milne, the post surgeon at Fort Pitt. Apparently, the physician had become so despondent that he cut his own throat with a razor. James Kenny wrote in his diary that Milne "had been at times Hipt or Lunatick."[56] Even Colonel Bouquet surrendered to melancholy when he learned that his beloved Anne Willing had unexpectedly married another man. It appears that the alluring Miss Willing harbored strong reservations about marrying a soldier. Acknowledging this reluctance, the colonel wrote to Anne, "If I should get rid of the continual occupation of a military life, I should of course feel a weariness of which I see nothing that would relieve me." He did admit, however, that if anything could change his mind, it would be her "persuasive eloquence." As it turned out, Bouquet did not act quickly enough to reassure the young woman: while he pined away at Fort Pitt, a young "Gentleman of Fortune" named Tench Francis quickly swept Anne off her feet. When Bouquet's good friend Captain Ourry broke the bad news, the colonel was struck with an "agitated spirit, like the ocean after the violent shock of an earthquake." Ourry's attempts at consolation did little to lift Bouquet from his "melancholy Solitude." The colonel informed Ourry that he intended to resign from the army and return to Europe. Perhaps from his sense of duty, Bouquet changed his mind and threw himself into his work in an effort to forget his heartache.[57]

There was plenty of work at Fort Pitt to distract Henry Bouquet from his lost love. With the French threat permanently removed, squatters of every description began to invade the trans-Appalachian frontier. In late March 1761 Sergeant Angus McDonald, who commanded a twelve-man garrison at Fort Burd along the Youghiogheny River, sent Colonel Bouquet a dispatch informing him that "here is people who has been Clearing Ground all winter" and were preparing to plant corn. McDonald, a former sailor from Scotland, was considered an "Intelligent & Carefull" soldier. Aware that allowing settlers in the region violated agreements with the Indians, he asked Bouquet what action should be taken. Bouquet ordered the sergeant to immediately "drive those People off." Despite McDonald's efforts the tide of immigrants continued unabated. By October the sergeant was again complaining to Bouquet that "here Comes Such Crowds of Hunters out of the Inhabitence as fills the woods at which the Indians seems very much disturbed and say the white people Kills all there Deer." This communication prompted Bouquet to post the following proclamation:

> Wheras by a Treaty held at East Town in the year 1758, and since ratified by His Majesty's Ministers, The Country to the West of the Alleghany Mountains is allowed to the Indians for their Hunting Ground, and as it is of the Highest Importance to His Majesty's Service, the Preservation of the Peace and a good understanding with the Indians, to avoid giving them any Just cause of Complaint, this is therefore to forbid any of His Majesty's Subjects to Settle or Hunt to the West of the Alleghany Mountains on any Pretence Whatsoever, unless such Persons have obtained leave in Writing of the General or the Governor's of their Provinces Respectively and produced the same to the Commanding Officer at Fort Pitt.

Further, Bouquet's proclamation warned transgressors that if they were apprehended for violating the order, they would be sent to Fort Pitt to be tried by military court martial.[58]

Colonel Bouquet's proclamation resulted in a swift and stern response from Virginia's governor, Francis Fauquier, who wrote to the colonel in January demanding further explanation. Fauquier informed the Swiss officer that his order had created "some Uneasiness in this colony" and reminded him that some settlers had already obtained a rightful patent to the land from the crown prior to the war. The governor also fumed over Bouquet's threat to try offenders under military law, asserting that "no person is liable to Martial Law or to tryal by Court Martial who is not in some Shape connected with the Military Department.[59]

Unintimidated, Colonel Bouquet shot back, defending his position: "For two years past these Lands have been overrun by a number of Vagabonds, who under pretence of hunting were making Settlements contrary to the Treaty made with [the Indians] at Easton. I issued the Said orders to prevent in the best manner I could those encroachments." The colonel believed he was justified in trying the squatters by court martial, he wrote, because the territory was outside the "known limit of one of the Provinces," where "there is no form of civil Judicature in force."[60] Standing firm, Bouquet informed the governor that unless he had express orders from General Amherst, no one, including those who maintained some prior claim, would be permitted to take possession of the land west of the Alleghenies.

Exasperated by Bouquet's terse military demeanor and his refusal to be intimidated by any civil authority, Fauquier appealed directly to Amherst. The general, wishing to "avoid any thing that can give the Colonies the least room to Complain of the Military power," wrote to Bouquet admitting that no military authority could prevent those Virginians holding patents issued prior to the Easton Treaty from taking up their claims. Bouquet continued to defend himself and made little effort to hide the fact that he was disappointed with the general's decision.[61] He insisted that he was a disinterested party in the Virginians' land grabbing, and he voiced indignation over their "Scandalous breach" of the Easton Treaty. In truth, however, the colonel himself was engaged in land speculation schemes along the Forbes Road. Evidence exists that the Swiss-born officer plotted with George Croghan to acquire property near Fort Bedford.[62]

The Indians of the Ohio Country were not alone in complaining of English attempts to settle their lands. To the east, along the Susquehanna, Teedyuscung also found settlers from Connecticut moving onto Indian land who based their asserted right to occupy the region on the transaction concluded with the Six Nations Iroquois at Albany in 1754. It mattered little to these Connecticut pioneers that the Iroquois themselves had disavowed the sale. In November 1762 Teedyuscung traveled to Philadelphia to appeal to Governor James Hamilton for help in expelling the invaders. The Delaware chief complained that 150 squatters, "furnished with all sorts of Tools, as well for building as Husbandry," had arrived on the banks of the Susquehanna. "Brother," he said to the governor, "Surely as you have a General of the King's Armies here, he might hinder these people from coming & disturbing us in our possessions." Since the entire matter of the Susquehanna lands had been laid before Superintendent of

Indian Affairs Sir William Johnson, Hamilton could do little but send a runner to warn the New Englanders not to settle on the lands. Hamilton also sent an express to Connecticut's governor, Thomas Fitch, outlining a history of the land dispute and reminding him that the matter must be settled by the king. Then Hamilton cautioned Teedyuscung "that no blood of the White People may be shed" and sent the chief back home to the Susquehanna.[63] Sir William Johnson had authority under the Easton agreement to adjudicate Teedyuscung's claims, but he seemed powerless to stop the Connecticut settlers. Even General Amherst could not control the tide of New Englanders whose insatiable desire for land would not be deterred.[64]

Indians to the north were also growing disgruntled over English land transgressions. General Amherst, wishing to institute a strong British presence along the portage road between lakes Ontario and Erie, decided to issue permits allowing some of his former officers to settle along the trail. One of these former soldiers, Walter Rutherford, planned to establish a tavern along the road. Rutherford also hoped to form partnerships with New York entrepreneurs and establish a freighting line between Fort Niagara and Lake Erie. This infuriated the western Senecas, who had for years been employed in hauling goods along the road. To these Indians it appeared that the English were not content with just taking their land but wanted to destroy their livelihood as well. When Sir William Johnson visited Fort Niagara in late July 1761, he learned that a "universal Jealousy and uneasiness appear amongst those of every Nation" as a result of the building that was taking place along the portage. When Johnson informed Amherst of the Seneca's discontent, the general disregarded the warning, saying, "they need not take umbrage at the Settlements on the Carrying Place, where People, Horses, Carriages etc. are absolutely necessary to keep up the Communication."[65]

Even the Great Lakes tribes living in the far western frontier were beginning to witness the British rapaciousness for Indian land. In April 1762 a young English adventurer and sportsman named Sir Robert Davers appeared at the gates of Fort Detroit accompanied by a Pawnee slave. Davers, the fifth baronet of Rushbrook, believed, following the suicides of two older brothers, that he was prone to mental illness. In an attempt to avoid a similar fate, he decided to come to America and live among the Indians. He found the Native American lifestyle suited him and began to make progress in learning their languages. Using Detroit as a base of operations, Davers spent a great deal of time on numerous expeditions up and down the lakes and rivers, presumably hoping to find an ideal location to stake a claim. He finally selected a small group of islands in the Detroit River and petitioned the Board of Trade in London for a land grant. While Sir Robert waited to hear if his petition had been approved, he wintered at the fort, where he proved splendid company to Captain Donald Campbell, the post commandant.[66]

From all quarters the nations of the Great Lakes and the Ohio Country witnessed the suffocating press of English attempting to root themselves in land that the tribes claimed. Indian leaders such as Teedyuscung provided dire warnings as to the consequences if this invasion were not curtailed. The Delaware leader told Pennsylvania governor James Hamilton, "It is the Indians' Lands and they will not suffer it to be settled."[67] The Indians around Fort Pitt echoed Teedyuscung's sentiments, convincing trader James Kenny that "it Greives ye Indians to see ye White People Settle on these Lands & follow hunting or Planting." In April 1762 Kenny scribbled in his journal that two Virginians who had settled near a tributary of the Monongahela called Redstone Creek had been killed by Indians. George Croghan, reported the incident to Sir William Johnson, remarking, "I Don't take it to be a National Merder butt Rather a kind of Robery as ye men were hunters and setling a plantation."[68] James Kenny also recorded that the Indians around Ligonier had attempted to drive out the British by poisoning the fort's water supply.[69] Incidents such as these underscored the growing resentment the Ohio Indians harbored against the English. Land issues were not the only source of their dissatisfaction, however, as General Amherst moved to implement new policies for dealing with the tribes that occupied the land beyond the mountains.

3

"If You Suffer the English among You, You Are Dead Men"

From his headquarters in New York Major General Jeffery Amherst was beset by a host of problems. By the summer of 1762, this hero of Louisbourg and conqueror of Canada stood by helplessly as his once lustrous star quickly began to dim. A lack of financial resources, the loss of political patronage, almost hostile provincial governments, dwindling troops, and vexing relations with the numerous Indian tribes, all conspired to trouble him. This tall, spare man with a protruding, aquiline nose had first come to the colonies as Britain's best hope for salvation in North America. Indeed, there had once been a time when Amherst's military fortunes were on the rise. Born in the county of Kent in 1717, Amherst had served as an aide to the rotund and inept Duke of Cumberland in the European theater of the Seven Years' War. Although Cumberland's military campaigns always seemed to end in disaster, Colonel Amherst displayed remarkable talent as a quartermaster, seeing to every detail in order to keep the army together while it was being decisively defeated by the French. When the duke was finally relieved of his command, Amherst managed to attach himself to the most illustrious soldier in England, Sir John Ligonier, an aging, distinguished officer who had fought with Marlborough a generation before. Through Sir John's patronage, Amherst came under the eye of the new secretary of state, William Pitt.[1]

Hoping to stem the tide of defeat that had plagued British forces since the eruption of war in the backwoods of Pennsylvania in 1754, Pitt determined to launch a broad, bold campaign against the French in 1758. To achieve that goal, the talented statesman believed a new cadre of young, resourceful officers needed to be recruited to conduct his military strategy. Consequently, Pitt elevated the forty-one-year-old Amherst to the rank of major general and placed him in charge of the expedition to conquer the French fortress at Louisbourg, which guarded access to the Saint Lawrence. Having accomplished this mission, Amherst moved on to the Lake George–Lake Champlain corridor in New York and seized the key French stronghold of Fort Carillon, known to the English as Ticonderoga, in 1759. The following year, Amherst finally put an end to the French military presence in Canada by capturing Montreal. For these efforts, the general had been knighted and was henceforth entitled to be addressed as Sir Jeffery Amherst. He had won his victories not through military genius or tactical ability but because of his unique administrative talents. During the campaign against Ticonderoga, Amherst had miraculously raised an army without a pound of financial assistance from the parent country. He carefully cultivated support from the provincial governors, obtained loans from the colonial assemblies, and maintained tight-fisted control of all expenses. His advance against the French fortress at the entrance to Lake Champlain was calculated and cautious. Unlike his predecessor, General Abercromby, Amherst did not sacrifice the lives of his soldiers in a doomed assault against the well-defended trenches of Ticonderoga. Instead, he laboriously maneuvered heavy siege artillery into range, making the French position untenable.[2]

Much had changed since Amherst's glory days at Louisbourg and Montreal. By the summer of 1762, his once powerful army had been reduced to a skeleton force as troops had been withdrawn from the peaceful North American continent in order to participate in attacks on French and Spanish possessions in the Caribbean. What few regular troops remained were concentrated in Canada or scattered thinly across the frontier at remote outposts like forts Pitt and Detroit. In addition, the home government maintained constant pressure on Amherst to economize. Pitt's aggressive and broad strategy to strike France around the globe had nearly bankrupted England. As the war continued in Europe and the West Indies, any available resources

General Jeffrey Amherst, Commander of British military forces in North America. Courtesy the William L. Clements Library, University of Michigan.

had to be diverted from a tranquil North America to battlefronts elsewhere. To further complicate Amherst's position, his principal bene-factor, William Pitt, had resigned. Instead of returning to England as a conquering hero, as he wished, Amherst was forgotten by the new regime and left to languish at his headquarters in New York.

The labyrinth of problems that General Amherst faced overwhelmed even his considerable administrative talents. During the late war, provincial assemblies had recognized the need for raising colonial militia forces and placing them under the command of English officers. Even so, the colonists had grudgingly complied with troop levies as they wrangled with crown officials and provincial governors over questions of how soldiers would be supplied and paid. In addition, the colonial governments tied militia recruitment to issues of their own power and authority. If the people were to be taxed in order to raise a defense force, then their representatives should have greater authority. With the end of fighting in North America, the assemblies regarded continued troop levies with suspicion in part because they traditionally feared a standing army under royal control as a usurpation of their own civil authority. Consequently, as regular British forces withdrew from North America to fight elsewhere, General Amherst found it increasingly difficult to maintain garrisons on the frontier of the newly expanded empire.

Amherst not only had to deal with irascible provincial assemblies but also had to contrive and implement a new policy for dealing with the various Indian tribes now under the British flag. Few in England or America doubted the need to place Indian affairs in the hands of some centralized authority. The chaos created by individual colonies treating with Indian tribes before and during the war had demonstrated this necessity. Any attempt to plan such a policy, however, without considering the multifaceted political and economic aims of the different tribes represented a major challenge. The Lords of Trade, a powerful group of royal officials charged with the administration of the colonies, instructed Amherst to consult with Sir William Johnson on Indian matters. The general found the Indian superintendent to be somewhat resistant to change, however. In Amherst's estimation Sir William was oblivious to the economic pressures the crown faced and simply requested more and more money to finance what the general considered to be a wasteful and dangerous Indian policy.

What ultimately prevented a solution to any of Sir Jeffery's problems, however, was a lack of financial resources and any concern from the home government. With England's debt of £150 million, there was simply little money left to spend on North America. In addition, British officials resumed their traditional "salutary neglect" of the

American colonies while they turned their attention to other, more urgent, concerns on the continent of Europe and elsewhere. The commander in chief of North America would have to develop his own policies and implement them without adequate economic support from England.[3]

In formulating his program to deal with the North American Indian tribes, Amherst relied on his talent for firm fiscal management and a contempt for Native peoples. During the late war with France, the general had watched with horror as his own Indian allies exhumed the bodies of slain enemy soldiers and scalped them, "as if it had been the greatest feast to them." Unaccustomed to these methods of warfare, the general was infuriated when many of the Iroquois who accompanied him on the Montreal campaign deserted, stealing a number of his boats along with weapons and other provisions. In short, Amherst, like almost every other officer in the British army, failed to fully appreciate the prowess of Indians in combat and regarded them as skulking, barbarous thieves and beggars. Incredibly, after the stunning defeats of General Braddock and Major James Grant before the gates of Fort Duquesne, European soldiers still underestimated the Indians' military superiority in the forests of America. In a letter to Pennsylvania governor James Hamilton, Sir Jeffery alluded to his contempt for their combat ability: "If they do not behave as good and faithfull allies ought to do, and renounce all acts of Hostilities against His Majesty's Subjects I shall retaliate upon them, and I have the might so to do tenfold every breach of Treaty they shall be guilty of and every outrage they shall Committ."[4] Amherst, of course, had never fought Indians and would soon learn that his claim of superiority over them was little more than foolish bravado.

General Amherst's first experience with Indian warfare unconnected to the larger struggle against France came when the Cherokees in the Carolinas rebelled against their former British allies in the summer of 1761. The uprising began when South Carolina's governor, William H. Lyttelton, imprisoned a group of Cherokee chiefs who had come to Charleston for a parley to ease already strained relations. In the opening phases of the war, the Cherokees held the upper hand, pushing back the frontier settlements to within seventy-five miles of Charleston. The Indians seized one frontier outpost, killing twenty-five members of the garrison. By the winter of 1761, however, the tide turned against the Cherokees, who found themselves isolated from potential allies and impeded by a lack of food and ammunition. The Cherokee rebellion soon subsided as the Indians sued for peace.[5]

One lesson that Amherst learned from the Cherokee uprising was that Indians deprived of arms and ammunition were less likely to prevail in a war.[6] As a cornerstone of his new Indian policy, therefore, the general intended to keep the Indians in short supply of powder and lead. In addition, he could see little need for supplying them with presents in order to foster and maintain peaceful relations; he considered this traditional practice wasteful. A side benefit of Sir Jeffery's policy would thus be sparing the crown unnecessary expense. In a letter to Sir William Johnson, Amherst outlined his new program:

> With regard to furnishing the [Indians], with a little Cloathing, some arms & ammunition to hunt with, that is all very well in Cases of Necessity; but as, when the Intended Trade is once Established they will be able to supply themselves with these, from the Traders, for their furrs, I do not see why the Crown should be put to that Expence. I am not neither for giving them any Provisions; when they find they can get it on Asking for, they will grow remiss in their hunting, which Should Industriously be avoided; for so long as their minds are Intent on business they will not have leisure to hatch mischief. . . . Services must be rewarded; it has ever been a maxim with me; but as to purchasing the good behavior either of Indians, or any Others, is what I do not understand; when men of what race soever behave ill, they must be punished but not bribed.[7]

Sir William Johnson, who understood Indian character and politics perhaps better than any other Englishman, strongly opposed General Amherst's new arrangements. Johnson had first come to America in 1738 as a twenty-three-year-old fortune seeker from Ireland. He arrived in the colony of New York well connected since his uncle, Sir Peter Warren, served as an admiral in the British navy. Settling in the Mohawk River Valley to manage his uncle's estate, Johnson established himself in the Indian trade and became highly respected by the Mohawks and other tribes of the Iroquois league. His influence grew to the point that the Mohawks and other members of the League

Sir William Johnson (1715–1774), oil on canvas by John Wollaston (active 1736–1767); c. 1751. Note the similarities between this and the Bouquet portrait. Courtesy the Albany Institute of History and Art, Gift of Laura Munsell Tremaine.

of Five Nations referred to him as "Warraghiyagey"—"the man who undertakes great things." Apparently, the young Irishman was also quite influential with the Mohawk women and reputedly fathered more than one hundred children with Indian concubines. Due to his growing prestige among the Iroquois, he was named superintendent of Indian affairs in the Northern Department in 1755 and assigned the task of recruiting Indian allies for the British army. Johnson won lasting fame and a knighthood as results of his victory over the French at Niagara in 1759. From that time on, the influential Lords of Trade listened intently to Sir William's advice regarding Indian affairs and usually deferred to his judgment. With such potent political connections and his influence over the Indian tribes, it is little wonder that Sir William became one of the wealthiest and most powerful men in the colonies.[8]

Warraghiyagey was keenly aware of the damage that Amherst's new policy would have on Indian relations, particularly among the tribes of the Great Lakes region that had yet to establish firm links with the British. Regarding the issuance of presents to Indian leaders, Sir William understood that such tokens enhanced the power and prestige of these chiefs among other members of the tribe. To the Indians, gift giving represented simple protocol in diplomacy and was often considered a form of tribute to their leaders and payment of rent for allowing the whites to build forts on Indian land.[9] Without such presents accommodationist chiefs such as Tamaqua and Teedyuscung would lose influence to more militant leadership. In addition, Johnson recognized that termination of gift giving would naturally cause the Indians to become suspicious of British intentions. In a letter to the Lords of Trade Johnson noted, "If we had no occasion for Frontier Posts, back Settlements, and an Indian trade, we might rest tolerably secure in our present possessions, without being at any expense in cultivating the friendship and affection of the Indians." But, he wrote, "as these things are Essential to the prosperity of the Provinces, and the encrease of his Majesty's Revenue we must I humbly apprehend endeavor to possess them [by] such means, as shall be most conducive to the Welfare of the one, and the extension of the other."[10] Johnson also made his thoughts known to William Pitt's replacement, Charles Wyndham, the Earl of Egremont. In a letter to the new secretary of state, Sir William wrote:

> Your Lordship will observe that the Indians are not only very uneasy, but Jealous of our growing power, which the Enemy [the French] (to engage them firmly in their interest) had always told them would prove their ruin, as we should by degrees Surround them on every side, & at length Extirpate them . . . from [the] treatment they receive from us, different

from what they have been accustomed to by the French, who spared no labor, or Expence to gain their friendship and Esteem, which alone enabled them to support the War in these parts so long whilst we, as either not thinking of them of sufficient Consequence, or that we had not so much occasion for their assistance not only fell infinitely short of the Enemy in our presents &ca to the Indians, but have of late I am apprehensive been rather premature in our sudden retrenchment of some necessary Expences, to which they have been always accustomed, & which on due consideration I flatter myself your Lordship will be of opinion they should be gradually weaned from, rather than be totally deprived of, as that cannot fail encreasing their Jealousy, and adding fuel to their discontent.[11]

Unlike General Amherst, Johnson was under no delusions regarding the Indians' capacity to wage desultory and bloody war on the border. To Johnson's mind the best way to prevent such conflict was to treat the Indians fairly and keep them supplied with the goods they needed to hunt and carry on other economic activities—not to threaten them with punishment for bad behavior. Johnson insisted that Amherst's plan would require garrisoning the remote outposts with "a verry large Regular Force at a Monstrous Expence to the Nation." "These Indians" he insisted, "conscious of their own Strength and Situation, will, unless kept in the best temper by Us, be easily persuaded to commit depredations on the Traders whose goods are a temptation to the Savages, thus once embarked they will not stop till they have spread Havock over all our frontiers."[12] Therefore, Sir William argued, the expense of providing the Indians with a few presents was still cheaper than fighting an Indian war. Unfortunately, the superintendent of Indian affairs depended on Amherst for funds to carry out such a program, and it was abundantly clear to Johnson that the general was "not at all a friend of Indians which . . . may have bad consequences one time or other."[13] Before officials in London got around to considering the merits of the two opposing policies, conditions in the land beyond the mountains had already deteriorated.

Sir William was not alone in endorsing a policy of benevolence toward the Indian tribes. George Croghan, Johnson's deputy Indian agent, also believed that a few presents of powder and lead were far cheaper than waging war against the Indians. "The Indians are a very Jelous peple," Croghan affirmed, "and they had great Expectations of being Ginerally Supplyed by us & from their poverty & Mercenery Disposition they cant Bear such a Dissapointment." "Undoubtedly," Croghan confided to Johnson sarcastically, "ye Gineral [Amherst] has his own Rason for Nott allowing any presents or ammunition to be given them, & I wish itt may have its Desired Effect Butt I take this opertunity to acquaint you that I Dread the Event as I know Indians cant long persevere."[14] Despite Croghan's protestations, Amherst insisted that the Irishman's expenses at Fort Pitt should be drastically reduced. This forced the deputy Indian agent to discharge six employees, leaving only one assistant, Alexander McKee.[15]

Sir William Johnson and his deputies were not the only ones who believed that General Amherst's Indian policy was flawed and dangerous. The commandant of Fort Detroit, Captain Donald Campbell, also believed that only a course of benevolence and good will would win the comradeship of the Indian tribes. By all appearances, Donald Campbell did not fit the image of an active British officer on the frontier. A fellow officer described the middle-aged Scotsman as "fat and unwieldy," and he was known to be extremely nearsighted. Nonetheless, his reputation for bravery and efficiency in the Royal American Regiment prompted General Robert Monckton to assign him to command the far western post along the Detroit River. Campbell, who spoke fluent French, set out to endear himself to the French inhabitants who remained about the fort following the British takeover in 1760. He hosted "a gathering every Sunday night" at his quarters where a "score of people of both sexes" came to socialize and play cards. In a letter to Colonel Bouquet, the captain revealed, "The women surpass our expectations, like the rest of America; the men very indifferent." One of Campbell's officers, Lieutenant James McDonald, agreed that the French citizens of Detroit "seem very well pleased with their change; And even acknowledge that the Capitulation was more favourable than they expected it would have been. They are very well satisfied with Captain Campbell."[16]

Campbell also worked hard to gain the trust and friendship of the Indian nations that lived near the fort. He recognized that, with France's withdrawal from Detroit, the British must fill the void in supplying them with certain essential provisions that they had become

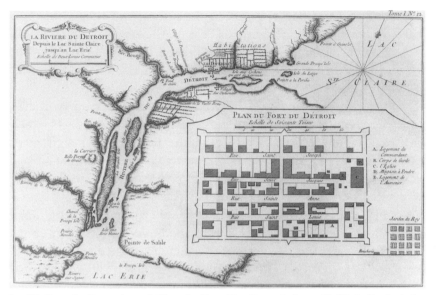

La Rivière du Detroit and Plan du Fort Du Detroit from Bellin's *Petit Atlas Maritime* (Paris, 1764). This view of the Detroit River was made in 1749 and shows the location of the fort (labeled simply *le Fort*), situated in the upper-center portion of the map. The fort is surrounded by the cleared fields of the French habitants. On the southern bank of the river, nearly opposite the fort, is the Ottawa village, while the Huron town is a short distance to the west. The Potawatomie village is located just west of the fort. The inset diagram of the fort reveals the compound's compactness. Courtesy the William L. Clements Library, University of Michigan.

dependent on. In December 1760 Captain Campbell wrote to Colonel Bouquet, "The Indians here are in great distress for want of Ammunition. I have had two of the Tribes that depends on Michillimakinac, that come at a great distance, they are absolutely Starving, as their whole Subsistance depends on it. I was obliged to give them what I could spare." Six months later the captain reported to Bouquet that he still felt obligated to offer visiting Indians "a present of Ammunition and Provisions," although he was fearful that his actions might incur Amherst's censure. Campbell was, he admitted, in a quandary over what measures to take: "I assure you I am much put to it, how to behave in Indian Affairs, as I have no orders on that head. . . . I have managed Things with the greatest Oeconomy possible, I am afraid they [Amherst and his staff] will find fault with soe much Provisions given to Indians, tho in our present Situation there was no help for it, I have done what I thought was best for the Service." In the same letter, Campbell also complained that the Indians were unhappy about the exorbitant prices charged by the English traders who operated out of Detroit.[17]

Despite the growing uneasiness caused by Amherst's new Indian policy, cross-cultural exchange and a spirit of cooperation between the Europeans and Indians did emerge on the trans-Appalachian frontier. Along the Muskingum River at the newly settled Delaware village of Tuscarawas, English carpenters built a house for Tamaqua. Colonel Bouquet also ordered artificers to construct "a Good Shingled House & several Stables & Cow houses" for another Delaware leader, known as Grey Eyes, who lived along the Beaver River about thirty miles from Fort Pitt. Further, Bouquet authorized the construction of a two-story council house for the Indians near the fort. The clapboarded structure included partitions, closets, stairs, and windows, all for the cost of less than £65. Surgeons at the fort provided medical care for the local Native Americans. The physicians learned a great deal from the Indians, who pointed out the benefits of many herbal remedies. Delaware and Mingo warriors also displayed other natural wonders for the English: periodically they would arrive at Fort Pitt carrying the teeth and tusks of the extinct wooly mammoth to show interested onlookers. Indians also served as guides for John Bartram, America's first botanist, and helped him collect specimens of vegetation unknown to the English world. Indians were, in fact, regularly employed as scouts, couriers, packhorse drivers, and laborers across the frontier. Through such employment the Native people became familiar with European economics. James Kenny, the post trader at Fort Pitt, who was accustomed to the simple barter system of merchandise for furs, began to record many cash transactions in his ledger. This destroys the long-held belief that Indians had no understanding of the value of money.[18]

Settlers and Indians often came into close contact in the forests of the Ohio Country. Midway along the trail between Fort Ligonier and Fort Pitt, a former sergeant from the Royal American Regiment named Andrew Byerly established a post house or relay station on a stream known as Bushy Run. The soldier, who served as a baker for the army, built his cabin near a small stream and kept a small herd of milk cows. Often Indians would pass by Byerly's Station and the sergeant's wife, Phoebe, always provided them with fresh bread and milk. One day, the Indians would reward Mrs. Byerly for her kindness.[19]

A darker, more sordid form of exchange was also taking place at Fort Pitt and other wilderness outposts. James Kenny recorded in his diary that only three men living at Pittsburgh did not have Indian mistresses. According to the Quaker trader, "degenerate squaws" prostituted their young daughters to civilians and soldiers alike. On the other hand, Kenny seemed particularly impressed by the character of an Indian named Jamey Wilson who had a white wife. According to Kenny, the woman "inclined to return to her own people," and Wilson brought her to the trading post with all of his worldly goods. There he informed his wife that "he loved her, [but] as she want'd to leave him, would let her go, so he divided his substance equally with her." Touched by the scene, Kenny characterized it as "an Instance of more self denial than many men of great Christian professions shews their poor Negros."[20]

While cooperation and cross-cultural exchange continued on the frontier, ominous signs of discontent among the Indians also emerged. The most pronounced indication of coming conflict arrived at Fort Detroit in the summer of 1761 in the form of a pair of Seneca emissaries named Kiasutha and Tahaiadoris. The two Iroquois called for a council among all the neighboring nations in order to plan a concerted strike against all the English forts. The name "Kiasutha," meaning "It sets up the cross," perhaps provides a clue to Kiasutha's long association with Europeans. Initially, he seemed well disposed toward the English, and as a young man had served as a guide to George Washington on his diplomatic mission to demand French evacuation of the Ohio Country in 1753. Later, however, the Seneca gravitated to the French sphere of influence and was one of the few Iroquois who participated in Braddock's defeat at the Monongahela. From that time on, Kiasutha demonstrated an implacable resentment toward the British. The missionary David McClure met Kiasutha years later and described him as a man of "martial appearance" with "a very sensible countenance & dignity of manners." His fellow diplomat at Fort Detroit, Tahaiadoris, was the son of Fort Niagara's former French commander Daniel Chabert de Joncaire and the half brother of the noted French partisan Philippe Thomas de Joncaire.[21]

Kiasutha. Little information is available regarding this portrait of the Seneca leader. The painting was featured as part of a series of commemorative China plates produced by Shenango Pottery in 1976. The date and artist are unknown. Courtesy the Lawrence County Historical Society, New Castle, Pennsylvania.

While the two Senecas harbored a definite affinity for their French allies, their hatred for the English came about as a result of more recent developments. Kiasutha and Tahaiadoris believed that they were "ill Treated" as a result of General Amherst's new policies and the British attempts to take away their land. The Indians believed they had "the greatest reason to believe by their behavior they intend to cut us off entirely." Incensed by Amherst's policies, the Seneca leaders came to Detroit to pass a large red war belt to the Ottawas, Hurons, Chippewas, and other tribes "from Nova Scotia to the Illinois, to take up the Hatchet against the English." The two Senecas informed the assembled tribesmen that as the British "have possessed themselves of our Country, it is now in our power to dispossess them & recover it, if we will embrace the opportunity before they have time to assemble together, & fortify themselves there."[22]

Perhaps because of his previous efforts to maintain good relations with them, friendly Indians informed Captain Campbell that the Seneca envoys had called for a council of all the neighboring tribes. Campbell sent these Indians to attend the council and report back to him regarding the plot that Kiasutha and Tahaiadoris laid out before the Detroit River tribes. In a well-conceived plan the Senecas hoped that the Ottawas and other tribes living near the fort would "Seize on the Traders, Murder the Garrison and make all the Plunder they cou'd." Then other nations such as the Delawares, Shawnees, and Miamis would fall upon the small posts scattered along the frontier as far east as Fort Pitt. Meanwhile the Iroquois, assisted by Delawares living along the Susquehanna, would cut British communications in central New York, thus isolating all the English forces west of the Appalachian Mountains. "Such Posts as they cou'd not take, they would starve out and so become Masters of their Country again." The single most important aspect of this plan was that all the tribes would act as one. Kiasutha informed the assembled chiefs that they "were but one people, & had but one Voice." The environment of the Ohio Country and Great Lakes, along with the experiences of the Great War for Empire, had brought these scattered nations together. Some had joined together in refugee villages along the Allegheny and Ohio rivers. Colonial and imperial policies that had precipitated the war with France had caused other Native Americans along the Great Lakes to identify with their brethren to the east. Indians everywhere witnessed the insatiable appetite of land-hungry Englishmen invading their homelands. Finally, General Amherst's new plan for Indian affairs convinced them that the English were intent on wiping them out. For years, historians would insist that the Ottawa leader Pontiac, who most certainly was present at this council, was responsible for bringing the tribes together. In fact, the people of the Eastern Woodlands had already forged an identity as one people.[23]

When Captain Campbell learned of the Seneca plot, he called the local tribes into council and informed them that he was well aware of their designs against the English. He admonished the two Seneca leaders, "I advise you with all my heart in the most friendly manner, to return home and ardently recommend it to your Chiefs and those of other Nations in Concert with you to quit their Bad Intentions and live in peace, for if they proceed in their Designs against the English it will terminate in their utter Ruin and Destruction." Tahaiadoris replied "that he would bury all bad thoughts [and] lay aside all thoughts of War and live in peace."[24] Captain Campbell was convinced of the Seneca leader's sincerity, and the conference adjourned. In all likelihood, the Indians reasoned that since their plot had been uncovered, there was no chance of achieving the element of surprise. The Senecas would bide their time and allow the war belts to continue circulating among the many western tribes.

The so-called Seneca Plot caused little alarm among the British military establishment. When news of the plan reached Colonel Bouquet back at Fort Pitt, the canny Swiss officer took the precaution of bringing the frontier inhabitants inside the bastions of the post and forming two companies of militia from the local citizenry to reinforce the garrison. He then called together Tamaqua and other Delaware leaders to convince them "of the rashness of the Enterprise and the bad Consequences that would attend it." In the end, however, Bouquet was persuaded that the entire plot would fail and that the Indians "could only flatter themselves to succeed by Surprise."[25] Back in New York General Amherst evinced equal complacency, disclosing that the intended uprising "never gave me a Moments Concern, as I know their incapacity of attempting anything serious, and that if they were rash enough to venture upon any Designs, I had it in my power not only to frustrate them, but to punish the Delinquents with Entire Destruction, which I am firmly resolved on whenever any of them give me cause."[26]

Other individuals, more intimately familiar with Indian affairs, did not take the Seneca Plot so lightly. Deputy Indian Agent George Croghan spelled out the Indians' grievances in his diary:

The Six Nations look on themselves to be ill Treated by the English General [Amherst], and in particular the Sinicas . . . say since the English has Conquered the french they insult the Sinicas, and won't let them travel thro' their own Country, they are forbid the Communication [along the Niagara portage]. Traders are not suffered to go amongst them, Powder and Lead is prohibited being sold to them, and the General is giving away their Country to be settled, which the King of England Promised to secure for their use, these steps they say appears to them as if the English had a mind to Cut them off the face of the Earth.[27]

Even before word of the Seneca Plot reached his fortified estate in the Mohawk Valley, Sir William Johnson sensed something was awry. In a letter to General Amherst Warraghiyagey stated that he was "verry apprehensive that something not right is brewing, and that verry privately among them. I do not only mean the Six Nations, I fear it is too generall. Whatever it be, I shall endeavour to find it out if possible."[28]

Sir William's plan to discern the temper of the various tribes involved traveling to Detroit and holding a grand council among them. In preparation for the meeting, the Indian superintendent requested that General Amherst supply him with certain trade items to be offered as presents to the Indian leaders. Sir Jeffrey informed Johnson "that the Amount of Goods, Supposed Necessary for the Indians, is really a large Sum" and struck from the list merchandise such as gun powder, lead, knives, and flints. Sir William quickly shot back, insisting that he "used all the frugality [for] the good of the Service," adding "that unless our Old, as well as New Indian Allies are allowed Amunition for their Livelyhood, or hunting, all Treaties held with, or Presents made to them will never secure their friendship, for they will in such case be Jealous of Us, as I find they are a good deal so already." In the end, Amherst relented, allowing Johnson to take some powder along to give to the Indians at Detroit.[29]

General Amherst ordered Major Henry Gladwin of the 80th Regiment of Foot to escort Johnson to Detroit with three hundred soldiers. Amherst also instructed Gladwin to relieve and reinforce the distant posts at Michilimackinac, St. Joseph, La Baye, Sandusky, and Ouiatenon—

all former French forts in the Great Lakes region. Gladwin was the
perfect choice for an expedition to the remote frontier. The thirty-one-
year-old officer had already experienced hard service in the forests of
America. He was a young lieutenant when he accompanied Braddock
on the ill-fated expedition to seize Fort Duquesne and was wounded
in the Battle of the Monongahela. Three years later, as a captain in
Thomas Gage's new light infantry regiment, Gladwin was again
wounded in the thick of battle as James Abercromby launched his
insane assault against the French fortifications at Ticonderoga. His
courage and tenacity inspired one historian to describe Gladwin as
"a superb example of England's bull-dog breed of soldiers."[30] Despite
this dogged quality, rough service in the wilderness had taken its toll
on Gladwin. After an arduous advance up the Niagara portage with
his regiment and a stormy crossing of Lake Erie in which a great
quantity of supplies was lost, Gladwin arrived at Detroit on September 1, 1761, wracked with malaria.

While Gladwin headed for Detroit, Sir William and an entourage
of Iroquois chiefs remained at Niagara to negotiate with the various
tribes that congregated around the fort. By this time Johnson had learned
of the Seneca attempt to enlist the Great Lakes tribes in a war against
the English. Angrily, the Indian superintendent called the Seneca chiefs
together and, in a tone only Sir William could get away with, severely
chastised them for their behavior. Johnson demanded that the Senecas
provide an explanation for fomenting such a plot and sending war
belts to the Great Lakes tribes. Following Indian custom, the Seneca
leader Sonajoana delivered his response the following day: "Brother
Warraghiyagey, what you declared to us yesterday has given us much
uneasiness especially, as we are not only innocent, but entirely ignorant of the whole charge against us. No such Message having been
ever to our knowledge sent by our nation." The chief suggested that
the belts may have emanated from their Seneca brethren living in
the Ohio Country. Sonajoana's suspicions underscored the fact that the
Indians living along the Allegheny and Ohio rivers had, once again,
asserted their independence from the Iroquois Confederacy. Since
1748, when Conrad Weiser first traveled to the multicultural village
of Loggstown, the Indians living in the region had insisted that they
spoke as one people, that they had kindled their own fire in the land
beyond the mountains, and that they did not accept the edicts of the

Major Henry Gladwin, painting by John Hall. Gift of Dexter M. Ferry, Jr. Courtesy the Detroit Institute of Arts.

Iroquois league. During the late war, Mingo warriors had ignored league neutrality and fought with their French fathers. Now, in 1761, the Ohio Country Senecas Kiasutha and Tahaiadoris took yet another step toward sovereignty from their cousins to the north by attempting to initiate a war without consulting the Iroquois council.[31]

Sir William had always believed that by controlling the Iroquois, he could supervise all the tribes regardless of their location. Surely no tribe or group of tribes would deny Iroquois leadership. In fact, that is exactly what had happened. Yet Warraghiyagey could not accept this new paradigm. He still believed that the war belts circulating among the Great Lakes warriors could do so only with the knowledge and acquiescence of the New York council. Therefore, he responded to Sonajoana by declaring that "your frivolous excuses that the Messengers lived Detached from you, have [no] Weight with me, being thoroughly convinced that they, or any Tribes of your Nation would not presume to undertake so dangerous an affair without your Concurrence & approbation." With this declaration Johnson returned the wampum belt given him by the Senecas, a gesture that indicated that he "paid no regard to what they had said." To prove their innocence, several chiefs offered to accompany Sir William to Detroit and address the council he planned to hold with the western tribes.[32] With that, the conference adjourned, and Johnson, with his entourage of Iroquois chiefs, set out for Fort Detroit to commence negotiations with the Great Lakes tribes.

When Sir William arrived at the post along the Detroit River on September 3, 1761, he found George Croghan had already assembled representatives from the Ottawa, Huron, Potawatomie, Chippewa, Miami, Shawnee, and Delaware nations for a grand council. While the Indians waited to hear the words of Warraghiyagey, the noted Indian superintendent spent some leisure hours being entertained at a ball Captain Campbell held in his honor. Major Gladwin, who had arrived several days earlier, was too ill to attend the party. Sir William opened the festivities at 8 P.M. by dancing with the enchanting, twenty-six-year-old Angelique Cuillerier, a French habitant who lived a short distance from the fort with her brother and parents. Johnson and this "fine girl" (as he confided in his diary) danced until five o'clock in the morning. This young French belle would, legend has it, have a compelling role in the horrible Indian war that was to follow.[33]

The ensuing grand council that convened near the palisades of Fort Detroit was the focal point for Sir William Johnson's new initiative in Indian diplomacy. He began by addressing the assembled chiefs with words of condolence for those warriors who had been slain in the war with France. He then asked them to hold fast to the ancient

Covenant Chain that bound the English colonies with the Indian world. In essence, he invited the western tribes to join that chain of friendship with a status equal to that of the Iroquois Confederacy. As the trader James Kenny noted, Sir William had in effect "cast off ye Onandago Yoke (of ye Six Nations) from ye Delawares, Shawanas, Wyondots, Picks or Tweetwees, & others to ye Westward which makes those Nations a Separate Power Independent of the Six Nations." Johnson intended to create a jealousy between the Iroquois and the other tribes that would prevent them from considering an alliance against the British. As Johnson later informed a British officer, "I did all in my power in private conferences to create a misunderstanding between the Six Nations and Western Indians, also between the latter and those of Ohio so as to render them jealous of each other."[34] Johnson then assured the Great Lakes tribes that the English had no desire to possess their lands and promised an increase in the volume of trade and a reduction in the price of goods. The superintendent concluded the conference satisfied that he had "left the Western Indians Extremely well Disposed towards the English" and that "unless greatly Irritated thereto they will never break the Peace Established."[35]

Perhaps Johnson's biggest miscalculation at Detroit was his underestimating the strong ties that existed between the Great Lakes tribes and those of the Ohio Country. While Johnson worked to "create a misunderstanding between the Six Nations and the Western Indians," his efforts served only to strengthen the already existing bond. Had the war belts emanated from New York Senecas, Johnson's strategy may have worked; but the call to war had come from the Ohio Country Indians. To further exacerbate the deterioration of relations between the English and the tribes living west of the mountains, militant leaders were beginning to embrace a new religious message coming from the Delaware villages deep in the Ohio Country.

In November 1762 Indians visiting James Kenny's trading post at Fort Pitt informed him of the teachings of a new prophet who had emerged among the Delawares living along the Tuscarawas River. Kenny recorded in his journal that this new prophet (whom Kenny called the "Imposter") had drawn a "plan" on deerhide and made copies to circulate among all the tribes in order to "shew them ye right way to Heaven." On the hide, the prophet had drawn earth at the bottom and heaven at the top. A direct line connecting the two realms denoted

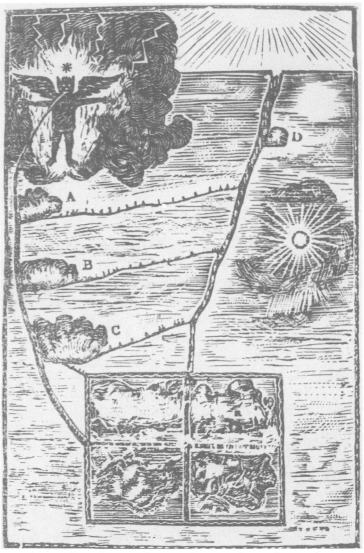

A rendition of Neolin's road map to heaven, drawn from information supplied by captive John McCullough. In his captivity narrative, McCullough stated that the inset square represented the earth. Indians situated in the boxes on the right-hand side of this square went immediately to heaven, while those to the left were forced to take a torturous path. To avoid hell (shown in the upper left corner) travelers had to "undergo a certain degree of Punishment, before they are admitted into heaven [B], and . . . each [of] those places are [*sic*] a flame of fire [denoted as A, B, and C on the map]." After the sinners had been sufficiently punished, they could pause to quench their thirst at a cool spring (marked D) before entering heaven. Neolin insisted that all the sinners living in the left-hand side of the square were those who had adopted the ways of the white man. The Delaware prophet sold the maps for one deer hide apiece. Drawing from Loudon, *Most Interesting Narratives.*

the path that the Indians had formerly taken to reach paradise and a square represented the presence of the white people. Many strokes emanated from the square, representing "all ye Sins & Vices which ye Indians have learned from ye White people"—obstacles, the prophet said, blocking the "Good Road" to heaven. The Indians who shared the drawing with Kenny disclosed that their prophet insisted that the only way to clear the good road was to "learn to live without any Trade or Connections with ye White people, Clothing & Supporting themselves as their forefathers did."[36]

Another white person who saw the prophet's drawing was John McCullough, who had been held captive by the Delawares since 1756. McCullough's description of the "hieroglyphics" was virtually identical to Kenny's. The young captive noted that the Indians sought to "purify themselves from sin, which they taught they could do by the use of emetics, and abstainence from carnal knowledge of the different sexes; to quit the use of firearms, and to live entirely in the original state that they were in before the white people found out their country." "Their prophet taught them, or made them believe," McCullough added, "that he had his instructions immediately from *Keesh-she-la-mil-lang-up*, or a being that thought us into being, and that by following his instructions, they would, in a few years, be able to drive the white people out of their country."[37]

Neither Kenny nor McCullough met this prophet, a young Delaware mystic named Neolin, or the "Enlightened One." Through incantations Neolin had fallen into a trance and visited with the "Master of Life." He was certainly not the first or only prophet to claim to have communed with the Great Spirit. As early as 1737 Conrad Weiser reported that a shaman had appeared before the Indians of the Susquehanna Valley, castigating them for trading their furs for rum. As punishment for this sin God had "driven the wild animals out of the country." More than a decade later the missionary John Brainerd learned of the teachings of a Delaware woman who claimed to have spoken with the Great Power. According to her vision, God had separately created the whites, blacks, and Indians, and each race should follow their own customs and beliefs. Still later, another Delaware prophet, named Papoonan, preaching from a village further up on the Susquehanna, scolded his people for growing "proud & Covetous, which causes God to be angry & to send dry & hot Summers & hard

Winters, & also Sickness among the People." Papoonan counseled his followers to purify themselves by "adhering to the ancient Customs & manners of their Forefathers." Another Delaware shaman, called Wangomend drew a chart for his Susquehanna followers that was very similar in content to the map Neolin would later create. Wangomend's drawing showed "Heaven and a Hell and Rum and Swan hak [white people] and Indiens and Ride [Red] Strokes for Rum," and his message was far more militant than those of previous prophets. Wangomend viewed the British as the cause of Indian decline and encouraged his followers to abandon European ways and immerse themselves in rituals of purification.[38]

Neolin's own vision began with a long journey through the spirit world. After traveling for seven days through this land, Neolin came to three forks in the road. After being turned back by fire along two of the trails, he finally encountered a woman of "radiant beauty" along the third path who directed him to "forsake all that thou hast with thee, and disrobe completely." She then instructed him to purify himself by bathing in a nearby river before meeting with the Master of Life. This portion of Neolin's vision symbolized the Indians' need to purge themselves of their "white ways" through purification. Finally, Neolin found himself seated before the Master of Life, who provided him with a set of detailed instructions to take back to the Indian people. These rules included refraining from drinking alcohol in large quantities and taking only one wife for life. The Master of Life admonished Neolin and all other Indians:

> This land where ye dwell I have made for you and not for others. Whence comes it that ye permit the Whites upon your lands? Can ye not live without them? I know that those whom ye call the children of your Great Father [the French] supply your needs, but if ye were not evil, as ye are, ye could surely do without them. Ye could live as ye did before knowing them,— before those whom ye call your brothers [the English] had come upon your lands. Did ye not live by the bow and arrow? Ye had no need of gun or powder, or anything else, and never-theless ye caught animals to live upon and to dress yourselves with their skins. But when I saw that ye were given up to evil, I led the wild animals to the depths of the forests so

that ye had to depend upon your brothers to feed and shelter you. Ye have only to become good again and do what I wish, and I will send back the animals for your food.[39]

Perhaps the most intriguing portion of Neolin's vision came when the Master of Life enjoined him from seeking vengeance on the French. According to the dream, the Master of Life told Neolin, "I do not forbid you to permit among you the children of your Father [the French]; I love them. They know me and pray to me, and I supply their wants and all they give you. But as to those who come to trouble your lands,—drive them out, make war upon them. I do not love them at all; they know me not, and are my enemies, and the enemies of your brothers. Send them back to the lands which I have created for them and let them stay there."[40]

For years historians have surmised that the Ottawa leader Pontiac later manipulated and reinterpreted Neolin's teachings to serve his own interests and that, unlike Neolin, Pontiac wished some dispensation for his brothers the French. More recent interpretations, however, indicate that Pontiac's relation of Neolin's teachings were true to the original vision. This seems entirely logical since the Ohio Country and Great Lakes people did not perceive the French and British in like terms. The Indians were acutely aware that their French fathers were not interested in "troubling their lands" and had not withheld vital supplies such as powder and lead. The French had always followed the ancient custom of gift giving. Some time later, far off in the Illinois country, those French fathers also learned of Neolin's vision and how Indian resentment was directed solely at the British. The Potawatomies living along the Illinois River informed a French emissary that "it was the Master of Life who was exciting them to war" and admonishing them "that if you suffer the English among you, you are dead men. Sickness, smallpox, and their poison will destroy you entirely."[41] Indeed, it seems quite clear that the French were to be spared from the wrath of the Indians who were growing ever more resentful and militant as the prophet's teaching spread from the Ohio River Valley to the Great Lakes and beyond.[42]

In order to purge English influence from the Indian world, the prophet exhorted his followers to partake of a curious herbal concoction known among the Shawnee as the "black drink." Back at Fort

Pitt James Kenny learned more about Neolin's vision through a Delaware informant called James Moccasin. The Indian told Kenny that "its agree'd to by their Whole Nation, to follow thire new Plan of Religion, & all their Boys are to be Train'd to ye use of the Bow & Arrow for Seven Years Then to Live intirely on dry'd Meat & a Sort of Bitter Drink made of Roots & Plants & Water . . . this is said to be Physick to purge out all that they got of ye White peoples ways & Nature." Throughout the Ohio Valley, Indians took to drinking the emetic "black drink" and going into the bushes to vomit. The practice grew to the point that the Shawnee village of Waketameki became known as "Vomit Town."[43]

The fact that Neolin's followers, according to James Moccasin. intended to train the young to once again use the bow and arrow underscores Native American dependency on firearms. The captive John McCullough later recalled a distinct community of Delawares who strictly followed the prophet's teaching. "I knew a company of them," McCullough remarked, "who had secluded themselves for the purpose of purifying from sin, as they thought they could do; I believe they made no use of fire-arms . . . it was said, that they made use of no other weapons than their bows and arrows."[44]

Without doubt, Neolin's messianic movement served to further unify the Ohio Valley Indians with the tribes of the Great Lakes. Ottawas, Potawatomies, Shawnees, Mingoes, and Delawares all came to believe that their plight resulted from the covetous behavior and drunkenness that had been brought among them by the British. The Master of Life was punishing them and the only way to effect their revitalization was to rid themselves of the English. The Moravian missionary Christian Frederick Post, who had once been instrumental in securing peace between the Indians and the English, was no longer certain if he would be welcome at the Delaware village of Tusca-rawas. When he arrived at their settlements, Post was alarmed to discover that Neolin "tells them [the Indians] he had a vission of Heaven where there was no White people but all Indians, & wants a total Seperation from us [the English]." Apparently, the Indians were no longer listening to stirring sermons about Christ's love and for-giveness from sin. In the fall of 1762, James Kenny recorded in his diary that "ye Imposter [Neolin] Prognosticates that there will be Two or Three Good Talks & then War."[45]

There were other warning signs that summer and fall. In mid-August Ohio Country Delawares joined their eastern kin from the Susquehanna and the Six Nations Iroquois to confirm the peace made at Easton in 1758 with the Pennsylvanians. Governor James Hamilton, who met the various tribes at Lancaster, was intent on securing the release of captives still held by the Indians living on the frontier and on seeking permission from the Six Nations to build yet another "strong house" along the west branch of the Susquehanna. From the outset, the Indians seemed disgruntled. In reply to Hamilton's request to build the trading post and fort, Seneca chief Kinderutie angrily replied:

> You may remember you told me, when you was going to Pittsburgh, you would build a Fort against the French, and you told me you wanted none of our lands; our Cousins [the Delaware] know this, and that you promised to go away as soon as you drove the French away, and yet you stay there and build Houses, and make it stronger and stronger every day. For this reason we entirely deny your request; you shall not have a road this Way.[46]

Another Iroquois spokesman bitterly complained that the English were "always longing after my Land." "You [the English] will serve me as you have done our cousins the Delawares," he added; "you have got all their land from them; all the land hereabouts belonged to them once, and you have got it all."[47] Indeed, even while those words were being spoken, hundreds of land-hungry settlers from Connecticut were invading the Wyoming Valley, land along the Susquehanna that was claimed as a homeland by Teedyuscung and the eastern Delawares. When the Lancaster conference finally adjourned at the end of the month, the Indians left "much dissatisfied." So disgusted were the Ohio Country Indians that they discarded along the road the presents given them by Governor Hamilton.[48]

With the approach of winter, signs of a great Indian uprising became more ominous. In December George Croghan wrote Colonel Bouquet, who was spending the winter in Philadelphia, to inform him that war belts were still circulating along the frontier. Having spoken with principal warriors among the Delawares, Shawnees, and Senecas, Croghan related that "they Say they Never Intended to make Warr on ye English Butt Say its full time for them to prepair to Defend themselves & thire Cuntry from us who they are Convensed Designe to make Warr on them." The Indians' conviction that the British were set to attack them, Croghan wrote, stemmed from the lack of powder and lead extended to them for hunting purposes. The Indians were also certain that as soon as all the captives were released, the English would launch their war. This was the principal reason, Croghan believed, that the Indians still retained so many prisoners. The quintessential Indian agent also reported to Bouquet that the Susquehanna Delawares had sent a war belt to their western kin, seeking aid in the coming conflict. With Senecas, Shawnees, and both eastern and western Delawares all alarmed and ready for war, Croghan issued an ominous prophesy: "I aShure you I am of opinion itt will Nott be Long before we Shall have Some Broyles [brawls] with them." Furthermore, he told Bouquet, "its Lucky that those Indians [the Ohio Country people] & ye Indians over ye Lakes are Nott upon good Terms with Each other att present how ever if any of them Should brake with us itt must End in a Gineral Indian Warr with us."[49]

At the end of January 1763, Captain Simeon Ecuyer, who was serving as the commandant at Fort Pitt in Colonel Bouquet's absence, reported that the Shawnees had confessed to him that the war belts Kiasutha and Tahaiadoris had taken to Detroit in the summer of 1761 were still circulating. According to the Shawnees, all the tribes had become convinced that the English intended to "make War against the Indians by their keeping Ammunition from them and settleing so many Forts in their Country."[50]

One might surmise that General Amherst would have been alarmed by the reports coming from the wilderness forts. After all, the few troops he had at his disposal were spread dangerously thin across the frontier. To the contrary, Sir Jeffery's contempt for Indians and his overarching confidence in the superiority of British martial power lulled him into a false sense of security. When George Croghan informed him of the ugly mood shared by all the tribes on the frontier, Amherst responded in typical fashion: "I See Nothing in the Intelligence, of any Consequence." The Indians' "power is altogether Insufficient," he declared, "while our Commanding officers are on their Guard; And Indeed I cannot think the Indians are so Blind to their own Interest as to Attempt any Mischief in those parts."[51] How conceited and foolish Amherst would soon appear.

4

"Drive off Your Lands Those Dogs Clothed in Red"

In November 1762 diplomats meeting at the palace of Versailles in Paris signed a preliminary peace agreement to end the long war between France and Great Britain that had begun on a Pennsylvania mountaintop in 1754. While the North American phase of the war had ended with the conquest of Canada in 1760, the bitter struggle continued elsewhere around the globe, from Europe to distant India. When Spain entered the conflict as an ally of France in January 1762, General Amherst was forced to relinquish his once great army in America for service in campaigns against French and Spanish possessions in the Caribbean. After a grueling siege that stretched through the heat of July and August, the strategic Spanish fortress at Havana, Cuba, finally fell to British forces. It was a great but costly victory. Upwards of five thousand British troops died from yellow fever or other tropical illnesses. The West Indies campaigns sapped the life from such notable regiments as the 42nd Royal Highlanders (the Black Watch) and Colonel Archibald Montgomery's 77th Highland Regiment. Just as victory celebrations over the fall of Havana broke out in London, the first boats bearing the remains of the army began arriving in New York harbor. One boatload of the Black Watch left Havana with 110 sick men aboard and anchored in New York with "hardly alive thirty odd." Most of the returning soldiers were placed in barracks that had been converted into hospitals.[1]

Although the toll in British lives had been high, the fall of Havana signaled that this world war was winding down. After another round of negotiations and some debate in Parliament over the terms of the treaty, a final peace agreement was signed in Paris on February 10, 1763. Under this treaty France ceded Canada, Florida, the interior of North America to the Mississippi River, and a number of islands in the Caribbean to Great Britain. Overnight, the size of the British Empire more than doubled, and with that expansion came the immense problems of defending and administering the newly won territory. One of the important questions facing British politicians was the disposition of the North American interior. Even before the cessation of hostilities, British policy makers had mused about the regulation of the frontier. One of the foremost concerns was the management of the numerous Indian nations that inhabited the region. Those who were knowledgeable about Indian relations, such as Sir William Johnson, insisted that the best way to keep peace in the forests of North America was to uphold promises made to the Indians regarding the preservation of their lands. The Lords of Trade and the Privy Council in London both agreed and issued firm instructions to Amherst and the various colonial governors not to permit settlement on lands claimed by the Indians. The situation was far too problematic, however, for these measures to have resolved the issue and assured the Indians. The colonial governors continued to press claims for land that the Indians had relinquished before the war, including areas already granted to the Ohio Company and other rival speculative ventures. These firms included powerful partners in Parliament who complicated the situation by delaying a final judgment on the issue. In addition, there were hundreds of squatters that the frontier military tried to eject from Indian lands with only marginal success. In all, the sudden change in the empire's size and status brought by this huge windfall of land produced a quagmire that would take time for Whitehall to sort out.[2]

A prime example of the inertia that characterized British policy toward the frontier can be seen in the land dispute that erupted in the Wyoming Valley of Pennsylvania. These lands along the Susquehanna were occupied by Teedyuscung's Delawares but claimed by Pennsylvania, Connecticut, and the Six Nations Iroquois. Since the

Easton Treaty of 1758, Teedyuscung had pleaded to every authority available to have the dispute resolved and to guarantee to him and his people a secure homeland. Despite these pleas, when the Delaware "king" returned home from the Lancaster conference in the fall of 1762, he found Connecticut settlers moving into the valley. These pioneers withdrew when threatened by Iroquois chiefs; however, they promised to return in the spring with a thousand more men and two cannons. Still, no one, from General Amherst to Pennsylvania governor James Hamilton, seemed inclined to use the force necessary to stop the invasion despite the London government's implicit instructions that Indian lands not be disturbed. Amherst, ever one to demand careful deliberation and planning, believed that it would be prudent to await instructions from his superiors before taking any action—even though he supported the Indians' position. In a letter to Amherst, the secretary of state, the Earl of Egremont, assured the North American commander that a plan to circumvent such disputes was "actually under Consideration."[3]

But implementation of this plan came too late to help Teedyuscung and his Delawares. On April 19, 1763, unknown arsonists set fire to the great chief's house while he slept inside. Within minutes, the remaining twenty cabins in the village of Shamokin were also put to the torch. Later it was claimed that the Six Nations Iroquois had ordered Teedyuscung's death in fear of his growing influence and reluctance to yield to their authority. The manner of his death makes this scenario seem unlikely. If the Iroquois wanted Teedyuscung dead, they simply would have traveled to Shamokin and tomahawked him. It seems more than coincidence that the Connecticut settlers returned to the Wyoming Valley to take up farming on Delaware land just two weeks after Teedyuscung's death. The destruction of Shamokin sparked the Indian uprising that would engulf the entire frontier west of the Appalachian Mountains.[4]

While the Delaware village of Shamokin smoldered in ashes along the Susquehanna, a new flame was set to ignite far to the west. The day after Teedyuscung's murder, Major Henry Gladwin, the commandant at Fort Detroit, wrote General Amherst of yet another war belt that had been circulating through the various Indian villages. This belt had been discovered at Fort Miami, where Ensign Robert Holmes and fifteen men of the Royal American Regiment guarded the portage between the Maumee and Wabash rivers. The Miami chiefs who surrendered the belt to Holmes reported that they had "Received [it] from the Shawnese Nation, & they Received it from the Delawares, & they from the Senecas, who are very much Enraged against the English." Gladwin noted that the Ohio Country tribes were all "Ill Disposed" toward the English and were "Tampering" with the Great Lakes Indians. Nevertheless, the battle-scarred veteran believed that their efforts would come to nothing.[5]

The source of this recent unrest stemmed from news of the preliminary peace agreement between England and France and the prospect that France would surrender all of its North American possessions to the English. At Fort Pitt George Croghan accurately gauged the mood of the Indians around Detroit and informed Sir William Johnson that "it appears that the Indians in them parts are very uneasy in their minds, since they have heard that so much of this Country is ceded to Great Britain, and indeed the Indian Nations hereabouts are full as uneasy, as 'till now they always expected Canada would be given back to the French on a Peace. They say the French had no Right to give up their Country to the English." Gladwin agreed. The Indians sensed, he believed, that with the French counterbalance permanently removed, the English would grow more and more powerful. "They [the Indians] say We mean to make Slaves of them, by Taking so many Posts in their Country, and that they had better Attempt Something now to Recover their Liberty, than Wait till We are better Established."[6]

In light of these ominous rumblings, Major Gladwin should have realized the vulnerability of his position at Fort Detroit. Located on sloping ground along the north bank of the Detroit River between lakes Erie and Huron, the fort was little more than an enclosed town and was never intended to withstand a military siege. An early map of the compound shows a number of buildings crowded along four parallel streets and enclosed by a rectangular palisade made of logs. Many of the seventy-odd structures within the fort had sharp peaked roofs and clapboard siding and were designed to serve as residences and shops for the French habitants. Also scattered throughout the post were storehouses, barracks, and officer's quarters and Saint Anne's Church, which served the parish founded by Jesuits when the town was first established as a trading center in 1701. The palisade walls were reinforced with earth on the inside and had a parapet from which soldiers could stand and fire on attackers below. In addition, blockhouses were placed at each corner of the compound and at strategic points over the three gates that served the fort. Outside the walls, for a distance of "ten miles on each side of the River," stood the farms and fields of the habitants. The seven hundred French residents who occupied these farms had all taken the oath of allegiance to Great Britain when Major Robert Rogers assumed control of Detroit in 1760, yet their loyalties were still a matter of conjecture.[7]

Aside from the suspect French habitants, Gladwin was also virtually surrounded by hundreds of disgruntled Indians. Several miles west of the fort, along the north bank of the river, resided the Potawatomies. According to a census of adult males made by Assistant Indian Agent Thomas Hutchins in the fall of 1762, there were about 150 men in this group. On the opposite side of the river lived the Hurons with a warrior population of 250. The Ottawas, also with about 250 warriors, were camped just across the river from Fort Detroit. In addition, Hutchins counted more than 300 Chippewas living in the area, although no contemporary map of the environs of Detroit designates a village site for these people.[8]

Against this formidable array Major Gladwin could count only two understrength companies of the Royal American Regiment; one company of independent rangers numbering twenty-three men; and a small contingent of officers and men attached to two naval vessels that plied the waters of Lake Erie. In all, there were no more than 140 officers and enlisted men to mount the ramparts, which formed a perimeter nearly four thousand feet long. Even if every able-bodied man was on constant duty, they would have to be spaced forty feet apart.[9]

Fortunately, the two armed ships anchored along the shore could provide protection from any assault from the river. One vessel, named the *Huron*, was a two-masted schooner sixty feet long and armed with six cannons mounted along the port, starboard, and bow. The other ship, the sloop *Michigan*, was slightly larger, with ten pieces of ordnance aboard. These vessels had been constructed above Niagara in 1761 under the supervision of Lieutenant Charles Robertson of the 77th Regiment. When the lieutenant arrived at Detroit with his tiny fleet in the fall of 1762, he hoped to navigate through Lake Saint Clair into Lake Huron. A sand bar prevented his passage through the lake, and he had to winter at Fort Detroit. With spring arriving, Robertson was anxious to explore Lake Saint Clair further, take soundings, and determine if his ships could maneuver into Lake Huron. On May 2 Robertson and two of his sailors set off in a small whaleboat with a military escort of six soldiers. The lieutenant was also accompanied by seventeen-year-old John Rutherford, who had been sent to Detroit by his uncle Walter, a former army officer involved in the Indian trade. Also tagging along in a small canoe was the English adventurer Sir Robert Davers and his Pawnee slave. Davers believed that the excursion would give him a splendid opportunity "to see further into the country."[10]

Even with Lieutenant Robertson gone, Major Gladwin could still count on experienced and dedicated officers from the Royal American Regiment to assist him. Aside from the amiable and talented Captain Campbell, Lieutenant Jehu Hay, from Chester, Pennsylvania, had six years experience on the frontier and had served as an assistant engineer and adjutant at Fort Niagara before coming to Detroit in 1762. Lieutenant Dietrich Brehm, who had served in the Dutch artillery before obtaining his commission in the regiment in 1756, had come to Detroit in 1760, when Robert Rogers took control of the post from the French. Another lieutenant from the Royal Americans, George McDougall, found life at Detroit quite pleasing and married a local French belle, Marie Francoise Navarre, in 1762. Just the opposite seemed to be true for Lieutenant James McDonald, who, having failed to win the heart of another Detroit habitant, fell "Ill from melancholy." One of the more courageous officers serving Major Gladwin was Captain Joseph Hopkins, who commanded the Independent Company of Rangers. A native of New England, Hopkins had served as sergeant major in Rogers's Rangers during the French and Indian War. After recruiting his own independent company, he had received his commission as a captain. Hopkins's lieutenant, Abraham Cuyler, came from a prominent Dutch family in Albany. He was not present at Detroit in the early spring, having been sent to Niagara to obtain supplies.[11]

On April 27 the Ottawa leader Pontiac called together all the tribes from the surrounding region for a grand council to convene on the Ecorse River about ten miles below Fort Detroit. The influential chief was determined to launch a surprise attack against the fort and wipe out the British garrison. The timing for this venture probably

Pontiac, painting by Jerry Farnsworth. There is no authenticated likeness of the Ottawa leader. This full-length portrait shows Pontiac as he may have appeared with an authentic headdress, bear-claw necklace, Woodland-style breechclout and moccasins, and war club. A bas-relief sculpture of Farnsworth's painting adorns the city building in Pontiac, Michigan. Courtesy the National Museum of the American Indian, Smithsonian Institution (catalog no. P11917).

coincided with the recent arrival of more war belts from the east and a realization that some effort must be made immediately to encourage the French not to surrender their country to the British. At the time of this council, Pontiac was perhaps forty-five to fifty years old, far past his prime as a warrior; yet his prowess in combat stretched back almost twenty years, and he was highly regarded by the Indians who resided around Detroit. In addition, he was a masterful orator and superb politician.

His appeals to the assembled Potawatomies, Ottawas, Chippewas, and Hurons were eloquent and convincing. A French habitant who apparently attended the council later related that Pontiac "spoke with so much eloquence that his narrative had just the effect upon them that he desired." The Ottawa leader echoed the discourse of the prophet Neolin and evoked the guiding hand of the Master of

Life in his plan to rid Detroit of the English. According to Pontiac, the Master of Life had directed the Indians to "drive off your lands those dogs clothed in red who will do you nothing but harm." The speech aroused the assembled warriors, who had been waiting for the right moment to strike. They had received the Seneca war belt two years earlier, and many more belts had passed through their villages since then. They had heard the warnings from the Ohio tribes that the English intended to starve and impoverish them and then "rub them out." The Indians residing near Detroit had no illusions about the evil designs of the British. For years, the French habitants had told them about British wickedness. Jesuit priests reputedly had added a question to the catechism taught to Indian children that asked, "Who killed Jesus Christ?" The answer: "The bloody English!" Little wonder, then, that Pontiac's message met with such an enthusiastic response. The Indians "listened to him as to an oracle, and told him that he had only to speak and they were all ready to do what he demanded of them."[12]

Indians rarely attacked a heavily defended position due to the considerable loss of life that could result and the difficulty of replacing large numbers of warriors killed in combat due to the tribes' relatively small populations. Apparently, Pontiac had already developed a strategy to gain entrance to the compound with a large number of warriors and then fall on the unsuspecting soldiers. In preparation for this coup the chief decided to undertake a careful reconnaissance of the fort. On May 1 Pontiac and fifty Ottawas approached the post and insisted on being admitted to perform a ceremonial dance for Captain Campbell. The post interpreter, Pierre Le Butte, convinced the sentries to allow the delegation to enter the compound. While Pontiac and a group of his warriors danced in front of Campbell's quarters, a handful of Indians quietly slipped away to prowl the narrow streets within the fort, noting the location of barracks, storehouses, and defenses. At the conclusion of the ceremony, Pontiac informed Major Gladwin that he would soon return with more of his people to smoke the calumet. With that, the Indians withdrew.[13]

Upon returning to his village, Pontiac began preparations for the surprise attack. He called together another council, at the Potawatomie village west of the fort. All the women in camp were ordered to withdraw, and Pontiac posted sentinels around the village. After all was secure, he delivered yet another impassioned speech to the assembled warriors:

> It is important for us, my brothers, that we exterminate from our lands this nation which seeks only to destroy us. You see as well as I that we can no longer supply our needs, as we have done from our brothers, the French. The English sell us goods twice as dear as the French do, and their goods do not last. . . . When I go to see the English commander and say to him that some of our comrades are dead, instead of bewailing their death, as our French brothers do, he laughs at me and at you. If I ask anything for our sick, he refuses with the reply that he has no use for us. From all this you can well see that they are seeking our ruin. Therefore, my brothers, we must all swear their destruction and wait no longer. Nothing prevents us; they are few in numbers, and we can accomplish it."[14]

The plans Pontiac made at the council called for him to approach the fort with a group of about sixty warriors, all armed with tomahawks, knives, or pistols hidden under their blankets. In addition, Indian women would enter the compound with shortened muskets under their clothing. At the appropriate moment, Pontiac himself would give the signal by turning over a wampum belt he would be carrying. He intended to present the belt to Major Gladwin with the white side facing up and then turn the belt over to the green side, which would be the signal to attack.[15]

The only problem with Pontiac's plan was that Major Gladwin learned all about it well in advance. For years historians have maintained a cottage industry in uncovering the identity of the informant who warned Gladwin of Pontiac's plan. Some of the likely candidates include an Ottawa warrior named Mahiganne who "was displeased with the evil behavior of those of his tribe"; an old Potawatomie woman named Catherine, who was later flogged by the Indians for supposedly revealing their plot; and a French habitant who visited one of the villages and noticed the warriors filing off the barrels of their muskets. One of the more romantic and sensational accounts credits the French belle Angelique Cuillerier, who had once danced the night away with Sir William Johnson, with revealing the plan to

Major Gladwin. In this tale young Angelique has fallen in love with an English trader named James Sterling. She learns of Pontiac's plans by eavesdropping on a council held between the Ottawa leader and her father, Antoine, who sympathizes with the Indians. Fearful that her lover will be killed in the ensuing massacre, she runs to the fort and relates her account to him. In turn, Sterling informs Gladwin. In fact, all of these stories have some credibility, and there is ample reason to believe that the major received a number of reports concerning Pontiac's plan to seize the fort.[16]

Regardless of who revealed the plot, Henry Gladwin was on his guard when Pontiac returned with hundreds of warriors on May 7. The Ottawa leader quickly realized that the entire garrison was under arms and posted at intervals throughout the fort. "We are greatly surprised, brother, at this unusual step thou hast taken, to have all the soldiers under arms," Pontiac told Gladwin. Attempting to cast off any suspicion, the chief said, "We would be very glad to know the reason for this, for we imagine some bad bird has given thee ill news of us, which we advise thee not to believe." Chagrined and bewildered over the fact that his plot had been uncovered, Pontiac could barely conceal his rage. After a brief exchange the Ottawa chief and his followers departed. Pontiac returned to the fort the following day and informed Captain Campbell that there was some obvious misunderstanding over the Indians' intentions. He told the officer that he would return the next day with his warriors to smoke the peace pipe. Major Gladwin used this interlude to shore up his defenses and remount his only three artillery pieces in commanding positions.[17]

On Monday, May 9, the soldiers standing guard along the parapet watched with apprehension as sixty-four canoes, "all full of Indians," glided across the river and came ashore near the fort. Already the fields outside Detroit were covered with hundreds of milling Indian men and women. Shortly afterward, Pontiac strode up to the gates and demanded that he and all his warriors be admitted into the compound in order to smoke the calumet. The post interpreter, Pierre Le Butte, informed the chief that only "twelve or fifteen of the leading men of his nation" might enter the fort. Pontiac angrily replied that "all his people wanted to smell the smoke of the peace-pipe, and if they could not enter he would not enter either." Realizing that his ruse to gain entry to the fort had been detected, the enraged Pontiac

Gladwin's council with Pontiac, May 7, 1763. According to one account, Pontiac intended to signal the attack against the garrison at Fort Detroit by turning over a wampum belt. When the Ottawa chief discovered the soldiers well armed and on guard, he decided to abandon his plan for a surprise attack and begin a siege of the fort. This sketch was used to illustrate an article about Pontiac's Uprising that appeared in *Harper's New Monthly Magazine* 22 (March 1861).

told Le Butte to tell Gladwin "that he may stay in his fort, and that I will keep the country." With that ominous warning, Pontiac turned and walked away. The siege of Fort Detroit had begun.[18]

Upon returning to his village, Pontiac picked up the hatchet and began to chant the war song. His followers needed no more encouragement and immediately set out to raid all the English houses that stood outside the walls of the fort. Although all the British settlers living outside the fort's confines had been warned that the Indians appeared troublesome, a few had not taken this admonition seriously. A party of warriors made their way to a small farm located about a mile from the fort. Without warning, they killed and scalped the occupants, a Mrs. Turnbull and her two sons. Then the Indians set the farmhouse on fire with the bodies of their victims inside. (The site of this attack was later known as Old Woman's Field.) Another party of Indians jumped in their canoes and paddled up the river to a spot known as Hog Island, where the British grazed their livestock. The Indians killed twenty-four head of cattle and quickly dispatched three soldiers working as herdsmen. They also mistakenly killed a habitant named Francois Goslin, whom they mistook for an Englishman. Then the Indians ran over to a nearby farm owned by a retired sergeant named James Fisher. Without hesitating, the warriors killed Sergeant Fisher, his wife, and two of his four children. They spared the maid and the other children and took them back to the Ottawa village. According to a local legend, several habitants went to Hog Island the following day to bury the slain soldiers and the Fisher family. When these same habitants returned to the island several days later, they discovered Sergeant Fisher's pale arm protruding from the grave. Shocked, the habitants covered the limb with earth. When they again visited the scene, however, they found the decaying arm once more jutting out of the fresh grave. The Frenchmen then fetched the local Franciscan priest, Father Simple Bocquet, who served as the pastor at Saint Anne's Church. After once again covering the grave with earth, Father Bocquet recited prayers and sprinkled holy water over the site. Sergeant Fisher's arm no longer rose from his grave.[19]

After butchering nearly all the English settlers outside Fort Detroit, the Ottawa, Chippewa, Huron, and Potawatomie warriors took positions "behind the Garden Fences and Houses in the Suburbs, and some Barns and Out-Houses, that were on the Side of the Fort next the Woods," whence they unleashed a brisk fire against the British troops behind the walls. The Royal Americans shot back and a lively firefight ensued. Meanwhile Pontiac ordered the Ottawas to break camp and cross to the north side of the river about three miles above the fort. This would prevent anyone from entering the post from the north or east. In the evening, a band of Chippewas arrived from the north and jubilantly reported that they had ambushed a small group of English soldiers on the Pine River near Lake Saint Clair. This was the exploration party under Lieutenant Charles Robertson that had left Fort Detroit to take soundings along the lake.[20]

Having departed Detroit on May 2, Robertson's crew traveled about sixty miles before arriving at a small sawmill that was being constructed by French habitants. Young John Rutherford, a member of Robertson's party, remembered that the French warned the British soldiers that the Indians were planning to ambush them upriver and that "they begged us with tears in their eyes for God's sake to return." While Robertson did not entirely doubt the veracity of the Canadian laborers, he was determined to continue on, believing that the Indians would not dare attack his party in broad daylight. He hoped to complete his soundings near the mouth of the Saint Clair River and then head back to Detroit before nightfall. With that, Sir Robert Davers and his Pawnee slave pushed off ahead of the slower-moving boat piloted by Robertson. Coming to a narrow stretch of the river, Sir Robert noticed a small Chippewa village on the shoreline. The Indians stood along the bank and motioned the English adventurer to come ashore. Davers realized that he could not escape and nosed his canoe to the riverbank, where he offered to smoke the calumet with the warriors.

When Lieutenant Robertson's slower-moving boat approached the scene, Davers urged the crew to continue on, knowing full well that the Indians were simply waiting for the entire party to arrive before striking. Suddenly, the river bank erupted with gunfire as the Indians sent a volley into Robertson's crew. The lieutenant and two of the soldiers aboard were immediately killed. While Rutherford attempted to bring the boat about, the Chippewas jumped into the water and seized the remaining crew members. In the meantime, Davers quickly maneuvered his fleet canoe across the river to the opposite side, but two Indians "leveled their pieces at him and brought him down. His body fell out of the boat into the river, which they picked up and brought on shore, cut his head off and buried his body; his head was also buried after the scalp was taken off." It was cruelly ironic that this English gentleman, who had come to America to escape suicidal tendencies by living with the Indians, died by their hands. The Chippewas then plundered the contents of the two boats. The following day, young Rutherford and the other captives were forced to witness the Indians roasting "small pieces of [Lieutenant Robert-son's] body . . . upon a stick at the fire." Peewash, the Chippewa who claimed Rutherford as his adopted son, assured him that "English-men's flesh was very good to eat." Later, one of the captured soldiers admitted to Rutherford that the Indians had forced him to partake of the cannibalistic feast. As the young captive later learned, the Chippe-was and some other tribes of the Great Lakes practiced cannibalism not "for want of food, but as a religious ceremony, or rather from a superstitious idea that it makes them prosperous in war."[21]

Back at Detroit the problem of provisions plagued both attackers and defenders from the very beginning. Major Gladwin realized that he had only about three weeks' worth of food on hand, enough to provide one pound of bread and two ounces of pork a day to each of his soldiers. He soon expected to receive additional supplies from Niagara, provided that the boats bearing the provisions could run the gauntlet formed by the Indians occupying both sides of the Detroit River below the fort. Recognizing that he could not rely solely on outside aid, Gladwin hoped to arrange for a cease-fire and take advant-age of the lull to gather more food from outside the fort. Pontiac, having failed to take Detroit by surprise, also recognized the need for food, powder, and lead in order to maintain a long siege. His only recourse was to commandeer these much needed provisions from the local French habitants whose farms and fields lined both sides of the river. Calling together a group of prominent French residents, Pontiac asked their advice on how to take the fort without a pro-tracted siege. Antoine Cuillerier, the father of the pretty Angelique, quickly emerged as the leader of the French who inhabited the area. The brother-in-law of Detroit's former French commander and a man whom Pontiac knew well and respected, Cuillerier and the other habitants urged Pontiac to negotiate with Gladwin for a peaceful surrender of the post. Accordingly, the Ottawa leader sent envoys to the fort to arrange a council with the English.[22]

A small delegation of French habitants and Indian chiefs arrived at Gladwin's headquarters and asked that Captain Campbell return with them to negotiate with Pontiac for a peaceful settlement to the crisis. Major Gladwin suggested that these emissaries be detained in the fort until Campbell's return, but the habitants assured Gladwin that his subordinate would be safe. The captain was eager to go and confident that he could reason with Pontiac and restore peace. He had been at Fort Detroit for three years, after all, and had worked hard to gain the trust and admiration of the Indians. Lieutenant George McDougall, who felt equally comfortable among the French and Indians on account of his marriage to a local French woman, accompanied Captain Campbell. After the two British officers passed through the gates of the fort and walked across the clearing, they were approached by a habitant named Claude Moran who "implored" Captain Campbell, "with tears in his eyes not to leave, saying if he went to the [Indian] camp he would never return."[23]

The conference took place at Antoine Cuillerier's house. When Campbell and McDougall entered, they could not help but notice Cuillerier sitting in the middle of the room wearing a laced coat and hat, as if he were invested with some sort of authority. The two British officers shortly learned the reason for Cuillerier's appearance and demeanor as Pontiac rose and addressed the assembly. He informed Cuillerier that he considered him to be the true commander of Detroit until the return of French troops. The Ottawa chief then turned to Campbell and McDougall and issued his terms for peace: the garrison must lay down its arms and give up its provisions, after which the Redcoats would be escorted eastward to the British fort at Niagara. Campbell responded with a plea for peace and then stated that he would take Pontiac's terms back to Major Gladwin. As the two officers were about to depart, Pontiac said to Campbell, "My father will sleep tonight in the lodges of his red children." With that, Campbell and McDougall ceased to be emissaries and became hostages.[24]

Some habitants returned to the fort to receive Major Gladwin's reply to Pontiac's terms, but the stubborn commander refused to negotiate until his officers were released. The following day, Pontiac and some of his principal chiefs ranged through the countryside commandeering more supplies from the French populace. The chief then ordered Captain Campbell to write out the Indians' demands for the capitulation of Detroit and had a Frenchman deliver them to Major Gladwin. The Ottawa leader modified his earlier terms to some degree by allowing the British to depart in the vessels anchored along shore. Pontiac also had "the Insolence to demand a Negro Boy belonging to a Merchant be delivered" to him to serve as his personal valet. Again, Gladwin responded that he had no intention of discussing any terms for the surrender of the fort so long as Campbell and McDougall remained as hostages. Meanwhile, the brief cease-fire did allow the British to take in additional supplies, allowing Gladwin to feel more secure in his position. Although not an expert in Indian warfare, he must have been assured by the local traders and loyal French habitants within the fort that Pontiac would never risk an all-out assault on the post for fear of sustaining too many casualties. Thus, the siege resumed, with Pontiac's warriors keeping a respectable distance from the walls of the fort.[25]

Unable to bring about Fort Detroit's quick capitulation through treachery, Pontiac had to conceive a new strategy to achieve his goal before he lost support among the allied tribes and habitants. The Ottawa chief contemplated having his warriors launch fire arrows against the wooden palisades and the structures within the fort. He asked a Frenchman to go to Father Bocquet and inquire whether God would be angry with the Indians if they accidentally set fire to Saint Anne's Church, inside the walls. The priest informed Pontiac that "God would be highly offended at such a step, and it was thereupon relinquished." Although Pontiac embraced the nativist movement of Neolin, that he would be concerned about offending the Christian God is not surprising. There is no reason to believe that he was inconsistent in his beliefs. Pontiac and the others who followed the Delaware prophet Neolin sincerely believed that the Master of Life and the Catholic God were one and the same. When some of the French balked at joining Pontiac in bearing arms against the English, he informed them that "all the English . . . must perish. It is the Master of Life who commands it. He has made known his will unto us,—we [the Indians] have responded, and you must carry out what He has said, and you French, you know Him better than we,—will you all go against His will?" During the siege, Pontiac himself attended Mass and allowed the habitants to enter the fort each Sunday to receive the Eucharist in Saint Anne's. Although the great Ottawa leader was not a true Christian convert, he was nonetheless instilled with a sense of spirituality that precluded his risking any insult to the Master of Life. Later he told the French that the Master of Life commanded him to "continue the War against the English . . . and not end it until there are no more red men."[26]

While not wishing to anger the Master of Life, Pontiac knew that he had to broaden his support to carry on the long siege. One group of Hurons living near Detroit had thus far remained neutral in the conflict due to the influence of the local Jesuit missionary, Father Pierre Potier. Pontiac went before Teata and Baby, chiefs of this band of Christian Indians and threatened them with annihilation unless they joined in the siege. With little recourse, the village agreed to add its perhaps sixty warriors to the attack after they had attended Mass on Thursday, May 12, the Feast of the Ascension.[27] After worship services the Hurons joined the Potawatomies stationed in the forest below the fort. These warriors began intense fire against the British soldiers sheltered behind the log palisades. At one point, the Hurons gained cover behind several barns that stood about sixty yards from the post. Gladwin ordered his artillery, loaded with red-hot iron and wire, to be aimed at the structures. The resulting barrage set the barns ablaze, and the Hurons scampered back to the woods out of range. During the attack, several Indians were killed and perhaps ten more wounded. From this point on, the cannon fire kept the enemy at bay.[28]

Like the Christian Hurons, many of the local habitants found themselves in a precarious position. If the British managed to withstand the siege, Pontiac's French collaborators would be branded as traitors and forced to relinquish their lands. If they refused to aid Pontiac, their produce and livestock would still be confiscated, and they might end up losing their lives. The French were thus "obliged to do what the Indians exact from us." One Frenchman lamented, "God alone can prevent our becoming the victims of the English and savages." Pontiac attempted to assure the habitants that he would reward them for their support. Whenever the Ottawa chief requisitioned cattle or other foodstuffs, he was careful to leave each habitant with a bill of credit drawn up on birch bark and inscribed with Pontiac's sign, a picture of an otter or raccoon. All of these supplies were stored at Antoine Cuillerier's house, where the Frenchman, as commissary, distributed the goods.[29]

More good fortune came Pontiac's way on May 13, when a convoy of five boats laden with supplies entered the Detroit River after a voyage across Lake Erie from Fort Niagara. The convoy, led by a Jewish trader named Chapman Abraham, came ashore at the home of a local Frenchman and was soon captured by some Hurons. The Indians immediately seized the goods, which included a considerable amount of rum and seventeen barrels of gunpowder. The Huron women, fearful that the rum would "cause their husbands to do more foolish things than they had already done," knocked in the heads of the liquor casks and spilled the contents. The startled warriors rescued only one eight-gallon barrel. Abraham and his crew were taken to the Indian villages, where some were tortured and killed. Abraham was tied to a stake to be burned alive. When he complained that the heat from the fire had made him thirsty, the Indians untied his hands and provided him with a bowl of scalding hot liquor. The unsuspecting trader took a sip and burned his mouth. Enraged, Abraham threw the remainder of the whiskey into the face of one of his captors. Awed by this defiant courage, the Indians released him from the stake and spared his life.[30]

Pontiac next sought support from his French "fathers" who still occupied outposts far to the west in the Illinois country. In a carefully crafted appeal revealing that the resentment of the Indians of the Ohio Country had inspired his rebellion, the chief reminded the French that they were "prisoners as well as we: It is vexing that the English, whom we are willing to adopt as brethren, should deceive so many nations. All that the Delawares and Shawany's [Shawnees] told us is now come to pass. They told us to be diffident to the English, they only seek to deceive you, and so it happeneth." He entrusted this message to a small group of Indians and two habitants, Jacques Godfroy and Mini Chesne. He also supplied his emissaries with a war belt to deliver to the Miamis, Kickapoos, and Mascoutens living farther south and west.[31]

Pontiac also dispatched warriors eastward toward the British outpost at Sandusky along Lake Erie. The small blockhouse, which the British had erected in the fall of 1761 for "purposes of keeping up the communication [and] keep[ing] the Canadians in proper subjection," was garrisoned by fifteen soldiers under the command of Ensign Christopher Pauli of the Royal Americans. Described by a fellow officer as a "very straightforward young man with an interest in engineering," Pauli had been stationed at the fort for nearly two years and had succeeded in planting a garden and making friends with the local Hurons who lived along the bay. On May 16 the ensign received seven Huron leaders from the nearby village who came to the blockhouse to smoke the calumet. Once admitted, the Indians seized the young officer and dragged him outside. To his surprise, Pauli "found his sentry Dead in the Gateway with the rest of the Garrison one

here and there all massacred, and the Fort surrounded by Indians."
The officer also noticed before being led away to Detroit that three
or four traders who had been operating out of the fort had also been
slain and one hundred pack horses laden with their trade goods
plundered. The first British fort had fallen.[32]

The next British outpost to be taken by the Indians was Fort Saint
Joseph. Located near present-day Niles, Michigan, the former French
fort was garrisoned by fifteen Royal Americans under Ensign Francis
Schlosser, an intemperate young officer whom the local French residents hated. On the morning of May 25, a small group of Potawatomies arrived at the fort and asked to speak with Schlosser. The
Indians pretended that relatives visiting them from Detroit wished
to meet the commandant. In reality, these so-called relatives were
warriors from Pontiac's camp bearing a war belt. Schlosser consented
and, while the Indians departed to retrieve their kinsmen, a local
French resident informed the ensign that the Potawatomies had "an
ill design" toward his meager garrison. The warning somewhat surprised the commandant, given the contempt that so many habitants
felt for him. The ensign sped to the barracks to place his men under
arms but found the room already crowded with Indians who were
ostensibly visiting with the garrison. Schlosser whispered to his
sergeant to attempt to get the men under arms and then went to his
quarters to meet with the other Potawatomies, who had returned
with their "relatives." The ensign was in the room only a few minutes
when he heard a scream emanating from the barracks. The Indians
quickly subdued Schlosser and led him outside, where, once again, a
British officer viewed a scene of terrible carnage. In a span of two
minutes, the Indians killed all but three of Schlosser's men. Like Ensign
Pauli before him, Schlosser was taken to Detroit as a hostage.[33]

Seventy miles southeast of Fort Saint Joseph stood another outpost
that the British had seized from French control after the surrender of
Montreal. Fort Miami, located along the Maumee River near present
day Fort Wayne, Indiana, was little more than a cluster of cabins and
storehouses enclosed by a log palisade. The fort's fourteen-man garrison was commanded by Ensign Robert Holmes, an experienced Indian
fighter from New Hampshire who had once been a member of Rogers's
Rangers. Despite the remote location of Holmes's assignment, he seemed
to adjust well to life at Fort Miami and took an Indian mistress. On

May 23 a French fur trader arrived at the fort and warned Holmes to be on his guard. The Frenchman claimed that while at the mouth of the Detroit River, he had heard cannon fire coming from the fort. The experienced ensign put his men on guard and ordered them to begin making cartridges. Four days later Holmes's Indian mistress came to the fort and asked him to come with her to the nearby Miami Indian village to bleed an old woman who was ill. Not suspecting treachery from his lover, the officer headed off for the Indian encampment. No sooner had he arrived at the village than two shots rang out, killing Holmes instantly. Upon hearing the gunfire, the sergeant of the post ran out of the fort and was quickly seized and made prisoner by the Miami warriors.

The rest of the garrison quickly shut the gates and climbed the ramparts to see a force standing outside that included John Welch, an English trader who operated out of Fort Detroit. Several days earlier Welch had been captured by Pontiac's emissaries on their way to the Illinois country to seek assistance from the French. Two of these messengers, the Detroit habitants Jacques Godfroy and Mini Chesne, now ordered the trader to speak to the Redcoats in English and inform them that their lives would be spared if they surrendered. The soldiers consulted with one another and decided to give up the post. The gates opened and the Indians poured in, carrying with them the mangled severed head of Ensign Holmes, which they tossed on the corporal's bed in the barracks. The Miamis killed four or five of the other soldiers and carried off the remaining Redcoats to Detroit.[34]

After the capitulation of Fort Miami, Pontiac's French and Indian emissaries from Detroit turned their attention toward Fort Ouiatenon, located along the Wabash River near present-day Lafayette, Indiana. Godfroy, Chesne, and their Ottawa companions told the local Weas, Kickapoos, and Mascoutens of their victory at Miami and the success of Pontiac's siege at Detroit. They passed the war belt to the local tribes and convinced them to devise a plan to take the fort. Lieutenant Edward Jenkins and his small garrison had no idea that hostilities between the British and Great Lakes tribes had commenced. On June 1 several local Indians came to the post and asked Lieutenant Jenkins to council with them at their village. As soon as the officer entered one of the cabins, the Indians seized him and forced him to order the remainder of his men to surrender. Unlike the soldiers at the other outposts,

Jenkins and his men were spared by the warriors due to the influence of several local habitants. The Weas, Kickapoos, and Mascoutens told the lieutenant that "they were sorry" for taking the garrison captive, "but they were Obliged to do it by the other Nations." Indeed, Pontiac's envoys quite possibly compelled the local Indians around Ouiatenon to strike the English or face the consequences from the Master of Life. Lieutenant Jenkins and his fortunate men were sequestered in the homes of some of the habitants for several months before being taken to the French forts in the Illinois country.[35]

The largest prize to be won by the Indians in this expanding war stood nearly three hundred miles north of Detroit at the narrows that separated Lake Huron from Lake Michigan. Fort Michilimackinac, established by the French in 1715 as a principal trading community for the entire upper Great Lakes region, was garrisoned by thirty-five soldiers under the command of Captain George Etherington of the Royal American Regiment. Alexander Henry, a young, enterprising trader who had first arrived at the outpost in the fall of 1761, described the fort as a complex covering two acres "enclosed with pickets of cedar wood." "Within the stockade," Henry wrote, "are thirty houses, neat in their appearance, and tolerably commodious; and a church in which mass is celebrated by a Jesuit missionary. The number of families may be nearly equal to that of the houses; and their subsistence is derived from the Indian traders who assemble here in their voyages to and from Montreal."[36]

While the Chippewa Indians who lived nearby were far removed from the tribes of the southern Great Lakes and the Ohio Country, they were, nonetheless, just as resentful of English rule. The old chief, Minavavana, told Alexander Henry shortly after the British assumed control over the narrows:

> Englishman, we are informed that our father, the King of France, is old and infirm; and that being fatigued with making war upon your nation, he is fallen asleep. During his sleep you have taken advantage of him and possessed yourselves of Canada. But his nap is almost at an end. I think I hear him already stirring and inquiring for his children, the Indians, and when he does awake, what must become of you? He will destroy you utterly.[37]

On June 2, 1763, a large number of Chippewa and Sauk Indians gathered outside the walls of Fort Michilimackinac to engage in a game of baggatiway, a contest that the French called lacrosse. Despite the growing tension between the local Indians and the fort's garrison, many of the soldiers went outside the gates to watch the contest. Just as the game reached a frenzied pitch, the ball sailed over the wall and into the fort. On the pretext of retrieving the ball, the Indians rushed the gates, grabbing knives and tomahawks concealed under the blankets of the Chippewa women standing nearby. Alexander Henry, who was preparing some letters inside his trading post, heard the high-pitched war cries and went to the window to ascertain the cause of the disturbance. There he witnessed "a crowd of Indians within the fort furiously cutting down and scalping every Englishman they found." Aghast, Henry "observed many of the Canadian inhabitants of the fort calmly looking on, neither opposing the Indians, nor suffering injury; and from this circumstance I conceived a hope of finding security in their houses." Henry dashed outside, jumped over a low fence, and ran into the home next door, which belonged to the French trader and former partisan ranger Charles Langlade. The Langlade family permitted Henry to hide in their loft and thus escape the initial carnage that took place on the fort's parade ground. Through a small aperture in the loft, Henry witnessed the final phases of the massacre. "The dead were scalped and mangled," Henry remembered; "the dying were writhing and shrieking under the unsatiated knife and tomahawk; and from the bodies of some, ripped open, their butchers were drinking the blood, scooped up in the hollow of joined hands and quaffed amid shouts of rage and victory."[38]

When the cries of the dying and wounded subsided, the Sauk and Chippewa warriors took stock of their triumph. Twenty-one British soldiers had been slain, and another seventeen men were held in captivity, including Captain Etherington. As the Indians began to plunder the fort the next morning, they discovered the young trader Alexander Henry, hiding in Langlade's house. Instead of tomahawking him to death, one Chippewa, named Wenniway, decided to adopt him to replace a brother who had been killed by the English during the war. The following day, June 4, a group of Ottawas arrived, angry that they had not been included in the attack. This somehow represented a breach of protocol, and the Ottawas confiscated the bulk of

The Conspiracy—Fort Michilimackinac, painting by Robert Griffing. In this stunning depiction by contemporary artist Robert Griffing, Chippewas discuss plans to attack the British garrison during a lacrosse game. Courtesy Paramount Press.

the Chippewas' captives and a portion of the plunder. With that, the Ottawas returned to their village, captives in tow, wishing to take no further part in the war. Captain Etherington convinced the Ottawas to spare the lives of his men with the promise of a sizable ransom once the prisoners had been redeemed at Montreal. To sweeten the pot, Etherington dispatched a group of Ottawas and French habitants to the far-off post known as Fort Edward Augustus (present-day Green Bay, Wisconsin) with a letter ordering the garrison there to abandon their position and join him at the Ottawa village. This would give the Indians even more hostages and, at the same time, guarantee the safety of the men at this remote post, who might otherwise be overrun by hostile Indians. Etherington thus believed that the best course was to combine both commands and place them under the protection of the Ottawas.[39]

On June 15 Lieutenant James Gorrell, the commander of Fort Edward Augustus, received the dispatch from Captain Etherington

ordering him to abandon his post. Gorrell called together the neighboring Sauk, Fox, Menominee, and Winnebago Indians and explained that
he was turning the fort over to them. He also informed them that the
Chippewas had attacked Captain Etherington at Michilimackinac.
As there was no love lost between the Chippewas and the tribes to
the west of Lake Michigan, the Sauk, Fox, Winnebago, and Menominee
chiefs agreed to escort Gorrell and his party to meet Etherington. As
a result the lieutenant arrived at the Ottawa camp without incident.
Once the English forces were combined, the Ottawas called the
Chippewas from Michilimackinac to council in order to "clear the
road" for the soldiers to depart for Montreal. The Chippewa chiefs
told Etherington and Gorrell that they wished to make peace with
the English and that they had been incited to attack the fort by war
belts coming from Detroit. This admission leaves little doubt that
Pontiac was behind the massacre, just as he had inspired the attacks
at Sandusky, Miami, Saint Joseph, and Ouiatenon. No longer fearing
another attack by the Chippewas, Etherington, Gorrell, and their commands boarded forty canoes and paddled toward Montreal, arriving
at the old French city on August 13, 1763.

Meanwhile, at Detroit Pontiac and his confederacy had realized
even more success gathering valuable supplies and ammunition from
the English. On May 21 Major Gladwin ordered the schooner *Huron*
with a crew of seven men to sail for Niagara to obtain fresh supplies
and reinforcements. The determined major instructed the ship's captain, a man named Newman, to remain at the mouth of the Detroit
River for several weeks before entering Lake Erie in order to await the
arrival of an anticipated convoy of supplies.[40] Once the ship anchored
at the mouth of the river, Pontiac deployed about thirty war canoes
loaded with warriors in an attempt to board the vessel. The bark of
the *Huron*'s cannons and the small-arms fire of the crew drove off the
Indians. Later the Ottawa leader put his hostage Captain Campbell
into the lead canoe and ordered him to convince the ship's captain
to surrender. The doughty Scotsman yelled to Captain Newman to do
his duty and fire on the canoes. Again, the cannons aboard the schooner
roared, and the Indians paddled for shore. The men aboard the sloop
realized, however, that they could not maintain their position at the
mouth of the river for long. Therefore, on May 26 the *Huron* entered
the open lake and sailed for Niagara.[41]

Pontiac and his followers understood that the presence of the sloop at the mouth of the Detroit River was a clear sign that Major Gladwin was expecting supplies and reinforcements from across the lake. Consequently, a large party of Indians traveled eastward along the shore of Lake Erie in hopes of intercepting such a convoy. At the same time, Lieutenant Abraham Cuyler, from Joseph Hopkins's ranger company, was returning to Detroit with ninety-six soldiers and 139 barrels of provisions loaded in ten large, bargelike vessels commonly used by the French to haul trade goods on the rivers and lakes of North America. As the boats skirted along the northern shore of Lake Erie, Cuyler and his men were completely unaware of the Indian war that had broken out on the frontier. On the evening of May 28, the command went ashore at Point Pelee, twenty-five miles from the mouth of the Detroit River. As the lieutenant and his men prepared to bivouac on the beach, one of the soldiers searched inland for firewood. Suddenly he came running back, screaming that a party of Indians were headed toward camp. Cuyler had little time to organize his men for an attack before the warriors were upon them. Knives and hatchets flashed in the darkness as the Indians hacked the unprepared soldiers to pieces. A wounded Lieutenant Cuyler and forty men managed to reach two of the barges and escape onto the lake, leaving behind the remainder of his rangers, who were either captured or butchered by the Indians.[42]

Two days later sentries stationed on the ramparts of Fort Detroit began cheering when they sighted a convoy of boats approaching from downriver. Their elation evaporated when they soon discovered that the barges were filled with Indians. A handful of soldiers who had been captured by the Indians during Cuyler's defeat were piloting the craft, serving as a human screen for the Indians aboard. When the first barge rowed past the sloop *Michigan*, the rangers steered the craft toward the fort. The Indians grappled with their prisoners in an attempt to redirect the boat toward the opposite bank. At the same time, the crew of the *Michigan* fired grapeshot across the river to disperse a group of warriors gathered along the shoreline. When the cannon belched its contents, the Indians in the barge dove into the water. One of the warriors pulled a soldier overboard with him, and both men drowned. The three remaining rangers paddled toward the fort while not less than fifty Indians fired at them from the opposite bank. Reaching the safety of the sloop, the three dauntless soldiers managed to save eight barrels of precious supplies, totaling "fourteen hundred pounds of flour, and a thousand pounds of bacon." The Indians in the remaining seven boats wisely chose to put ashore before reaching the fort. They forced their prisoners to unload the provisions and transport them overland to Pontiac's camp. While a few of the rangers were spared for adoption into the tribe, most were tortured and killed, after which "those [Indians] who had not engaged in killing fell upon the dead bodies and hacked them to pieces, cooked them, and feasted upon them." One Frenchman who observed the horrid scene recorded in his journal, "I could never finish if I wished to undertake it, the complete description of the cruel sacrifice and the sad end of all the unfortunates." The prizes gained from Cuyler's convoy gave Indian morale a considerable boost. As one French observer reported,

> The barges were loaded with powder and lead in bars, which was lucky for the Indians, who were running short. There was also flour and bacon, each barge carrying a ton of each, and liquor and fresh provisions for the officers of the Fort. The liquor caused great disorder in the camp; the savages got drunk and fought among themselves, and the taunts exchanged led to the death of two young braves the next day.[43]

The Indians were further reinvigorated on the last day of May, when a party of more than two hundred Chippewas led by the great chief Wasson arrived from Saginaw Bay to reinforce Pontiac. With the arrival of these Chippewas, the force surrounding Major Gladwin's tiny garrison increased to more than eight hundred warriors. The leadership dynamic among the Indians also changed. Wasson was an influential warrior-chief with a remarkable ability to unify the various tribes of the Great Lakes region. In addition, the Chippewas, who now outnumbered the Ottawas around Detroit, were more inclined to take direction from one of their own kinsmen than from Pontiac. With his stature diminished, Pontiac no longer exercised absolute authority over the siege of Detroit.[44]

Just as things began to look up for the Indians surrounding Detroit, however, the fortunes of war quickly turned against them. On June 3 one of Cuyler's rangers escaped from his captors and made his way into the fort under the cover of darkness. The former hostage brought news of the final terms of the Treaty of Paris that officially ended hostilities between Great Britain and France. Confirming this report was a letter brought by a local habitant who came into the post later in the day. Taken by the Hurons as part of the spoils from Cuyler's command, this communication described the terms of the peace settlement, and Gladwin read the letter to the French habitants inside the fort. It fairly warned the local community that no French army from the Illinois Country would come to reclaim Detroit. The wiser habitants realized that they must make peace with the English or face the consequences once the British had reasserted control over the region. Naturally, confirmation of the final treaty was welcome news to the beleaguered garrison, and that evening Major Gladwin ordered the band to perform a concert to celebrate the event.[45]

Apparently, word of the French father's surrender to the English spread through the Indian camps as well. On June 10 a party of Potawatomies approached the walls of the fort and asked to speak with Major Gladwin. The Indians wished to exchange Ensign Schlosser and several soldiers captured at Fort Sandusky for two Potawatomie chiefs whom the British had been holding as hostages since the start of the siege. When the Indians confessed that "they were led into the War by Pondiac," Gladwin "advised them to disperse & mind to their hunting & planting, for if they persisted it would end in their utter Ruin." To Lieutenant Hay, who observed the conference from the ramparts, the emissaries seemed humiliated by Gladwin's reproach and "hung their Heads." Several days later the Potawatomies returned and once again informed Gladwin that they were forced into the war by Pontiac and the Ottawas. Gladwin responded by asking the chiefs "if they were the Slaves of Pondiac?" He further stated that their tribesmen would not be released until all of the prisoners held by the Potawatomies were delivered up to him. The Indians departed promising to send corn to the fort to feed the garrison. On June 15 Washee, a principal Potawatomie chief, came to the fort and after intense negotiations released Ensign Schlosser and two soldiers in exchange for one of the Indians Gladwin held hostage. Washee further promised to redeem the rest of his prisoners for the remaining captive held by the British and, moreover, assured Gladwin that his band was "not concerned in the War, nor would be." This overture by the

Potawatomies encouraged other Indians to approach the fort to discuss peace terms. The Hurons, who were under the influence of the Jesuit missionary Father Potier, entered the post by a secret gate and pledged to Major Gladwin that they were "peacibly inclin'd." The commandant offered them "a flag, which they accepted in sign of union, and departed without any other conclusion." The following day, Chief Washee again returned with a delegation of other defectors—part of the recently arrived Saginaw Chippewas who, despite the influence of the powerful Wasson, insisted that "they had not entered into the War at all, that their Hearts were the same as the Puttawattamees." Major Gladwin informed all of these emissaries that "the only thing they could do to convince him of their good intentions wou'd be to give up the rest of their Prisoners and go to their villages and tend to their Corn & hunt."[46]

Gladwin was also encouraged when a man named Repus, identified as an Indian slave, came into the fort to inform the major that he had seen the schooner *Huron*, returning from Niagara with supplies and reinforcements, at the entrance to the Detroit River. At long last, after more than a month and a half of unrelenting siege warfare, the garrison at Detroit could expect relief.

In the meantime, Pontiac's fortunes continued to decline. On June 18 a Jesuit priest, Father Pierre Du Jaunay, arrived from Michilimackinac with word of the British defeat at that post. Du Jaunay was accompanied by eight Chippewas led by Kinonchamek, son of the powerful chief Minavavana, whose warriors had carried out the successful attack on the fort at the straits. After setting up his camp two and a half miles above Detroit, Kinonchamek received messengers from Pontiac's village. According to a habitant (whose identity is unknown), the young chief treated these diplomats "pretty coldly" and informed them that he would hold a council with Pontiac that afternoon. Kinonchamek then called several French residents "to give information about matters since the beginning of the siege by the Indians, and concerning all that had been done by Pontiac's orders." Several Shawnees and Delawares, recently arrived from the Ohio Country, accompanied Kinonchamek to the council ground.

The young Chippewa leader opened the conference by boasting of the victory over the British at Michilimackinac, exclaiming, "We have learned at home, my brothers, that you are waging war very differently from us. Like you, we have undertaken to chase the English out of our territory and we have succeeded. And we did it without glutting ourselves with their blood after we had taken them, as you have done; we surprised them while playing a game of lacrosse." Then, addressing Pontiac directly, Kinonchamek chastised the Ottawa leader: "But as for thee, thou hast taken prisoners upon the lake and the river, and after having brought them to thy camp thou hast killed them, and drunk their blood, and eaten their flesh. Is the flesh of men good for food? One eats only the flesh of deer and other animals which the Master of Life has placed on the earth." This statement was patently false since some of the Chippewas had indeed partaken in ritualistic cannibalism after the massacre at Michilimackinac; however, there is some reason to believe that Kinonchamek and his father, Minavavana, had not approved of such ancient rites and had punished those warriors who participated in the gory feast. "Moreover," Kinonchamek said, continuing his denouncement, "in making war upon the English thou hast made war upon the French by killing their stock and devouring their provisions, and if they refuse thee anything thou hast had thy followers pillage them."[47]

After the Chippewa chief finished his tirade against Pontiac, a leader from the nearly extinct Erie nation rose and spoke on behalf of the Delawares:

> My brothers, we have also fallen upon the English because the Master of Life by one of our brother Delawares told us to do so, but he forbade us to attack our brothers, the French, and thou hast done so. . . . We see well what has obliged thee to do what thou hast done to our brothers, the French: it is because thou hast begun the war ill-advisedly and art now in a rage at not having been able to take the English in the Fort. . . . We desired to come to thy assistance but shall not do so.[48]

Pontiac was stupefied and speechless after this severe rebuke. He gave no explanation or defense for his actions, and the council adjourned. Three days later Kinonchamek and the Chippewas from Michilimackinac broke up their encampment and returned to the straits.

Following the censure he had received from the Chippewas and the continued resilience of the British troops inside Fort Detroit, Pontiac was anxious to score some victory in the protracted siege to restore his tarnished reputation. Consequently, he targeted the schooner *Huron*, which was slowly making its way up the Detroit River. The vessel, piloted by Captain Newman, carried twenty-two men from the 30th Regiment of Foot, twenty-eight men from Lieutenant Cuyler's rangers who had survived the Huron attack along the shore of Lake Erie, and 150 barrels of provisions. On June 23 large numbers of Indians passed the fort heading downstream to intercept the schooner. Most of these warriors took a position on Turkey Island, where the river narrowed, enabling them to be within musket range when the ship passed. To protect themselves from the shipboard artillery, the Indians constructed makeshift barricades from tree trunks, branches, and earth. Then they waited. About six o'clock that evening the wind rose, allowing Captain Newman to continue his ascent toward Fort Detroit. Expecting an attack, most of the British soldiers were hidden below deck, and the Indians could see only about a dozen men aboard the vessel. As if by design, the wind died just as the *Huron* neared the island. The ship dropped anchor directly across from the concealed Indian breastworks. Emboldened by the appearance of so few men aboard the vessel, the warriors boarded canoes after nightfall and attempted to surround the ship. A keen-eyed sentinel spied the approaching birch-bark canoes, and Captain Newman quickly ordered the men who were below deck to come up and take positions "along the gunwale with weapons in their hands; in silence, all ready, with cannon loaded." Newman coolly instructed the soldiers to wait until the Indians were within range, whereupon he would signal them to fire by striking the deck with a hammer.

Suddenly an eruption of musket and cannon fire illuminated the Detroit River. Cannon balls tore through several canoes, and fourteen Indians were killed before the startled warriors recovered from their shock and paddled back to shore. The Indians stationed behind their barricade on Turkey Island opened fire, and five soldiers aboard the *Huron* suffered wounds during the nightlong attack. At daylight Captain Newman weighed anchor and allowed the slow-moving current to take the vessel back downstream to the mouth of the river in order to wait for a more favorable wind. Finally, on the last day of June, the schooner dropped anchor at Fort Detroit to the great joy and relief of Major Gladwin and his beleaguered garrison.[49]

The misfortunes accompanying Pontiac's efforts to conduct a protracted siege of Detroit certainly diminished the zeal with which the Indians had begun the war. With the arrival of reinforcements and supplies from Niagara, the Indians surrounding the fort may well have considered abandoning their efforts to rid their country of the British. Powerful forces were at work, however, that continued to inspire the Ottawas, Potawatomies, Hurons, and Chippewas who surrounded the garrison, not the least of which was the fact that the war had been ordained by the Master of Life. The Indians' belief that the Creator would sustain them guided their efforts and encouraged them to persevere. Too, the Great Lakes tribes probably still clung to the hope that the French father would wake up and eventually renew the war with the English. Many habitants and Indians, refusing to believe the report regarding a final peace treaty, said that "Major Gladwin had made the Declaration himself to pacify the Indians." Still others, who may have been inclined to believe the news from Europe, continued to hope that the French would come to their senses and reclaim the country. This is evident from the fact that Pontiac's emissaries continued to travel to the Illinois Country throughout the siege to convince the French commanders to provide them with arms and ammunition. Regardless of their setbacks at Detroit, the Indians drew encouragement from the victories that had been won elsewhere in the Great Lakes region. The British outposts at Michilimackinac, Sandusky, Saint Joseph, Ouiatenon, and Miami had fallen. As Pontiac had predicted, Gladwin could keep his fort and the Indians would control the country.[50]

Yet another reason for the Indians' continued resolve was the forceful character of Pontiac himself. For some years now, historians have argued about the extent and significance of Pontiac's personal role in the Indian uprising.[51] In an effort to prove that the war was not a "conspiracy" conceptualized and orchestrated by some Indian Svengali, these historians have denigrated Pontiac's overall influence.[52] This interpretation, however, tends to underestimate the Ottawa leader's personal magnetism, the power of which is evident in the fact that Pontiac maintained a considerable degree of control and respect despite the setbacks suffered by the Indians around Detroit and the censure he received from some of his Indian allies. Following the arrival of the *Huron*, Pontiac was astute enough to call a council with the wavering French habitants. At this conference the chief handed war belts to the leading Frenchmen, declaring, "My brothers, I am tired of seeing our lands encumbered by this carrion flesh [the British], and I hope you feel the same. . . . I have already told you, and I say it again, that when I began this war it was for your interest as well as ours." Pontiac then appealed to the habitants' religious beliefs and sense of loyalty, challenging them to "remain French as we are, or altogether English as they are." While this stirring appeal had little influence on the older Frenchmen, a number of young habitants rose and accepted the war belt, pledging to do all in their power to capture the fort. Pontiac's council with the habitants underscores his ability as a leader able to command the respect necessary to maintain a fragile coalition.[53] With that, the siege continued.

Indeed, despite the troops' jubilation over the arrival of the *Huron*, events early in July forced them to realize that their position at Detroit remained precarious—they were still hemmed in by hundreds of hostile Indians. On July 2 Lieutenant George McDougall, who had been taken hostage with Captain Campbell, effected a miraculous escape from his French and Indian captors under the cloak of darkness. McDougall had implored Campbell to escape with him, but the captain, being corpulent and nearsighted, feared that he would slow down his friend and be recaptured anyway. Two days later Major Gladwin ordered Lieutenant Jehu Hay with thirty men to sally out of the fort to destroy an entrenchment the Indians had constructed about a quarter mile from the stockade. The Indians observed Lieutenant Hay's party advancing on the entrenchment and began to fire at the British. As one witness to the skirmish recorded, "Hay was not disconcerted but animated his men by his example [to advance toward] the enemy, and charged on in the face of the fire." Major Gladwin, watching the skirmish from the ramparts of the fort, prudently ordered Captain Joseph Hopkins and twenty more men to go out and reinforce Hay. With the approach of Hopkins's company, some of the warriors fled, but a resolute group remained steadfast in the entrenchment and continued to fire at the troops. Hopkins sent a small party to flank the Indians. With bullets whining from two directions, the remaining Indians could no longer hold their position. They jumped up and began to run away, closely pursued by Hay's men. The retreat came too late for several of the warriors; two Indians were killed and several others wounded. One of the soldiers, who had at one time been held captive by the Indians, paused to scalp a young Chippewa chief, waving the grizzly trophy at the fleeing warriors and taunting them derisively.[54]

The Chippewa who was killed and scalped was the nephew of the great Saginaw leader Wasson. Enraged at the news, the vengeful chief went to Pontiac's camp and demanded that Captain Campbell be given up to him. Wasson told Pontiac, "My brother, I am fond of this carrion flesh which thou guardest. I wish some in my turn,— give it to me." To preserve his alliance, Pontiac reluctantly turned Campbell over to Wasson. The chief took the unfortunate captain to his camp and tomahawked him to death. Wasson then "took out his Heart & eat it reaking from his Body." Afterward, the Chippewas beheaded the corpse, cut off the limbs, and threw the torso into the Detroit River, where some habitants later recovered and buried the remains.[55] When the garrison at the fort learned of Campbell's death, it forcibly reminded them that they were still besieged by a desperate foe. In commenting on poor Campbell's fate, Lieutenant James McDonald remarked, "I must Own, I never had nor Never shall have, a Friend or Acquaintance that I valued more than Him."[56] When a Pennsylvania newspaper reported the circumstances surrounding Campbell's death a month later, the correspondent vowed that measures "will be employed . . . in taking such Revenge for the Butcheries committed by the Barbarians, as shall be a Lasting Monument of the Wrath of Injured Britons; and be sufficient to deter the Beasts from ever attempting the like hereafter."[57] This bit of bravado from a newspaper correspondent in Philadelphia provided little comfort to the beleaguered garrison at Detroit or the other white inhabitants of a frontier ablaze.

5

"A General Panick Has Seized This Extensive Country"

For nearly a month Sir Jeffery Amherst sat idly at his headquarters in New York completely oblivious to the conflagration that had already consumed the frontier. Despite all the warnings of unrest beyond the Appalachian Mountains, the general believed that the Indians could never mount a serious threat to British military occupation of their country. The commander in chief had grown restlessly tired of America and longed to return to England and his dilapidating estate Riverhead. His desire to be recalled had become even more urgent in recent months as word filtered back to him from England that his wife, Lady Jane, was deep in the throes of insanity. Surprisingly, General Amherst's first indication of Indian unrest came not from Detroit but from the environs of Fort Pitt.[1]

On May 27, 1763, the trader James Kenny found business at his trading post unusually brisk. A small party of Delawares arrived at his store, appearing to be "in an unusual hurry." The Indians traded eighty pounds of fur for "a Good deal of Powder & Lead & wanted more Powder," but Kenny told them he had none left to spare. While Kenny bartered with the Delawares, Indians were also at other trading posts dealing away their furs for ammunition. That same day a Delaware chief named Turtle's Heart came to the fort and went to visit the deputy Indian agent, Alexander McKee, who was operating as the principal liaison between the British and the Indians in George Croghan's absence. The Delaware leader asked McKee when he would be returning to the settlements in the East. The agent replied that he planned to journey back over the mountains in about ten days. Strangely, the chief insisted that McKee depart "that Day or in four Days at the furthest or else he should not expect to see him alive more & signified as if ye Indians was just ready to Strike."[2]

Other ominous warnings were issued that May 27 at the Delaware villages to the west. At Tuscarawas Thomas Colhoon and seven assistants were engaged in trading operations with the Indians. Colhoon was a personal friend of the great leader Shingas, their relationship stretching back to the time when the trader had his carpenter make a coffin for Shingas's departed wife. Perhaps to repay that kindness, the Delaware chief, accompanied by Tamaqua and other leaders, came to Colhoon's camp to inform him that an uprising had broken out on the frontier and that a war party was on its way to attack him. The chiefs admonished the trader, saying, "The Nations that have taken up the Hatchet against you, are the Ottawas and Chepawas. And when You first went to speak with these People, You did not consult us upon it." Obviously, the Delawares were disgruntled by Sir William Johnson's decision to bring the western tribes into the Covenant Chain with the English in 1761. Tamaqua and the other leaders insisted that they wanted no part in the pending conflict. "We thought Your King had made Peace with us and all the Western Nations of Indians," Tamaqua exclaimed, "for our Parts we joyn'd it heartly, And desired to hold it allways Good, and You may Depend upon it we will take Care not to be Cheated or drawn into a war again." The Indians admitted that they were, nonetheless, wedged between the Great Lakes tribes and the English, which left them helpless to avoid the conflict. The Delawares urged Colhoon and his men leave all their trade goods and other possessions behind and depart at once. They further instructed an old chief named Daniel and two other warriors to escort the traders safely to Fort Pitt. The next day, as Colhoon and his men passed Beaver Creek, they were ambushed by a war party hiding along the trail. Colhoon and three of his assistants dove from their horses into the bushes and managed to escape. The Indians killed the other traders. After wandering around through the dense forest,

Colhoon and his remaining men eventually struck the Venango Trail and headed south to the safety of Fort Pitt. The traders fully believed that Daniel and their other guides had deceived them and led them into the ambush. The Delawares in the war party, however, had also shot at their own kinsmen; Daniel returned to Tuscarawas with a bullet hole in his saddle.[3]

At Fort Pitt the small garrison of 145 men of the Royal American Regiment was hardly prepared to bear the brunt of an Indian war. Although the outpost was relatively large, with sixteen pieces of ordnance at hand, spring floods had severely damaged the compound and destroyed a considerable quantity of flour and other rations. Due to Colonel Bouquet's absence in Philadelphia, the fort was commanded by a fellow Swiss officer, Captain Simeon Ecuyer. The meaning of his name, "squire," suggests that Ecuyer might have come from a military family. Certainly the forty-three year old captain had seen extensive military service in Europe before coming to America with Henry Bouquet in 1756. Ecuyer was an astute and wily soldier, and the flurry of trade in powder and lead that the Indians were conducting outside the fort aroused his suspicion. On May 28 he sent Alexander McKee to the Indian villages near the fort to ascertain the reason for the unusual trading activity. McKee returned to report that the Delawares and Mingoes had all abandoned their homes.[4]

That same day Ecuyer's worst fears were realized when a war party of Delawares attacked Colonel William Clapham's settlement along the Youghiogheny River about twenty-five miles from Fort Pitt. Clapham was an old Indian fighter from Massachusetts who had come to Pennsylvania during the Seven Years' War to assist Benjamin Franklin in establishing a series of forts to protect the frontier. He arrived at Pittsburgh in 1760 and eventually entered into a partnership with George Croghan to develop a settlement in the Youghiogheny valley. The Indians who attacked Clapham's plantation were led by a young Delaware warrior named the Wolf who was a son of the noted chief Keekyuscung. The Wolf hated the English for throwing him in the guardhouse at Fort Pitt for stealing horses in November 1762. He managed to escape several weeks later and harbored a lasting grudge against the whites for their rough treatment of him. Despite Clapham's experience as a soldier, he was not on his guard that day when the Wolf struck. The war party tomahawked and scalped the colonel, killed his wife and one child, and murdered another man and woman employed at the settlement. Several other men working in the nearby fields managed to escape and brought word of the massacre into Fort Pitt.[5]

The next morning, Captain William Trent, another experienced frontiersman who ran a trading post in partnership with George Croghan, appeared outside James Kenny's store and awoke the Quaker trader with the news concerning the raid at Clapham's settlement. Kenny must have realized that this was the uprising that many of his Indian customers had been predicting for some time. The alarmed Quaker wasted little time in gathering up his personal belongings and setting out for Philadelphia. While Kenny was making his way to safety in the east, Captain Ecuyer received more bad news. Two soldiers working at a sawmill about a mile from the fort had been killed and scalped by the Indians. Convinced that a full-fledged uprising had commenced, the captain hurried off several dispatch riders to Colonel Bouquet in Philadelphia to inform him of the recent depredations. "I think the uprising is general," Ecuyer wrote, "I tremble for our posts. I think according to reports that I am surrounded by Indians. I am neglecting nothing to give them a good reception."[6]

The captain then set to work preparing Fort Pitt for a siege. He ordered all civilians living outside the fort to abandon their homes and seek sanctuary inside the compound and organized more than one hundred of the male refugees into a militia company under the command of Captain Trent. He then directed his soldiers to sally out and dismantle the shanties and other structures located in what was called the Upper Town along the Monongahela River. All the buildings in the Lower Town, which stood adjacent to the fort along the Allegheny, were burned to the ground. The men hauled the building materials from the Upper Town into the fort and used some of the "heavy planks" to form a firing barricade atop the fort's earthen ramparts. This was accomplished by driving stakes into the top of the earthworks and then attaching two planks, with a gap between them, to the stakes. The soldiers could then fire from atop the ramparts without exposing themselves to the enemy. Other boards were used to build platforms to mount all the artillery pieces on the fort's five bastions. Inside the compound, Ecuyer ordered his men to construct ovens and a forge, and barrels filled with water were strategically placed on each bastion in case the Indians sent fire arrows into the fort. He also requisitioned all the gunpowder from local merchants and stored it in the magazine. In addition, the men went out and herded all the cattle and oxen to pasture within sight of the palisades. In a letter to Colonel Bouquet, the captain gleefully stated that he had placed beaver traps along the earthen ramparts. "I would be happy to send you one," he told Bouquet, "with a savage's leg in it."

After all of this preparation Captain Ecuyer believed he was ready to repel any attack. "Our men are high spirited," he informed Bouquet, "and I am glad to see their good will, and speed with which they work . . . all very determined to conquer or die." Ecuyer noted that the Indians kept a respectable distance from the fort. "They do not dare to show themselves as yet," he wrote Bouquet; "perhaps they are weak; it is not my business to go look for them." The Indians later attempted to draw Ecuyer's force out of the fort by setting fire to both the sawmill and George Croghan's estate, but the experienced captain was too clever to fall for such a ruse. He boasted to Bouquet, "They would like to decoy me and make me send out detachments, but they will not fool me. I am determined to hold my post, spare my men and not expose them unwisely." The captain was correct in his assumptions concerning the enemy's tactics. Due to their reluctance to sustain large numbers of casualties in a direct attack, the Delaware, Mingo, and Shawnee warriors who surrounded the fort were content to keep the garrison bottled up inside the compound and hope to draw out small parties that could be quickly overwhelmed. While keeping the larger garrison at Fort Pitt hemmed in, the Indians felt secure in sending small war parties streaming north and eastward to ambush anyone found along the line of communication and to attack the weakly defended forts and settlements on the frontier. Despite Captain Ecuyer's bravado the cunning warriors of the woods had effectively neutralized his formidable command.[7]

Captain Ecuyer's first dispatches, carried by courageous Indian couriers attached to the British, arrived at Colonel Bouquet's headquarters in Philadelphia on June 4. Bouquet quickly forwarded the intelligence to General Amherst in New York. At first the general did not consider the Indian activities around Fort Pitt to be of much consequence. He responded to Bouquet by writing, "I am persuaded this Alarm will End in Nothing more than a Rash Attempt of what the Senecas have been threatening and which We have heard of for some time past." The general was convinced that "the Post of Fort Pitt, or any of the Others Commanded by Officers, can certainly never be in Danger from such a Wretched Enemy as the Indians are." For safety's sake, however, Amherst decided to assemble the light infantry companies from the 17th Regiment of Foot and the 42nd and 77th Highland Regiments and hold them in reserve at Staten Island in case they would be needed. The general was confident that this force could "Chastize any Nation, or Tribe, of Indians that Dare Commit Hostilities on His Majesty's Subjects." Exuding his usual contempt for Indians, Amherst told Bouquet, "I only Wait to Hear from You what further Steps the Savages have taken, for I still think it cannot be anything General, but the Rash Attempts of that Turbulent Tribe the Senecas, who Richly Deserve a Severe Chastizement from our Hands, for their Treacherous Behavior on many Occasions."[8]

After receiving rumors of the hostilities perpetrated by Pontiac's warriors to the west, however, Amherst at last became convinced that he was dealing with an Indian uprising of ominous proportions. On June 12 he wrote to Colonel Bouquet, "I Find the Affair of the Indians, appears to be more General than I had Apprehended. I Cannot Deferr Sending you a Reinforcement for the Communication." The general set two companies of light infantry from the Highland regiments on the road to Philadelphia to join Bouquet and gave the colonel complete authority to utilize them as he saw fit, urging him to waste no time in restoring order. "If the Indians have really Cutt off any of our Garrisons," Amherst wrote, "no time must be Lost in Retaking the Posts, & Securing them, so that We may keep Entire Possession of them." Little did Amherst realize at the time that five of his western fortresses had already fallen to the Great Lakes tribes and the smaller outposts on the Pennsylvania frontier were dangerously exposed to attack.[9]

Indeed, the tiny garrisons to the north of Fort Pitt—at Venango, LeBoeuf, and Presque Isle—each comprising perhaps only twelve to fifteen men, were particularly vulnerable to Indian attack. Captain Ecuyer sent out a total of eight couriers in an attempt to warn these forts, but in each case the men were either killed, wounded, or driven back by prowling Indians.[10] East of the forks of the Ohio lay the undefended relay station at Bushy Run, located midway between forts Pitt and Ligonier. At the first alarm, Ecuyer sent the three men who had escaped from the Clapham massacre to warn Andrew Byerly, who ran the station. When the messengers arrived at Byerly's, they convinced him to go with them to bury Clapham and his family. The former soldier left his wife and four children behind at their cabin. Phoebe, Andrew's wife, was certainly in no condition to travel, having given birth to their fourth child only three days before. Mrs. Byerly, however, was one of those proverbial hardy pioneer women. She had immigrated to America from the canton of Berne in Switzerland, the same homeland as Henry Bouquet. The colonel would often stop at Bushy Run Station and reminisce with Phoebe "about the lakes and the Alps, and friends in the far away land of their nativity." Sometime after Andrew departed with the messengers from Fort Pitt, an Indian appeared at the Byerly cabin. In the past, whenever this warrior had come to Bushy Run Station, Mrs. Byerly had always graciously treated him to a bowl of milk and some fresh baked bread. Perhaps to repay her hospitality, the Indian warned her that she must depart with her family before daylight. After scrawling a note to her husband on the cabin door, Phoebe Byerly gathered up her children and headed east toward the sanctuary of Fort Ligonier. It was a tedious journey as Mrs. Byerly rode horseback cradling her infant in her arms while another child, only two years old, was strapped to her back. The two older Byerly children—Michael, aged twelve, and Jacob, only three—tried to drive the family's small herd of milk cows through the forest. The cattle were not very cooperative, and when the family heard the distant war cries of the Indians behind them, it seemed prudent to abandon the livestock and hurry on to Ligonier. After traveling through the night, the Byerly's managed to reach the fort safely.[11]

The timely warning given to the Byerlys was not the only act of kindness shown by the Indians during the opening phases of the uprising. About a mile from Fort Ligonier stood the homestead of settler Robert Means. Means had come to the valley with his wife and eleven-year-old daughter, Mary, shortly after the conclusion of Forbes's campaign. Often the Means family traveled to the fort, where Indians and settlers gathered to trade and partake in intercultural festivities. At one such encounter a Delaware warrior known as Maiden Foot became enamored with little Mary. The child reminded Maiden

Foot of his own sister, who had recently died. Sometime later, when rumors of an Indian uprising reached the vicinity of Ligonier, Mrs. Means and her daughter gathered their few belongings and began the short journey to the fort. Suddenly, several Delaware warriors jumped from the brush, seized the couple, took them into the woods, and tied them to a tree. The frontier mother and her little girl must have been terrified, not knowing what fate the warriors planned for them. Then Maiden Foot appeared, cut them loose from their restraints, and guided them back to their cabin, where Robert Means was frantically searching for his family. The Delaware directed them to a place of safety in a ravine. Before departing, Maiden Foot took a handkerchief belonging to the little girl that was embroidered in black silk thread with the name "Mary Means." Many years later Mary married an army officer named Kearney who participated in the Battle of Fallen Timbers against the Little Turtle confederacy. After the American victory, Kearney and some fellow officers were roaming the battlefield when they came across an old Indian sitting on a log. The ancient warrior recounted how he had fought against the white man all his life and now wished to live in peace. When the soldiers inspected the pouch the Indian was carrying, they found a white handkerchief with the name "Mary Means" stitched into the cloth. Kearney, who was familiar with his wife's harrowing tale, brought the Indian to his home near Cincinnati, Ohio. The reunion between Maiden Foot and Mary must have been particularly poignant for the old Delaware lived out the remainder of his life with the Kearney family. When he died in 1798, Mary had a headstone erected over his grave that read: "In Memory of Maiden Foot, an Indian Chief of the Eighteenth Century, who died a Civilian and a Christian."[12]

While the Means and Byerly families managed to escape massacre at the hands of the Indians, other settlers were not so fortunate. Within days of the initial outbreak at Fort Pitt, word of an Indian war spread through the small, isolated settlements that dotted the wilderness, and hundreds of families fled their farms and rough-hewn cabins in absolute terror. Colonel John Armstrong, a Pennsylvania militia commander, arrived at Carlisle and found "the state of the frontier . . . already thrown into great confusion & difficulty," as horror-stricken pioneers poured into the town from their abandoned homesteads. These petrified farmers were no match for the stealthy war parties scouring the woods in search of defenseless frontier settlers. Contrary to the popular image of the stalwart frontiersman dressed in buckskin, defending his log cabin with his trusty long rifle, many of the inhabitants living on the border were unarmed. During the French and Indian War the Anglican missionary Thomas Barton traversed the backcountry and noted that "not a Man in Ten is able to purchase a Gun. Not a House in Twenty has a Door with either Lock or Bolt to it." Little had changed in the years following the conflict. At Fort Pitt Captain Ecuyer distributed tomahawks and firearms to the settlers who crowded into the fort. Colonel James Burd of the Pennsylvania militia arrived in the frontier community of Northampton to find the tiny village with only four muskets, three of them unfit for service. Even the frontiersmen who owned weapons found it difficult to obtain sufficient quantities of powder and lead. Colonel Armstrong, hoping to stem the tide of refugees streaming into Carlisle, complained that "ammunition is greatly wanted throughout the country." Even those wilderness inhabitants who were fortunate enough to possess a firearm and were adequately supplied with ammunition were not necessarily proficient in the use of their weapons. The typical frontier settler was likely to be a recent immigrant or former servant who came from a country or background where most people spent their entire lives tilling the soil as farmers and where there was no long-standing tradition among the European colonists of gun ownership or use. When these people arrived on the exposed frontier they tended to retain their agrarian customs and demonstrated little skill in marksmanship.[13]

In Philadelphia Colonel Henry Bouquet began planning for a relief expedition to clear the Forbes Road and bring supplies and reinforcements to Fort Pitt. The same logistical problems that had plagued the British army during the 1755 and 1758 campaigns surfaced once more. Bouquet found it impossible to obtain gunpowder in the city and could only hope that he would be able to purchase some from the traders along his line of march. While flour was plentiful, the colonel had no way of transporting the precious cargo. He wrote to General Amherst requesting bags for carrying the flour on the backs of packhorses. While Bouquet was certainly relieved by the news that the Highland companies were in motion to join him, he still hoped that Governor Hamilton could recruit additional provincial troops.

Knowing the chronic obstinacy of the Pennsylvania Assembly in refusing to support the proprietor's appeal for defensive appropriations, Bouquet realized there was little chance of help from that quarter. He informed Amherst that "the Governor will do everything in his Power for the Service, but he expects no Assistance from his assembly if the are called upon." Moreover, even if Hamilton was successful in raising a militia contingent, Bouquet's experience in the late war told him that they would be next to worthless for offensive operations. For the most part, Pennsylvania's provincial forces consisted of recent immigrants, former indentured servants, and common laborers who had little or no military experience. Nonetheless, Bouquet wanted such troops to garrison the weakly defended forts along the line of communication. The security of these outposts was crucial to keep that line open and to restore order in the hinterland. Like Captain Ecuyer, Bouquet was deeply concerned for the safety of these forts, especially those at Ligonier and Bedford.[14]

Like Fort Pitt, the post at Ligonier was in too poor a state of disrepair to repel an Indian attack. Due to General Amherst's false sense of security and miserliness, the wooden stockade and fascine batteries were rotting away. Lieutenant Archibald Blane, a Scotsman who was determined "with fixed resolve to do [his] utmost what ever may happen," commanded the small garrison of one sergeant and seven privates of the Royal American Regiment. With the local inhabitants streaming into the fort for protection, Blane organized a militia of approximately forty men and set them to work strengthening the perimeter of the compound. The lieutenant's preparations came none too soon, for a war party appeared at the edge of the timber on June 2 and began firing on the fort. The cautious and frugal Blane later related that "I contented myself with giving them three Chears, without spending a single shot upon them." As the day wore on, the Indians continued their fire and began to work their way toward the cover of buildings that stood near the post's outer works. To deny the enemy this cover, Blane sent out a detachment led by his sergeant to set fire to the structures. Foiled by that wise decision, the Indians faded back into the forest. Upon learning of this incident sometime later, General Amherst failed to appreciate Blane's wisdom. "I Cannot help Expressing my Surprise, that on the Appearance of a few Indians, all Out Houses should be Burnt & Destroyed," the general complained,

Fort Ligonier—Sketched on the Spot—30th June 1762, by Lieutenant Archibald Blane; ink, pastel, and chalk on paper. This view shows the horizontal log curtain wall and bastions on the eastern side of the fort. Courtesy Fort Ligonier, Pennsylvania.

"for I can See no sort of Necessity for that, on the Approach of so Despicable an Enemy as the Indians are, without any kind of Warlike Implements, but those of Ill provided Small Arms."[15]

Fifty miles to the east of Ligonier stood Fort Bedford, another important outpost along the line of communication. The fort, with its garrison of twelve Royal Americans, was commanded by Captain Lewis Ourry. Colonel Bouquet's closest friend, the captain had consoled the Swiss commander when Anne Willing married another man. Ourry, who was two years older than Bouquet, came from a family steeped in military tradition. His father, a French Huguenot, had fled his homeland to escape persecution and had held a commission in the British army for nearly sixty years. Ourry's three brothers served in the Royal Navy. His own military career began in 1747, when he was commissioned a second lieutenant in the Churchill Marines. He came to America with Henry Bouquet in 1756 and served as a quartermaster on the Forbes Expedition. Although, like many British officers, Captain Ourry had a distinct contempt for provincials, when word reached his outpost of an impending Indian uprising to the west, he became dependent on this class of soldiers to help maintain his post.[16]

Captain Ourry wrote to Bouquet on June 1 regarding the defenseless state of the frontier: "The nakedness of this [line of] Communication, and the weakness of the Garrisons in general, have induced the Savages to renew their barbarous Hostilities." In common with Ecuyer and Blane, Ourry organized the settlers swarming to the fort into a militia company of 155 men and provided them with arms and ammunition. To intimidate any Indians who may have been lurking about the fort, the captain staged a display of force by hoisting "a New Union Flag" over the parade ground, "which was Saluted with three Volleys from the whole line." He sent a dispatch to Colonel Bouquet assuring him that the men were "in good Spirits, & resolved to Stand by here. So that I am in no pain for this Post." In private, however, Ourry commented on the lack of gunpowder and supplies on hand. "If any Troops come up," he wrote Bouquet, "they must bring Powder, for we have very little here & that damaged. . . . I will deffend the Rats in the Stores [storehouses] to the best of my Abilities. I wish I could convert them all into men. [Then] I would not begrudge them all the Stores they daily continue to eat & destroy."[17]

Captain Ourry was fortunate in at least one regard. He managed to cull from his militia a small group of "Excellent Woods Men, disguised like Indians & well versed in their method of traveling & acquainted with their Haunts." These more experienced frontiersmen could be relied on to conduct scouting forays in search of the enemy and to carry dispatches through hostile territory to Ligonier. Ourry's rangers included Christopher Lems and John Proctor, resourceful Indian fighters who had participated in John Armstrong's raid on the Delaware village of Kittaning back in 1756.[18] Throughout the first days of June, Ourry sent out patrols to scour the country for Indians and worked tirelessly to get his fort in shape. "Since the allarm I never lie down 'till about twelve," he wrote Bouquet, "& am walking about the fort between 2 & 3 in the Morning, turning out the guards." The indefatigable commander had pens built for the cattle and sheep, filled all the barrels with water, and made necessary repairs on all the gutters "to receive & collect the drops from heaven." Despite these

Herculean efforts, by June 9 the captain had grown more despondent and apprehensive. In a dispatch to Colonel Bouquet he admitted, "My greatest Difficulty is to keep my undisciplined Militia from straggling by two's & three's to their dear plantations, thereby exposing themselves to be Scalped & weakening my Garrison." He assured Bouquet that he would "use all Means to prevail on them to stay till some Troops come up." Closing the letter, Ourry wrote, "I long . . . to hear the Grenadiers March, & to see some more Red Coats."[19]

With the two Highland companies on the march to Philadelphia, Henry Bouquet wrote to Amherst outlining his plan of operations for a relief expedition to the West. "I propose to march to Fort Pitt, with a Convoy of Flour, Sheep, and some Powder, which will be kept ready at Shippensburg; and in escorting back the Horses and Drivers, clear the Forts of all useless People, and leave Sufficient garrisons upon the communication to keep it clear and open to further Supplies." Due to the few troops at his disposal, Bouquet suggested that the small forts at Venango and LeBoeuf be abandoned and the troops from these posts be sent to either Fort Pitt or Presque Isle. To continue maintaining a presence at Venango and LeBoeuf, the colonel argued, "Is very precarious, and would require more men than we can Spare, without any visible advantage." Replying, the stubborn Amherst refused to consider Bouquet's suggestion: "Altho the Posts at Venango and LeBoeuf may be of Little Advantage to Us, yet I Cannot think of giving them up, at this time, if We Can keep them, as such a Step would give the Indians Room to Imagine themselves more Formidable than they really are; and it would be much better We never Attempted to take Post in what they call their Country, if upon every Alarm We Abandon them." Little did the obstinate Amherst realize that by the time he penned this response to Bouquet, all of his forts along the Venango Trail had already fallen to the Indians.[20]

For years historians have maintained that the Indians who ravaged the frontiers of Pennsylvania in the summer of 1763 were led by the Seneca chief Kiasutha. To be sure, the Ohio Country leader was an implacable foe of the English and had taken the first step toward war back in the fall of 1761 by circulating war belts among the tribes of the Great Lakes. On June 6, 1763, the Senecas living about Fort Niagara received "a Belt from the Indians about Pittsborough, to take up the Bloody Hatchet." The war belts were accompanied by the scalps taken from the victims of the Clapham massacre and the soldiers killed at the sawmill near Fort Pitt. Curiously, this war belt had been sent by a "Seneca Chachim [Sachem]" with a message for his tribesmen at Niagara to evacuate the area around the fort. This sachem could very well have been Kiasutha, and it is hard not to see his hand in the passage of this war belt, since he was the principle Seneca leader about Fort Pitt. Less than a week after the initial outbreak at the forks of the Ohio, all the Senecas to the north had been apprized of the uprising. Now these warriors, who held a long-standing grudge against the British, were ready to strike.[21]

The first outpost to fall to the Senecas was Fort Venango, located at the confluence of French Creek and the Allegheny River. When the French abandoned the region in 1759, they burned the fort they called Machault to the ground. In its place the British constructed a smaller outpost with earthen bastions and curtain walls. Inside they erected a large two-story log blockhouse measuring about sixty feet square. The fort was occupied by an imprudent lieutenant named Francis Gordon and a garrison of perhaps fifteen Royal Americans. Several Delaware and Mingo villages stood nearby. On June 16 a number of Indians approached the fort and entered the compound by subterfuge. Local legend holds that the warriors used the same ruse that the Chippewas employed to gain entry into Michilimackinac—a game of lacrosse. Once inside, the Mingoes butchered the entire garrison except Lieutenant Gordon. Perhaps to justify their attack on the fort, the Indians forced Gordon to write a letter detailing their grievances against the English. In this document the Mingoes maintained that they believed, given the number of forts that the British occupied in the region and the scarcity of gunpowder provided to the Indians, that the British intended "to Possess all their Country." After Gordon completed this manifesto, the Indians slowly roasted him to death.[22]

After burning Venango to the ground, the Indians moved north toward Fort LeBoeuf. Like Venango, LeBoeuf consisted of little more than a large blockhouse within an earthen enclosure and a few out-buildings scattered about. The compound was commanded by Ensign George Price, an experienced officer who had served in one of the Pennsylvania provincial battalions before gaining a commission in the Royal American Regiment. Price had two corporals and eleven enlisted men under his command, and there was also a woman staying at the fort. The soldiers at LeBoeuf were already on guard, having received word from Fort Presque Isle that the Indians to the west were besieging Detroit. On the morning of June 18, a small group of Indians appeared at the fort and, telling Ensign Price that they were on their way south to fight the Cherokees, requested that they be supplied with powder and lead for their journey. Price refused, and the Indians went off, only to return with thirty more warriors. The Indians then asked Price to open the door of the blockhouse and give them a kettle to cook their food. When the ensign refused this request, the Senecas, perhaps joined by some Delawares, broke into a nearby storehouse and began shooting at the blockhouse. The Indians also shot fire arrows onto the roof of the structure, compelling soldiers to clamber up to the top and extinguish the flames. The reign of fire arrows continued into the evening, when the men on the roof finally came down to inform Price that they could no longer put out the flames. Though the soldiers begged their commander to let them attempt an escape, Ensign Price was adamant, exclaiming, "We must fight as long as we can, and then die together."

At last, as the soldiers choked on the dense smoke now engulfing them, Price relented. He ordered the men to take an axe and chop through a narrow window in the back of the building. Under the cover of darkness, Price and all his men managed to escape while the enemy was focused on the front door of the stronghold. The refugees crawled to a pine swamp from which a soldier named John Dortinger claimed he could lead the group safely to Fort Venango. Through a dense forest as black as pitch, the men, along with their lone female companion, traveled all night. At one point six of the soldiers and the woman became separated from Price and the rest of the group. When the ensign and the remnants of his command reached Venango the following day, they found the fort burned to the ground and the charred bodies of the garrison lying in the smoldering embers. The men continued their flight down the Venango Trail, finding several of Captain Ecuyer's couriers lying dead and mutilated along the road. Finally, on the morning of June 26, Price and his men slipped through the cordon of Indians and reached the safety of Fort Pitt. Four more soldiers and the woman came straggling into the fort the next day. Presumably the other two men perished in the woods or were killed by Indians.[23]

Fort LeBoeuf, 1763. This small British outpost was little more than a block-house surrounded by a wooden palisade. From George Albert Dallas, *The Frontier Forts of Western Pennsylvania* (1916).

After destroying Venango and LeBoeuf, the Senecas moved on to the larger and stronger outpost at Presque Isle, situated on the shore of Lake Erie. Colonel Bouquet had personally overseen the construction of this fort and had deemed it "impregnable to Savages." Commanded by Ensign John Christie, the post contained a garrison of twenty-nine Royal Americans and several civilians, including one woman. At dawn on June 20 Christie and his men awoke to find themselves surrounded by Indians. The Senecas and Delawares from the Ohio Country had been joined by Pontiac's Ottawas, Chippewas, and Hurons. At last, a true pan-Indian confederation had been achieved. In all, there were about 250 warriors, and they poured a brisk fire into the fort from two hills overlooking the site. The Indians cleverly had dug foxholes into the sandy soil to protect themselves while they shot fire arrows onto the roof of the main blockhouse. The Royal Americans fought back, killing several Indians who ventured too close to the fort's earthen curtain wall. Trying to extinguish the fires the Indians set, Christie's soldiers quickly used up the water stored inside the block-house, so they began digging a well inside the structure. After two days of fighting, the Indians penetrated the fort's parade ground, where they set fire to the officers' quarters.

What must have been particularly discouraging to Christie's beleaguered command was the fact that they could see the schooner *Huron* several miles offshore. The vessel was returning to Detroit with Lieutenant Abraham Cuyler and his relief force of fifty men. For some unexplained reason the ship could not sail into the harbor or approach close enough to the fort to use its artillery against the attacking Indians. In addition, the one landing craft on board the *Huron* could hold only ten men. Had Cuyler attempted to send his troops ashore to relieve the fort, the Indians would simply have picked them off as they landed. Consequently, the lieutenant watched helplessly from the deck of the schooner as the Indians tightened their circle around Ensign Christie's command.[24]

Finally at midnight on the 22nd, one of the Indians who spoke French called out to Christie "that it was in vain for him to pretend to hold out, for they could set fire to the Blockhouse when they pleased, & if he would not surrender they would burn and torture every man that he had." In response the ensign asked if any of his attackers could speak English. A white man came forward who had once been a captive but was now part of the enemy force. The renegade told Christie that the Indians wanted only to take over the compound and that the soldiers would be free to depart to Fort Pitt. The lieutenant pondered his predicament throughout the night. The following morning, Christie and his command marched out of the blockhouse and surrendered. Instead of setting the garrison free, however, the Indians divided up their captives. During this process one soldier named Benjamin Gray managed to make his escape by hiding in the bushes. Eventually, he made his way to Fort Pitt to report the harrowing tale of Presque Isle's fall. The Hurons claimed Ensign Christie, four of his men, and the one woman as their hostages and took them back to Detroit, where two of the soldiers were tortured and put to death. Later, after the Hurons began to waver, they turned Christie, one soldier, and the woman over to Major Gladwin.[25] Presumably, the remainder of Christie's men were either killed or redeemed at a later time.

In the span of one week, the Senecas and their allies had, by taking three British outposts, severed the line of communication between forts Pitt and Niagara. Truly, the Indians were the masters of their country.

While woodland warriors ravaged the frontier outposts to the north, Captain Simeon Ecuyer continued to hold on at Fort Pitt. Despite the formidable state of his defenses, the captain could not prevent the drain on his provisions and the crowded, unsanitary conditions that prevailed inside the perimeter. Altogether, there were nearly 550 people jammed into the compound, including 104 women and 106 children. In a letter to Bouquet Ecuyer complained, "We are so crowded in the fort that I fear disease, for in spite of all my care I cannot keep the place as clean as I should like; moreover, the smallpox is among us." To combat that scourge of mankind, Ecuyer set up a makeshift hospital under the fort's drawbridge.[26]

Further complicating Ecuyer's situation, once the Indians had completed their destruction of the forts at Venango, LeBoeuf, and Presque Isle, they began to intensify their attacks against him. On June 22 a small group of Indians drove away some horses and cattle grazing in the pasture near the fort. Later that day "a great number of Indians appeared on each river and on Grant's Hill" (the hill overlooking the fort where Major James Grant's forces had been attacked and defeated in 1758) and began firing at the fort. Captain Trent reported in his journal that James Thompson, a civilian, went out in an attempt to locate his horse and "was killed and scalped in sight of the fort." Another soldier was wounded by musket fire during the attack. The firing subsided when Captain Ecuyer ordered an exploding shell to be discharged in the Indians' direction. Nevertheless, the cordon of warriors surrounding the fort continued to tighten as they moved ever closer to the outer bastions under the cover of darkness. At one point during the night, a sentinel standing guard gave out the "All's well" call only to have nearby Indians mimic him. Most certainly, the situation was not "all's well" at Fort Pitt.[27]

On June 24 two Delaware leaders, Turtle's Heart and Maumaultee, came before the fort under a flag of truce to confer with Captain Ecuyer. The chiefs opened the parley by informing Ecuyer that "a great number of Indians," representing six different nations, had surrounded him and that all the English forts to the north and east had been "burn't and cut off." Out of the regard that the Delawares still had for the English, however, the chiefs had come to offer the garrison an opportunity to depart and "Pass safe to the inhabitants," meaning the inhabited parts of the colony that existed east of the mountains. In the spirit of diplomacy, Captain Ecuyer thanked the Delawares but informed them that he intended to defend the fort "against all the Indians in the woods." Furthermore, the Swiss officer told them, three separate armies were on the move to relieve the fort and crush the Indian rebellion. He advised the chiefs to reaffirm their friendship with the English and depart in peace. Turtle's Heart and Maumaultee promised to deliver the message to the other tribes surrounding Fort Pitt and told Ecuyer that they would return with a response. That same afternoon the chiefs once again appeared before the walls of the fort. They pledged to "continue to hold fast to the Chain of Friendship" and requested that the commander give them some provisions and liquor for their return journey home. Ecuyer provided the Delaware leaders with an astounding six hundred rations, but among the array of supplies was a more sinister gift. Captain Trent, who was present during the parley, later recorded in his journal, "Out of our regard to them we gave them two Blankets and an Handkerchief out of the Small Pox Hospital. I hope it has the desired effect."[28]

Smallpox was the bane of the frontier, indiscriminately decimating both European and Indian communities. Once the disease had been introduced into a community, it spread quickly, usually before the telltale rash developed among its victims to warn of the impending plague. As the disease progressed, the rash became more severe and pronounced, forming into oozing pustules that covered the entire body but frequently concentrated on the face and extremities, especially the soles of the feet and palms of the hand. In some cases these secreting pustules combined into a nocuous mass. Such was George Croghan's experience with the disease in 1762, during negotiations with the Indians at Easton. One observer noticed that the Indian agent had "the pox so bad that he cant live long having a hole at the bottom of his belly that runs constantly." The seeping wound forced the proud Irishman to wear a Scottish kilt. Sir William Johnson wrote to his subordinate suggesting that he treat the affliction as a venereal disease. Fortunately, Croghan survived the deadly virus without the serious impairments that were common such as blindness, deformity, and horrific scarring.[29]

Some historians who have investigated the infamous smallpox incident at Fort Pitt have claimed that the English attempt to use germ warfare against the enemy had a far greater impact in ending the Indian uprising than British military strategy or force of arms. According to these scholars, English perfidy decimated the Indian population of the Ohio Country as smallpox spread like fire throughout the confederated tribes. Close examination of the incident, however, indicates that the British experiment in biological warfare may well have been a failure. To begin with, there is no doubt that British military authorities approved of attempts to spread smallpox among the enemy. On July 7 General Amherst suggested to Colonel Bouquet, "Could it not be contrived to Send the Small Pox among those Disaffected Tribes of Indians? We must, on this occasion, Use Every Strategem in our power to Reduce them." Bouquet responded that he would attempt to introduce the disease through blankets "that may fall in their Hands, and take Care not to get the disease myself." Upon learning of Bouquet's plan, Sir Jeffery instructed his subordinate, "You will Do well to try to Innoculate the Indians, by means of Blankets, as well as to Try Every other Method, that can Serve to Extirpate this Execrable Race." At the time of this exchange, neither Amherst nor Bouquet knew that Captain Ecuyer, without authorization, had already put the plan into motion. Equally significant, the Indians also attempted a crude form of biological warfare of their own when they poisoned the well at Fort Ligonier in the summer of 1761 "in hopes to Hurt ye People" living there. While this in no way exonerates the English, it does remind us that there is nothing more brutal in human experience than war, regardless of which side may be right or wrong. Perhaps worth pondering in this connection are the words the French explorer La Salle once found carved in a wooden plank at the abandoned Fort Crèvecoeur in the heart of the American wilderness: *Nous sommes tous sauvages* ("We are all savages").[30]

Having established that it was deliberate British policy to infect the Indians with smallpox, it is also important to examine whether the plan succeeded. An undetermined number of Indians did become infected at some point during the war. Much less certain, however, is how the Indians contracted the disease. In March 1765 the Delaware chief Killbuck told Sir William Johnson that "the Shawanes lost in three Months time 149 Men besides Women & Children by Sickness above a year ago, also many of them dyed last Summer of the Small Pox, as did Several of their Nation." This statement would indicate that the epidemic took hold sometime later than the summer of 1763, when the blanket incident occurred. Another reputed witness to the smallpox outbreak among the Indians was Gershom Hicks, a renegade held by the British at Fort Pitt as a prisoner of war in April 1764. According to a deposition Hicks made to Captain William Grant, "the Small Pox has been very general & raging amongst the Indians since last spring and that 30 or 40 Mingoes, as many Delawares and some Shawneese Died all of the Small Pox since that time." Hicks's statement contradicts the account given by Killbuck in asserting that the Mingoes and Delawares were the hardest hit by the disease, not the Shawnees. Hicks also claimed that the epidemic began in the spring of 1763, long before Ecuyer presented the chiefs with the infected blankets. Also important, however, is that Hicks later admitted to Captain Grant "that the greatest part of his former story was False." Ironically, the evidence most often cited by historians to prove British treachery is the statements of Killbuck and Hicks. While these two accounts indicate that smallpox devastated the Ohio Country people, they also disclose that the epidemic was not likely not caused by Ecuyer's distribution of infected blankets.[31]

There is additional evidence strengthening the case that the British failed in their attempt to unleash germ warfare upon their enemies. On July 26, a full month after Turtle's Heart and Maumaultee received the infected blankets from Captain Ecuyer, the same two chiefs once again appeared before the fort to parley. Since the incubation period for smallpox is about two weeks, these two Indian leaders should have exhibited the full range of symptoms from the disease by this time. The records from this meeting make no mention of the Indians suffering from any infirmities. Although it is plausible that both chiefs had at one time already contracted smallpox and acquired immunity, it is more likely that Ecuyer's attempt to spread the disease failed. Had the scheme succeeded, the Indians investing the fort would have been reeling from the plague. They would certainly have abandoned their siege, vacated their disease-infested camps surrounding Fort Pitt, and moved to healthier environs. On the contrary, the Ohio Country tribes persisted with the siege through July with unflagging determination to wipe out the English at the confluence of the three rivers.[32]

The most probable source of the smallpox epidemic that struck the Indians during the late summer of 1763 was not British perfidy but the Indians themselves, who contracted the disease while raiding isolated wilderness settlements. During the uprising, the captive John McCullough lived at the Delaware village of Mahoning, near present-day Newton Falls, Ohio. He later recalled that warriors from the village "committed several depredations along the Juniata; it happened to be at a time when the smallpox was in the settlement where they were murdering, the consequence was, a number of them got infected, and some died before they got home, others shortly after." According to another source, approximately eighteen Delawares under the leadership of Shamokin Daniel conducted a raid through the Juniata Valley in early July. McCullough also noted that "those who took [smallpox] after their return, were immediately moved out of the town, and put under the care of one who had had the disease before," which indicates that the Indians clearly understood that once a person had survived smallpox, that person was immune to the virus. In sum, the Indians may well have received the dreaded disease from a number of sources, but infected blankets from Fort Pitt was not one of them.[33]

While conditions at Fort Pitt continued to deteriorate as the siege wore on, the forts to the east fared no better. Indians maneuvering around Fort Ligonier kept Lieutenant Archibald Blane ever vigilant. With supplies dwindling, the lieutenant grew increasingly despondent, confiding to Colonel Bouquet, "I hope soon to see yourselfe, and live in dayly hopes of a reinforcement. I wish you was here, you would live upon hope as well as I." Blane's wish for reinforcements was answered on June 17, when militia lieutenant Christopher Lems and eighteen of his woodsmen cut their way through from Fort Bedford. The frontiersmen reached Ligonier just in time to help repel another Indian attack. During this engagement a small party of Lieutenant Blane's militia sallied from the compound to assault four Indians who stood defiantly at the edge of the clearing. The warriors melted into the forest at the approach of the soldiers. As the whites returned to the fort, a party of perhaps one hundred Indians suddenly rose up from the banks of Loyalhanna Creek and attempted to cut them off. Fortunately, a "deep Morrass" prevented the Indians from overtaking the militiamen, and all of them returned safely to the gates of the outpost. According to Lieutenant Blane, the warriors then fired a barrage of "upwards of 1000 shot" at the fort, but none of his men was injured. Frustrated in their attempt to dislodge the defenders, the warriors then proceeded to kill livestock and burn nearby cabins.[34]

Further to the east at Fort Bedford, Captain Lewis Ourry found himself in an equally dire predicament. As he had predicted, the nearby settlers, who had flocked to the fort with the first alarm of an uprising, began to feel more secure and gradually drifted back to their homesteads. This left the captain with only twelve Royal Americans to defend the fort. A concerned Ourry wrote to Bouquet, "I should be very glad . . . to see some troops come to my Assistance. A Fort with five Bastions cannot be guarded, much less deffended by a Dozen Men. But, I hope God will protect us all."[35]

One bright moment for the small garrison at Bedford came with the arrival of the intrepid George Croghan, who entered the post on June 14. Croghan had departed Philadelphia at the first news of the outbreak and made his way across the frontier at an astonishing pace. He stopped in Shippensburg long enough to recruit twenty-five men to garrison Fort Lyttleton, a small way station east of Bedford. Realizing that Lyttleton was a key relay along the trail, Croghan deemed the post's maintenance essential to securing the line of communication. To outfit this expedition Croghan drew upon his own personal stores in town and distributed powder, lead, and other provisions to the men. After securing Lyttleton, the Indian agent rode on to Fort Bedford. In spite of the persistent threat of attack against the weakly defended outpost, Croghan and Ourry could not resist partaking of a plentiful supply of Madeira, claret, and other beverages that Ourry kept in stock. Perhaps the alcohol helped bolster their spirits as supplies continued to dwindle. While the two men shared a bottle of wine, they were forced to burn Captain Ourry's last candle, prompting Croghan to write to Colonel Bouquet, "I hope you wont Lett us be Long in the dark." Ourry, adding his own sentiments on the fort's bleak prospects, told Bouquet, "I long to hear the Bag Pipes."[36]

On June 17 the tranquility that had lured many frontier settlers away from the sanctuary of Fort Bedford was shattered as roving war parties struck the remote homesteads that dotted the forest. "This moment I return from the Parade," wrote Captain Ourry, "Some scalps taken up Dening's Creek yesterday and today, some Families murder'd, & Houses burnt, have restored me my Militia; who are now convinced by fatal Experience, that my Advice Should have been taken." A total of seven settlers died in the raid, including James Clark, who had established a farm about twelve miles from the fort. A scouting party sent out by Captain Ourry to assess the damage found Clark's body scalped and "inhumanly mangled," with a spear protruding from his remains.[37]

The sudden raids around Bedford and other outlying areas brought the terrified backcountry people once again streaming into the frontier forts and settled communities. One unidentified man at Fort Cumberland, located south of Bedford, wrote of the distress of these refugees: "it was a most melancholy Sight, to see such Numbers of poor People, who had abandoned their Settlements in such Consternation and Hurry, that they had hardly any thing with them but their Children. And what is still worse, I dare say there is not Money enough amongst the whole Families to maintain a fifth Part of them till the Fall, and none of the poor Creatures can get a Hovel to shelter them from the Weather, but lie about scattered in the Woods."[38]

With the situation on the Pennsylvania frontier growing ever worse, Colonel Bouquet continued to mount a relief expedition. As reports trickling in from the backcountry underscored the immensity of the uprising, the chief problem confronting both Bouquet and General Amherst was the chronic lack of troops. When Amherst finally grasped the severity of the situation in mid-June, he realized that the two light infantry companies of Highlanders he had sent to Philadelphia would not be sufficient to quell the disturbance. On June 18 the general sent a third company of the 42nd Royal Highland Regiment, along with eleven artillerymen, to join Bouquet. Finally, perhaps due to his growing frustration, Amherst sent marching orders to the remainder of Scottish troops held in reserve at Staten Island. This final contingent consisted of 171 men of the 42nd and 102 members of Montgomery's 77th Highland regiment. Amherst doubted that the men of the 77th would be of much use to Bouquet, because they were "so feeble and weak with the West India Distemper." The total number of Highlanders and artillerymen sent to the frontier—including officers, pipers, and drummers—was no more than five hundred. When Colonel Bouquet inquired whether some recent recruits from the 34th Regiment of Foot might be made available to him, Amherst snapped back, "I have already told you, that all the Troops from hence, that Could be Collected, are Sent you . . . so that should the whole Race of Indians take Arms against Us, I Can do no more."[39]

In fact, General Amherst could have done more. At the time of the Indian uprising, there were about 8,000 troops under his command in North America. Nearly half of these soldiers were stationed in Canada as occupation forces. Of the rest, 1,700 men were garrisoning

British possessions in Nova Scotia, Cape Breton Island, and Newfoundland. This left less than three thousand troops to man the posts in the thirteen colonies. Of this number, nearly 1,300 were stationed in upper New York, and another 450 occupied forts in the South. In short, the general had detailed a meager force of roughly five hundred men to maintain the peace on the trans-Appalachian frontier. By the end of June, Amherst had already lost more than 220 of these troops with the destruction of so many frontier forts and the defeat of Cuyler's command. This left only the small garrisons at Detroit, Pitt, Ligonier, and Bedford. Had the general respected his Native American adversaries, he could have detached a portion of the troops stationed in the relative serenity of Canada to reinforce the beleaguered outposts along the border. Instead, Amherst sent Bouquet a handful of convalescents that were recuperating in New York.[40]

Both Amherst and Colonel Bouquet hoped that Pennsylvania's governor, James Hamilton, would prevail on his acrimonious assembly to authorize recruitment of militia to garrison the various provincial forts guarding the main lines of communication. To press the matter, Bouquet wrote to Hamilton describing the defenseless state of the frontier: "The Inhabitants, in their present Position, are utterly unable to defend their scattered Plantations, and should they be so lucky as to reap their Harvest, they have no Means to save it from the Flames." In urging the governor to exert himself in raising a provincial militia, Bouquet especially appealed to Hamilton to recruit "two or three Companies of Hunters & Woodsmen" who could be employed "in a more fatiguing & dangerous Duty." While making these appeals, the colonel confided to General Amherst that even if Hamilton succeeded in raising the militia, the troops would not be ready to take the field for at least six weeks. Consequently, Bouquet wasted no time in organizing his relief force and collecting supplies for his expedition.[41]

On June 25 Bouquet left Philadelphia with a contingent of Royal Americans to rendezvous with the first two light infantry companies of Highland troops. Although these Scots were considered convalescents, they were nonetheless determined and courageous soldiers. From the time they first landed in America in 1756, the Highlanders had been regarded with awe. With their skirling bagpipes and their plaid kilts, badger-skin sporrans, and jaunty bonnets, the Scottish troops must have made an impressive sight when they first disembarked at New

Captain John Campbell, painting by unknown artist, c. 1762. Campbell served in both the 77th and 42nd Highland Regiments. He is shown wearing the distinctive uniform of the Highland soldiers in America— kilt, bonnet, checkered hose—and armed with an officer's musket and basket-hilted sword. Some historians insist that the broadsword was discarded by Highland troops in America; however, examples of these weapons were unearthed at archeological digs at Fort Ligonier. Courtesy the Trustees of the Black Watch Regimental Museum.

York. One observer recalled that "when the Highlanders landed they were caressed by all ranks and orders of men, but more particularly by the Indians. On the march to Albany, the Indians flocked from all quarters to see the strangers who, they believed, were of the same extraction as themselves." Others saw the similarity between the Woodland Indians and the Scots, including General Forbes, who once jokingly referred to the Highlanders as "cousins" of the Cherokees. Likewise, the French labeled them *les sauvages sans culottes*. The Highlanders and Indians had more in common, however, than the fact that neither wore pants; they also shared an indomitable warrior spirit. One British officer noted, "The Highlanders seem particularly calculated for this country and species of warfare, requiring great personal exertion; their patience, sober habits and hardihood—their bravery, their agility and their dress contribute to adapt them to this climate and render them formidable to the enemy." In short, the Highlanders seemed more like warriors than soldiers.[42]

Bouquet was also fortunate in that the troops he was destined to meet at Carlisle were elements of light infantry companies, organized in America to fight the peculiar kind of war dictated by the environment and the nature of the enemy. British officers were not wholly unaccustomed to dealing with irregular warfare, for they had encountered partisan activity in various European conflicts. Nonetheless, they were still unprepared to combat the adroit tactics developed by Indian warriors in the forests of North America.[43] Consequently, English officers had begun training some of their soldiers during the French and Indian War to contend with the "bush fighting" that was a deadly and all-too-common feature of warfare in the colonies. During the conflict with France, General John Campbell, the Earl of Loudoun, sent a number of his officers, including men from the 42nd Regiment, to train with the indefatigable ranger Major Robert Rogers. Rogers took these men under his wing and provided them with a set of written rules specifically designed to govern their conduct in wilderness combat. These ranging rules included such matters as marching so as to prevent ambush and discovery, protecting the flanks of the column when engaged in battle, advancing and retreating by taking advantage of the cover of trees, and firing at particular targets rather than delivering mass volleys, which seldom found their marks in the dense forest.[44]

Many of these British officers whom Rogers had trained were later incorporated into the newly created 80th Regiment of Foot under the command of Colonel Thomas Gage. Having already tasted the bitter sting of Indian battlefield tactics at Braddock's defeat, Gage armed and equipped his men in a fashion that made them more mobile in the woods. Known as Gage's Light Infantry, the 80th Foot generally carried shortened muskets whose browned barrels gave off no glint in the dark forest. Originally, the regiment's personnel wore brown coats to better conceal themselves in the brush, but by 1763 Gage's troops had reverted to wearing the red uniform. These innovations quickly spread throughout the British army as other regiments, including the Black Watch, incorporated light infantry companies into their organizational structures.

Despite these commendable efforts, the British regulars were still no match for the resourceful Woodland Indian warriors. This was due in part to the Redcoats' commitment to certain precepts that were ineffective in combating Indians. For example, British regulars, despite the circumstances of campaigning in dense forest, were trained to fire in volleys or by platoons. While this tended to deliver maximum firepower, it proved to be practically useless against an enemy concealed behind trees or crouching among the bushes. At the same time, for the Redcoats to detonate their blistering volleys, they needed to be in an open file, exposing them as targets to the enemy. In short, fundamental tactics dictated by the very essence of British military discipline and order proved to be entirely unsuited for the forests of North America.[45]

The Highlanders who marched toward Carlisle to rendezvous with Bouquet were seasoned veterans of campaigns from Ticonderoga to Havana, accustomed to deprivation and hard fighting. They were commanded by tough, experienced officers. Some—including Captain John Graham and lieutenants Archibald Campbell and Charles Menzies—had trained with Rogers's Rangers. Other officers, such as Captain William Grant and John Smith, had fought heroically against the French at Ticonderoga and had been wounded in that terrible slaughter. The overall command of the Scots went to Major Allan Campbell, who had joined the 42nd Regiment in 1744. No stranger to wilderness warfare, Campbell had been "actively employed at the head of Grenadiers and Rangers, clearing the way for the army" during the campaign against Ticonderoga in 1758. During the assault on the fort, the major was severely wounded by a musket ball in the thigh. With such experience, it is little wonder that his fellow officers regarded Campbell as a steady and brave soldier.[46]

When Colonel Bouquet reached Carlisle on June 28, he found the advance unit of two light infantry companies waiting for him. Also greeting him was a frontier community in a state of upheaval. The colonel described the situation he faced in a letter to Amherst: "A general Panick has Seized this extensive Country, and made the Inhabitants abandon their Farms & their Mills." The town teemed with refugees who had fled their homes in the interior at the first alarm of an Indian uprising. "Every Stable and Hovel in the Town," the *Pennsylvania Gazette* elaborated, was crowded with miserable Refugees, who were reduced to a State of Beggary and Despair; their Houses, Cattle, and Harvest destroyed . . . it was most dismal to see the Streets filled with People, in whose Countenances might be discovered a Mixture of Grief, Madness and Despair; and to hear, now and then, the Sighs and Groans of Men; the disconsolate Lamentations of Women; and the Screams of Children. . . . And that on both Sides of the Susquehanna, for some Miles, the Woods were filled with poor Families, and their Cattle, who make Fires, and live like Savages.[47]

Adding to Colonel Bouquet's consternation was the fact that none of the supplies, pack animals, or wagons that he had requested had arrived in Carlisle. To make matters worse, the colonel was compelled to share the meager provisions he had brought from Philadelphia with the destitute refugees who congregated at his tent. To avoid wasting any more time in relieving the western posts, Bouquet fired off a series of letters to various government contractors to hasten to Carlisle the necessary supplies. He instructed Robert Callender, a former provincial officer and trader who managed the government's horse contract for the firm of Plumstead and Franks, to collect three hundred pack animals with two horse masters and eighteen drivers and send them to the staging area at Carlisle.[48] He then contacted the freighting firm of Slough and Simon to send him thirty-two wagons loaded with sixty thousand pounds of flour. To facilitate the freight haulers' contracting so many wagons, Bouquet informed the local magistrates of Lancaster County that he would, if necessary, impress the transports for government service.[49] Bouquet also purchased from local traders thirty-six barrels of gunpowder, each weighing eighty-four pounds, and requested that an additional twenty barrels—along with flints, musket balls, and paper cartridges—be rushed to him from the ordnance stores in New York.[50] Lastly, the colonel set about purchasing livestock in order to feed the hungry soldiers on the march and the beleaguered garrisons to the west. Miraculously, by July 3 he had managed to collect one hundred head of cattle and two hundred sheep![51]

Concerned with the tenuous security of forts Bedford and Ligonier, Colonel Bouquet ordered Lieutenant Donald Campbell from the 77th

Highlanders and Lieutenant James McIntosh from the Black Watch to take thirty men and proceed immediately to the relief of Ligonier. Bouquet warned the two officers to observe "the greatest order and Caution to avoid being Surprised by the Savages particularly at night." Furthermore, his instructions read, "in case you Should be attacked, you are to force your Way thro' the Enemy, who will never Stand when vigorously charged; and are only dangerous to People who appear to fear them."[52] After Campbell and McIntosh departed, the colonel ordered the remainder of his two light infantry companies to set out to reinforce Bedford. Having seen to every possible detail necessary to organize his relief force, Henry Bouquet could do little else but await the arrival of the larger contingent of Highlanders en route from New York. The colonel then sat down and made out his last will and testament.[53]

As Bouquet labored at Carlisle to redeem British fortunes, the situation on the frontier continued to worsen. On June 30 a party of fifteen farm laborers working George Croghan's fields were attacked by a war party less than a mile from Fort Bedford. The *Pennsylvania Gazette* excerpted a report from Bedford describing the attack: "Eight o'clock. Two men are brought in, alive, tomahawked and scalped more than Half the Head over. —Our Parade just now presents a Scene of bloody and Savage Cruelty; three Men, two of which are in the Bloom of Life, the other an old Man, lying scalped (two of them still alive) thereon: Any thing feigned in the most fabulous Romance, cannot parallel the horrid sight now before us."[54]

The Indians not only continued to prowl around the forts on the line of communication but also intensified their attacks against remote pioneer communities. On July 10 a war party swooped down on the home of William White, located along the Juniata River about thirty miles west of Carlisle. White and three other men, along with a young boy, were asleep on the floor of the cabin when the Indians silently crept up and began firing into the house. Wounding three of the men, the Indians then set fire to the cabin. Only one of the occupants, William Riddle, managed to escape the burning dwelling by climbing through a window in the loft. Later that day, the same Indians attacked Robert Campbell's house, about a mile and a half from the White homestead. Campbell and five other men were sitting down for the afternoon meal when the warriors burst into the cabin. In the ensuing melee, the Indians tomahawked one of the settlers. Then a man named George Dodds grabbed a rifle and killed one of the intruders. The other Indians fled the cabin and began shooting at the house from positions outside. Dodds and one other man climbed up to the loft and broke through the roof to make their escape. The Indians fired at the men on the roof, killing Dodds's companion instantly. As bullets whizzed around him, the redoubtable Dodds managed to leap to the ground and scamper away to safety.[55]

While small war parties raided the settlements along the Juniata, other Indian bands attacked homes in the Tuscarora Valley. One raiding party entered the cabin of William Anderson just as the elderly man was sitting down to read his Bible. The Indians killed the old man along with his son and adopted daughter. When word of these atrocities reached Carlisle and Sherman's Valley to the west, search parties formed to chase down the marauders and bury their victims. One of these groups, made up of twelve men led by William Robison and his two brothers, entered the upper end of Tuscarora Valley through Bigham's Gap. As they passed through the valley, the men observed the devastation wrought by the Indians. John Graham's house had been burned to the ground, and the Collinses' farm had been destroyed and a number of hogs killed. As the avengers approached an abandoned homestead belonging to a man named Nicholson, twenty-five Indians who had been waiting in ambush jumped up and fired. William Robison was one of the first whites to fall, his belly full of buckshot. The remainder of the group broke and ran for their lives. The Indians managed to catch and kill four of the settlers before breaking off pursuit. No longer threatened with retaliation, the war party set about torching the entire Tuscarora Valley, razing houses and barns, destroying corn in the fields, and burning grain stacks. The churches of Philadelphia later took up a collection to relieve the refugees from the valley, using the $2,942.89 raised to buy food, muskets, gunpowder, and lead.[56]

Pennsylvania was not the only colony plagued by roving bands of Indians. On July 13 a small war party appeared just outside Cresap's Fort, located along the North Branch River in western Maryland. The fort was little more than a stockade surrounding the house of Thomas Cresap, an old trader and frontiersman who had come to the area in 1752 as a member of the Ohio Company. The small band of Indians fired on a group of farmers who were shocking wheat in the field and killed one of the men. The following day, the Indians attacked sixteen settlers who were resting only about a hundred yards from the fort. On July 15 Samuel Wilder along with three men and several women set out for his cabin, situated less than three hundred yards from Cresap's stockade. Suddenly, "the Indians to the amount of 20 or upwards rush'd on them from rising ground." A party of settlers sallied from the fort and fired at the Indians, killing one warrior. The Indians returned fire, slaying Wilder and another man named Wade. One Indian, apparently undeterred by the gunfire surrounding him, leaped upon Wilder's lifeless body, plunged his knife into his back, and then methodically "divided his Ribs from the Back Bone." The warrior's act of bravado cost him his life when Cresap's son, Michael, shot the Indian and then scalped him. The three days of skirmishing around Cresap's Fort convinced the old frontiersman to pack up his family and move eastward to safer territory.[57]

Further to the south, in western Virginia, a large war party of sixty to eighty Shawnees, led by the noted chief Cornstalk, raided the pioneer settlements of Muddy Creek and Greenbriar. At one point, the Shawnees stopped at cabins belonging to Frederick Lea and Filty Yolkum, gaining the settlers' confidence by claiming that they were on their way to fight the Cherokees. Lea and Yolkum offered to feed the Indians, who then turned on the men and killed them. Cornstalk and his warriors perpetrated a similar ruse when they reached Greenbriar. They approached the home of Archibald Glendennin, where a number of families had gathered for a feast. The Indians were invited to join the pioneers and partake of three fat elk that Glendennin had killed. The slaughter began when one old woman, desiring an herbal remedy, showed her injured leg to a warrior and inquired how it might be cured. The Indian responded by burying his tomahawk in her skull. In the melee that immediately erupted, the Indians killed every white man present and took the women and children into captivity. As the Indians were marching their captives back to their village the following day, Mrs. Glendennin handed her infant to another woman and managed to escape by stepping into the bushes. When the baby began to cry, the Indians noticed that Mrs. Glendennin was missing. One of the warriors grabbed the infant and remarked, "I will soon bring the cow to her calf." When the woman did not respond to the cries of her child, the disgusted Indian killed the baby and threw the body on the trail. The distraught mother continued her flight until she reached her home, where she buried her dead husband by covering him with fence rails.[58]

To the north, other Indians struck the two-story blockhouse and stockade belonging to the Kuykendall family, which stood overlooking the South Branch River. In a sharp skirmish Abraham Kuykendall was wounded by a musket ball that a surgeon later removed, charging Kuykendall five pounds, ten shillings, for his services. Afterward, the Virginia House of Burgesses refused to reimburse the wounded man because he had not been employed in the militia at the time. Also during this raid the Indians captured Abraham Kuykendall's brother, Jacob, and took him to their village in Ohio. The captive remained in Indian hands for ten years. When he finally returned home in 1773, he was dismayed to discover that his wife, presuming him dead, had married another man. Like those in Pennsylvania, the settlers of Maryland and Virginia were absolutely powerless to defend themselves against the type of warfare waged by the Indians. With no other recourse many fled for their lives. By mid-July more than a thousand men, women, and children had abandoned their homes to seek refuge in tiny civilian forts or more settled communities far from the frontier.[59]

While Indian war parties continued to overrun the backcountry, back in Carlisle, Colonel Bouquet was still frantically working to put his relief column in motion. On July 5 another company of Highlanders arrived at Carlisle, and Bouquet quickly dispatched them to escort cattle, sheep, and horses to Fort Loudon, a small provincial outpost west of Shippensburg. This would allow the livestock to rest and recover by the time Bouquet and the main force arrived. The escort, commanded by Lieutenant James Robertson of the 77th Highland Regiment, followed in the wake of the first relief columns sent to reinforce the garrisons at Bedford and Ligonier. That first contingent of reinforcements, under the command of lieutenants Campbell and McIntosh, arrived at Bedford on July 3, much to the joy of Captain Ourry. To quell the fears of the local inhabitants, Ourry retained the thirty Highlanders for four days before sending them to reinforce Lieutenant Blane at Ligonier. Knowing that their small force would be vulnerable to ambush along the trail, Campbell and McIntosh departed

Bedford in the dead of night on July 7. The troops were guided by four "good Woodsmen" under the leadership of Philip Baltimore, an experienced scout and wagon master. With stealth and daring, the troops arrived safely at Ligonier on the morning of the ninth "without seeing any of the Enemy." Indians still lurked near the fort and, that evening, fired several shots at the garrison.[60]

On July 11 Captain Robertson arrived at Fort Bedford, having deposited his cattle, sheep, and horses at Fort Loudon. Finally, after more than a month of tense vigilance and sporadic hostilities, Captain Ourry could breath a sigh of relief. He wrote to Bouquet, "Captn Robertson's Arrival has given me great ease, for my Militia was a vast fatigue to me, & I could not depend Sufficiently on them to Sleep o'Nights."[61]

With Bedford and Ligonier now temporarily secure, Bouquet had only to clear the Forbes Road and bring relief to Fort Pitt. From the beginning of the siege, Bouquet had counseled Captain Ecuyer to be frugal with his food supplies. Quartermaster returns from the fort, which had been carried to Colonel Bouquet by daring express riders and loyal Indian scouts, convinced him that Ecuyer's supplies were sufficient to sustain the garrison until the relief expedition arrived. Unbeknownst to the colonel, however, these returns were misleading. Fort Pitt's commissary of provisions, Captain William Murray, had failed to take into account supplies of flour and corn that had either been destroyed by the flood in March or consumed by weevils. It is also quite likely that, as a result of Captain Ecuyer's rationing, a large supply of food had been stolen from the quartermaster stores. Whatever the cause, the garrison had lost nearly a month's supply of flour. Some of the merchants and traders inside the fort began to sell their meager cache of corn at the exorbitant price of one dollar per bushel. With more than four hundred mouths to feed, Ecuyer's food supplies dwindled fast.[62]

Finally, on July 10 Major Allan Campbell and the remainder of Bouquet's relief force reached Carlisle. The major's command consisted of 168 members of the Black Watch regiment and 109 of the 77th Highlanders, or a total of 277. Of this number, nearly 15 percent were still listed as sick due to the ravages of malaria contracted while the men were campaigning in the West Indies. Bouquet informed Amherst that Campbell's troops arrived "greatly fatigued" from their march.

The soldiers were permitted to rest for a week while Bouquet finished collecting enough wagons to transport his supplies. At last, amidst the oppressive heat of July 15, the colonel's caravan departed Carlisle. It must have presented an odd and colorful sight. Altogether, the command included 271 frazzled Highlanders, their pipers and drummers setting the pace of the march; 24 Royal Artillerymen, who must have felt out of place since there were no cannons in the convoy; 165 Royal Americans, some of whom spoke only their native German dialects; and a motley crew of 50-odd civilian teamsters and herders who drove the wagons and escorted the livestock herds. This mixed force of Scots, Germans, English, and Irish, all led by a Swiss soldier of fortune, underscored the international flavor of the British colonies in the eighteenth century. It also emphasized the fact that General Amherst had scraped the bottom of the barrel to collect a relief force whose mission was to stem the tide of the greatest Indian uprising ever manifested on the frontier.[63]

Henry Bouquet was under no delusions about the challenges his small command faced. He confided to his friend Ourry that the tiny column represented "the only present Resource of this Part of the Country, open to all the Ravages of that bloody Race. Should we meet with a Check, the Consequences are evident." The colonel did not reveal his apprehensions to Amherst, however, promising the general that he would "take an adequate revenge on the Barbarians." Needless to say, Sir Jeffery was equally determined to exact retribution on the warring tribes and informed Bouquet that he "wished to Hear of no Prisoners, should any of the Villains be met with in Arms."[64]

"The Excessive heat, bad roads [and] immense loads of Forrage" made Bouquet's march across Pennsylvania a grueling experience. The command moved slowly, and Bouquet was compelled to carry some of the sick Highlanders in the wagons. The conditions ruined "Men, Horses & Cattle," the colonel related. On July 19 the expedition reached Fort Loudon, where men and animals received a day's rest. While encamped at the fort, Bouquet received the disturbing news that the Pennsylvania Assembly would not authorize the newly raised militia to be placed under his command. The legislators firmly believed that no Pennsylvania troops should be used to conduct offensive operations against the Indians. Instead, the militia should be retained at the provincial forts along the Susquehanna River to defend the more

Along Laurel Ridge, painting by John Buxton. The artist depicts soldiers of the 60th Royal American Regiment resting after a grueling march along Forbes Road. Scenes such as this would have been common during Bouquet's march to relieve Fort Pitt during Pontiac's Uprising. Courtesy John Buxton and Paramount Press.

settled regions. Lieutenant Colonel James Robertson, an aide to General Amherst, had tried to persuade the assemblymen "that the Indians could not by a defensive plan be prevented from ravageing the frontiers," but his arguments had made no headway. A disgruntled Bouquet wrote General Amherst, "I hope that we shall be able to save that infatuated People from destruction in Spite of all their Endeavors to defeat your vigorous measures, I meet everywhere with the Same backwardness, even among the most exposed of the Inhabitants; which makes every thing move on heavily, and is disgusting to the last degree."[65]

Undaunted by the Pennsylvania government's lack of cooperation, Bouquet slowly pushed deeper into the interior. Bad roads and washed-out bridges further deterred the progress of the march. In a letter to Colonel Robertson, Bouquet complained that it took him thirty-six hours to travel only three miles. The bad roads, rough terrain, excessive heat, and increasing likelihood of encountering a dangerous enemy force caused some soldiers to desert. As the command penetrated deeper into enemy territory, Bouquet ordered that the Highlanders fan out into the forest to serve as flankers to protect the column. To his exasperation, the colonel soon discovered that the Scots were wholly unsuited for such service in an unfamiliar country. As he related to Colonel Robertson, "I labour under a great Disadvantage for want of Men used to the Woods, as I cannot send a Highlander out of my Sight without running the risk of losing the Man; which exposes me to a Surprise from the skulking Villains I have to deal with." Despite such adversity, Bouquet's relief column plodded on, arriving at Fort Bedford on July 25.[66]

While the men and draft animals rested, Colonel Bouquet set about reoutfitting his command. Broken-down wagons were repaired, fresh horses replaced animals worn out from the march, and some additional supplies, including musket balls, were collected. The colonel also was fortunate enough to recruit fourteen frontiersmen, under the command of Captain Lemuel Barrett to serve as rangers. Barrett and his men resided in the Cumberland Valley and for years had been exposed to the harsh conditions of frontier living and the constant danger of Indian attacks. The ranger detachment included Lieutenant Joseph Randall, who once served in a Pennsylvania militia battalion; Elias Jarrett, who left behind a wife and six children to join Bouquet's expedition; and John Jemison, whose little sister Mary had been carried off by Indians during the French and Indian War.[67] With the experienced rangers along, the colonel would no longer have to worry about his flankers getting lost in the woods. As Bouquet prepared to set out for Fort Ligonier, he decided to leave behind an officer and thirty men from both of the Highland Regiments who were too weak to continue the march.[68]

Bouquet's column cleared Bedford on July 28 and headed toward Fort Ligonier. Not knowing whether Fort Pitt still held out against the besieging warriors, the colonel sent a loyal Cayuga named John Hudson to deliver a message to Captain Ecuyer. In the letter, Bouquet informed the captain, "I shall do what I can to intice the Enemy Indians to march against me," thereby providing relief to the fort. Little did Bouquet expect that virtually all the Indians surrounding Ecuyer's outpost would sally out to meet his small command at Bushy Run.[69]

6

"THE BRAVEST MEN I EVER SAW"

While Henry Bouquet's column plodded along the trail to relieve the beleaguered forts in the Ohio Country, another expedition was racing to lift the siege against Fort Detroit. General Amherst's first inclination of trouble among the tribes of the Great Lakes came more than a week after he learned of the outbreak of violence around Fort Pitt. Major John Wilkins, the commandant at Fort Niagara, informed Amherst of the defeat of Lieutenant Abraham Cuyler's supply convoy along Lake Erie. Finally, on June 21, the commander in chief received his first dispatch from Major Gladwin providing him with details of the siege at Detroit. Major Wilkins, who had forwarded Gladwin's letter, reported that he had taken the liberty of rushing a small force of fifty-four men to Gladwin's assistance. This was the same relief force that had witnessed the fall of Presque Isle. More troops were desperately needed, and the general dispatched his aide-de-camp, Captain James Dalyell, to head for Albany and begin assembling a larger relief expedition. This force was to consist of men from the 55th Regiment of Foot who were stationed in the town and whatever New York provincials Dalyell could induce to join the command. From there, he was to march westward to Fort Ontario, where more troops of the 55th Regiment were garrisoned. Amherst instructed the captain, after collecting these soldiers, to head immediately to Niagara, pick up what troops could be spared from that garrison, and then proceed across the lake to Detroit.[1]

James Dalyell is perhaps best described as a rash and ambitious soldier. The son of a baronet, Dalyell had entered the army as a lieutenant in the Royal American Regiment before being transferred to the 80th Regiment of Foot. During the war with France, he had served with distinction along the Lake George–Lake Champlain corridor and campaigned with Rogers' Rangers. With the influence of family and friends back in England, he had procured a captaincy in the prestigious 1st Regiment of Foot or Royal Regiment in September 1760. From there, the young officer joined General Amherst's official family. The general's high regard for Dalyell may have stemmed from the shared scorn with which the two viewed Indians. Without question, both of these officers underestimated the fighting prowess of these woodland adversaries.[2]

After arriving at Albany, Dalyell consulted with Sir William Johnson. Since the beginning of the uprising, the Indian superintendent had been working feverishly to ascertain the reasons for the outbreak, determine which tribes were involved, and obtain assurances from the Iroquois Confederation that it would hold fast to the Covenant Chain of friendship with the English. Sir William was not at all surprised by the uprising, considering all the warnings he had directed to Amherst concerning the general's miserly and contemptuous policies. The superintendent had realized that Sir Jeffery's refusal to allow the distribution of gifts to the Indians would eventually lead to increased hostility toward the British. In a letter to the general dated June 26, Johnson offhandedly chided the commander: "t'is What I have often been induced to expect, knowing [that the Indians] will consider friendship as verry trifleing when unattended with Gifts which might bind them by Motives of Interest to preserve peace." Nonetheless, the great Warraghiyagey promised Amherst that he would use all of his influence and power to preserve peace with the Iroquois. Sir William was pleased to report to Amherst that he had received assurances from the Onondaga council "of their inclination to remain quiet." However, he was quick to inform the general that such assurances from the Iroquois could be maintained only by providing the Indians with presents "purchased at a moderate expence."[3]

While Sir William worked to keep the Iroquois at peace, Captain Dalyell attempted to recruit men for a militia unit to accompany him to Detroit. All of his endeavors proved fruitless, and he informed General Amherst that not a man could be induced to enlist. Although failing to raise volunteers in Albany, Dalyell was joined by a most useful recruit—Major Robert Rogers, the legendary ranger leader. Following his successful 1760 mission to take control of the French outposts along the Great Lakes, Rogers had fallen on hard times. He had campaigned against the Cherokees in South Carolina for nearly two years but suffered constantly from malaria. When he finally returned to New England in late 1762, he was forced to subsist on half pay as a captain in a disbanded New York provincial company. The salary was insufficient to keep creditors from hounding him continuously to pay off long-standing debts that had accumulated during the war with France. To make matters worse, Rogers languished as a peacetime soldier, for whom daring raids and narrow escapes were but a distant memory. Rogers thus jumped at the chance to resurrect his sagging career and participate in one more military expedition.[4]

Not wishing to waste any more time attempting to recruit volunteers, Dalyell marched off with his small command of regulars toward Lake Ontario, where he hoped to rendezvous with additional troops. As his expedition headed westward through the Mohawk River Valley, the captain was surprised when a small contingent of twenty-eight New York militiamen finally joined him at Schenectady. This company of volunteers had been induced to enlist largely through the efforts of Sir William Johnson. With these added reinforcements the captain pushed on, reaching Fort Ontario on June 28. Dalyell hoped to cross Lake Ontario to Fort Niagara as quickly as possible but was delayed because the lake was "too tempestuous to venture on it out of the Harbour." Before stripping the garrison at Fort Ontario, he had to await the arrival of replacement troops from the convalescing 17th Regiment of Foot, which was slowing marching from the city of New York. Finally, on July 3, Dalyell's relief force pushed off in twenty-two whaleboats. The command consisted of 179 men from the 55th Regiment, 28 New York militiamen, and 6 men from the Royal Artillery. Dalyell was guided by Major Rogers and seven volunteers who had been organized into a ranger detachment.[5]

After skirting the shore of Lake Ontario for three days, Dalyell arrived at Niagara, where he prevailed on Major John Wilkins to supply him with forty light infantrymen from the 80th Regiment. Dalyell wasted little time in marching his troops across the portage and casting off in his whaleboats toward Detroit. The expedition reached the ruins of Fort Presque Isle on the afternoon of July 15. The victorious Indians had burned the blockhouse to the ground, and the charred bones of the soldiers protruded through the ashes. To quell any alarm among his men, Dalyell informed them that General Amherst had ordered the post to be abandoned and that the bones were merely the remnants of supplies destroyed by the departing troops. The experienced Robert Rogers knew better. In a letter to his wife he correctly surmised that the blockhouse had been destroyed with fire arrows and the garrison massacred.[6]

From Presque Isle Dalyell made his way along the southern shore of Lake Erie, reaching the deserted ruins of Fort Sandusky on July 26. Here too the captain confronted the horrible aftermath of another Indian victory. General Amherst's "desire of having a Speedy Retaliation made, Should the Savages have Committed any Insults on the upper posts," must have been ringing in Captain Dalyell's ears as he ordered a reconnaissance inland to the supposed location of a Huron village. Leaving behind Captain James Grant with a portion of the 80th Foot to guard the boats, Dalyell and Major Rogers led a sortie of 160 men toward the Indian camp, about six miles from the burned fort. The command arrived at the village around 8 A.M., only to find it deserted. The soldiers set fire to the bark-covered lodges and nearby cornfields before countermarching to their boats. After spending the night on an island in Lake Erie, the expedition set sail for Detroit. Assisted by a fair southerly wind, the flotilla reached the mouth of the Detroit River about three o'clock in the afternoon and went ashore on a small island. Since there had been no direct communication from Major Gladwin since mid-May, Captain Dalyell could not be certain that Fort Detroit had not already fallen to the enemy. Consequently, he decided to proceed upriver under the cover of darkness.[7]

At dusk Dalyell's boats pushed off. Fortunately, "a fog so dense that one could not see a step in front of him" enshrouded the water course, masking the ascent. Throughout the night, the troops rowed cautiously and silently up the Detroit. The command was guided by Jacques Lacelle, a Detroit merchant and fur trader who had been recruited at Niagara. The Frenchman tried to keep the boats in midstream. Just before dawn, however, he strayed close to one bank. Suddenly gunfire erupted from the Huron village that stood on the shoreline. From the opposite bank more shots rang out as the Potawatomies, startled by the musket fire, opened up with their own ragged volleys. Lacelle eventually managed to steer the lead boat toward the center of the river. As the men continued to row, Dalyell ordered his artillerymen to return fire with the swivel guns mounted on the bows of four boats. During the sharp exchange, fourteen of the captain's men suffered wounds. Nonetheless, the determined troops rowed through the cross-fire and entered the water gate of the fort.[8]

For Major Gladwin the sight of twenty-two boats filled with 280 reinforcements must have brought immense relief. For more than two months, he had weathered a protracted siege waged by hundreds of Indians. His small command had maintained a constant watch on the ramparts and firing platforms, straining their eyes to spy some relief. Throughout this harrowing and stressful time, the major had been reinforced only once, when Lieutenant Cuyler sailed up the river in the schooner *Huron* with a meager fifty men.

Throughout the grim standoff, Gladwin had remained resolute. Following the assassination of Captain Campbell, the major had retaliated by ordering the *Michigan* to sail across the river and shell Pontiac's village. It took the vessel so long to move into position that the Ottawa leader had plenty of time to evacuate the camp. The shot from the *Michigan's* cannons destroyed a number of Ottawa lodges and compelled Pontiac to relocate his village three miles upriver where it was somewhat protected by an intervening swamp. The other Indian nations surrounding the fort realized that their villages were also exposed to attack by the sloop, and that took the fight out of some of them. On July 9 a group of Hurons came into the fort to sue for peace. The Indians surrendered Ensign Christie, the dispirited commander of Fort Presque Isle, along with seven other prisoners.[9]

Enraged by the audacity of the English soldiers in bombarding his camp, Pontiac vowed to destroy the vessels anchored outside the fort. Perhaps on the advice of one of the friendly French habitants, Pontiac directed his warriors to construct a raft that would be set ablaze and would float downstream into the hull of the *Michigan*. The plan failed when the current took the fiery raft past its intended target. Undeterred, the Indians constructed several more fire rafts. This time, the gun crew aboard the ship fired several rounds at the Indians attempting to direct the rafts, which sent them scurrying for the shore. The unguided fire rafts once again drifted by the sloop and schooner without causing any damage. Despite these setbacks the Indians continued to take potshots at the fort and the vessels anchored nearby. These pinprick attacks usually prompted Major Gladwin to order a sortie from the fort against the encroaching warriors. Aside from these minor clashes, nothing of importance happened at Detroit until the arrival of Captain Dalyell's relief expedition.

The troops that Dalyell brought to Detroit increased the size of the beleaguered garrison to nearly five hundred men, not counting the number of traders and habitants who had sided with the British. Captain Dalyell was convinced that this force was large enough to provide adequate protection for the fort and simultaneously mount a retaliatory attack against the ringleader of this uprising—Pontiac. The imprudent and ambitious officer immediately pressed Gladwin to permit him to take a strike force and pay a surprise visit to the Ottawa village. The major, who was well acquainted with the Indians' strength and fighting capabilities, strongly disagreed. He believed that Pontiac "was too much on his Guard" to fall prey to such a surprise attack. Perhaps Dalyell countered that the recent overtures of the Hurons and Potawatomies indicated that the number of hostile Indians was dwindling. Gladwin and others, however, were skeptical about of the new peace initiatives coming from these tribes. James Sterling, one of the merchants bottled up in the fort, predicted that the Potawatomies and Hurons would eventually "recommence and join the enemy" in the siege. In the end, Dalyell won the debate when he revealed to Gladwin Sir Jeffery Amherst's explicit desire for a "speedy retaliation" against the Indians.[10]

Having won his argument, Captain Dalyell began making preparations for his surprise raid on Pontiac's camp. Waiting for nightfall on July 30, 247 of Fort Detroit's "best troops" stripped down to light marching order and fixed bayonets. At 2:30 A.M. the gates of the fort swung open, and Dalyell's strike force filed out into the foggy darkness. The raiding party consisted of troops from all three regiments present at Detroit, as well as twenty rangers under the leadership of Captain Hopkins and eight volunteers from among the merchants and traders. The command was guided by one of the French interpreters, Jacques St. Martin, and a loyal habitant named Jacques Duperon Baby. The advance guard, which marched about twenty yards in front of the main body, was made up of twenty-five light infantrymen under the direct commanded of Lieutenant Archibald Montgomery Brown of the 55th Regiment of Foot. Captain Dalyell commanded the main body of Redcoats with the assistance of Captain Robert Gray of the 55th Foot and Major Rogers. Captain James Grant, an experienced light infantry officer, brought up the rear. Major Rogers, who should have commanded the entire sortie, was no doubt astounded when the troops set out along the road to the Indian camp in a column of two abreast, with no flankers to probe the fields, orchards, and houses that lined the road to the left. To the right of the road was the sandy shore of the Detroit River. Dalyell had at least been canny enough to put two of the whaleboats, mounted with swivel guns, into the water in order to parallel his march up river.[11]

Pontiac was well informed of this surprise attack. As one observer at Detroit wryly noted, "We could never do anything in the Fort without [the Indians] knowing." In all likelihood, a habitant sympathetic to the Indians had managed to get word to Pontiac of the impending attack. The Ottawa war leader responded by posting hundreds of his warriors behind the picket fences and in the fields that lined the left side of the river road. More Indians concealed themselves opposite a long bridge that crossed Parent's Creek, about two miles from the fort. Evidently, Pontiac's goal was to check the British advance at the bridge, then cut off their retreat by sweeping up behind the rear guard from the left side of the road.[12]

Lieutenant Brown's advance guard was midway across the bridge when Pontiac's concealed warriors opened fire. The initial volley either killed or wounded most of Brown's light infantry. The lieutenant himself fell with a musket ball through the thigh. Captain Gray, with a detachment from the main body, rushed forward under heavy fire to secure the bridge and carry off the wounded Redcoats. About the same time, Captain Grant's rear guard drew fire from the Indians hidden behind the picket fences and ditches lining the road. The captain ordered his men to face left and deliver a volley into the enemy. He

Lieutenant John Montresor's 1763 map of Detroit drawn near the end of Pontiac's siege. Close examination reveals the locations of the various Indian villages that surrounded the fort. The Ottawa, Huron, and Potawatomie camps are located in the same vicinity as noted in Bellin's 1749 map (see page 83). Pontiac's camp, marked "C" on Montresor's map, is located along the riverbank northeast of the fort and just to the right of where Parent's Creek empties into the Detroit River. Courtesy the William L. Clements Library, University of Michigan.

then rushed forward and secured one of the houses that faced the road. Inside were two Frenchmen who informed Grant that Pontiac's warriors, about three hundred in number, had been waiting for the British for some time and that the Indians intended to cut off any avenue of retreat.

Captain Dalyell, whose thigh wound was slight, hobbled back along the line of Redcoats and joined Grant in the house. Grant informed Dalyell of Pontiac's intended trap and encouraged the commander to either push forward immediately or secure the wounded and retreat in good order. Dalyell then returned to the front, where Captain Gray had succeeded in pushing the enemy from a low ridge in front of the bridge. This provided a lull in the fighting that allowed the British to place their wounded men in one of the whaleboats. At this point, Captain Dalyell hesitated, not knowing whether to attempt to continue his march toward Pontiac's village or order a general retreat. An hour elapsed before the Indians once again took up concealed positions and began firing at the British soldiers deployed along the road. Dalyell, finally convinced that a further advance was futile, returned to Grant's position and ordered the captain to execute an about-face and secure the line of retreat by taking possession of the houses and orchards that rimmed the road. Dalyell then limped back to the bridge to organize the rear guard.

As the Redcoats began their long retreat back to the fort, the Indians grew bolder and increased their fire. The soldiers made easy targets in the middle of the road. As the troops slowly fought their way back toward Detroit, the resourceful Major Rogers noticed intense gunfire coming from one of the houses along the road. With a small detail of soldiers, Rogers stormed the house and chased out the Indians. From this new stronghold the major and his men could fire on the Indians in the outlying fields and cover the retreat.

Another party of warriors, who had entrenched themselves behind a pile of cordwood and in a depression left by a recently dug cellar, poured a deadly volley into the rear guard and held up the retreat. Dalyell ordered Captain Gray and his company of Redcoats to make a headlong charge toward this enemy position in order to dislodge the Indians. During the successful assault, the daring Gray fell with a bullet in his stomach and another in his thigh. As the retreat resumed, Dalyell glanced back and spotted a wounded sergeant of the 55th Regiment lying helpless by the side of the road. What Captain Dalyell lacked in judgment he made up for in bravery as he hobbled back to help the wounded soldier. Pontiac's brother-in-law, an Ottawa warrior named Geeyette, was lying concealed nearby. He sprang up from his hiding place and motioned for Dalyell to drop his pistol and surrender. When the captain refused, Geeyette raised his musket and killed him. Unable or unwilling to recover the captain's body, the remainder of the rear guard continued its retreat.[13]

As the rear of the column came opposite Major Rogers's position, some of the soldiers carried the wounded Captain Gray into the house. The situation appeared bleak for the beleaguered men inside as the Indians, in ever increasing numbers, focused their fire on the house. Just then, the two boats appeared near the shore and discharged several rounds of grapeshot toward the warriors surrounding the house. The Indians scattered, giving Rogers time to load Captain Gray and the other wounded men into the boats. As the vessels pushed off with their cargo of wounded soldiers, Rogers resumed the retreat. The Indians continued to press the rear of the column, and Rogers, with about thirty men, "was obliged to take Possession of another House" in order to hold back the onslaught of Indians trying to overwhelm the retreating Redcoats.

Once inside, the dauntless major ordered his men to hastily build breastworks behind the windows by piling up beaver skins that they found in the house. The encroaching Indians gave up their pursuit of the retreating column to focus their attack on Rogers's men. The ranger leader, who had been in harrowing predicaments more than once, found himself surrounded by at least two hundred warriors. The interior of Rogers's stronghold became a scene of pandemonium as bullets pierced the flimsy walls and the rooms filled with acrid, dense gun smoke. The house belonged to a habitant named Jacques Campau who had secreted his family in the cellar when the battle began. The Frenchman now stood on the trap door leading to the basement in order to prevent frightened soldiers from seeking shelter among the women and children. Some of Rogers's men found a keg of whiskey and set about getting drunk, while others kept up a deadly fire against the Indians outside. The siege of Campau's house lasted for more than two hours until at last, about eight o'clock in the morning, the two whaleboats returned to deliver a barrage of grape- and round shot toward the gathering warriors. The Indians withdrew, and Major Rogers and his men finally made their way back to the sanctuary of Fort Detroit. The battle, that would forever be known as Bloody Run, was over.

In all, Captain Dalyell's rash "surprise attack" had cost the lives of eighteen British soldiers, with another forty wounded. Had it not been for the courageous stand made by Major Rogers, many more men would have been overwhelmed and killed by the Indians. In contrast, Pontiac lost only six warriors.[14] It was, as merchant James Sterling later recalled, a "damned drubbing the Savage Bougres Gave us."[15]

Heartened by his victory over Dalyell, Pontiac grew even more resolved to take Fort Detroit. After the battle, the habitants discovered a number of British soldiers lying dead in their orchards and fields. The captive John Rutherford remembered seeing Captain Dalyell's heart roasting over an Ottawa fire. The incident was so horrendous and revolting that Rutherford determined to make his escape. He stole away in the night and managed to safely reach the fort the next day. When General Amherst learned of Dalyell's death, he offered a reward of £100 to anyone who would kill Pontiac. Later, the vengeful commander added an additional £100 as an "inducement for a Daring fellow to attempt the Death of that Villain." "I will add it with pleasure," Amherst wrote. "His Death would be some small satisfaction for the loss of poor Dalyell."[16]

Following his triumph at Bloody Run, Pontiac invited the leading habitants to a feast. One of these Frenchmen, Peter Descompts Labadie, later remembered that there was plenty of food but no liquor available. After the sumptuous banquet Pontiac asked Labadie, "How did you like the meat? It was very good young beef, was it not? Come here, I will show you what you have eaten." With that, the Ottawa chief opened a sack lying nearby and pulled out the severed head of an English soldier. Labadie turned and vomited.[17]

While Captain Dalyell's forces were being overwhelmed outside Detroit, the Redcoats at Fort Pitt were fighting their own desperate battle against a combined force of Mingoes, Delawares, Shawnees, Ottawas, and Hurons. Throughout the month of July, the garrison had noticed an increase in the number of Indians surrounding the fort. Canoes filled with warriors were observed passing the fort on both the Monongahela and Allegheny rivers. At one point, Captain Trent counted fifty-seven Indians on horseback riding along the opposite bank of the Allegheny. Quite likely, these were warriors who were returning from raiding activities in the East. As Colonel Bouquet's relief force crept westward and cleared the line of communications, many of these war parties fell back to Fort Pitt. Also at this time, food supplies began to run low for both besiegers and the besieged. Captain Ecuyer had been forced to send out men to the nearby garrison garden under armed guards to cut and tie corn and gather other vegetables. From behind their palisades the soldiers spied Indians in the same fields cutting wheat. It was altogether apparent to the men inside Fort Pitt that the siege was reaching a climax. As the number of hostile Indians grew, so did the demands on their food supply. With the approach of Bouquet's small army, the Indians realized that unless they could compel the garrison to surrender, they had either to take the outpost by assault or to give up the siege.[18]

On July 26 a delegation of chiefs came to the gates of the fort to parley with Captain Ecuyer. The tribal leaders included Grey Eyes, the prominent Delaware chief whose house had been constructed by Colonel Bouquet's carpenters. Also present was the great warrior Shingas, who had wreaked havoc on the Pennsylvania frontier during the French and Indian War. A chief by the name of Big Wolf and four other headmen represented the Shawnees at the council. Interestingly, Maumaultee, the Delaware who had been given smallpox-infected blankets by Captain Ecuyer, appeared among the delegation, in perfect health. Tissacoma, a Delaware chief, opened the conference, saying, "Brothers, On your first coming to this place, we were the first Nation you contracted a Friendship with; after this you extended, a Belt of Friendship across this Country, the End of which reach'd those Nations over the Lakes Toward the Sun Setting." Explaining that the Delawares had tried to hold fast to the Belt of Friendship, Tissacoma admonished the English: "You sent us word that you were so firmly Seated here that you were not to be removed; Brothers you have Towns & places of your own; you know this is our Country; & that your having Possession of it must be offensive to all Nations therefore it would be proper, that you were in your own Country where our Friendship might always remain Undisturbed." The chief then complained about the "large Armies" and "Strong Forts" that the British brought to the Ohio Country and beyond. "You have no Body else to Blame, but yourselves; for what has happened," Tissacoma asserted. With that, the Delaware leader produced a string of wampum that had been received from the Ottawas and other tribes to the west. The trinket represented a dire warning to the British that if they did not abandon the fort, they would all be killed. The parley then adjourned and the Indians returned to the opposite bank of the river to await Captain Ecuyer's reply.

In the poetic eloquence that was a hallmark of Indian diplomacy, Tissacoma had made clear the source of the uprising. Ever since 1758, when Christian Frederick Post traveled to Tamaqua's village at Kuskuski to affirm that the English would someday go back across the mountains, the people of the Ohio Country had been waiting for that promise to be fulfilled. The French fathers were long gone, and the definitive Treaty of Paris had made it clear to the Indians that they would not return. Throughout this period the British had kept the Indians in a state of near destitution by refusing to trade in powder and lead, an act that convinced many of them that the English intended to wipe them out. Trade prices had remained intolerably high, while settlers continued to pour over the mountains. Little wonder, then, that the Ohio Country people and the Indians of the Great Lakes had seized on the prophetic teachings of Neolin and instituted a savage war to expel the whites from their land.[19]

Captain Ecuyer was unmoved by Tissacoma's oration. The following day, he delivered his response to the chiefs, arguing that, "these Forts was to protect you & your trade, which you have been often told. With regard to your Lands, we have taken none only such parts as our Enemies the French did Possess. You Suffered them first to settle in the Heart of your Country without molestation, and why would you pretend to turn us out of it now; who have always been friendly and Kind to you." Ecuyer then delivered his own warning to the assembled chiefs: "I will not abandon this Post; I have Warriors, Provisions, and Ammunition plenty to defend it three Years against all the Indians in the Woods, and we shall not abandon it as long as a white Man Lives in America." "This is our Home," the captain exclaimed. "You have attacked us without reason or provocation, you have Murdered & plundered our Warriors and Traders, you have took off our Horses and Cattle, and at the Same time you tell us, your Hearts are good towards your Brothers the English; how can I have faith in you and believe you are Sincere?" After this scathing rebuke, Ecuyer advised the chiefs to collect their families and return to their villages. The disheartened Indians then turned and walked away. This was their final attempt to convince the British to peacefully leave the forks of the Ohio.[20]

The day after the parley, the British inside Fort Pitt observed Indians crossing over the river, and Captain Trent warned the garrison that an attack on the outpost was imminent. By midafternoon the assembled warriors had moved into position close to the fort's ramparts, and they began firing. The Indians were situated along the banks of both rivers and kept up a hot fire against the fort all day and night. Captain Ecuyer gave orders to each man not to fire "without seeing his target." One soldier was killed during the attack and seven others wounded, including Captain Ecuyer, whose left leg was grazed by an arrow. The Indians were so close that they were able to launch fire arrows into the fort, damaging the "Governour's House and the Barracks," but the women of the garrison formed a bucket brigade and helped quench the flames.[21]

The following day, the Indians continued their attack with vigor. As canoes loaded with warriors rushing to reinforce the assault crossed the river, Ecuyer's artillerymen opened up with a discharge of round shot from their six-pound cannon. One of the projectiles severed an Indian in two and forced the others in the canoe to jump overboard and swim for their lives. Nonetheless, the Indians continued to creep closer to the fort and kept up their incessant gunfire. By digging holes in the riverbank, the warriors managed to keep themselves well concealed, but occasionally an Indian showed his head and was picked off by the Redcoats. Captain Trent noted in his journal that the garrison had succeeded in killing "several of them from the Fort—one of them wounded and drowned in the River attempting to swim over and five more seen carrying out of the Canoe on the further side of the Ohio supposed to be wounded." During the night, the Indians crept up to the perimeter ditch located just beyond the walls of the fort. To dislodge them, the soldiers lit and tossed hand grenades into the trench.[22]

The Indians continued their attack on the fort until the afternoon of August 1. Then, just as abruptly as it had started, the gunfire ceased. Captain Trent noted, "We saw large numbers [of Indians] crossing from this to the opposite side of the Ohio with their baggage." The reason for the hasty departure was that the Indians had intercepted the Cayuga courier John Hudson, who was carrying dispatches from Colonel Bouquet to Captain Ecuyer. The assembled warriors tore open the letters and forced a white captive to read the contents. With this intelligence the Indians besieging Fort Pitt realized that they had to sally out to contend with this new threat or abandon their efforts to take the fort and retreat to their sanctuaries along the Muskingum. The Hurons and Ottawas present vowed "they would not make peace while one of them was alive." The Delawares, however, were divided. Tamaqua, who had always been a peace advocate, decided to depart "with a party of warriors" to his town. While Tamaqua and a few of his followers may have felt it was fruitless to fight the English any longer, many more Indians were not ready to give up their holy war. Hundreds of Mingo, Delaware, Shawnee, Huron, and Ottawa warriors turned eastward to lay a trap for Bouquet's approaching column.[23]

The following day, the Indians released John Hudson, and he crossed the river to deliver one of Colonel Bouquet's dispatches to Captain Ecuyer. The Cayuga courier told Ecuyer that the Indian warriors surrounding the fort numbered around four hundred and that most of them were on their way to attack Bouquet. The captain enlisted Hudson to return to Bouquet that evening with a warning to be on his guard against a likely Indian ambush set up along the road between Ligonier and Fort Pitt. Ecuyer found another volunteer to try to get through to Bouquet the following day. In this second dispatch the sly captain added a cryptic postscript that erroneously indicated that other troops were marching from Lake Erie to attack the Delaware villages deep in the Ohio Country. Ecuyer probably reasoned that if the courier was captured by enemy forces and the contents of the letter revealed, the Indians would be inclined to think that their homes and families were being attacked by the British. Fort Pitt's commandant could do no more to assist Bouquet's arrival. With food supplies all but depleted, the fate of the fort's garrison rested on Henry Bouquet's tiny army.[24]

On August 2, after another grueling five-day march, Bouquet's command arrived at Ligonier. Fully expecting the Indians to attempt to ambush his command, the colonel decided to leave his wagons behind and transfer a supply of flour onto the backs of about 340 pack animals. He was also forced to leave behind thirty more men too weak to continue the march. After giving his weary soldiers two days' rest, Bouquet departed for the final leg of his journey. Due to sickness and desertion the command numbered less than five hundred men, not counting the assortment of civilians who accompanied the troops in order to drive the packhorses, cattle, and sheep.[25] Family tradition states that Andrew Byerly and his son Michael marched out with the troops in hopes of recovering some of their property, which had been abandoned when the family fled their home at Bushy Run Station.[26] The first day's march took the relief force about twelve miles before Bouquet made camp along the road for the evening.[27]

Early the next morning, August 5, the troops resumed the advance with the rangers serving as flankers on either side of the column of Redcoats. The advance guard was led by Lieutenant James Dow of the Royal American Regiment, who was serving as quartermaster for the expedition. Dow was followed by the main body of troops and the long pack train of horses laden with flour for Fort Pitt. Bouquet was determined to push his command as far as Bushy Run Station, where they would halt and refresh themselves at the stream. The colonel planned to resume the march after dark and pass over Turtle Creek, which was flanked by "high and craggy hills." It was in this "dangerous Defile of Several miles" that the experienced Bouquet expected the Indians to be waiting in ambush.[28]

As the command pushed on through the rolling countryside dense with majestic white and black oaks, the day grew increasingly hot, and the Redcoats looked forward to quenching their thirst at the stream known as Bushy Run.[29] By one o'clock in the afternoon, the troops had traversed about seventeen miles and were only a scant mile from their destination. The command was stretched out along the trail for more than a half mile between two rolling hills. Suddenly, gunfire and war whoops erupted at the head of the column. As Lieutenant Dow's advance guard passed by one of the hills to the right of the road, the combined Indian force rose from their ambush and fired into the column. Although a number of British soldiers dropped with this initial discharge, Dow held his ground and ordered his men to wheel right and deliver their own volley at the darting warriors. The lieutenant was credited with personally killing two Indians and wounding a third before being shot through the body.

At the first sound of gunfire, Colonel Bouquet ordered his men in the main column to strip off their burdensome packs and prepare for action. He then sent forward two light infantry companies of the Black Watch to reinforce Dow's advance guard. With daring and resolution, the Scots rushed on through the forest and engaged the enemy concealed along the hillside. Unlike Braddock's forces that had been defeated at the Monongahela years before, Bouquet's men displayed unusual coolness under fire and avoided becoming snarled in confusion. The Highlanders seized the initiative and drove the Indians from the important high ground. From this position they were able to keep the enemy temporarily at bay.[30]

Having relinquished the commanding hill to the Highlanders, the warriors quickly resorted to their proven battlefield tactic of enveloping the enemy in a half-moon formation. Darting from tree to tree, the Indians spilled along both sides of Bouquet's column and joined other warriors who were already lying "in ambush in some

One Mile to Bushy Run Station, painting by Robert Griffing. This epic canvas depicts the action on August 5, 1763, when Bouquet's relief column was attacked by the Indians near Bushy Run. A spirited charge by the Highlanders is dislodging the Indians from the nearby knoll on the right. Other warriors, however, are beginning to envelop the column's flanks. Courtesy Paramount Press.

high grounds which lay along the flanks of the army." This maneuver drove Lemuel Barrett's rangers, who were in the woods on either side of the command, back to the main column. One unidentified British soldier later recalled that the Indians "galled our troops with a most obstinate fire."[31]

With the enemy tearing at his flanks, Bouquet must have realized that unless he took decisive action, a repeat of Braddock's debacle was quite likely. He ordered his entire line to charge the Indians and dislodge them from their firing positions. The Redcoats, with bayoneted muskets firmly in hand, pushed through the woods and succeeded in forcing the Indians back. As Colonel Bouquet soon discovered, however, the charge gave the soldiers very little advantage, "for as soon as they [the Indians] were driven from one Post, they appeared on another."[32]

After sweeping the enemy from the commanding hillside and along his flanks, Bouquet heard firing at the rear of his column, where the pack train and livestock were located. The colonel had no recourse but to give up the hotly contested hill and fall back to protect his convoy of supplies. Slowly and deliberately, the Redcoats retreated in an orderly fashion. This was no rout as Braddock had suffered. As the British fell back, their retreat was covered by soldiers who staunchly stood their ground and allowed for an organized withdrawal.

To protect his supply train, Colonel Bouquet directed his officers to establish a defensive perimeter around the pack animals and livestock. This stand was made on the top of a rolling hill that covered about ten or twelve acres and dropped precipitously on one side. Dubbing this site "Edge Hill," the colonel later described it as "a comodious Piece of ground, & just Spacious enough for our Purpose." While a number of the frightened packers hid in the bushes, Bouquet ordered his men to remove the flour bags from the horses and pile them up in a circle. Then the soldiers placed their wounded comrades inside this makeshift redoubt for protection. Outside the flour-bag fort, the unflinching Highlanders and experienced Royal Americans took up position according to their respective companies and began to fire at the Indians, who darted from tree to tree with amazing agility. Through the dense gun smoke swirling around the battlefield, a Redcoat would occasionally detect the slender form of an Indian warrior, his body covered with red and black paint, as he moved swiftly through the forest.

The firing continued throughout the afternoon, and casualties among the more exposed British troops began to mount. Typically, the British soldier was trained to fire his Brown Bess musket in a rigidly sequenced fashion that from an entire company, produced a continuous field of firepower. Because this technique was not designed to pick out individual targets, however, the detonations had little impact on a concealed enemy. The stealthy Indians, on the other hand, were able to creep close to the British lines, quickly rise, and fire at specific targets. The only way that the Redcoats could keep the enemy at a respectable distance was to sally from the defensive perimeter with fixed bayonets and drive the Indians from their places of concealment. One Highland soldier, Robert Kirk, remembered that "when they came close up, we gave them our whole fire, and rushed out upon them with fixt bayonets; the Indians are not very well used to this way of fighting."[33] Another factor that may have helped to keep the Indians at bay were the long rifles in the hands of Lemuel Barrett's rangers.[34] These weapons had a far greater range and were deadly tools in the hands of experienced marksmen. Unfortunately, there were too few rifles among Bouquet's besieged forces to keep the Indians at a distance. By late afternoon the colonel counted more than sixty of his men either killed or wounded. Among the dead were Captain-lieutenant John Graham and Lieutenant James McIntosh of the Black Watch regiment. Respite from the terrible carnage that engulfed Colonel Bouquet's command came only as darkness fell over the battlefield.

Once night fell, Bouquet took stock of his distressing situation. Inside the circle of flour bags, his wounded men groaned and cried out for water. All along the defensive perimeter, the men who were fit to stand guard also suffered from thirst and fatigue. A considerable number of packhorses were either dead or had bolted from the battlefield. With such a large number of wounded men and so few pack animals, Bouquet could neither retreat nor continue the advance toward Fort Pitt. Despite the gravity of the moment, the colonel felt duty bound to pen a full report to General Amherst detailing his desperate situation. "Whatever our Fate may be," Bouquet wrote, "I thought it necessary to give your Excellency this early Information, that you may, at all Events, take such measures as you will think proper with the Provinces for their own Safety, and the Effectual relief of Fort Pitt, as in case of another Engagement, I fear insurmountable difficulties." The colonel went on to praise the leadership of Major Campbell and the "cool and steady behaviour of the Troops, who did not fire a Shot without orders, and drove the Enemy from their Posts with fixed Bayonets." Despite these accolades probably few of the soldiers hemmed in at Bushy Run believed there was much glory in this type of warfare. Far from home in a strange land, fighting an enemy they could not even see, let alone understand, the grim Redcoats felt nothing but despair. An unidentified British officer at the battle expressed this bleak outlook: "In an American campaign every thing is terrible; the face of the country, the climate, the enemy. There is no refreshment for the healthy, nor relief for the sick. A vast unhospitable desart, unsafe and treacherous, surrounds them, where victories are not decisive, but defeats are ruinous; and simple death is the least misfortune which can happen to them."[35]

Early the next morning, the Indians resumed the attack "by Shouting and yelping" in an attempt to frighten and intimidate the British. The soldiers caught sight of the Delaware chief Keekyuscung, who was hiding behind a tree and hurling insults at the British in perfect English. Robert Kirk distinctly heard the Indians boast to Colonel Bouquet "that they would have his scalp before night." The Mingo leader Kiasutha was also present, exhorting the warriors to press closer upon the Redcoats. As the morning wore on, the Indians, "under Favour of an incessant fire, made Several bold Efforts to penetrate [Bouquet's] Camp." With each assault the Highlanders sallied from their defensive position to drive the enemy back. One British officer recalled that these bold attacks were "very smart, and bloody, many being killed and wounded on both Sides, the Indians still continuing to behave with uncommon Bravery." Colonel Bouquet also acknowledged the enemy's determination, remarking that they "fought with the greatest bravery and resolution." Indeed, seeing British soldiers continue to fall emboldened the warriors even more. They were clearly quite convinced that the line of Redcoats would give way at any moment and they would be able to overrun the remaining soldiers. Bouquet also realized that his position was becoming untenable and that, sooner or later, the enemy would indeed swarm over his command. It was at this desperate moment that the colonel devised a stratagem that would turn the tide of battle at Bushy Run.[36]

Throughout the two-day engagement, Bouquet had been quick to realize that bold bayonet charges had little effect on an enemy who would simply give way and then reappear at a different point. His only hope was to encourage his opponents to concentrate their forces at a particular location and then draw them out into the open where his troops could engage them. Experience also taught Bouquet that the best way to entice the Indians out into the open was to make them believe that his soldiers were giving up the fight and retreating. The colonel had once counseled Major James Grant to utilize this same plan outside Fort Duquesne during the French and Indian War. Instead, the foolhardy Grant had let himself be drawn into an Indian ambush, and his force had been annihilated. Bouquet believed the tactic had merit nonetheless, and he often advocated its use in conversations with fellow officers.[37] At Bushy Run Bouquet finally had an opportunity to put the stratagem into practice.

While the colonel planned his feigned retreat, one of the officers, perhaps Lemuel Barrett, pointed out that a number of troops could fall back over the eastern brow of the hill, where their movements could be observed only by a few Indians stationed in the rear of the circle.[38] These soldiers could then be positioned so as to effect a flanking maneuver against those Indians who would congregate to assault the command from the west.

At about ten o'clock in the morning, Colonel Bouquet called his officers together to brief them on his plan and instruct them how to position their men to execute the maneuver. When everything was ready, Bouquet ordered two light infantry companies, stationed on either side of the trail on the western side of his perimeter, to fall back inside the circle. The gap created by this withdrawal was filled by two other companies that had been posted on either side of the light infantry. This weakened the circle, leaving the western side thinly defended. As expected, the observant Indians interpreted this movement as the beginning of a British retreat. They immediately pressed an attack from the west and advanced against the weakened position with "heavy fire." In the meantime, Major Campbell took charge of the light infantry companies that had moved inside the perimeter and directed them to continue through the circle and fall back over the eastern brow of the hill as if they were continuing the retreat.[39] Once they were out of sight, the major reformed his men into a line of battle.

On the other side of the hill, the Indians were now confident that they could overrun Bouquet's position, and many of them threw down their muskets, grasped their tomahawks, and "rushed on in Clusters, quite exposed," toward the weakly defended front. With all their attention riveted on the thin line in front of them, the howling warriors did not notice Major Campbell's light infantry companies come crashing through the forest. As the Scots moved deftly around the brow of the hill, they drove the Indians before them, rolling up the enemy's right flank. When the major's men reached a spot only yards from the enemy's exposed position, the Highlanders stopped and fired a deadly volley at point-blank range into the confused warriors. Undaunted, the Indians "resolutely returned the Fire, but could not Stand the irresistible Shock of the [Scots], who rushing in among them, killed many of them." With broadswords and bayonets the Highlanders slashed and

PLAN OF THE **BATTLE** NEAR **BUSHY-RUN**,

Gained by Colonel Bouquet, over the

Delawares, Shawanese, Mingoes, Wyandots, Mohikons, Miamies, & Ottawas;

on the 5.ᵗʰ and 6.ᵗʰ of August 1763.

Survey'd by Thos. Hutchins, Assistant Engineer.

REFERENCES.

1. Grenadiers	7. Entrenchment of Bags
2. Light Infantry	for the Wounded
3. Battalion Men	x. The Enemy
4. Rangers	8. First Position of the Troops
5. Cattle	◫◫ Graves
6. Horses	

Plan of the Battle near Bushy Run, drawing by Thomas Hutchins (1765). This map, drawn on the scene, clearly shows the British positions during the engagement and details Bouquet's flanking maneuver (lower right), which routed the Indians. From William Smith, *An Historical Account of Colonel Bouquet's Expedition* (1765). Courtesy Fort Ligonier, Pennsylvania.

stabbed at their opponents with a vengeance. Totally unprepared and unaccustomed to this type of warfare, the Indians bolted, running parallel to the British lines. The Highlander Robert Kirk vividly remembered the scene: "We met them with our fire first, and then made terrible havock amongst them with our fixt bayonets, and continuing to push them everywhere, they set to their heels and were never able to rally again."[40] Then, without warning, the desperate warriors received a second shock as another company of light infantry and a body of grenadiers under Captain Basset, rose up from their crouched positions along the defensive perimeter and delivered another heavy volley into the panic-stricken Indians. After discharging their Brown Bess muskets, Basset's men jumped up and joined in the charge against the stunned enemy. The Indians who had been stationed on the left flank were held in check by the fire from the rest of Bouquet's men positioned along the top of the hill. They could do nothing but stand "in awe" as the ferocious Highlanders butchered their fellow tribesmen. Completely routed, the combined Indian force fled in terror as all four companies of Highlanders drove them through the forest. The pursuit continued for over a mile as the maddened Scots attempted to overtake the fleeing Indians. At last the soldiers halted and took a position on the hilltop that had been the scene of action on the first day of the battle.

The Battle of Bushy Run, the most complete victory the British ever achieved over Native American warriors, was over. It was an astonishing blow to the Indians, who were unaccustomed to sustaining such high casualties. In their hysterical flight they left twenty dead warriors on the field. This was unprecedented among Native American fighters, who usually risked all to take away their fallen comrades. One of the bodies left behind was that of Keekyuscung, who had once predicted before Christian Frederick Post that there would "be a great war, and never come to peace again." "From the Marks of Blood & other Circumstances," the Redcoats estimated that many more Indians had been killed or wounded. After the battle, Colonel Bouquet remarked, "Our brave Men disdained so much to touch the dead Body of a vanquished Enemy that scarce a Scalp was taken, except by the Rangers & Pack Horse Drivers." A particularly fleet-footed Highlander managed to capture one Indian and led him back to the camp. One of Barrett's rangers approached the soldier and asked, "What

The Highland charge at Bushy Run. This illustration, which accompanied an 1861 article about the battle, is one of the earliest artistic renditions of the event. From *New Harper's Monthly Magazine* 22 (October 1861).

are you going to do with that fellow?" "I am taking him to Colonel Bouquet," replied the Scot. "If you want one, there are plenty of them running yonder in the woods, and you may catch one for yourself." The ranger then drew a pistol and shot the Indian through the head.[41]

Atop Edge Hill, Henry Bouquet viewed the carnage left by the two days of determined fighting. Fifty dead Redcoats were strewn about the battlefield, and another sixty men, including four officers, had been wounded.[42] These casualties underscored the fierce determination of the doughty Scotsmen and prompted Bouquet to proclaim that "the Highlanders are the bravest Men I ever saw, and their behavior in that obstinate affair does them the highest honor."[43]

The colonel realized that his first concern was to bring some relief to the wounded men who had been suffering from thirst for two days. Accordingly, the soldiers set about constructing litters to transport their fallen comrades. Since so many draft animals were either dead or missing, Bouquet had no recourse but to destroy a large portion of the flour destined for Fort Pitt. Without pausing to bury their dead, the British formed into line along the trail and marched on to Bushy Run. No sooner had the troops established their camp at the stream than a party of Indians returned and fired at them. Without orders, the light infantry grabbed their muskets and charged through the woods once more, dispersing the enemy without loss.[44]

The next day, the column resumed the march. The defeated and demoralized Indians made no further attempts to halt Bouquet's progress other than to fire some "Scattered shots along the Road." It was slow going as the crippled command inched its way toward Fort Pitt—no doubt an excruciating journey for the wounded men being carried in litters hoisted by their fellow soldiers. Bouquet was particularly impressed with the behavior of Lieutenant Dow, who, though desperately wounded in the stomach, never complained and was anxious only about obtaining an officer's commission for his son.[45]

After traveling three days, the command halted at John Metcalfe's farm along Nine Mile Run, less than ten miles from Fort Pitt. The Indians had burned Metcalfe's cabin and barn, but a portion of the crops remained in the fields, and Bouquet's men were able to harvest a little Indian corn, beans, and other vegetables to satisfy their hunger. While the Redcoats piled up Metcalfe's fence rails to build their campfires, the colonel dispatched a scout to carry word to the fort of his impending arrival. At daybreak the next morning, the scout arrived at Fort Pitt to inform Captain Ecuyer that Bouquet's command would be arriving that day. Ecuyer dispatched Captain Ralph Phillips with a detachment to escort Bouquet's column to the fort. Later that morning, the soldiers standing along the ramparts watched nervously as parties of Indians crossed the Ohio River brandishing the scalps they had taken at Bushy Run. That night Bouquet's triumphant but bloodied column finally straggled into the fort.[46]

The next day, August 11, Colonel Bouquet set about writing official dispatches informing General Amherst and Pennsylvania governor James Hamilton of his safe arrival at Fort Pitt. The Swiss commander did not downplay his achievement when he announced to Amherst, "It is with great Pleasure I can acquaint you that we have been so happy as to Execute the General's orders in throwing a supply of

Provisions into this Fort, And in Humbling the savages by the most compleat defeat they ever Received in the woods." Bouquet was equally boastful when he informed the Pennsylvania governor that "the most warlike of the savage Tribes have lost their Boasted Claim of being Invincible in the Woods." The news of Bouquet's victory quickly traveled eastward with his official dispatches. Lieutenant Blane at Fort Ligonier, the first officer to receive the good news, hurriedly wrote Bouquet congratulating him on "being the first Person that has ever throughly convinced these Rascals of their inability to cope with us." Further down the line at Fort Bedford, Bouquet's friend Lewis Ourry sent similar congratulatory remarks: "I believe you have given the Savages such a Dose as has effectually cured them of the Itch of meddling with us, for they have not appeared on this Communication Since."

Reports of the victory finally reached Philadelphia on August 24, and church bells clanged throughout the night to celebrate the news. Governor Hamilton penned a letter to Bouquet thanking him for his "Victory and triumph over the Indians." The *Pennsylvania Journal & Weekly Advertiser* was equally laudatory, reporting that "the Indian Army was composed of 8 different Nations, and as Braddock, and Grant were conquered on that Road, they expected to have served Col. Bouquet in the same Manner; but thank God they have been disappointed." "We hope," the paper went on, "the Province of Pennsylvania will reap the Sweets thereof, and many be convinced, that Indians are no more invulnerable than other Men, when attacked on equal Terms, and especially by British Troops." The final, and perhaps most significant, praise heaped on Colonel Bouquet and his troops for the victory at Bushy Run came from the king himself. On January 5, 1764, the following order was posted at army headquarters in New York:

> His Majesty has been graciously pleased to signify to the commander in chief, his royal approbation of the conduct and bravery of Col. Bouquet, and the officers and troops under his command, in the two actions of the 5th and 6th of August; in which, notwithstanding the many circumstances of difficulty and distress they laboured under, and the unusual spirit and resolution of the Indians, they repelled the repeated attacks of the Savages, and conducted their convoy safe to Fort Pitt.[47]

As the years passed, the plaudits conferred on Bouquet and the men at Bushy Run continued. I. D. Rupp, in one of the first histories of western Pennsylvania, published in 1846, extolled the accomplishments of Bouquet's forces: "The signal victory gained over the Indians by Col. Bouquet . . . so dismayed them, that they not only gave up all designs against Fort Pitt, but withdrew from the frontiers." Five years later, Francis Parkman, who published the first general history of what became known as Pontiac's Uprising, declared, "The battle of Bushy Run was one of the best contested actions ever fought between white men and Indians." These accolades continued well into the twentieth century. When Howard Peckham crafted his highly acclaimed study of Pontiac's Uprising in 1947, he proclaimed that as a result of Bouquet's victory, "the crisis in western Pennsylvania was past; only a few Indians showed themselves around Fort Pitt again." As late as 1966, when Niles Anderson wrote the official guidebook for the Pennsylvania Historical and Museum Commission, he declared that the engagement "was a major victory—a decisive battle—in quelling the 1763 Indian uprising."[48]

Since the late 1960s, historians studying the Battle of Bushy Run have tended to downplay Bouquet's achievement, claiming either that the engagement was not as decisive as previously supposed or that the Swiss commander should only be credited with delivering "a lucky blow."[49] Earlier accolades bestowed on Bouquet certainly overstated the battle's significance. The engagement did not totally destroy the Indians' capacity to wage war against the Redcoats. It did, however, sap their fighting strength enough to cause them to abandon their siege of Fort Pitt. As a consequence, the Indians were never again formidable enough to cut off a strategic British outpost. Had the fort fallen or the garrison surrendered, it would have provided the Indians with a considerable amount of supplies, especially powder and lead. This would have allowed them to continue the war for a longer period. In addition, the fall of the most important of all British forts would have given the enemy an important psychological and spiritual impetus. Bouquet's offensive also reopened the line of communication from Philadelphia to the West. This was a strategically critical precondition to contemplating any future military operations. In sum, Bouquet's triumph must be considered a significant turning point in the war.

In addition, this victory should be recognized as much more than just "a lucky blow" against a resourceful enemy that had time and again bested its English adversary on the field of battle. Henry Bouquet's understanding of Native American battlefield tactics led him to develop his own stratagem of feigning a retreat and catching the enemy completely off guard. The subsequent flanking maneuver provided the necessary shock to propel the Indians into a full retreat. Bouquet fully understood that the enemy, no matter how determined, could not stand up to this type of stunning attack. Perhaps the only "lucky" element of the victory was the fact that Henry Bouquet was in command that day at Bushy Run.

After his arrival at Fort Pitt Colonel Bouquet's immediate concerns were to remove any noncombatants from the outpost and to bring up the remainder of the supplies that had been left behind at Ligonier. Bouquet ordered Major Campbell to take four hundred soldiers and escort the women and children eastward to Ligonier, from which point the militia would conduct them further east to Bedford. The colonel's order to evacuate the "useless people" was too much to bear for Dr. Robert Boyd, surgeon's mate and post physician. Before coming to Fort Pitt, the good doctor had apparently seduced a girl and "took her young & innocent from her parents without their knowledge." Boyd, believing that it would be "both dishonorable and villainous to Seduce a virtuous Girl and then turn her off," appealed to Bouquet to allow the young woman to stay with him. Undoubtedly, Dr. Boyd did not relish spending the winter at the remote frontier outpost without companionship. There is no record as to whether the colonel relented to Boyd's appeal.[50]

From the beginning of the campaign, General Amherst had been adamant that, once Bouquet had effected the relief of Fort Pitt, he should forge ahead and reestablish the British line of communication northward to Presque Isle. Due to the high number of casualties suffered at Bushy Run, however, Bouquet realized that further offensive operations would be impossible to execute unless provincial troops could be pried away from their defensive positions along the Susquehanna. The day after his arrival at Fort Pitt Bouquet once again appealed to Governor Hamilton: "If the Provinces would now Enable us to follow this Lucky Blow we might drive the Indians over the lakes or Compell them to sue for peace but it cannot be attempted with

Prudence with the Troops I have left, And if we give them time to recover of their Pannick we may have the whole to do over again."[51] After making his appeal to Hamilton, Bouquet could do nothing else but inform the commander in chief that there were simply not enough troops left to open the road to the north and reoccupy Fort Presque Isle. Lord Amherst fumed over Pennsylvania's lack of resolve and fired off a dispatch to Hamilton expressing his surprise "at the infatuation of the People in your Province, who tamely look on while their Brethren are butchered by the Savages, when, without doubt, it is in their Power, by exerting a proper Spirit, not only to protect their Settlements, but to punish any Indians that are hardy enough to disturb them." The Pennsylvania Assembly considered Amherst's remarks to be both insulting and erroneous. In a written statement to Hamilton, the assembly members reminded the governor that they had approved the recruitment of seven hundred men for frontier defense and that it would be wholly unfair to release these troops for offensive operations beyond the borders of Pennsylvania without some assurances that the other colonies would also participate in such activities. Besides, the assembly argued, Pennsylvania forces were already engaged in an offensive expedition against the Delawares living at Great Island, along the West Branch of the Susquehanna.[52]

On August 26 Colonel John Armstrong of the Pennsylvania militia wrote Bouquet from Carlisle that "a party of Volunteers chiefly from the East side of the River [Susquehanna] betwixt One hundred & two in number are gone up the West Branch of Sasquehanah" in order to punish the Delawares at Great Island. The majority of these Indians belonged to Teedyuscung's band and had fled their homes at Shamokin after the venerated chief had been murdered by the invaders from Connecticut. From Great Island Teedyuscung's son, Captain Bull, had vowed to avenge his father's death. In preparation for their campaign, the Pennsylvanians sent the noted interpreter Andrew Montour to scout the West Branch and report back to Fort Augusta as to the disposition and strength of the Delawares living along the river. Just as the expedition was getting under way, the Pennsylvania volunteers encountered Montour returning downriver in a canoe. The mixed-blood frontiersman reported that the Delawares at Great Island were "bad Indians, and that [the troops] might use them as they pleased." Some of the militia questioned Montour's loyalty and suspected that the frontiersman had warned the Indians of the column's approach up the West Branch. One citizen-soldier named William Patterson, convinced that the Indians would be waiting to ambush the troops, decided to return to Fort Augusta. The remainder of the command, determined to strike the Indians in their villages, continued upriver.[53]

On August 27 the volunteers crested Muncy Creek Hill and encountered "a large party of the great island warriors." In the sharp skirmish that followed, the Delawares engaged the Pennsylvanians "briskly for some time; but, after an hour's hot firing they were obliged to run, with considerable loss." During the fight, four volunteers were killed and another four men were wounded. According to several participants, the Pennsylvanians killed a Delaware leader named the Snake and at least ten other warriors. At nightfall the militia made camp near the battlefield and set about tending to the wounded men. Without warning the Indians returned and crept into a nearby thicket. The warriors were so close that the soldiers could hear them cock their muskets. The Delawares sent a volley into the camp, but the Pennsylvanians held their fire, fearful that if they emptied their weapons all at once, the Indians would rush in among them with knives and tomahawks. Throughout the long night, the opposing parties exchanged insults. When the Indians heard some of the wounded soldiers moaning, they remarked that it sounded as if the white men were sick. The Pennsylvanians replied that if the Indians came any closer "they would serve some of them as they had done the Snake."[54]

During the harrowing night, six militiamen became separated from the main command. Unable to locate their comrades in the darkness, the men decided to strike out and find their own way back to Fort Augusta. Led by George Allen, who claimed to be familiar with the trail, the volunteers stumbled through the night until daybreak, when they came upon the path leading back to the fort. They continued southward until one of the soldiers spied a column of smoke coming from a campfire along the trail. Allen and his men crept up to the fire and discovered three Delawares preparing breakfast. The Pennsylvanians raised their muskets to fire just as the Indians sprang up crying, "Don't shoot brothers, don't shoot!" The soldiers lowered their weapons. The Pennsylvanians quickly recognized at least one of the Indians. Ironically, he was known among the whites as George Allen and had taken that name from the very militia leader who now leveled his musket at the surprised Delawares. The trembling Delawares hastily explained that they had been to Bethlehem to trade with the Moravians and were returning to their village along the West Branch. Convinced that these Indians were part of the same party that had attacked the soldiers the day before, Allen and his men decided to take their prisoners back to Fort Augusta. Along the way, the Pennsylvania men discussed their hostages' fate. One man suggested that if they took the Indians back to the fort, the officers would release them or send them to Philadelphia, where the Quakers would protect them. Finally, the vengeful militiamen decided to kill the Indians. Prodding the Delawares to march ahead, the soldiers raised their weapons and fired. The three Indians fell to the ground, and the white men ran up and scalped them. Collecting their grisly trophies, the soldiers turned to walk away. Suddenly, the Delaware named George Allen jumped up, as if "raising from the dead," and bolted into the forest to make his escape. Eventually, George Allen, scalped and wounded, made his way back to Great Island, where he "threatened to take his revenge on George Allen."[55]

Following the skirmish at Muncy Creek Hill, the Pennsylvania militiamen believed that they had chastised the Indians sufficiently to discourage further raids into the frontier settlements. By the beginning of October, however, war parties from the West Branch resumed their raids among the Moravian settlements in northeastern Pennsylvania. On October 13 the *Pennsylvania Gazette* printed a letter from the region that read in part, "I cannot describe the deplorable Conditions this poor Country is in: most of the Inhabitants of Allen's Town, and other places, are fled from their Habitations. I cannot ascertain the Number killed, but that it exceeds 20." The paper also report that "Yost's Mill about 13 miles from Bethlehem, was destroyed and all the People that belonged to it, excepting one young Man, cut off."[56]

With such devastation continuing along the frontier, Colonel Armstrong mounted another expedition of three hundred militia to strike the Indian villages along the West Branch of the Susquehanna. When Armstrong reached Great Island, he found the first village deserted. Undeterred, the expedition continued upstream in search of the enemy, yet every time Armstrong's men approached an Indian encampment, however, the inhabitants would flee. Nonetheless, the colonel's men were able to destroy seven towns and over three thousand bushels of corn.[57]

While Armstrong cut a swath of destruction up the West Branch, another party of 104 vengeful Pennsylvanians, under Major Asher Clayton, proceeded from Fort Augusta up the North Branch of the Susquehanna. On October 17 Clayton's command came upon the ruins of the town that had been established by Connecticut settlers following the death of Teedyuscung. Two days earlier a party of more than a hundred Delawares under Captain Bull had swooped down on the Connecticut invaders and wiped them out. One unidentified man in Clayton's command described the horrible carnage left by the Indians: "We buried the dead—nine men and a woman—who had been most cruelly butchered. The woman was roasted, and had two hinges in her hands—supposed to be put in red hot—and several of the men had awls thrust in their eyes, and spears, arrows, pitchforks, etc. sticking in their bodies." Clayton's men finished burning the houses and destroying the crop of corn before returning to Fort Augusta. Captain Bull had finally exacted his revenge.[58]

The meager offensive launched by the Pennsylvania militia did little to alleviate the situation that Colonel Bouquet faced west of the mountains. Throughout August and September Bouquet waited anxiously for reinforcements from the provinces in order to resume his own offensive against the Indians. The colonel was further discouraged when he received orders from Amherst calling for the reduction of British troops in North America. General Amherst had received the orders to reduce his command in May but had forestalled implementing them until after the relief of forts Pitt and Detroit. The reduction called for the total disbandment of the 77th Highland Regiment and drastic reductions in the Black Watch battalion. In addition, Amherst ordered Bouquet to send three entire companies of the Royal American Regiment to South Carolina to replace independent companies that were being disbanded there. That the commander in chief would so foolishly order such dramatic curtailments in the number of troops on the frontier during the throes of an Indian war seems almost incredible. Yet the miserly Amherst, never one to question a directive from London aimed at saving money, insisted that the reductions be implemented as soon as possible. More astounding is Amherst's hope that Bouquet could push on to Presque Isle and reestablish the outpost with so few troops.[59]

In addition to the troop reductions, Amherst insisted on continuing the destructive policies that had helped to ignite the Indian war. When Sir William Johnson suggested that some gifts be distributed to various tribal leaders in order to sway other Indians toward peace, Amherst's response was stern:

> I am fully convinced of your Exerting your utmost endeavors for the good of the service, and have no doubt but you will pay the strictest regard to . . . Economy. The late defection of so many tribes, in my opinion ought to lesson the Expenses in your departments; The measures they have occasioned to be taken for reducing them will create a very heavy and unavoidable expense to the Crown. Their punishment must be previous to the treating with them, and when that shall happen, all they can expect is forgiveness, and a Trade, under proper regulations, opened to them. But as to presents, it would certainly be the highest presumption in them to expect any. Justice they shall have, but no more; for they can never be considered by us as a people to whom we owe rewards; and it would be madness, to the highest degree, ever to bestow favors on a race who have so treacherously, and without provocation on our side, attacked our Posts, and butchered our Garrisons.[60]

The frontier diplomat George Croghan finally had enough of Amherst and his shortsighted policies. Despite the chicanery and scheming that always seemed to swirl around him, Croghan knew Indians. For years he had repeatedly warned that Sir Jeffery's policies would lead to an Indian war, yet the general had chosen to ignore Croghan's advice. The frustrated Indian agent told Colonel Bouquet that "No Regard was had to any intelligence I sent No More then to my opinion." As a consequence, the Irishman decided to submit his letter of resignation to Amherst and go to England to petition the crown for compensation for the financial losses he had incurred during the war. Other "suffering traders" asked Croghan to represent their interests as well and to request that the king grant the group a large tract of land in the Illinois country to offset their combined losses. While in London, Croghan informed the Lords of Trade that the Indians had "killed and captivated not less than two thousand of his Majesty's subjects, and drove some thousands to Beggary and the greatest distress, besides burning to the ground nine Forts or Blockhouses . . . and killing a number of His Majesty's Troops and Traders, whom they plundered of goods to the amount of not less than one hundred thousand pounds." While Croghan may have exaggerated the losses sustained by these "suffering traders," the forfeiture of trade goods was substantial. At Fort Pitt William Trent computed his own estimate of the losses sustained by the various trading firms and determined that £45,000's worth of trade goods had been taken by the Indians. In addition, Trent claimed that eighty-eight traders and their employees had been either killed or taken into captivity.[61]

One of the men captured by the Indians during that bloody summer was Isaac Stewart. Quite likely, Stewart was serving as an employee of Thomas Colhoon, or one of the other traders who operated out of Fort Pitt. Regardless of where or when Stewart was taken by the Indians, his captivity narrative ranks as one of the most bizarre tales emanating from Pontiac's War. Stewart related that he was captured about fifty miles west of Fort Pitt along with other white men and taken to an Indian village along the Wabash River. While their fellow captives were tortured to death by the Indians, Stewart and a Welshman named John Davey were spared through the intercession of one of the village women, known as Rose. The two men remained with the tribe for two years until they were redeemed by a Spaniard who took them westward to the Mississippi. Stewart claimed that they then ascended a river that was called "la Riviere Rough, or Red River." Traveling upstream for seven hundred miles, the party encountered "a nation of Indians remarkably white, and whose hair was of a reddish colour." Davey informed Stewart that he could converse with these Indians since they spoke a language "being very little different from the Welch." The Indians told Davey that their ancestors had come from a foreign land and had settled along the coast of what Stewart believed was western Florida. After the Spanish arrived, these people fled to their present location. To prove their story the Indians "brought forth rolls of parchment, which were carefully tied up in otter skins, on which were large characters, written with blue ink." While the Welshman Davey decided to remain with his new-found kinsmen, Stewart and his Spanish companion continued westward, traveling another five hundred miles and eventually crossing "a ridge of mountains . . . from which the streams run due west [the

Continental Divide]." At the foot of the mountains, the two adventurers discovered gold in the streambeds. Stewart claimed that he and the Spaniard returned by a different route and ended up at a Spanish outpost near the mouth of the Missouri River. There Stewart bid his traveling companion goodbye and made his way cross-country to South Carolina. If Isaac Stewart's incredible saga is to be believed, then he was perhaps the first person of British descent to cross the Rocky Mountains, nearly forty years before Lewis and Clark.[62]

Back at Fort Pitt, Colonel Bouquet must have bristled when he read General Amherst's directive to reduce the number of troops on the frontier. Despite these reductions, the Swiss commander still hoped to resume his offensive against the Ohio Country Indians before the onset of winter. Bouquet was briefly encouraged in September 1763 by reports that Colonel Adam Stephen of the Virginia militia was recruiting a thousand men to march to Fort Pitt and take the field against the Shawnees living on the Ohio. On learning of Stephen's efforts, Bouquet dashed off a flattering letter to the Virginian, saying, "You would have command of the most promising Expedition that has been attempted yet against the Savages and obtain great honor to your Government & to yourself, by So great & Seasonable a service." Stephen soon replied to Bouquet with the predictable objection: who was going to pay for the troops? On October 23 a dejected Bouquet wrote back to Stephen: "I have no reason to expect that the General [Amherst] will engage the Crown on that Account, into any other Expences than those of Provisions, and the Ammunition that might be wanted." So ended any further possibility of continuing the war that fall. Henry Bouquet could hope only that the troops at Detroit could strike a crushing blow against the enemy. On September 30 he wrote to Major Gladwin, "I flatter myself that . . . you have by this time dispersed the Enemy, and obtained some Satisfaction [for] their infamous Barbarities . . . The Fate of this War depends intirely on your Successes."[63]

7

"Nothing Remains in Our Heart but Good"

While Henry Bouquet's campaign in the Ohio Country came to a close in the late summer of 1763, the stalemate at Fort Detroit continued. The defeat of Dalyell's force in late July gave the Indians surrounding the fort only a fleeting sense of triumph. Despite the losses the British had suffered at Bloody Run, the garrison was still stronger than at the start of the siege, which meant that it would be increasingly difficult for Pontiac to take the fort. The reinforcements also provided the fort's original defenders with some respite from their long ordeal. As Lieutenant Jehu Hay noted in his diary, "Since the Detachment arrived the Garrison has been less fatigued than before, as instead of everybody lying [upon] the Works, a . . . picket of 80 Men & three Subalterns took their place every Night." Major Gladwin felt secure enough to send out skirmish parties to take control of several houses near the fort. Another sortie of sixty men led by Captain Hopkins boarded some of the whaleboats in the dead of night in an attempt to launch a surprise attack on the Potawatomie village south of the fort. The boats became separated in the thick fog engulfing the river, and a coordinated attack could not be made. It was daylight before Hopkins and his men could regroup. Having lost the crucial element of surprise, the soldiers returned to the fort.[1]

On August 6 the schooner *Huron* returned to Detroit after crossing Lake Erie to obtain supplies. While the eighty barrels of provisions were certainly a welcome sight for the garrison, Major Gladwin realized that with so many mouths to feed, the food would not last long. With Detroit's garrison reinforced, Gladwin concluded that he no longer needed the protection of the vessels at the fort's water gate. He accordingly directed that both the *Huron* and *Michigan* set sail to obtain even more supplies. The boats were made ready, and fifteen men who had been wounded in Dalyell's defeat went aboard for the journey to Fort Niagara. The former captive John Rutherford also agreed to return to Niagara to oversee the acquisition of supplies. The vessels cast off on August 13, and the Indians on the river's shoreline did not even bother firing at them. When the two ships reached the landing above Niagara Falls, Major Wilkins wasted no time in sending supplies and reinforcements upriver from Fort Niagara for the return voyage to Detroit. The *Michigan* set sail first, on August 26, with John Rutherford and a small relief column of seventeen men led by Captain Edward Hope. Also aboard was Lieutenant John Montresor of the Royal Engineers. Montresor was an experienced campaigner, having fought alongside Braddock in 1755 and with General Wolfe at Quebec. Several Mohawks, bearing peace belts from Sir William Johnson to the Indians of Detroit, also took passage on the sloop.[2]

With failing wind the *Michigan* made little progress on the first day of the voyage and was forced to drop anchor after sailing less than fourteen miles. Lake Erie had gained a reputation for the sudden and unpredictable tempests it could raise, and the next morning the crew was lashed by a violent storm. Lieutenant Montresor recorded in his journal that "the Vessel Labored immensely in an immense high Sea." To make matters worse, the boat sprung a leak, and a group of men hurried below deck to work the pumps while other soldiers feverishly bailed water and threw the heavy artillery and eighty barrels of provisions overboard. Years later, John Rutherford recalled the surreal scene aboard the *Michigan:*

> Dread and consternation was painted on every countenance and I was surprised to find myself the least moved of all, which must have been owing to my having been for some time so much exposed and inured to danger. While some

were stripping themselves to swim, others cursing and swearing at their companions for not working, others praying, and some drinking brandy. I looked tamely on, after finding I could be of no assistance.[3]

The storm eventually dashed the sloop against the shore near the mouth of what was called Catfish Creek (present-day Eighteen Mile Creek) in southwestern New York. All the men clambered safely ashore, where the experienced Montresor put them to work building a log breastwork and earthen redoubts in the event of an Indian attack. While the soldiers worked to construct their makeshift fortifications, the sailors went aboard the scuttled *Michigan* to salvage what supplies they could. In the meantime, Captain Hope sent a courier back the short distance to Niagara to ask Major Wilkins to forward reinforcements until the damaged sloop could be repaired.[4]

When the courier arrived at Niagara with news of the mishap, Major Wilkins rushed off a relief force consisting of one hundred men from the 46th and 55th regiments under Captain Gavin Cochrane. These reinforcements arrived at Montresor's fortified camp on September 2, just in time to help ward off an assault by a combined force of Senecas, Ottawas, and Chippewas. The Indians maneuvered undetected to within fifty yards of the breastwork before opening fire. In the initial discharge, three soldiers fell dead. The British returned fire and blasted the enemy with two rounds from a swivel gun that had been salvaged from the wrecked sloop. After two hours of fighting the disheartened Indians retreated into the forest. The attack on Montresor's camp demonstrated that the Indians had devised a new strategy to prevent Detroit from receiving supplies and reinforcements. Instead of trying to stop the ships after they had already sailed into the Detroit River, the combined tribes were determined to hover close to Niagara in hopes of ambushing the supply shipments there.[5]

The schooner *Huron*, which departed for Detroit after the *Michigan*, sailed across the lake without incident. The vessel, which carried forty-seven barrels of flour and 160 barrels of pork, was piloted by Joseph Horssey, an industrious shipwright who had been engaged in hauling goods across Lake Erie since the end of the French and Indian War. Horssey's crew consisted of a first mate named Jacobs and ten soldiers from Fort Niagara. Also aboard were six Mohawks who were carrying diplomatic overtures from Sir William Johnson to the Hurons.

Horssey and his crew arrived at the mouth of the Detroit River on September 3, and the Mohawks asked to be put ashore in order to approach the Huron village by land. While the Indians were disembarking, two habitants in a canoe rowed alongside the *Huron* in an attempt to sell vegetables to the crew. Horssey refused to permit the Frenchmen to board the schooner, and they paddled away, but not before noting that only ten men defended the vessel.[6]

The Frenchmen in the canoe wasted little time in paddling to Pontiac's village to inform him that the troublesome craft was carrying only a handful of Englishmen. About nine o'clock that night three to four hundred Indians jumped into their canoes and paddled downstream to intercept the *Huron*. By this time the vessel had already begun its ascent up the river and was anchored for the evening in a narrow channel about nine miles below the fort. A sentinel aboard the schooner did not spy the enemy until the Indians were less than one hundred yards away. The cannon attached to the bow spewed its deadly contents toward the oncoming canoes, but the Indians kept on and swarmed around the boat. The crew took to their muskets but had time enough to fire only one round before the warriors began to crawl up over the side of the vessel. Dropping their firearms, the embattled Redcoats grabbed lances to ward off the enemy. While many of the Indians attempted to scramble up to the deck, others used their tomahawks to hack away at the *Huron's* heavy rope anchor line. Some Indians even attempted to crawl through the cabin windows. In the bloody hand-to-hand fighting that took place on the deck, Horssey and one soldier were killed, and four more men were wounded. When the Indians finally succeeded in cutting through the anchor rope, the *Huron* slowly drifted around, sweeping a number of the canoes aside. The first mate Jacobs tried desperately to rally the crew by shouting, "Stand by, my brave Fellows, to the last, and then blow up the Vessel!" A white captive who was with the Indians heard Jacob's cry and warned the warriors what was about to happen. Suddenly the Indians abandoned their attack and made a hasty retreat in their birch-bark canoes. Later, the British learned through informants that fifteen Indians were killed in this bizarre naval engagement and another thirteen wounded—a high casualty count by Native standards.[7]

The next morning, Major Gladwin ordered a detachment of Redcoats under Captain Hopkins's command to row down the river in whaleboats and escort the *Huron* back to the fort. Only after the battle-scarred craft finally docked at the outpost did the garrison fully appreciate how desperate the engagement had been. The merchant James Sterling later commented that "the attack was the bravest ever known to be made by Indians & the defense, such as British subjects alone are capable of—the bayonets, spears, lances on board her are dy'd with Indian blood like Axes in a slaughter house." Later General Amherst ordered that special medals be struck and presented to the surviving crew members.[8]

While Pontiac's efforts to interrupt the flow of supplies to Fort Detroit continued to fail, Indians to the east along the Niagara portage remained vigilant in the hope of waylaying a convoy destined for the beleaguered outpost. Throughout the long summer of 1763, the British succeeded in transporting a meager amount of supplies and reinforcements across the narrow road that followed the winding course of the Niagara River. Surprisingly, the Redcoats had done little to fortify the valuable trail. At the southern end of the road, just above the falls, stood Fort Schlosser, which guarded the docks where goods were transferred from the wagons to boats for the voyage across Lake Erie. The only other defense along the trail was Fort Demler, a tiny outpost located less than two miles below Devil's Hole, the spectacular whirlpool that swirled violently in the river's deep gorge. With such meager security the narrow portage trail was particularly prone to ambush. On September 14 Seneca warriors who had been silently monitoring British activities along the carrying place finally found their opportunity to strike.[9]

A small wagon train escorted by a sergeant and twenty Redcoats was returning from Fort Schlosser to the lower landing at Fort Demler. The convoy crossed a wooden bridge that straddled a small rivulet atop the steep escarpment. At the bottom of the precipice raged the whirlpool. Without warning, hundreds of Indians jumped out of the underbrush and attacked the surprised soldiers and wagoners. The Senecas rushed in among the startled Redcoats, furiously slashing and hacking them to pieces with knives and tomahawks. The Indians shoved the wagons and draft animals over the cliff, sending them crashing to the bottom of the gorge. When a teamster named John Stedman, who was mounted on a horse, attempted to break out of the trap and ride back to Fort Schlosser, some Seneca warriors grabbed the bridle of his mount and tried to lead him into the underbrush. The resourceful teamster drew his knife and cut the bridle, spurring his horse forward to escape amid a hail of musket balls. Stedman and another wagon driver were the only men to survive the ambush.[10]

Downstream at Fort Demler Lieutenant George Campbell and two companies of the 80th Light Infantry heard the gunfire coming from Devil's Hole. With a handful of other officers, Campbell rallied about eighty men and charged up the steep escarpment to rescue the convoy. The relief column rushed forward along the narrow trail with the lieutenant and the other officers in the lead. Suddenly, an overwhelming number of Indians stepped onto the roadway and delivered a devastating volley of musket fire into the head of the column. Campbell and all of his officers toppled over dead, and the Senecas again rushed in among the stunned Redcoats. The Indians made short work of the soldiers. Only a handful of men managed to escape the slaughter. Sixteen-year-old Lemuel Matthews, a drummer boy with the 80th Regiment, stood aghast as his comrades were hacked to pieces. Preferring suicide to butchery, Matthews leaped from the top of the escarpment to the chasm below. Miraculously, the boy's leather drum strap caught on a tree branch and left him dangling above the raging river and rocks below. From his perch above the Niagara River, Matthews could hear the shrieking warriors on the road above finishing off the wounded soldiers. It was all over in minutes. When Major Wilkins and a relief party from Fort Niagara arrived at the scene the next day, they were shocked to discover the mangled bodies of their fallen comrades. One of the officers with Wilkins's relief force reported that "we found Lieut. Campbell and Sixteen Men on the road all stript and scalped and thirty-two in the same situation which the Enemy had thrown down the Rocks which with what men we found dead afterwards we can make out seventy six-kill'd and eight or nine wounded." The massacre at Devil's Hole was the most devastating defeat suffered by British forces during Pontiac's Uprising.[11]

The interruption in the flow of supplies and reinforcements from Niagara, combined with the wreck of the *Michigan*, left Major Gladwin in a precarious position. He now had only the *Huron* available to keep open his line of communications. The vessel would be kept in constant service, sailing back and forth across Lake Erie. On one such excursion the *Huron* picked up the survivors from the *Michigan* and carried them to Detroit. This force arrived at the fort on October 3, bringing with them 185 barrels of provisions. It was hardly enough food to feed the garrison for another three weeks. The long siege was taking its toll on even the most seasoned Indian fighters. Major Rogers, who had been cooped up in the fort since Dalyell's defeat, wrote to Amherst, "The Indian War will not end for Ten Months should Fifteen Hundred men be sent to Chastize them." Gladwin was equally glum. On October 7 he confided to Sir William Johnson, "What with business, vexation, and disappointment, I have scarce had time to think of any friend, much less write to them. . . . I am brought into a scrape, and left in it; things are expected of me that cant be performed; I could only wish I had quitted the service seven years ago, and that somebody else commanded here."[12]

Little did the melancholy Gladwin realize that his opponents were also tiring of the siege. Following the failed attempt to take the *Huron*, many of the Indians surrounding Detroit concluded that further resistance toward the British was useless. Provisions commandeered from the habitants were being quickly depleted, and without further plunder Pontiac's forces would not be able to sustain the siege through the winter. The warriors realized that they had precious little time to hunt and collect food to feed their families. In addition, Pontiac's rhetoric was wearing thin, and even some of the Ottawas questioned his ability as a war leader. One group of disgruntled Ottawas openly broke from Pontiac and chose to follow the leadership of Manitou. It is also possible that smallpox had finally reached the villages surrounding Fort Detroit. On October 9 Lieutenant Montresor recorded in his journal that "an Epidermical disorder rages amongst the Enemy, the Wiandots [Hurons] particular, by first a Shivering, then a fever, attended with Blotches, and in 2 days Expire."[13]

Finally, on October 11, a Mississauga chief named Wabbicomigot came into the fort to parley with Gladwin. He assured the commandant that he spoke for all the Miamis and Chippewas in expressing a desire to make peace with the English. Gladwin listened intently and informed Wabbicomigot that he did not have the authority to make peace, but if General Amherst "was thoroughly convinced of their sincerity everything would be well again." With only enough rations to last another two weeks, the major used this lull in the siege to take in twenty bushels of wheat and other provisions purchased from the habitants. A few days after the parley with Wabbicomigot, more Chippewas entered the fort to negotiate. As a sign of good faith, the Indians released six captives who had been held in their village. On October 17 Gladwin received the Chippewa chief Wasson and the Ottawa leader Manitou. It is not known if the major realized that he was negotiating with the Indian chief who had brutally murdered Captain Campbell. With provisions still low, Gladwin had little recourse but to listen to the peace entreaties delivered by Wasson. Both influential chiefs expressed their desire to resume peaceful relations with the British and promised to abandon the siege and move to their hunting grounds. The next day, the Potawatomies came into the fort and pledged to break up their camp and "retire for the winter to hunt." Almost every day, the garrison could see Indians in heavily loaded canoes paddling away. Pontiac's siege was unraveling.[14]

On October 29 a storm dumped four inches of snow on Fort Detroit, prompting Lieutenant Montresor to proclaim "an Entire appearance of winter, the Cold very intense and the ground impenetrable." The storm that blew in from the west brought with it an important emissary from the Chevalier Pierre Joseph Neyon de Villiers, the French commander in the Illinois country. When final confirmation of the Treaty of Paris had reached Neyon in late September, he had immediately dispatched a cadet named Dequindre to communicate the peace with all the Indian tribes in the vicinity and to the French habitants at Detroit. Neyon's message to the Indians read:

Open your Ears, that it may penetrate even to the Bottom of your Hearts. The great Day is come at last, whereon it has pleased the Master of life to inspire the great King of the French, and him of the English to make Peace between them, Sorry to See the Blood of Men Spilt so long. It is for this reason they have ordered all their Chiefs, and Warriors to lay down their Arms. What Joy you will have in seeing the French & English smoking with the same Pipe, and Eating out of the same Spoon, and finally living like Brethren. Leave off then, My Dear Children the spilling of the Blood of your Brethren the English. Our Hearts are now but one. You cannot strike at present the one without having the Other for an Enemy, so if you continue Hostilities you will have no Supplies, and it is from them, that you are to expect them.[15]

Neyon's dispatch left no room for doubt in the minds of Pontiac and his remaining followers. The French king was not going to wake up. With no hope for assistance from the French, Pontiac had little recourse but to terminate his siege and beg Gladwin for a truce. The next day the great Ottawa war chief sent a brief message to the major:

> The word which my Father [the French] sent me to make peace, I have accepted; all my young men have buried their hatchets: I think that you will forget all the evil things which have occurred for some time past. Likewise, I shall forget what you may have done to me, in order to think nothing but good. I, the Saultiers [Chippewas from Sault Saint Marie], the Hurons, we will come to speak when you ask us. Give us a reply. I am sending this council to you in order that you may see it. If you are as good as I, you will send me a reply. I wish you good day.[16]

Major Gladwin promptly responded to Pontiac's overture by again stating that he did not have the authority to make peace. He promised the Ottawa leader that he would communicate this desire for peace to General Amherst. After penning this reply, the major quickly sent off a dispatch to Amherst suggesting "as things are circumstanced it would be for the good of His Majesty's Service to accommodate Matters in the Spring; by that time the Savages will be Sufficiently reduced for a want of Powder, and I don't imagine there will be any danger of their breaking out again." "No advantages can be gained by prosecuting the War," Gladwin explained, "owing to the difficulty of catching them, add to this the Expence of Such a War, which if continued, the intire ruin of our Peltry Trade must follow." The major estimated that the Indians had "lost between 80, and 90, of their best Warriors; But if your Excellancy Still intends to punish them further for their Barbarities, it may be easily done without Expence to the Crown, by permitting a free Sale of Rum, which will destroy them more effectually than Fire & Sword."[17]

Thus, with little more than a whimper, the siege of Detroit came to an end. After receiving Gladwin's reply, Pontiac packed up his village and moved south, where he wintered along the Maumee River. With tranquility restored and not enough provisions to sustain such a large garrison, the major sent Robert Rogers with 240 men back to New York. Of all people, Gladwin should have rejoiced over the termination of the lengthy siege. But the weary major had to remain behind, to languish yet another winter at the remote outpost. A relief force of six hundred men commanded by Major Wilkins set out for Detroit in early November but was turned back after a violent storm wrecked the boats, drowning sixty-seven soldiers. The despondent Gladwin wrote to Bouquet, "I am heartily wearied of my command. . . . I hope I shall be relieved soon, if not, I intend to quit the service for I would not chuse to be any longer exposed to the villainy and treachery of the settlements and Indians." Gladwin's only reward for his stubborn defense of Fort Detroit was a promotion to the rank of lieutenant colonel.[18]

Another person who could not celebrate the end of the siege of Detroit was Sir Jeffery Amherst. On October 7 the general received word from London that his request to return home had finally been granted. After quickly disposing of his personal affairs, Amherst wasted little time in drawing up a plan for operations against the Indians in the spring. The general proposed that a new establishment of provincial troops be raised in the colonies to act in concert with regular forces under the command of colonels John Bradstreet and Henry Bouquet. Bradstreet would drive the Indians from Niagara to Detroit, while Bouquet would launch an expedition from Fort Pitt deep into the Ohio Country. With little fanfare, on November 18 the conceited Amherst boarded a sloop named *Weasel* and set sail for England. Amherst expected to be hailed as a conquering hero when he returned home. Instead, the general faced recriminations and accusations from a ministry that had lost significant public support as a result of the Indian uprising. George Croghan, who was still in London when Amherst arrived, gleefully wrote of the general's compromised position to Sir William Johnson: "Ginberal Amhersts Conduct is Condemned by Everybody and has been pelted away in the papers. The Army Curse him in publick as well as the Merchants."[19]

Reviled in England, Amherst was even more vehemently scorned in America. His departure was cause for celebration among some of his own officers. The defender of Fort Pitt, Captain Simeon Ecuyer, reported to Colonel Bouquet, "What universal cries of joy and what bumpers of Madeira are drunk to his prompt departure." Bouquet's friend and fellow officer, Lewis Ourry, was more direct in commenting on Amherst's departure, quipping, "bon Voyage!"[20]

Amherst's replacement was Major General Thomas Gage, a reticent and capable officer and administrator who had none of the conceit and arrogance of his predecessor. Gage had come to America at the beginning of the French and Indian War, in which he had gained experience in fighting Indians with Braddock. In the vanguard at the Battle of the Monongahela, Gage was slightly wounded while attempting to repel the Indian onslaught. The engagement taught him the advantages of having Indian allies and the utilitarian function that rangers and scouts could have while campaigning in the wilderness. Gage discovered, however, that irregular rangers were "not very alert in obeying orders," which undermined his confidence in their abilities. Consequently, he lobbied for the creation and command of a regiment of regular light infantry troops to do battle in the forests of North America. This unit, the 80th Regiment of Foot, proved quite valuable in the war against France and its Indian allies. Though Gage lacked confidence in provincial rangers, he showed little contempt for America or Americans. He counted among his friends and acquaintances Pennsylvanians such as Robert Morris and Benjamin Franklin and Virginians such as George Washington. Gage even married an American woman, Margaret Kemble, who came from an elite New Jersey family.[21]

Gage's promotion to commander in chief was welcome news to colonial officials and military officers alike, for he was recognized as tactful, good-natured, and modest. Following the cessation of hostilities with France, Gage was appointed military governor of Montreal, a sensitive position that required a great deal of administrative and diplomatic skill. Perhaps the most pointed difference between the new commander and his predecessor was Gage's willingness to defer in matters pertaining to Indian affairs to the Indian superintendent, Sir William Johnson. Perhaps the general realized that the task of subjugating the warring Indian tribes would be vexing and complicated enough without his attempting to micromanage the Indian superintendency. When Gage assumed command of His Majesty's forces in North America, fellow officer Frederick Haldimand hinted at the adversity the new commander would face: "I am very sorry, Monsieur, to see you charged with the cares of such a harassing war; the honor

Major General Thomas Gage, painting by John Singleton Copley, c. 1769. Courtesy Yale Center for British Art, Paul Mellon Collection, Yale University.

that you may acquire cannot be compared to the unpleasantness to which you will be exposed, and what is even worse, no one in Europe will realize the difficulties you must surmount."[22]

For the time being, General Gage would have few Indian disturbances to worry about. Winter weather and military setbacks suffered at Detroit and Pittsburgh had driven the Indians into their winter camps. An uneasy period of relative calm had descended on the frontier. Both Indian and Englishman understood, however, that this serenity represented only a temporary truce. The two sides had reached no tangible or definitive accord. George III had taken a step in the right

direction in October 1763 by issuing a royal proclamation barring
settlement beyond the Appalachian Mountains. This so-called Proclamation Line did nothing, however, to remove the British military
presence in the trans-Appalachian frontier. The tribes of the Ohio
Country and Great Lakes had entered the war convinced that the
English had sent troops to their land with the intention of rubbing them
out. The Indians probably had little, if any, faith in the king's present
orders to white settlers to withdraw from their lands. After all, the insatiable pioneers and land speculators had paid no attention to the previous
agreement, made at Easton in 1758, to preserve Indian land. Indeed,
wealthy investors and entrepreneurs such as George Washington, Henry
Fitzhugh, and Richard Henry Lee had already drawn up plans to solicit
the crown for a land grant as far west as the Mississippi River.[23] In
addition, there had been no effort to adjust the repugnant trade policies
and practices that kept the Indians in a perpetual state of abject
poverty. In all, the tribes could discern no progress toward redressing
their grievances with the English. The Master of Life still beckoned
them to defend what they considered to be their last sanctuary.

Sir William Johnson realized that the issues which had caused the
uprising were unresolved and that hostilities would resume with the
coming of spring. He had little time to formulate a plan that would
restore tranquility to the ravaged frontier. Johnson also became convinced that his dabbling in balance-of-power diplomacy—which had
elevated the status of the Delawares, Shawnees, and Great Lakes
tribes to a position of parity with the Iroquois—had been a tragic
mistake. In particular, he had failed to appreciate the significance of
the growing influence of the Delawares among the other refugee tribes
of the Ohio Country. Consequently, when Johnson removed the "Onondaga yoke" from the Delawares and embraced the Great Lakes tribes
as equals to the Iroquois in the Great Chain of Friendship, he further
undermined the flagging authority of the League of Six Nations.[24]
This, in turn, gave the western Senecas, whose interests were closer
to those of the western tribes, an opportunity to break ranks with the
other nations in the Iroquois confederation and assume a position of
great influence among the Indians of the Ohio Country and Great
Lakes. This diplomatic strategy had not ignited the great uprising by
itself, of course. Amherst's inflammatory policies, white encroachment
on Indian lands, and deteriorating trade conditions, had also exacerbated

the volatile situation. Perhaps Johnson's greatest mistake had been his inability to appreciate the power of Neolin's messianic rhetoric. This is particularly odd since Warraghiyagey had always exhibited great sensitivity to cultural and religious factors in treating with Indian nations. Since the Indians were secretive about Neolin's message, perhaps Sir William never knew of the movement and, therefore, was unable to counter its influence. Johnson nevertheless understood by the winter of 1763–1764 that the only way to rectify his previous diplomatic failings was to punish the Senecas for breaking away from the confederation and to restore the power, prestige, and authority of the Iroquois.

To attain his objectives, Johnson first worked to isolate the hostile Seneca faction from the rest of the Six Nations. He refused to receive the tribe's envoys and demanded that the Senecas make satisfaction for their transgressions by surrendering any claims to land along the Niagara portage. To hasten Seneca subjection, the superintendent even threatened to send other Six Nations warriors to fight any Senecas who remained bellicose. This produced the desired effect in that many New York Senecas abandoned their belligerency for fear they would lose even more land. Little by little, the Indians meekly came to Sir William to sue for peace. The superintendent's conditions for such an armistice were harsh: the Senecas were forced to cede all their territory along the Niagara portage, deliver up any hostages in their custody, discontinue their relationship with the Ohio Country tribes, and "hold fast [to] the Covenant Chain." Most of the New York Senecas agreed to comply with the superintendent's demands, leaving only warriors who resided in the Ohio Country still hostile toward the British. These Indians followed the leadership of Kiasutha and Mingo chiefs living along the Muskingum River.[25]

After isolating the more warlike Senecas from the rest of that nation, Warraghiyagey turned his attention to the Delawares, Shawnees, and Mingoes. With little difficulty he persuaded the Six Nations to mount a campaign against these recalcitrant tribes. The Iroquois were more than willing to participate in such an endeavor since it would serve to punish these former subjects for their disloyalty and force them to yield once again to Iroquois hegemony. Unlike Amherst, who found the use of Indian auxiliaries repugnant, General Gage enthusiastically endorsed the plan.[26]

In his attempt to subjugate the Delawares, Johnson summoned the noted frontiersman and interpreter Andrew Montour. On February 9 he instructed the mixed blood to lead a force of nearly two hundred Iroquois warriors (chiefly comprised of the Oneida, Tuscarora, and Mohawk nations) against hostile Indian villages along the Susquehanna River. Sir William was careful to outfit this expedition with all the "provision, Arms, Snow-Shoes & everry article [of] Ammunition excepted." Fully equipped, Montour's war party set out in three feet of snow to wreak destruction on the enemy. The first blow was struck on February 26, when Montour's warriors surrounded a Delaware village located near the forks of the Susquehanna. The Iroquois rushed into the unsuspecting camp and apprehended forty-one Delawares, including Captain Bull. While the prisoners were being bound, Captain Bull boasted of killing twenty-six Englishmen since the spring of 1763. After sending his prisoners under an armed escort to Sir William Johnson, Montour continued up the West Branch, where he succeeded in destroying three more Delaware and Shawnee towns consisting of "130 Good & well built Houses of Square timber Chimneys etc. with all the little out Settlements they [the Indians] had along the River on both sides, destroying their Cows, Hogs Horses etc. to a considerable amt. Also their takeing away all the goods & provision which they had hid under ground."[27] Johnson's plan of sending the Iroquois against the enemy tribes proved to be most effective. All the Delawares and Shawnees living along the Susquehanna River fled to other sanctuaries along the Scioto and Muskingum rivers, deep in the Ohio Country. As Sir William had predicted, the Delawares and others had much more to fear from Iroquois warriors "than the best Troops in the World."[28]

With a majority of the Senecas back in the fold and a severe blow delivered to the Delawares and Shawnees, Johnson next had to deal with the disaffected tribes near Detroit. Due to the considerable number of Indians who inhabited the region, Sir William deemed it foolhardy to send Iroquois war parties against them. He estimated that the Ottawas, Hurons, Potawatomies, Chippewas, and others included more than three thousand warriors. The Iroquois, discounting the Senecas, could muster at best no more than nine hundred men to send against the western tribes. After conferring with General Gage, the superintendent concluded that it would be prudent to accept the overtures of peace that had been offered by the Great Lakes tribes. Johnson reasoned that because the tribes were by then in abject poverty due to the cessation of trade and lack of support from the French, they would be inclined to accept the British presence in return for a resumption of trade. Warraghiyagey insisted, however, that the Indians should still make some concessions for their recent hostilities. He recommended to General Gage that the Great Lakes people deliver up any captives in their midst, dissociate themselves from the French, and banish the Jesuits from their villages. With this last demand Johnson revealed his Anglo-Protestant prejudice. He was unjustifiably convinced that the Jesuits were chiefly responsible for stirring up trouble among the Indians. Gage wholly agreed with Johnson's recommendations. "It is true that the Indians of Detroit, particularly the Ottawas under *Pondiac* . . . have acted warmly against Us," he wrote, "but they have been brought to their senses by Losses and Distress." The Indians had, Gage further stated, been "reduced to a want of every necessary, particularly Ammunition. They have been taught their Folly, by their sufferings, which is all we can desire, and not our Business to push those Indians to extremities. . . . I think it is our Interest, if we find them sincere, to close with them . . . and be thereby enabled to turn our whole force against the Rest."[29]

Thanks to Sir William Johnson's Herculean diplomatic efforts, by the spring of 1764, General Gage likely presumed that the upcoming campaign against the Indians would be little more than a mopping-up exercise. Both Gage and Johnson, however, underestimated the continued recalcitrance and resolve of the Ohio Country people. On February 24 six Indians attacked a small detachment of soldiers who were gathering wood outside Fort Pitt. Colonel Bouquet rightly concluded that the incident "seems to indicate a design [on the Indians' part] to continue the War, & probably to infest soon [the line of] Communication." A month later a small war party, lying in ambush along the Forbes Road, pursued a dispatch rider named Caleb Kennedy. The next day, March 24, the same Indians killed a settler named George Dobson near Fort Bedford.[30]

As the arrival of spring continued to warm the trans-Appalachian frontier, the raids escalated. On April 14 Gershom Hicks made his way to Fort Pitt, claiming to have escaped from the Delawares. Hicks maintained that the Indians were nearly destitute from a lack of powder and lead and that smallpox had greatly reduced the fighting spirit of the Ohio Country tribes. Captain William Grant, commanding the fort in Colonel Bouquet's absence, became suspicious of Hicks when shots rang out across the Allegheny River. The captain, sensing that Indians were skulking about the fort, began to interrogate Hicks to determine if he had any knowledge of Indians in the vicinity. For some reason, Hicks broke down and confessed that he had been with a small war party of seven Delawares who were spying on the fort. When the renegade further admitted that much of what he had told the captain earlier had been a lie, Grant threatened to hang the man unless he divulged the full truth about his involvement with the Indians and their intentions. Hicks revealed that his war party had come from a village near the headwaters of the Hockhocking River, deep in the Ohio Country. The Indians had stolen past the forts along the Forbes Road and attacked an isolated settler's cabin in Sherman's Valley, killing a husband and wife and kidnapping two children. Upon their return the Delawares convinced Hicks to enter Fort Pitt and attempt to gather intelligence regarding "what Provisions, Ammunition and Troops was in this Fort." Hicks also claimed that other war parties were in the vicinity and that the Delaware chief White Eyes had recently made an agreement to purchase twelve whaleboats filled with powder, lead, and other provisions from French traders along the Mississippi. Perhaps most disturbing, Hicks maintained that "soon in the month of May, the Ottawas & Weyondots, were to joyn with the Delawares & Shawanies, expecting to make in all about eight hundred; and that they were to keep all in a Body this Year; and that at the late Council it was to be proposed, to take this Post [Fort Pitt]; and if they miscarried, to then attempt Ligonier and Bedford, which they knew they could easily Destroy." Hicks insisted that the Indians hoped to gain entrance into the fort "under pretence to hold a Council . . . and that if they were Admitted they would endeavor to Surprize the Garrison and Murder them All."[31]

While the attack on Fort Pitt that Hicks spoke of never materialized, the raids along the Pennsylvania and Virginia frontier intensified with the coming of summer. On May 26 near Fort Cumberland, "a large body of Indians fell on a party of white people working in a field, then they killed 15 and wounded 16 more." By the first of June, reports filtering back from the Virginia frontier indicated that "within eight days upwards of 40 persons have been killed." The *Pennsylvania Gazette* reported on June 14 that Indians had struck a group of settlers near Fort Loudon: "three families were cut off, 13 of whom were killed, and their bodies together with their habitations burnt."[32]

The worst atrocity occurred in Pennsylvania's Conococheague Valley. On July 26 Schoolmaster Enoch Brown instructing twelve children in a simple log schoolhouse. Without warning, four young Delaware warriors burst into the room. Brown desperately pleaded with the Indians to spare the lives of the children. Instead, one of the Indians shot Brown in the chest and scalped him. The warriors then began to tomahawk and scalp all of the children. Hearing the shot, a few of the local farmers ran to the schoolhouse, where they found the lifeless body of Brown, who was still clutching his Bible. Strewn about the bloody room were the bodies of nine dead children. One little girl, though scalped, had managed to crawl through a window and was found sitting next to a nearby spring washing the blood from her face. The horrified settlers also discovered another child, named Archic McCullough, who was still alive inside the schoolhouse. Though scalped and bleeding, young Archie was creeping around the room, rubbing his hands over the faces of his dead companions, trying to recognize them.[33]

The same war party also killed a pregnant woman named Susan King Cunningham who lived in the vicinity of the schoolhouse. Mrs. Cunningham was murdered while on her way to visit a neighbor. The Indians bludgeoned the woman to death, scalped her, and then ripped open her abdomen, placing the lifeless fetus next to her body. Incidents such as the Enoch Brown Schoolhouse Massacre and the murder of Susan Cunningham underscore the horrific nature of the Indian's holy war to preserve their lands and way of life—a war without mercy. The brutality demonstrated by this particular Delaware war party, however, was not condoned by all the tribe's members. When the young Delawares returned to their village along the Muskingum, displaying the scalps of the children they had murdered, an old chief called the Night Walker rebuked them as cowards.[34]

In retaliation for the atrocities committed by the Indians during the spring and summer of 1764, the Pennsylvania Assembly voted to reintroduce its infamous scalp bounty system. The act, which was endorsed by the new governor, John Penn, provided $134 "for the scalp

of every Indian enemy, above the Age of Ten Years, produced as
Evidence of their being killed." The government would pay $50 for
every female scalp. One man who attempted to collect a reward for
Indian scalps was David Owens, a so-called renegade who lived among
both the Delawares and Shawnees. Owens was the son of an Indian
trader and at one time had deserted from a New York militia company.
Thereafter, he lived with the Indians and married a Delaware woman
and had three children with her. One night, while on a hunting trip
with his family and several other Delawares, Owens brutally murdered his wife and children as they quietly slept by the campfire. He
also shot two Delaware warriors who were related to his wife. After
spending the remainder of the night calmly sitting among the corpses,
the fiend scalped his victims and traveled to Philadelphia to seek a
reward for the grizzly trophies. Governor John Penn, recognizing Owens
as a "fellow not [of] the best Character," refused to pay the reward,
but he offered Owens employment as a courier and interpreter. Owens's
depravity offers yet further proof that the savagery of Pontiac's Uprising worked both ways.[35]

Throughout the bloody spring and summer of 1764, Colonel Henry
Bouquet remained restlessly idle. The old problems of raising provincial forces and gathering supplies once again hampered his ability
to strike back at the Indians. Bouquet had at his disposal only eight
companies of the Black Watch regiment and another six companies
of Royal Americans—in all, less than eight hundred men scattered
throughout the frontier. General Gage, fully aware of Bouquet's predicament, instructed his subordinate, "Disappointed in the hopes of Reinforcements of provincial Troops . . . Your first Consideration must be
only defensive measures, and the means of preserving Fort Pitt, and
the posts of Communication; which have cost so much Blood and
Treasure." The general was hopeful nonetheless that the colonies
would eventually provide the troops necessary to carry on offensive
operations.

For this reason he frequently corresponded with Bouquet and his
other commanders in order to develop a strategic plan for the upcoming
campaign. This plan, which had first been suggested by Amherst,
involved sending Colonel John Bradstreet with a mixed force of regulars, provincials, and Iroquois to ascend the Niagara portage. Bradstreet
would then sail westward along the southern shore of Lake Erie to

the enemy villages located at Sandusky. After destroying these settlements, the colonel would direct his troops toward Delaware and Shawnee strongholds along the Scioto River. Another expedition, led by Colonel Bouquet, would depart from Fort Pitt and march westward toward the Indian villages located along the Muskingum. Gage hoped that this two-pronged movement would, at the very least, prevent the Indians on the Scioto and Muskingum from cooperating with one another and create a panic amongst them. At most, the two independent expeditions could operate like a pincer, trapping the Indians between them.[36]

Clearly, the success of Gage's plan hinged on the continued pacification of the confederated tribes near Detroit, especially Pontiac's Ottawas. Should these Indians once again rise up against the English, Colonel Bradstreet could find himself caught between the Detroit tribes and the Delawares and Shawnees living along the Scioto River. In early April 1764 Major Gladwin, still at Detroit, reported with relief that "the Indians here are still quiet at their hunting grounds." There was, however, little news of Pontiac or his intentions. Then, on April 14, General Gage received word by way of a packet ship from New Orleans that the great Ottawa war chief was headed west into the Illinois country in an attempt to recruit the tribes of that region to join him in the war against the British. Gage also learned that Pontiac hoped to make a final appeal to the French commander Major Pierre Joseph Neyon de Villiers to resume the war.

Apparently, the chief was not convinced of the sincerity of Neyon's earlier message to the Detroit tribes to lay down their arms and join in the great peace that had been made in Paris. After traveling twenty-one days, Pontiac reached Neyon's headquarters at Fort de Chartres, on the east bank of the Mississippi River. Pontiac opened the conference with the French commander by saying, "The Master of Life who deliberates everything has had regard to the prayers which I have made to Him. . . . I come to discover to thee my heart and to know of thee thyself what thou thinkest." The chief lied to Neyon about the status of his siege: "I have left my army at Detroit, who continue there the war against the English and who will not end it until there are no more red men. They would rather die with their tomahawks in their hands than live in slavery with which the English menace them." Still hoping to convince the French to resume hostilities against the British, Pontiac appealed to Neyon to heed the words of the prophet Neolin:

> Thou knowest the Master of Life; it is He who had put arms in our hands and it is He who has ordered us to fight against this bad meat [the English] that would come to infect our lands. If I was the first red man that held this opinion, thou might say, "Pontiac is a liar"; but the Abenakies, the Iroquois, the Shawnees, the Chippewas, in short all the nations of the continent hold this discourse and they are correct. All the answers to the demands I have made thee are to bury my tomahawk. Think then, my father, that thou goest against the orders of the Master of Life, and that all red men conform to His will. Thus I pray thee to talk to me no more of a peace with the English, because I hate them.[37]

Neyon, after listening intently to Pontiac's address, responded by repeating that it was the will of the French king that the Indians and English live in peace. He then chastised the chief for attempting to incite the Illinois tribes into a war that would lead to their destruction. In the end, Neyon offered Pontiac no powder, lead, or other supplies and instructed him to go back home and remain peaceful. With that, Pontiac departed. The chief remained in the Illinois country until July, still hoping to exhort the Indians there to join him. Perhaps he also spent time trying to convince local French traders to supply him with powder and lead. In the end, all his efforts failed, and the once powerful war leader returned to his village along the Maumee River.[38]

When Gage learned the details of Pontiac's attempt to cajole the French into continuing the war, he denounced the chief "As a Savage, possessed of the most refined Cunning and Treachery natural to the Indians." The general hastily sent a dispatch to Gladwin to be on his guard against Pontiac: "If you can clearly prove that he makes peace for want of means to carry on the war, and that you plainly see, we are to expect further proofs of his treachery, the moment he has it in his power to exert it, we must not be guilty of so much weakness and folly, as to wait the Stroke, but prevent it by surprising him and his Crew and putting the whole to the sword." The general reasoned that the other Great Lakes tribes would welcome Pontiac's execution "as they will see themselves the necessity of such a measure to restore tranquility to the country. I believe many of them will be glad to be freed from the trouble they are often brought into by this turbulent and enterprising Savage, who seems to bully and make himself dreaded by all the tribes round the country."[39]

For the most part, the Indians around Detroit had grown tired of Pontiac's rhetoric and had elected to follow new leaders, who wished to restore peace with the English. When it became apparent to General Gage that the Indians of Detroit were no longer inclined to resume the war, he turned his attention to the unfinished task of subjugating the still-hostile Delawares and Shawnees residing in the Ohio Country. By the beginning of July, everything was ready for Colonel John Bradstreet to launch his punitive expedition against the Indians of Sandusky and the Scioto River.

Bradstreet, the son of a British army officer, had gained an enviable reputation during the French and Indian War. In 1758 he had led an expedition that captured the French stronghold of Fort Frontenac, located at the mouth of the Saint Lawrence River on Lake Ontario. Amherst had rewarded Bradstreet by making him quartermaster general of British forces in North America. The colonel now seemed a perfect choice to lead such a dangerous mission. Before the campaign concluded, however, many officers in the British army, from General Gage down, would accuse Bradstreet of being duped by the Indians and conducting himself in a dishonorable fashion.[40]

Before Colonel Bradstreet could begin his push toward the Scioto, he first had to secure his supply line. The massacre at Devil's Hole had made it all too apparent that the Niagara portage was extremely vulnerable. Consequently, the indefatigable army engineer Lieutenant John Montresor set about erecting a series of log redoubts, spaced roughly one thousand yards apart, to protect the strategic trail along the Niagara River. The colonel also had to arrange for transports and supplies. He ordered Captain Joshua Loring to Oswego to oversee the construction of massive whaleboats, forty-six feet long, large enough to carry twenty-seven men and three weeks' provisions. In the meantime, Major Thomas Mante, acting as Bradstreet's aide-de-camp, worked to collect powder, lead, rations, and other supplies for the campaign. While General Amherst had been miserly in his prosecution of the war, it seems that Gage would spare no expense in preparing to do battle with the resourceful tribes of the forest.[41]

Colonel Bradstreet also wished to secure a force of Iroquois allies to serve with his command. To this end Sir William Johnson sent messages to the Six Nations chiefs directing them to send warriors to rendezvous at Niagara in July. Johnson also planned to use this gathering to formalize peace with the Senecas and any of the Great Lakes tribes that might wish to restore the Chain of Friendship with the English. The Indian superintendent offered explicit instructions to Bradstreet regarding how to command his Indian auxiliaries: "It will be necessary on Seeing the Indians to address them with affability," Johnson suggested, and "to see that they are properly cloathed, & armed, also victualled plentifully, with a Dram likewise Morning & Evening." The superintendent also appealed to Bradstreet to frequently counsel with the Iroquois, especially before undertaking any "unexpected or sudden movement."[42]

On July 7 Sir William Johnson arrived at Niagara to conduct his grand council with the assembled tribes. The sight must have been gratifying to Warraghiyagey. Complying with his will, more than seventeen hundred Indians had gathered around the fort. For three weeks the superintendent met with each delegation and formalized agreements with various bands of Ottawas, Chippewas, and Hurons. Johnson liberally dispensed rum and £25,000 in presents to the Indians. At the end of the council, Sir William met with the Senecas, who meekly informed him that they would comply with all the articles of peace. As a gesture of their sincerity the Indians delivered up thirteen hostages.[43]

By the time Johnson had finished his negotiations with the Indians, Bradstreet had assembled his expeditionary force and was prepared to set off for the West. The command consisted of nearly 341 regulars from the 17th and 55th regiments of foot; 766 provincials from New York, Connecticut, and New Jersey; seventy-three sailors to pilot the whaleboats; and more than 250 Indian allies. On August 8 the large flotilla departed Fort Schlosser and entered Lake Erie. As the command approached the ruins of Fort Presque Isle, gale-like winds forced the boats ashore at a point known as L'Ance aux Sevilles.[44]

There on August 12 a party of ten Indians approached Bradstreet's camp. The warriors claimed to be a delegation representing the Delawares, Shawnees, Hurons, and "the five Nations of Indians inhabiting the Scioto plains." The envoys explained to Bradstreet that they had been informed that a great army was coming against them and that they had immediately called in all their war parties from the frontier. They begged the colonel to show them mercy and assured him that they were empowered to conclude a peace with the English. Bradstreet should have been suspicious of this sudden change of heart on the part of the Delawares and Shawnees. If they were truly sincere in their desire to bring an end to the hostilities, why had they not traveled to Niagara to confer with Sir William Johnson, the only man authorized to conclude peace with the warring tribes? Instead of sending these envoys to Johnson, Bradstreet determined to finalize a peace treaty with the Indians himself. The colonel insisted that the Indians gather all their hostages at Sandusky and prepare to deliver them up when he arrived. All the chiefs of the various tribes must also be present to ratify the peace. Bradstreet further demanded that the Indians agree to "relinquish their claims to the Forts and Posts the English now have in their Country and that the English shall be at Liberty to build and erect as many Forts or Trading Houses as they may find necessary." Lastly, the colonel declared that in the future, the Indians must give up any tribal member who kills or plunders any white person. Retaining six of the diplomats as hostages, Bradstreet then sent the remaining Indians back to their villages to inform their kinsmen of the proposed council at Sandusky.[45]

Bradstreet departed the next day and, by August 23, reached Sandusky Bay. He was met by a delegation of chiefs from the Miami and Scioto rivers. Wishing to keep the English army away from their villages, the Indians asked for more time in order to collect their hostages. Again, the naive Bradstreet agreed to the request. Had he marched his force overland toward the Indian towns, the warriors would have been much more eager to accept terms of peace. The colonel apparently harbored grandiose dreams of subduing all the Indians of the Great Lakes without firing a shot. Consequently, he decided to invite the various tribes that occupied the Illinois country, as well, to come to Detroit to make peace. Before departing for Detroit, Bradstreet decided to dispatch Captain Thomas Morris of the 17th Foot with a boatload of presents to visit the western tribes and make overtures of peace.[46]

Captain Morris was accompanied by a motley and dangerous crew comprising two servants, twelve Indians from the Miami River, and five Mohawks who were ordered to row the boat filled with presents.

Morris's guide was none other than Jacques Godfroy, the Detroit habitant who had served as an emissary for Pontiac and had helped to plan the massacre of the British garrison at Fort Miami. The captain was also accompanied by an Ottawa chief named Atawang who had a village along the Maumee River and by the notorious Chippewa leader Wasson, who had brutally murdered Captain Campbell outside Fort Detroit. Needless to say, Morris had no idea as to the character of the company he was keeping, or he might have refused to go on such a dangerous mission.[47]

On August 27 Morris and his party approached a Miami Indian village located on the banks of the Maumee River. Suddenly Morris and his party found themselves surrounded "by Pondiac's army, consisting of six hundred savages, with tomahawks in their hands." Morris later recorded the tense moment in a letter to Colonel Bradstreet: "In a word, I gave myself over for lost, especially as I could observe them to be even more exasperated than curious, tho they gazed at me as at a Monster." The Indians conducted Morris into the town and directed him to sit down on a large bearskin spread on the ground. Presently, Pontiac himself came and sat down beside Morris. The great Ottawa leader asked the captain if he had come to tell lies like the rest of the Englishmen. The chief insisted that the "French king was not crushed as the English had reported, but had got upon his legs again." As proof, Pontiac presented a letter stating that a large French army had landed in Louisiana and was preparing to march up the Mississippi Valley. Morris tried to assure Pontiac that the message was a fabrication. When the council resumed the following day, Pontiac told the French interpreter Godfroy, "I will lead the nations to war no more; let 'em be at peace if they chuse it: but I myself will never be a friend to the English. I shall now become a wanderer in the woods; and if they [the British] come to seek me there, while I have an arrow left, I will shoot at them." To Morris's relief, the chief then rose to address the other tribal leaders, declaring, "We must not kill ambassadors."[48]

After the council adjourned, Morris and his liberated party continued up the river, pausing at various Indian camps to deliver their peace overtures. At one point the captain "met an Indian on a handsome white horse, which had been General Braddock's, and had been taken ten years before when that General was killed on his march to Fort du Quesne." The peace delegation reached the ruins of Fort Miami on September 7, where they were met by "almost the whole village, who had brought spears and tomahawks, in order to dispatch [Morris]; even little children had bows and arrows to shoot at the Englishman who was come among them." The Indians pulled Morris across the shallow river, stripped him, and brought him bound into the village, where he was tied to a stake. The captain was certain that torture and death were to follow. Then a Miami chief named Pacanne rode into the village and ordered his warriors to release the captain. "If you want meat," declared the chief, "go to Detroit, or upon the lake (meaning go face your enemies the English) and you'll find enough. What business have you with this man's flesh, who has come to speak with us."

The relieved Morris learned that the town was filled with Kicka-poo, Mascouten, and Ouiatenon Indians who wanted no part of a peace with the English. Also present in the village were a delegation of fifteen Delawares and Shawnees who had come bearing war belts to distribute to the various western tribes. The Shawnees and Delawares begged the Miamis to put Morris to death and "loaded the English with the heaviest reproaches; and added, that while the sun shone they would be at enmity with [the British]." While sparing his life, Pacanne advised Morris to proceed no further and return to Detroit as quickly as possible. Having already escaped death on several occasions, the captain readily concluded that his peace mission should be immediately aborted. With that, Morris hastily "struck into the wood with Godfroy." After traveling more than 240 miles, the captain arrived safely at Detroit on September 17. It had been a har-rowing mission, and Morris was able to report to Colonel Bradstreet that the western tribes were far from being reconciled to the British interest.[49]

While Captain Morris was negotiating with Pontiac and the western tribes, Bradstreet continued on his journey to Fort Detroit, arriving at the outpost on August 26. The approach of this large flotilla of men and supplies was certainly a welcome sight to the steadfast garrison. Major Mante noted that the fort's defenders, "having sustained a long and severe blockade, during which they had experienced the want of every necessary of life, required more than ordinary refresh-ment. It may, therefore, be easily conceived, how the transition to ease and plenty, effected by the Colonel's arrival, operated on their spirits."

Perhaps no one was more thrilled to witness Bradstreet's approach than Henry Gladwin. At last the weary soldier could go home.[50]

The hundreds of Ottawa, Chippewa, and Potawatomie Indians who gathered around the fort were also awed by the size of Bradstreet's army. With so many Redcoats camped near Detroit, Bradstreet encountered little difficulty in convincing the Indians to accept his demands for peace. Chief Wasson, speaking on behalf of the assembled Ottawas and Chippewas, told Bradstreet, "Tis God's will our hearts are now altered. . . . Tis God's will also, there should be peace and tranquillity all over the face of the earth and of the waters. Everything that was done last year bad, was done by the old warriors, without cause: We have turned them on one side." Bradstreet's terms were identical to those offered the Delawares and Shawnees: the Indians must give up all their hostages, reject the French, and become subjects of King George III. After concluding his peace with the Indian nations around Detroit, the colonel and his command departed for Sandusky to conclude matters with the Delawares and Shawnees.[51]

When Bradstreet arrived at Sandusky on September 18, he was met by a delegation of Delaware, Shawnee, and Miami Indians who informed him that they needed more time to collect their white hostages. Once more the colonel acquiesced to their request but moved his command up the Sandusky River in order to be in closer proximity to their villages. While encamped along the river, the colonel received a letter from General Gage severely chastising him for concluding a peace treaty with the Delawares and Shawnees that did "not contain the smallest satisfaction to the Nation for the Traitorous Proceedings or the horrid and cruel Massacres those Indians have been Guilty of from their first Insurrection to within these few Weeks." Continuing his condemnation of Bradstreet's treaty, Gage decried the absence of even one article in the agreement that would "deter them [the Indians] from recommencing their Butcheries the next Year and cutting our Throats the first Opportunity." The general reminded Bradstreet that he had been given express orders to attack the Shawnees and Delawares and to "offer" peace only to the other tribes. After upbraiding his subordinate, Gage informed the colonel that he would not "confirm any Peace so derogatory to the Honor and Credit of His Majesty's Arms amongst the Indian Nations." Gage closed by ordering the colonel to "act as much as possible in concert with Colonel Bouquet."[52]

As General Gage alluded in his letter, Bouquet was nearly ready to begin his own campaign against the warring tribes holed up along the Muskingum River. Gathering the necessary troops and supplies for his expedition had been a long and protracted ordeal for Bouquet. It was not until May 20 that the Pennsylvania Assembly had authorized the recruitment of one thousand militiamen to participate in the proposed campaign. It took Governor John Penn another eleven days to agree to pay the £55,000 necessary to arm and equip the provincial forces. More delays ensued when the assembly demanded that all back pay due the militia had to be satisfied before new troops could be raised. This required an additional four weeks before the governor could come up with the funds. Bouquet also had to settle unpaid bills owed to government contractors before they would begin to arrange for new supplies and transports for the army. The colonel became so frustrated that he wrote to General Gage, "I flatter myself that you will do me the favor to have me relieved from this Command, as I begin to feel my strength unequal to the burthen and fatigues of it."[53]

Slowly, Bouquet's efforts began to pay off. By the first week of August, two battalions of the Pennsylvania troops rendezvoused at Carlisle to begin the march to Fort Pitt. Governor Penn traveled from Philadelphia to animate the soldiers and transfer formal command to Colonel Bouquet. Addressing the provincials on August 5, the governor reminded them of the "repeated and unprovoked barbarities" perpetrated on the citizens by the Indians. He encouraged them "to do honour to their country" and promised "that they could not but hope to be crowned with the same success, as they were to be united with the same regular troops, and under the same able commander, who had by themselves, on that very day, the memorable 5th of August in the preceding year, sustained the repeated attacks of the savages, and obtained a compleat victory over them." Notwithstanding Governor Penn's words of encouragement, a large number of provincials had their doubts about the success of the campaign, and more than two hundred deserted within the first week, carrying with them all their weapons and equipment.[54]

When the army reached Fort Loudon, Bouquet received word of Bradstreet's treaty with the Delawares and Shawnees. The colonel was astonished by the terms of the peace and complained to General Gage, "Had Col. Bradstreet been as well informed as I am, of the horrid

Perfidities of the Delawares and Shawnesse . . . he never could have compromised the Honor of the Nation by such disgraceful conditions." As Bouquet continued his march to Fort Pitt, more evidence surfaced indicating that the Ohio Country tribes had no intention of fulfilling the promises made to Bradstreet. Christopher Lems, the ranger captain who operated out of Bedford, wrote to Bouquet that he had found the mangled corpse of a man named Isaac Stimble, lying a short distance from the fort. Tracks indicated that the unfortunate man had been ambushed by a party of thirty to forty Indians. Two days later, on August 25, the Indians killed a woman near Fort Cumberland. The bold warriors crept near enough to Bouquet's camp to attack a lone sentinel who was guarding the livestock herd. As the expedition inched closer to Fort Pitt, the colonel received more distressing reports of enemy atrocities. Alexander McKee, the interpreter and deputy Indian agent from Fort Pitt, was returning to Pittsburgh after carrying dispatches to Colonel Bradstreet when he found the head of an unidentified man stuck on a pole in the middle of the trail. This was a clear warning from the Delawares not to come any closer to their villages.[55]

Bouquet reached Fort Pitt on September 18, 1764, and was surprised to find several Delawares, including the chief known as Captain Pipe, waiting to see him. The Indians had arrived at the fort the day before to inquire whether or the rumors about the peace made by Colonel Bradstreet were true. Bouquet informed the Indians that they had already violated the agreement by continuing their depredations on the frontier. "As I now consider You as a People whose Promises I can no more trust," the colonel told them, "I was determined to attack you. . . . But I will put it once more in your Power to prevent your total Destruction and save yourselves and your Familys, by giving us Satisfaction for the Hostilitys committed against us." Bouquet then instructed the Indians to go to their villages and tell the tribal leaders to come and meet with him. Bouquet further demanded that the tribes collect all of their hostages and be prepared to deliver them up. To insure that the Indians would return with an answer, he retained Captain Pipe and another tribesman as hostages. The warriors then crossed back over the Allegheny and made their way to the Delaware villages along the Muskingum.[56]

After the Delawares departed, Bouquet wasted little time making final preparations for his campaign. The assembled twelve hundred troops, which must have made an awe-inspiring sight at the fort, represented the largest military force stationed at the forks of the Ohio since General Forbes's campaign back in 1758. The backbone of the expeditionary force consisted of the battle-tested regulars from the 42nd and 60th Foot. The 316 Highlanders were commanded by Lieutenant Colonel John Reid, a career soldier from Scotland who had participated in the grueling campaign in the West Indies in 1762. The 113 Royal Americans who accompanied the expedition were under the command of Major Jacques (James) Marcus Prevost, whose older brother was the overall commander of the regiment. Like Bouquet, Prevost hailed from a Swiss Huguenot background and had been in America since the beginning of the French and Indian War. In support of the regulars were nearly five hundred Pennsylvania provincials under the command of lieutenant colonels Asher Clayton and Turbutt Francis. Clayton was an experienced Indian fighter who had been wounded during Grant's defeat in 1758. Francis, on the other hand, seems to have had little experience in campaigning against Indians and owed his commission to his family's prominent status. Francis's younger brother, Tench, had been the man who stole away and married Colonel Bouquet's sweetheart, Anne Willing.[57]

Many of the men who enlisted in the ranks of the Pennsylvania battalions had experienced firsthand the horrors of Indian warfare and were eager for revenge. Wives and children of some soldiers had been murdered or taken into captivity. Among the men was Lieutenant James Smith, who had himself been taken captive by the Indians during Braddock's campaign in 1755. He lived with the Indians for nearly five years before he escaped and returned home to the Conococheague Valley. When the Indians began to raid the settlements in the summer of 1763, Smith organized a group of young men into a ranger company in a futile attempt to protect the valley. Smith's rangers were outfitted and dressed "in the Indian manner, with breech-clout, leggings, mockesons and green shrouds." Smith recalled, "In place of hats we wore red handkerchiefs, and painted our faces red and black, like Indian warriors." Because of their appearance, the men became known as the Black Boys. Smith relinquished command of his rangers in order to accept a commission in one of the Pennsylvania battalions.[58]

Appreciating the value of experienced frontiersmen like James Smith, Bouquet employed a large contingent of volunteers from Virginia.

These woodsmen, commanded by Major John Field, were selected to march in advance of Bouquet's main column. Field's experience as an Indian fighter perhaps predated that of everyone else in the army. He had fought with both Braddock and Forbes and had commanded various militia units on the Virginia frontier throughout the long and bitter years of border conflict. George Washington regarded Field as an "extremely active, brave, and zealous officer." There was little chance that the army would be caught in an Indian ambush with Field screening the advance.[59] To round out Field's ranger force, Colonel Bouquet also enlisted small groups of frontiersmen from both Maryland and Pennsylvania.

To guide the expedition, the colonel selected a quartet of experienced traders who were intimately familiar with the Ohio Country. Alexander Lowrey, the chief guide, was born in Ireland and settled with his family in Lancaster County, Pennsylvania, in 1729, where his father opened a trading post. Alexander started his own trading firm in partnership with Edward Shippen in 1744. Five years later, the French and Indians killed Lowrey's brother during a trading expedition in the Ohio Country. During the onset of Pontiac's Uprising, Lowrey lost most of his trade goods in an Indian attack. Like many men on this expedition, Lowrey may have been motivated to sign on by a desire to settle scores. Perhaps the most curious appointment that Bouquet made in preparing for his campaign was to select the notorious scalp hunter David Owens to serve as his interpreter.[60]

As usual, Bouquet saw to every detail in organizing his command. He ordered special rifle companies to be established among the Pennsylvania battalions. The men in these companies were selected from among the best shots in a marksmanship contest in which winners received a cash prize. Bouquet's employment of these special "riffelemen" underscores his talent for incorporating innovative ideas into military doctrine. Rifled weapons were as yet uncommon among regular European military forces. During the French and Indian War, some British officers discovered that their Indian adversaries often favored the weapons over more conventional smoothbore arms. While acknowledging that firepower took precedence over accuracy in combat, Bouquet realized the advantage of having the best marksmen armed with rifles. The colonel ordered the officers to inspect each man's weapon every morning.

Drawing on his experiences in Indian warfare of the year before, the colonel carefully prescribed an order of march and camp configuration that offered the best protection against a surprise attack. He insisted that the soldiers march in complete silence six feet apart. The colonel further directed that the one thousand packhorses and the supply wagons, cattle, and sheep be carefully guarded by infantry and light horse troops. To chart the progress of his march, Bouquet assigned the army engineer Lieutenant Thomas Hutchins to make detailed maps of the route, taking note of special topographical features, river courses, and Indian towns. The colonel was even so thorough in his plans as to make out a list of the six "Promoters of the War" that he hoped to capture and eventually execute. The list included the Wolf, the warrior who had murdered the Clapham family near Fort Pitt, and the Delaware prophet Neolin.[61]

The expedition crossed the Allegheny River on October 3 and traveled down the Ohio to the old village of Loggstown, which the half king Monacatootha had destroyed in 1754. After crossing the Beaver River, the mile-long column left the Ohio behind and proceeded west toward the Muskingum. In the next eleven days, the command marched an uneventful ninety-two miles until reaching the Tuscarawas branch of the Muskingum, the site of an abandoned Indian village once inhabited by Tamaqua. It was here, on October 14, that two couriers returning from Colonel Bradstreet's command approached Bouquet's camp. The two men explained that they had been captured by a party of Delawares and taken to their town sixteen miles away. When the Indians had become aware of the close proximity of Colonel Bouquet's army, they had released the couriers, directing them to take a message to the commander stating that they were prepared to discuss terms for peace at Tuscarawas. The message was signed with the marks of eleven Delaware chiefs and warriors, including Killbuck and the great prophet Neolin. Bouquet agreed to meet with the Indians and moved his camp several miles downstream on the Muskingum so as to be closer to their villages.[62]

The council was held on October 17 under a "conference bower" that Bouquet's soldiers erected. At last, Henry Bouquet came face-to-face with the Indians who had fought him at Bushy Run and had spread terror throughout the border. The delegation was led by none other than Kiasutha, the Seneca headman who had helped to instigate

the conflict. Turtle's Heart, the Delaware chief who tried to convince
Captain Ecuyer to surrender Fort Pitt, was also present. Perhaps most
important, two Delaware leaders who had always advocated peace
and accommodation—Tamaqua and Custaloga—also came to meet
with the colonel. Although the significance of their presence was
probably lost on Bouquet, it was a strong indication that the peace
faction had finally gained the upper hand among the Delawares. Also
significant was the presence of only one Shawnee chief, Keissinaut-
chta, at the council.

As befitting his status as a half king, Kiasutha opened the negotiations by holding out a string of wampum and proclaiming to Bouquet,
"In the name of all the Chiefs here present, of the Senecas, Delawares & Shawanese, we clean your Ears that you may hear what
they are going to say, which is nothing but good." This was a common
salutation at the beginning of each council, and it illustrates the use
of metaphor in Native American conversation and diplomacy. For
the Indians, the forests were seething with spirits—both good and
bad. Consequently, anyone traveling through this metaphysical environment could be seduced by thoughts of evil or influenced by bad
intentions. Thus, Kiasutha's remarks were part of a timeless discourse
designed to clear away any preconceptions Colonel Bouquet may have
developed about the Indians' sincerity.[63] "It's owing to the Western
Nations & our foolish Young Men," the Seneca chief continued, "that
this War happened between us. It is neither your fault nor ours. . . .
Now we have thrown everything bad away & nothing remains in
our Heart but Good . . . what we say comes not only from our Lips,
but from the bottom of our Hearts." As proof of his sincerity Kiasutha
produced a magnificent wampum belt made from ten rows of shell
beads. He then informed Bouquet that the Indians were prepared to
return all the white prisoners in their hands. As a sign of good faith
the Indians then released eighteen white prisoners, promising to bring
in the remainder of their hostages as soon as they could collect them
from the other villages.

As was customary, Bouquet did not reply immediately to Kiasutha's speech. Protocol demanded that any response be carefully
considered and then delivered the following day. Due to "the badness
of the Weather," the council did not reconvene until October 20. When
Bouquet finally delivered his reply to Kiasutha's oratory, he did not

Bouquet's conference with the Indians on the Muskingum, 1764. This sketch by eyewitness Thomas Hutchins originally appeared as a cartouche illustrating his 1765 map of the campaign. The drawing shows Bouquet seated within the arbor and being addressed by an Indian leader holding a wampum belt. Nearby stand a Highland soldier and what appears to be a member of the Royal American Regiment. Also noticeable are a white woman captive with her mixed-blood child (to the right of the arbor) and another Native woman clutching what may be a white infant captive (left foreground). This Indian woman appears to be crying over the thought of losing her adopted infant. Courtesy Fort Ligonier, Pennsylvania.

adopt a conciliatory tone. He claimed that the chief's attempts to blame the Great Lakes tribes and the "foolish young men" were a mere pretense. "You have begun this War without the least Reason or Provocation whatsoever," Bouquet said. The colonel went on to register a long list of atrocities that the Indians had committed during the war, including the murder of Major Clapham, the murder and plundering of numerous traders, the attack on Fort Pitt, and the killing of Schoolmaster Enoch Brown and his pupils. "Your conduct has always been equally perfidious," Bouquet added. "You promised at every former Treaty, as you do now, that you would deliver up all your Prisoners . . . but you have never complied with that nor any of your Engagements." Bouquet demanded, as a condition to any further negotiations, that the Indians bring in all their prisoners within twelve days. To further intimidate the Indians, Bouquet announced that he would continue his march up the Muskingum River toward their villages and that a chief from each of the nations should accompany him. After this stunning rebuke, the council adjourned, and the Indians returned to their towns to collect their hostages.[64]

On October 25 Bouquet's army reached the forks of the Muskingum (present-day Coshocton, Ohio), where the colonel ordered that another bower be "Erected for receiving the Indian Deputies & holding Conferences with them." Once the Redcoats had made camp, white hostages began trickling into the British lines. There were many heart-wrenching scenes as the Indians parted with their adopted loved ones. Some of these captives had been held since childhood and had forgotten their native languages. Indian husbands, sobbing and wailing, bade farewell to wives as adopted white children were torn screaming from their Indian parents. In some cases captives came into camp bound in order to prevent them from fleeing back to the Indian villages. When Tamaqua and Custaloga brought in fifty-seven hostages, the chiefs explained that "our reasons for doing it tonight, is perhaps some of them may attempt to run away. You can take better care of them than we." Not all the captives were despondent over their redemption. A number of men among the Pennsylvania troops enjoyed tearful reunions with wives and children. In all, the Indians released 206 white captives.[65]

As the release of hostages unfolded, Colonel Bouquet recognized that the Shawnees were reluctant to comply. He also noticed that Shawnee tribal leaders shied away from the frequent conferences and negotiations that were taking place between the Ohio Country people and the British. Indeed, the Shawnee villages were bitterly divided over whether to make peace with the Redcoats. Perhaps one reason for this continued defiance was the growing influence of a mixed-blood Shawnee leader named Charlot Kaské. Kaské, whose father was German, had married a white woman captive. Thus his children were three-quarters European. Nonetheless, he hated the English and was recognized as a great war leader among the Shawnee. Like Pontiac, Kaské had a strong attachment to the French and had traveled to the Illinois country to seek material support from the commander of Fort de Chartres. The Shawnee leader later provided the French governor of Louisiana with a list of forty-seven Indian villages "that desire to die attached to the French, while defending their lands up to the last drop of their blood." Despite this profession of loyalty, French officials rebuffed Kaské's appeals and encouraged him to bury the war hatchet. French traders living in the Illinois country, however, gladly sent the Shawnees sixteen hundred pounds of powder and lead to continue the war against the British. This ammunition was being distributed among the Shawnee villages just as Colonel Bouquet began his negotiations with the Ohio Country people along the Muskingum.[66]

While some Shawnees, emboldened by a fresh supply of powder and lead, wished to continue the fight, others were uncertain. Kaské was away in the Illinois country trying to drum up support from the French. Without their influential leader the more militant Shawnees had to yield to the increasing pressure coming from their grandfathers the Delawares and their brothers the Senecas. A Shawnee headman named Red Hawk came to Bouquet with thirty-six prisoners and promised that the rest would be delivered up in the spring at Fort Pitt. With winter fast approaching, Bouquet had little recourse but to accept the Shawnee's overtures of peace.[67]

Once a truce had been negotiated with the reluctant Shawnees, Colonel Bouquet was ready to deliver his final demands to the assembled Indians. They had to agree to put an immediate end to all hostilities; they must redeem the remainder of their hostages at Fort Pitt as soon as possible; and they had to send delegations to Sir William Johnson to formalize the peace. To insure compliance, Bouquet demanded that each nation supply him with Indian hostages to take back to Fort Pitt. The Indians agreed to all of the colonel's stipulations.[68]

With cold weather pressing on them, Bouquet's men broke camp on November 18 and began the long march back to the forks of the Ohio. A number of Indians traveled with the troops in order to remain close to their adopted wives and children. The grief-stricken warriors came into the military camp bringing fresh game and other provisions for their loved ones. When the column reached Fort Pitt on November 28, many frontier settlers were waiting to receive their long-lost family members. These reunions were not always joyful, since many of the hostages had become acculturated to Indian ways. Later, a Shawnee chief named Lawoughqua pleaded with the English settlers: "We have taken as much Care of these Prisoners, as if they were our own Flesh, and blood; they are become unacquainted with your Customs, and manners, and therefore, Father we request you will use them tender, and kindly."[69]

Those captives who did not have family waiting for them at Fort Pitt continued the journey with Colonel Bouquet to the settlements east of the mountains. At every hamlet anxious family members gathered in the hope of being reunited with their wives, children, brothers, and sisters. One of the more touching legends of Pennsylvania's frontier history comes from one such reunion. According to the story, when Colonel Bouquet and his redeemed hostages arrived at Carlisle in January 1765, a large crowd assembled hoping to find some family member. One old German woman named Leininger paced back and forth in front of the line of captives. Her two daughters, Regina and Barbara, had been captured by the Delawares shortly after Braddock's defeat in 1755. Barbara, who was older than Regina, managed to escape from the Indians in 1759 and eventually returned home to her family. Nothing was known of Regina's fate, however, and her mother had given up on the prospect of ever seeing her again. Finally Mrs. Leininger stood before a slender young girl dressed in Indian garb. The child bore some resemblance to the daughter she had lost, but nothing the old woman could say brought any sign of recognition from the youngster. Finally, Colonel Bouquet stepped forward and suggested to Mrs. Leininger that she sing a hymn or song that might be familiar to the child. As the distraught woman began to sing Regina's favorite hymn, the child's memory of her past life came rushing back, and she flung herself into her mother's arms.[70]

With the final return of the captives, the great Indian uprising of 1763–1764 came to an end. Neither side could claim any decisive victory in the conflict. The British army had expended thousands of pounds sterling and hundreds of lives in its failed attempt to subdue the nations of the Ohio Country and Great Lakes. While Bouquet's expedition to the Muskingum wrested some concessions and hostages from the Indians, they remained in their homelands, defying any form of absolute British subjection and still insisting that the trans-Appalachian region belonged to them. Accordingly, they expected the British to pay tribute for permission to erect forts and other establishments on Indian land. They also remained adamant that trade with them be conducted on a fair and equitable basis. Above all, they expected the British to keep their promise to prohibit settlement on their lands. In the end, Gage, Johnson, Bouquet, and the powerful Lords of Trade agreed that accommodation was infinitely preferable to a protracted, costly, and bitter war.

On the other hand, the Indians had failed to push the English back across the mountains as the Master of Life commanded. Slowly and grudgingly they realized that the French father was not going to wake up and assist them in repelling the English invaders. Without trade or plunder the tribes lacked the means to continue their struggle indefinitely. They could no longer fight and feed their families at the same time. While they had, in many cases, proved their superiority on the field of battle, their own numbers had been greatly reduced by war, famine, and disease. In addition, the Ohio Country people, having attempted to assert their independence from the Six Nations, were dejected to find themselves once again gravitating toward Iroquois hegemony. Like their British adversaries, the Indians were utterly exhausted by the war. Now both sides were willing to seek accommodation and improved relations through new diplomatic initiatives.

While British authorities and the Indian nations groped for peace, however, other forces worked to undermine any such reconciliation. The beleaguered frontier settlers who had borne the brunt of Indian warfare for ten years were not so quick to forgive and forget. They nourished deep-seated resentment not only against the Indians but also toward the provincial and imperial authorities that had failed to protect them. Buried deep inside this smoldering hatred and resentment lay the seeds of revolution.

8

"THE ENDS OF THE AMERICAN EARTH"

When Henry Bouquet returned to Philadelphia in January 1765, the local citizenry hailed him as a conquering Caesar. In recognition of the "great services" he had rendered to the province, the General Assembly of Pennsylvania passed a resolution extending to Bouquet "a most sincere and hearty thanks." Other letters of congratulation came from Gage, Sir William Johnson, and Virginia governor Francis Fauquier. Like the Pennsylvania Assembly, the Virginia House of Burgesses passed a resolution congratulating Colonel Bouquet. Despite these accolades the weary commander decided to resign his commission and return to Europe. According to British military custom and law, foreign-born officers were refused general rank in the army. Bouquet's only hope for promotion rested on his application to become a naturalized citizen. After nearly ten years of campaigning on the harsh frontier, it appeared as if the colonel's dreams would never be realized. In accepting this "sad prospect," he once again appealed to General Gage to be relieved of command and allowed to return home. The general ignored Bouquet's petition, conjecturing that his services might still be required until peace with the Indians had been formalized by Sir William Johnson.[1]

While the good citizens of Philadelphia celebrated Henry Bouquet's glorious achievements, they were far from happy with the imperial government that he served. By mid-April news reached the colonies of Parliament's passage of the Stamp Act, a measure designed to help offset the exorbitant cost of colonial defense. This tax was only the latest reflection of the changing attitude that British policy makers had adopted at the end of the French and Indian War.

After the Treaty of Paris was concluded in the spring of 1763, officials in London recognized the need to develop a new strategy for administering the vast American empire that England had acquired. It was rash to believe that the trans-Appalachian frontier could be simply carved up to create new colonies. If anything, the late war had taught policy makers in Britain that the various provincial assemblies had already grown too powerful. To create even more such unresponsive appendages would be foolhardy. Since the French and Indian War had been largely a costly contest for control of Canada and the western frontier, King George's ministers agreed that keeping and governing all this hard-won territory required greater imperial authority, not less.

Officials at Whitehall also recognized the need to keep the colonists themselves tied to Great Britain's economic and political influence. To allow unrestrained settlement west of the mountains would increase the provincials' economic and political independence from the parent country. In addition, such a tidal wave of development in the western lands would create friction, and perhaps another costly and bloody war, with the aboriginal inhabitants. Consequently, even before the great Indian uprising of 1763, London officials were already drawing up plans to control the development of the interior. Pontiac's War accelerated these plans. The Indian conflict made it clear to British officials that they needed greater imperial authority over the trans-Appalachian frontier. They quickly realized that a handful of so-called "savages" in the forests of America could easily threaten and disrupt the fruits of His Majesty's triumph over the forces of Louis XV. Therefore, in October 1763 ministers in London put the finishing touches on a proposal that was known as the Proclamation Line of 1763.[2]

Simply put, the Proclamation Line was designed to prohibit unrestrained settlement in the lands recently wrested from France. Another provision of the law required that all traders must obtain a permit from any of the provincial governors before conducting their business in Indian territory. Policy makers in Great Britain hoped that this provision would not only help prevent unscrupulous traders from victimizing hapless Indian consumers but also fulfill London officials' desire to maintain control over the colonies, quell Indian unrest, preserve the lucrative trade with the tribes, and save a fortune on military defense. Instead, the measure served to unite three disparate groups in colonial America.

From the perspective of provincial settlers, the Proclamation Line represented a hindrance to their seeking opportunity in the rich farmland of the Upper Ohio River Valley and beyond. After all, the frontier folk reasoned, had their blood and toil not helped the parent country gain this land from France? Now that same government proclaimed that they should be denied the fruits of that victory. Many colonists defied the porous barrier and set about the task of carving homes out of the forbidden wilderness. Others, realizing that their claims to any of the land in the West might be nullified whenever the region was officially opened for settlement, hesitated to take up residence, clear forests for planting, and make improvements that might later be seized from them.[3]

The great merchants of Philadelphia and other inland seaboard towns who amassed fortunes from the Indian trade also believed that the proclamation infringed on their rights to free enterprise by restricting trade to a few outposts. They claimed, with some legitimacy, that similar restraints that had been imposed by General Amherst had served to retard trade, squelch competition, inflate prices, and frustrate Indian consumers. Royal officials, on the other hand, were more concerned about the unscrupulous and dangerous aspects of a trade in which rum, powder, lead, and scalping knives seemed to be the most sought-after commodities.

Lastly, the Proclamation Line infuriated wealthy and influential land speculators who hoped to reap a fortune in the development of the trans-Appalachian frontier. Thomas Jefferson, George Washington, Richard Henry Lee, and Patrick Henry, to name a few, were poised to obtain lucrative land grants from the king at the end of the war. The planters of the Virginia tidewater were particularly eager to apply for land grants in the Ohio Country and further south in Kentucky. Many of these aristocrats found land speculation to be a way out of mounting debt that resulted from fluctuating tobacco prices. Pontiac's

War and the Proclamation Line dashed their hopes of finding solvency in the development of western lands. George Washington found the measure to be particularly onerous. He believed, however, that the restriction on settlement would eventually be lifted. To his friend William Crawford, Washington wrote, "I can never look upon that Proclamation in any other light (but this I say between ourselves) than as a temporary expedient to quiet the minds of the Indians & must fall of course in a few years especially when those Indians are consenting to our Occupying the Lands." Later Washington became less certain of his chances of acquiring a large land grant and began to turn his fields to wheat production rather than rely on the whims of the tobacco market.[4] British officials could not know when they first concocted the Proclamation Line that the measure would help to make colonial America a crucible in which resentful and defiant social strata would come together. Within this cauldron of discontent can be found the ingredients for revolutionary agitation.

Just as news of the Proclamation Line was filtering through the colonies, another incident occurred on the frontier that foreshadowed the spread of revolutionary sentiment in the backcountry. On December 14, 1763, amid a driving snowstorm, a body of perhaps fifty armed settlers from the community of Paxton swooped down on the peaceful Christian Indians of Conestoga Manor, brutally murdering six of the unsuspecting residents. For years, these Indians had lived along the Susquehanna River under the tutelage of Moravian missionaries. When Pontiac's War erupted, many of the pioneer farmers of the region believed, without foundation, that the Conestoga people were spies for the warring tribes to the west. As the war intensified, rumors increased among the frightened frontier inhabitants that many nearby Christian Indians were in league with the hostile Delawares and Shawnees. A number of these peaceful Indians living on the frontier fled their homes and begged Governor Penn to give them sanctuary in Philadelphia. The governor obliged, placing the frightened refugees on Province Island in the middle of the Delaware River. Paxton's Presbyterian minister, John Elder, wrote to Penn in September suggesting that the Conestogas also be removed from the area for their own protection. For some unknown reason the governor failed to take action on Elder's request, leaving the Conestoga Indians defenseless against the rage of the Scots-Irish and German settlers living in the backcountry. After the massacre, Penn sent out a proclamation to the magistrates of Lancaster County to apprehend the men responsible for the murders.[5]

Fourteen Indians who were away from the Conestoga village at the time of the attack managed to find sanctuary in Lancaster, where Sheriff John Hay placed them in the community workhouse. At two o'clock on the afternoon of December 27, another party of these so-called Paxton Boys rode into Lancaster, burst open the workhouse door, and in the span of ten minutes, horribly butchered the remaining fourteen Indian men, women, and children. After scalping and mutilating the dead Indians, the Paxton Boys mounted their horses and rode away. Lancaster resident William Henry, one of the first men to reach the jail, vividly described the scene: "I ran into the prison yard," Henry recalled, "and there, oh what a horrid sight presented itself to my view. Strewn throughout the jail were the mangled bodies of the helpless victims." "Towards the middle of the jail yard," Henry continued, "along the west side of the wall, lay a stout Indian, whom I particularly noticed to have been shot in his breast; his legs were chopped off with a tomahawk, his hands cut off, and finally a rifle ball discharged in his mouth, so that his head was blown to atoms." After burying the victims of this gruesome massacre, the sheriff gathered all of their personal belongings. Among those effects was a parchment detailing a treaty that the Indians had made with William Penn in 1701.[6]

Horrified by the murders, Governor Penn issued another proclamation offering a reward of £200 for information leading to the apprehension of the Paxton ringleaders. Penn was further alarmed when he received a letter from Lancaster County magistrate Edward Shippen revealing that "many of the Inhabitants of the Townships of Lebanon, Paxton, and Hanover, in Lancaster County, were forming themselves into a Company of 200 Men, to March to Philadelphia, with a design to kill the Indians on the Province Island." Suddenly, the Pennsylvania Assembly, which for years had squabbled with the governors over military appropriations, beseeched Penn to call out the militia to protect the city. Within hours, the anxious lawmakers passed "An Act for preventing Tumults and Riotous Assemblies and for the more speedy and effectual Punishing of the Rioters." In addition, the Indians were moved to an old barracks in the city, and carpenters constructed redoubts to protect the building. Panic and pandemonium

Massacre of the Indians at Lancaster by the Paxton Boys in 1763. This nineteenth-century lithograph does not quite convey the horror of the massacre perpetrated on these peaceful Indians. From John Wimer, *Events in Indian History* (1841). Author's collection.

gripped the community on February 4, when rumors spread that the Paxton Boys were on the march and now numbered more than a thousand. Benjamin Franklin helped organize the citizens into nine companies to defend the capital.[7]

On February 5 the church bells of Philadelphia rang out to announce the approach of the Paxton Boys. The frontiersmen, numbering perhaps 250, halted at Germantown, where several clergymen from the city tried to dissuade them from going any further. One Quaker onlooker described the Paxton Boys as "a set of fellows, dressed in blanket coats and mocassins, like our Indian traders, or back-country wagoners: they were armed with rifles and tomahawks, and some of them had a brace of pistols besides." The insurrectionists appointed Matthew Smith and James Gibson to represent them in conversations with the ministers. Smith and Gibson informed the clergymen that "the people in and around Philadelphia lived at their ease and in plenty, and had no idea of the distress and trouble of the poor frontiers, and the want of protection and many other evils." The men demanded that the Indians being protected in the city either be given up to them or expelled from the colony and that the government redress their grievances.[8]

Two days later, government representatives Benjamin Franklin, Joseph Galloway, Benjamin Chew, and Thomas Willing rode out to Germantown to negotiate with the Paxton men. Franklin and the others promised that if the angry westerners agreed to disperse, the governor and assembly would consider their demands. Smith and Gibson wrote out a long statement titled "A Declaration and Remonstrance" that outlined their complaints against the government. After identifying themselves as "his Majesties faithful and loyal Subjects," the men demanded that all Indians be removed from the inhabited regions of the colony, that no trade should be conducted with any Indians until all the captives held among them were released, that stronger measures of defense be made to protect them, that citizens wounded by Indians be cared for at public expense, and that the interior counties be given greater representation in the assembly. This final point was particularly important to the Paxton Boys. At that time, the Pennsylvania Assembly consisted of representatives from eight counties. The three eastern counties that included Philadelphia and the surrounding area had twenty-six representatives, while the five western districts had only ten assemblymen. Consequently, the frontiersmen believed that their interests were not being amply addressed.[9] They were also convinced that the eastern counties were controlled by the Quaker faction, which was always reluctant to provide resources for provincial defense.

Having delivered their demands to government authorities, the rioters were content to return to their homes. Immediately after the mob had dispersed, a bitter propaganda campaign filled with satire ensued between government supporters and detractors. Philadelphia printers circulated a series of pamphlets debating the justification for the Paxton Boys' actions and Quaker involvement in Indian affairs. While the polemical exchange between these rival factions seems narrowly focused, the Paxton Boys' insurrection did raise issues of broader importance. The entire affair underscored the feeling frontier inhabitants had that their government was unresponsive to their needs. For this reason they demanded greater representation in that government. The actual murder of peaceful Indians demonstrated that these disgruntled pioneers had a propensity for violence and would take matters into their own hands rather than rely on duly constituted authority, whether that authority resided in Philadelphia or London. Also, despite the Paxton Boys' professions of allegiance to King George III, many of these men were not English. For the most part, the interior counties were inhabited by Scots-Irish, Irish, and German immigrants whose ties to Great Britain were less concrete than those of the English settlers in Pennsylvania. While none of these issues and implications in themselves can be directly linked to revolutionary movement a decade later, they certainly contributed to the tempest of resentment that eventually brought about the final break with England.[10]

As the clamor over the Paxton Boys' insurrection subsided, the citizens of Philadelphia turned their attention to other issues. When Colonel Bouquet began planning his expedition to the Muskingum in the spring of 1764, politicians once again bickered over the proprietor's contribution to providing resources for colonial defense. Perhaps Governor Penn had the Paxton Boys' rebellion in mind when he finally agreed to concede the proprietary prerogative and provide a one-time contribution to the militia bill. This allowed Bouquet to muster his provincial forces and finally launch a successful campaign into the heart of the Ohio Country. With Bouquet's triumphant return to Philadelphia in early 1765, Pennsylvanians could look forward to a return to peace and prosperity. Then word arrived of the passage of the Stamp Act.

Historians have generally acknowledged that Parliament's efforts to exact revenue from the colonies in order to offset the cost of colonial defense did not particularly raise the ire of Pennsylvania's frontier inhabitants. Indeed, no tumultuous riot like the one that occurred in Philadelphia during the summer of 1765 took place at Carlisle, Bedford, or Fort Pitt. No protest broadsides nor records from clandestine meetings of the Sons of Liberty have been found emanating from Harris Landing or Ligonier. It would be a mistake, however, to conclude that none of the law's provisions impacted frontier society. The act called for a revenue stamp to be affixed to all legal documents, including court pleas, will probates, contracts, and deeds. Perhaps more irritating was the fact that violators could be tried in admiralty courts without the benefit of a jury of peers. While no extant document records frontier objection to the Stamp Act, broader issues surrounding the measure—including questions over sovereignty, land titles, local autonomy, and representation—were matters that deeply concerned westerners.[11]

While the eastern seaboard communities of North America rose up in resistance to the Stamp Act, backcountry farmers were trying to rebuild their lives following Pontiac's War. Most of the frontier inhabitants had returned to their homesteads following Bouquet's march to the Muskingum. There was much work to be done rebuilding homes and barns that had been burned to the ground by the Indians. Without question, most frontier folk were more concerned about the prospects of a permanent peace with the Ohio Country tribes than they were about British tax measures.

By the spring of 1765, that permanent peace still eluded the backcountry. The Indians of the Ohio Country, who had pledged to travel to New York to meet with Sir William Johnson, still had not arrived. In addition, General Gage was deeply concerned that the influence of recalcitrants such as Pontiac and Charlot Kaské might spark hostilities in the Illinois country. This was all the more likely since Great Britain had not yet extended its authority in the region, where military outposts were still occupied by French troops. Even worse, French traders still roamed throughout the territory and were more than willing to sell arms and ammunition to the Indians. Sir William Johnson was acutely aware that the key to peace in the Illinois territory rested with none other than Pontiac. As the superintendent informed General Gage, "Some Steps should certainly be taken without delay for the Gaining possession of the Illinois, without which we shall never be at rest, and the Gaining of Pondiac . . . is absolutely necessary." Gage agreed: "This fellow [Pontiac] shou'd be gained to our Interest, or knocked in the head." Gage reasoned that if peace could be established with the great Ottawa leader, all the other nations of the Illinois territory would follow suit.[12]

To encourage the Ohio tribes to fulfill their commitment to make a formalized peace, as well as to pave the way for British occupation of the Illinois country, Sir William Johnson called on the one man who, above all others, had the most experience in dealing with Indian affairs—George Croghan.[13] The Irishman had returned from England frustrated over his failure to extract any compensation for the losses incurred by the so-called "Suffering Traders" during Pontiac's Uprising. Upon his arrival in New York Croghan called on General Gage, from whom he learned that the only Indians not yet committed to peace were Pontiac and the Illinois tribes. At this point Croghan struck on a scheme to win over the Indians, allow for the peaceful occupation of the Illinois territory by British forces, and recoup his staggering losses, all at the same time. Croghan proposed that the general send him to the Illinois region to make peace with the Indians and "obtain their consent to His Majesty's Troops, peaceably, possessing that Country." Gage was delighted with Croghan's offer and promised to supply him with a small military escort and enough presents to distribute among the Indians to convince them of English good will. Along the way, the Irishman would pause at Fort Pitt, where he would coax the Shawnees and Delawares into sending their ambassadors to negotiate with Sir William Johnson. Croghan also expected to use his diplomatic credentials to forward private trade goods to Fort Pitt, thereby giving him the upper hand over competitors when trade was legally restored.[14]

Before striking out for Fort Pitt in late January 1765, Croghan stopped in Philadelphia to make arrangements with the Quaker trading firm of Baynton, Wharton, and Morgan to transport £15,000's worth of trade goods to Fort Pitt. Less than £3,000 of those goods were designated as government items to be distributed as presents for the Illinois Indians. The remainder of the cargo was made up of private trade goods, including rum and gunpowder. Croghan then sent a message to Fort Pitt to his partner Alexander McKee, telling him to inform all the Ohio Country tribes to gather their furs and be ready to do business. He cautioned McKee to keep the Indians and their furs away from the fort until he arrived so as not to raise the commanding officer's suspicion. Croghan further urged his partner not to reveal his plans to open up the trade. Having concluded these clandestine business arrangements, Croghan set off for the West.[15]

It was not unusual for the frontier settlers to see convoys of supplies moving along Forbes Road. For years, Baynton, Wharton, and Morgan had worked as government contractors, supplying the western forts with military goods and other provisions. What made the pack train that passed through the Conococheague Valley in early March so unusual was that the caravan bypassed the main trail in favor of back roads and deer paths. What may have also raised suspicions among backcountry inhabitants was the person leading the convoy of eighty-one packhorses—Robert Callender, one of George Croghan's trading partners. Word spread quickly that illegal trade goods were passing through the valley. William Duffield and a body of armed settlers made several attempts to reason with Callender, arguing that to forward the goods to the West at this time "would be a kind of murder, and would be illegally trading at the expence of the blood and treasure of the frontiers." The traders ignored these appeals and continued their march to the base of Sideling Hill. There Callender and his men were met by eleven armed men thinly disguised as Indians with their faces painted black. It was James Smith, the former provincial lieutenant, and a group of his Black Boys. Smith posted his men along the trail and ordered them to begin shooting the pack-horses. Callender and his men, fearing for their lives, called out, "Pray, gentlemen, what would you have us do?" Smith ordered the men to unload the remaining horses, pile up the goods, and depart immediately. After Callender and his men left, the Black Boys set fire to all the goods they deemed to be contraband.[16]

The frightened traders went immediately to nearby Fort Loudon and reported the ambush to the post commandant, Lieutenant Charles Grant from the Black Watch regiment. Grant quickly dispatched Sergeant Leonard McGlashan and a dozen Highlanders to the scene in order to recover any of the goods not yet destroyed and apprehend any of the Black Boys who might still be lurking in the vicinity. When the sergeant and his squad reached Sideling Hill, they encountered a small party of men wearing new blankets. Assuming these blankets were part of the trade goods, McGlashan ordered the men to halt. The Black Boys scattered, but the sergeant and his detail managed to run down two men and take them into custody. After making a thorough search of the area, the Highlanders started back for the fort with their prisoners in tow. Along the way, McGlashan and his men encountered fifty men "all armed, with their thumbs upon the locks of their Guns." The sergeant did not flinch when one of the angry settlers threatened to shoot him unless he released the prisoners. Instead,

James Smith's Encounter with the Indians. This 1841 lithograph shows James Smith being taken captive by Indians. Smith, who lived among the Ohio Country people for four years, later adopted Indian tactics to disrupt trade caravans bound for the frontier. His actions ignited a backcountry rebellion that was a precursor to the American Revolution a decade later. From John Wimer, *Events in Indian History* (1841). Author's collection.

McGlashan ordered his men to disarm and capture as many of the rebellious frontiersmen as possible. Most of the men in the crowd fled, but the Highlanders managed to capture four more frontier farmers. With fixed bayonets the sergeant and his squad continued on to Fort Loudon with their prisoners.[17]

On March 9 Lieutenant Grant peered out from the walls of Fort Loudon to see a large body of armed frontiersmen gathering on a hill just beyond the woods line. Grant hastened his small force of Highlanders to climb to the firing platforms and ordered that the gates of the fort be closed. He sent a messenger to find out the reason for "Such a Mobb" appearing before "the King's Fort." James Smith came to the stockade to parley with Grant. He told the Scottish officer that the prisoners being held inside the compound must be immediately released. Grant defiantly informed Smith that he intended to send the accused men under armed escort to stand trial at Carlisle. The Black Boys' leader responded that his men were "Determined to fight the Troops, & Die to a Man Sooner than let them prisoners go to Gaol." Surrounded by an angry and resolute crowd of backcountry settlers that outnumbered his garrison by nearly ten to one, Grant decided to send couriers to Bedford requesting reinforcements. Before the end of the day, Smith's Black Boys had captured twice as many couriers as Grant had prisoners. Inside the fort, a nervous Robert Callender, realizing that the standoff could quickly escalate into violence, agreed to post bail for the prisoners, and Lieutenant Grant reluctantly released the men. As a precaution, the lieutenant insisted on retaining the firearms that the men had been carrying at the time of their arrest. Rather than go to Carlisle to stand trial, the accused vandals appeared before a local magistrate and were all exonerated.[18]

When word of the Black Boys' actions reached Philadelphia, Governor Penn and General Gage launched an investigation into the incident and its causes. With very little effort they discovered that the uprising was the result of George Croghan's effort to circumvent the Royal Proclamation of 1763 by sending trade goods to the frontier without proper authority. The Indian agent sheepishly defended himself to his superior, Sir William Johnson, claiming that he had intended only to transport the goods to Fort Pitt to be stored until trade was legally reopened. While Gage and Penn placed the blame squarely on Croghan, they were still alarmed at the news that "lawless Ruffians" prowled the frontier seeking to take the law into their own hands. One observant frontier trader noted at the time that the actions of the Black Boys "far exceeds the Paxton affair."[19] While many Pennsylvania officials such as John Armstrong and Chief Justice William Allen sympathized with the plight of the Conococheague settlers, prominent merchants in Philadelphia were aghast at the conduct of the Black Boys. The *Pennsylvania Gazette* labeled the Black Boys "hot-headed, stiff people" and condemned the conduct of those who "seized and destroyed [the trade goods]."[20]

Sensing that neither military officials nor provincial authorities were going to do anything to stop the illicit trade, the settlers of the Conococheague grew determined to again take matters into their own hands. Public notices were displayed in taverns throughout the valley declaring that all freight haulers must obtain a pass from the local magistrates before passing through the region. On May 6 another convoy of goods stopped at Fort Loudon en route to Pittsburgh. This time the pack animals bore military items, but the convoy master, Ralph Nailer, failed to have his freight inspected by the local magistrates. After depositing his goods at the fort, Nailer and his drivers took their horses to graze in a nearby meadow. They suddenly found themselves surrounded by the Black Boys, who tied the freight men to trees and flogged them. Once again, Lieutenant Grant sent out Sergeant McGlashan with a detail of Redcoats to apprehend the assailants. When the Highlanders reached the scene, the Black Boys fired on them. McGlashan and his soldiers returned the fire, wounding one of the suspects.

Before the end of the day, another crowd of perhaps three hundred frontiersmen assembled outside Fort Loudon. Magistrate William Smith, the brother-in-law of James Smith, approached Lieutenant Grant and demanded to inspect the goods being stored at the post. Grant belligerently refused, claiming that the cargo was being transported by government orders. The lieutenant then produced a permit signed by the commanding officer at Fort Pitt, giving the caravan the right of passage. Justice Smith countered that "the Commanding officer's pass was no pass, and that no Military Officer's pass would do without a Magistrate's pass." Loudon "was not a King's Fort," he argued, "nor was this the King's Road . . . five Hundred men wou'd not Escort up these Goods without a Magistrate's pass."[21]

Throughout the spring of 1765, tension continued to escalate in the Conococheague Valley. Freight caravans were routinely halted for inspection by local magistrates. The Black Boys even detained and interrogated military express riders along Forbes Road. A particular sore point among the incited frontiersmen was the firearms that Lieutenant Grant had confiscated from local inhabitants and still retained at Fort Loudon. In late May James Smith and his band intercepted Grant while he was out riding. The Black Boys tied the lieutenant to a tree and threatened to take him into the Carolina wilderness unless he agreed to surrender the guns. Grant defiantly told the Black Boys that they "would be dealt with as Rebells," to which Smith replied that "they were Ready for a Rebellion." Fearing that the insurgents would carry out their threat to whisk him off to the Carolina mountains, Grant finally agreed to post a £40 bond, promising to turn over the confiscated weapons within five weeks. After his release the outraged officer refused to honor this commitment.[22]

The Black Boys' rebellion came to a head in November when the Conococheague inhabitants learned that General Gage had ordered Grant's transfer to Fort Pitt. The general wisely deduced that the lieutenant's presence in the valley was a continuing source of irritation to the settlers. The Black Boys were determined, however, not to allow Grant to leave until he had honored his agreement to return the confiscated firearms. On November 16 hundreds of rebellious valley residents once again surrounded Fort Loudon. After demanding that Grant surrender the guns, they opened fire on the fort. For nearly two days the Black Boys kept up their siege of the outpost, "firing some thousands of Shot" against the stockade walls. Finally, Grant agreed to release the weapons to one of the local magistrates, and the Black Boys withdrew. Two hours later a detachment from Bedford arrived to escort Grant to Fort Pitt.[23]

Grant's transfer from Fort Loudon restored peace to the Conococheague Valley. The Black Boys reunited four years later, however, when they concluded that trade with the Indians once again threatened the security of the frontier. Ironically, the band again plundered trade goods being conveyed by Robert Callender. When British troops apprehended some of the bandits and imprisoned them at Fort Bedford, James Smith and his ragtag crew assaulted the fort and compelled the officer in charge to release the accused men. In his memoirs, Smith proudly proclaimed, "This, I believe was the first British fort in America, that was taken by what they called American rebels."[24]

Like the earlier Paxton Boys affair, the Black Boys' rebellion demonstrated that frontier inhabitants had lost faith in both the crown and their own provincial authorities to protect their interests. James Smith and his neighbors were thus more than willing to rely on their own elected officials rather than a distant authority in Philadelphia or, for that matter, London. A full ten years before the gunfire on Lexington Green, these Americans had become convinced that their rights were being usurped by unscrupulous traders, British military officers, and proprietary interests. With ample justification the historical novelist Neil Swanson has labeled James Smith "the First Rebel."[25]

Meanwhile George Croghan was determined to carry out his daunting mission to facilitate a final peace with the Ohio Country tribes, pave the way for British occupation of the Illinois territory, and seduce Pontiac into accepting English stewardship. With suspicion mounting over his role in the Black Boys affair, perhaps the Irishman thought it best to focus on his diplomatic initiative rather than the restoration of a profitable trade. Croghan reached Fort Pitt on February 28 accompanied by Lieutenant Alexander Fraser, a former Highland officer from the disbanded 78th Regiment of Foot. General Gage had selected Fraser to carry dispatches to French officials in the Illinois territory, paving the way for British occupation. When the two men arrived at the fort, they were disappointed to find that none of the Delaware, Shawnee, and Mingo leaders had yet assembled. Not only was Croghan anxious to forward the Ohio Country chiefs on to Johnson Hall to discuss final peace terms, but he also hoped to recruit a delegation of Indians to accompany him to the Illinois country. Croghan realized that to reconcile the western tribes to English hegemony, he would need the support of the Shawnees and Delawares. Therefore, the Indian agent had no recourse but to await the arrival of the Indian leaders before departing down the Ohio on the second phase of his mission. After waiting nearly three weeks, Fraser became impatient and decided to strike out for the Illinois territory without Croghan. Unable to dissuade the officer from making such a dangerous journey, Croghan supplied Fraser with an interpreter and several Indian guides. On March 22 the lieutenant cast off down the Ohio River with a handful of soldiers from the Royal Highland Regiment.[26]

On April 1 four Delaware runners arrived at Fort Pitt to explain why the tribe was tardy in coming to speak with Croghan. The Indians informed the agent that the villages were divided over how the peace terms with the British should be negotiated. According to their story, the great prophet Neolin had once again "been called up to Heaven, by the Great Spirit, who told him, that he must acquaint his Nation, that before they made Peace with the English, they must consult the Quakers of Philadelphia, who would direct them, how to make a lasting Peace." These Delaware messengers wanted Croghan to bring the Quakers to Fort Pitt to negotiate on their behalf. Needless to say, the shrewd agent had little interest in having Quakers meddle in Indian affairs. He directed the couriers to return to their villages and inform the chiefs that only Sir William Johnson was authorized to provide them with a lasting peace. Croghan further insisted that the Delaware leaders come to Fort Pitt immediately.[27]

After receiving Croghan's terse reply, the Indians slowly began to arrive at the forks of the Ohio. Kiasutha came with 125 warriors and many women and children. The astute and experienced Croghan regarded the Seneca leader as "a Sencable good Tempered Indian" and recognized that he had considerable power and influence among the Indians of the Ohio Country. Indeed, the once recalcitrant warrior was now eager to restore peace and reopen trade with the British. Once Kiasutha's people had gathered, other tribes began to filter into the fort. Custaloga, Tamaqua, and Newcomer arrived in mid-April, bringing with them the holy man Neolin. In a private conversation with Croghan Neolin reiterated the details of his most recent meeting with the Master of Life. The prophet told the Irishman, "We are sensible of the misunderstanding, that has been between us, & know we ought to be as one People, having but one Father. God, when he first made us, on this Earth, considered us, as his People, & gave us directions, in what manner to Live, & now this second time has discovered himself to me, acquainting me with the method, we ought to pursue, & to live agreeable to his desire. He spoke to me concerning all the People which inhabit this Continent." The Master of Life now decreed, Neolin related, that the Indians and English live in peace and that both sides must "comply with his request."[28]

Finally, by the first week of May, more than four hundred Indian warriors had collected outside the walls of Fort Pitt to listen to Croghan's message. He began by chastising the assembled tribes for their tardiness and for their failure to send delegates to meet with Sir William Johnson. He then assured them that as soon as they fulfilled the promises made to Colonel Bouquet along the Muskingum, a free and open trade would resume. He requested that they appoint a delegation to accompany him to the Illinois country to meet with the western tribes. After Croghan finished speaking, Kiasutha addressed the chiefs, encouraging them to honor the commitments they had made the previous fall. Addressing Croghan, the Seneca leader also admonished the English: "your Brethren, the Delawares, and Children, the Shawanese, are willing to comply with everything you required of them. Now, do not act as you have done for a Year or two before those late Troubles, when you prohibited the sale of Powder, Lead, and Rum. This conduct gave all the Nations in this Country a suspicion that you had bad designs against them."

After Kiasutha's remarks the Delaware and Shawnee chiefs stood up one by one and acknowledged that henceforth, they would refer to the English as "father," as they had previously addressed the French. Croghan received assurances that all the tribes would immediately appoint delegates to go to meet with Sir William Johnson and that other tribal leaders would accompany him to the Illinois territory. Before the conference adjourned, the Indians released another twenty-four hostages as an act of good will.[29]

Croghan could not have been more satisfied with the results of his negotiations with the Ohio tribes. He obtained their assurances that they would go directly to Sir William Johnson to formalize the peace, he had secured the release of an additional twenty-four hostages, and he had arranged to have Shawnee and Delaware leaders accompany him to the Illinois. The Irishman was now anxious to depart on the second leg of his mission and try to catch up with Lieutenant Fraser and his party. On May 15 the Indian agent and his delegation cast off in two flat-bottomed boats to meet with the western nations.[30]

Unbeknownst to Croghan, Lieutenant Fraser had already made his way to Fort Chartres and delivered his dispatches to the French commander, Louis St. Ange de Bellerive. Fraser soon discovered that the Kickapoo and Mascouten warriors who lived near the outpost were still ill disposed to any British presence in their country, and St. Ange urged the Englishman to escape from the fort as quickly as possible. Undaunted, Fraser insisted on completing his mission by holding a grand council with the Indians to inform them of the upcoming British occupation. As the lieutenant dined with St. Ange, "Pontiac with eight of his followers rushed in to the room" and seized him. The French commander interceded, promising Pontiac that he would turn the officer over to the Indians the next morning.

The next day, Lieutenant Fraser boldly went to visit several Illinois chiefs to inform them that the Shawnee, Delaware, and Seneca tribes had all agreed to make peace with the British and that George Croghan was on his way to settle differences with them, as well. Fraser was acutely aware that local French traders continued to encourage the Indians to resist English occupation. They plied the warriors with lies concerning a French resurgence in the region and provided them with ammunition to carry on the war. Fraser was also convinced that Pontiac still incited the western tribes to maintain their belligerence toward the English. The lieutenant realized that to save his own life and secure peace with the Illinois tribes, he must persuade the Ottawa leader of the British government's good intentions.

When Pontiac met with Fraser, he was surprised to learn that the Shawnees and Delawares had actually followed through on their promises to reconcile with the Redcoats. The chief realized that without the support of the Ohio nations, further resistance was hopeless. He therefore agreed to at least listen to Fraser's overtures for peace in council with the other Illinois chiefs.

That afternoon, more than five hundred Indians assembled around the fort to hear Fraser's address. The lieutenant opened the council by reiterating that the Ohio tribes had made amends with the British and that George Croghan was on his way to treat with them as well. Pontiac then rose and "accepted the Belt of Peace since his father [the French] had advised him to it, and since [Fraser] had apprized him that the Delawares, Shawanise, and Iroquois had made peace." He explained that, while "he had acted as a Principle in the war he did not begin it; that he on the contrary received the war belt from those very nations which . . . now had made peace." To celebrate the moment, Fraser provided the Indians with "a hundred & thirty pots of Brandy at the Extravagant price of twenty livres each pot."[31]

The fragile peace that Fraser concluded was soon threatened by the Shawnee leader Charlot Kaské, who arrived at the fort claiming to possess a war belt from the French governor of Louisiana. Kaské "assured all the Indians that [the governor] would send them Presents frequently and Traders sufficient to supply them with Ammunition & Arms to carry on the War." Once again the Indians living around the fort wanted to kill Fraser. Undoubtedly, Pontiac recognized that Kaské's tirades were nothing more than lies, and he interceded to save the lieutenant's life. Fraser appreciated the chief's good will, observing, "He is the Person who seems most inclined to peace of any amongst them, and it is much to be wished that He may be prevail'd on to make Peace, as it will probably be of longer duration than any made without him. He is in a manner Ador'd by all the Nations hereabouts, and He is more remarkable for His integrity and humanity than either French Man or Indian in the colony."[32]

Believing that he could do no more to reassure the Indians of his peaceful intentions, Fraser decided to depart the Illinois and float down the Mississippi to New Orleans. Before leaving, the officer gave Pontiac some presents and instructed him to go to Ouiatenon, along the banks of the Wabash River, where he might expect to find George Croghan. The lieutenant then set off and reached New Orleans without incident on June 16, 1765.[33]

While Fraser floated safely down the Mississippi, George Croghan was just entering the contentious territory. After passing the mouth of the Wabash River on June 6, Croghan and his Indian delegation continued down the Ohio for another six miles before making camp. The next day, the agent dispatched several Indians to Fort Chartres in an attempt to make contact with Lieutenant Fraser. At dawn the following morning, a war party of eighty Kickapoos and Mascoutens sprang from the bushes and attacked Croghan's camp. During the surprise encounter, two white attendants and three Shawnees were killed. Croghan was also wounded in the attack and later commented to a friend, "I got the Stroke of a Hatchet on the Head, but my Scull being pretty thick, the hatchet would not enter, so You may See a thick Scull is of Service on some Occasions." Once the Kickapoos and Mascoutens learned that they had killed three Shawnees, they begged for forgiveness, explaining that the French traders "had spirited them up telling them the English were coming with a body of Southern Indians [Cherokees] to take their Country from them and inslave them." Fearing reprisal from the Shawnees, the Kickapoos and Mascoutens released the whole Ohio Indian delegation. They insisted, however, that Croghan and the other white men with him must be retained as prisoners until they had received final word from their chiefs in regard to a peace with the English. With that, the Kickapoos and Mascoutens struck off for their villages along the Wabash, leading their captives.[34]

After a grueling march in which the wounded Croghan suffered greatly from "the excessive Heat of the Weather and Scarcity of Water," the Indians and their prisoners reached the abandoned Fort Ouiatenon on June 23. Mascouten and Kickapoo chiefs scolded their warriors for their unwarranted attack and ordered that Croghan and his men be immediately released. Still fearful that the Shawnees might take revenge upon them, the Indian leaders indicated that they were eager to negotiate peace with the English. After four days of consultation Croghan joyfully recorded in his journal, "I was lucky enough to reconcile those Nations to His Majesties Interest & obtain their Consent and Approbation to take Possession of any Posts in their Country which the French formerly possessed." In the days that followed, the Irishman also negotiated peace agreements with the Miami Indians.[35]

Finally, on or near July 18, Pontiac arrived from Fort Chartres to meet with Croghan. For the first time, the accomplished Indian agent had an opportunity to size up the Ottawa chief and found him to be "a shrewd Sensible Indian of few words [who] commands more respect amongst those Nations, than any Indian I ever saw could do amongst his own tribe." In fact, by this time Pontiac commanded greater influence over the Illinois Indians than he did among his own people. After some preliminary negotiations Pontiac agreed to accompany Croghan to Detroit for a grand council of all the Great Lakes tribes.[36]

It was perhaps fitting that the peace conference between Pontiac and Croghan was to be held on the same ground where so much bloodshed and destruction had taken place. The chief had not been back to Detroit since he had abandoned his siege in the fall of 1763. Much had changed since then. A larger and stronger British garrison occupied the fort, and Pontiac's former nemesis, Major Gladwin, had been replaced by Colonel John Campbell. Another change had taken place among the Great Lakes tribes: the alteration in Pontiac's status as a great leader. Men who were experienced in Indian affairs, such as Sir William Johnson and George Croghan, believed that the Ottawa chief's influence was still absolute among these nations. They had no way of knowing that due to his failure to take Fort Detroit, Pontiac had, in effect, been deposed by many of the tribes that lived along the lakes. The attention that George Croghan showered on the chief disturbed many of the other Indians and may have created considerable jealousy among tribal leaders at Detroit.[37]

The grand council convened on August 28 with representatives from all the Great Lakes tribes present. Wasson came with his Chippewas; Teata spoke for the Hurons. There were also Potawatomies,

Piankashaws, Miamis, Kickapoos, and Mascoutens present—in all more than five hundred warriors. Despite his waning influence, the Ottawas chose Pontiac to serve as their spokesman. When his turn to speak came, the chief declared his intention to live at peace with the British and offered up his pipe to be taken to Sir William Johnson as a symbol of good faith. Pontiac also called for a resumption of trade, including that in ammunition and rum. He further complained that the French had never purchased the land from the Indians and that he hoped the English would offer them some compensation for the forts and trading posts that the British requested in their territory. Before the conference adjourned, Pontiac and the other chiefs agreed to meet Sir William Johnson in the spring and sign formalized peace agreements.[38]

While George Croghan parleyed with the Great Lakes tribes, Henry Bouquet embarked on a new assignment, more deadly than any he had faced before. On April 15, 1765, General Gage notified Bouquet that the king had promoted him to the rank of brigadier general. Due to the commander's stunning achievements, George III had dispensed with the prohibition on promoting foreign-born officers to high military rank. The promotion induced Bouquet to give up any thoughts of resigning from the army and returning to Europe. Gage ordered his new brigadier to take command of the turbulent Southern District, with its headquarters at Fort Saint George in Pensacola, Florida.[39]

When Great Britain acquired Florida in the 1763 Treaty of Paris, officials had hoped to establish a lively and profitable trade relationship with the Spanish possessions in the Gulf of Mexico. However, the same British navigation laws that proved vexing to merchants along the eastern seaboard colonies prevented such commerce from developing. In addition, fierce disputes over authority had erupted between the civilian governor, George Johnstone, and military officials in West Florida. Johnstone believed that he had the power to distribute troops on the frontier to protect settlements. Military officers, such as Pensacola commander Ralph Walsh, refused to comply with the governor's orders. Britain's secretary of state, the Earl of Halifax, attempted to clarify the situation by informing Johnstone that in matters purely of a military nature, officers were obliged to take orders only from the commander in chief, General Gage, or his brigadier assigned to the colony. Halifax admitted that in the absence of a brigadier, the governor could indeed issue directives for the distribution of troops. Clearly, Bouquet's presence in West Florida was an absolute necessity.[40]

Another more familiar problem that confronted the Southern District involved Indian affairs. The powerful Choctaw and Creek Indians who inhabited West Florida were suspicious of the new English regime. Like their counterparts to the north, these troublesome tribes resented British presence in their territory and were disturbed by the paucity of trade that they had once enjoyed from both the Spanish and the French. As the Indian superintendent for the Southern District, John Stuart, put it, the tribes of West Florida seemed to possess "an inveterate Hatred to the English." It seemed that the war-weary Bouquet was once again entering a maelstrom of rivalry, contempt, and danger.[41]

More than likely, Henry Bouquet was well aware of the challenges he would face with his new command. His reluctance to leave Philadelphia, however, had less to do with the onerous duty that awaited him than with the prospect of parting from a new love who had entered his life. He had ceased pining for Anne Willing the minute he encountered Peggy Oswald, the daughter of an old sea captain. Bouquet became smitten with the young woman and considered her "the dearest concern of my life." He planned to ask for Peggy's hand in marriage until he received the dreaded orders to take command of the Southern District. Before departing on the final leg of his voyage to Pensacola, the general wrote to her expressing his gratitude for the salve she had given him to ward off the mosquitoes he would encounter. Expressing his undying affection, he concluded the letter, "When Shall I See you again, When shall I be happy? While I breathe I shall remain irrevocably Yours."[42]

General Bouquet arrived at his new headquarters on August 23 with all the finery that befitted his rank. On the dock at Pensacola the ship's crew unloaded a multitude of boxes and chests containing all his personal items—china, pots and pans, a scarlet frock coat with gold lace, two green umbrellas, a silver-mounted sword, paint, furniture, a brace of pistols, casks of wine and sherry, a rifle and musket, striped curtains, and mosquito netting. Bouquet was also accompanied by three African slaves whom he had recently purchased en route. All of these luxuries, however, could not compensate for the deplorable conditions at the dreary and inhospitable outpost. The dilapidated storehouses and barracks were enclosed by an irregular, rotting wooden stockade. All around the fort were disease-infested swamps and dense forests. Worst of all, an epidemic of yellow fever was ravaging the entire garrison.[43]

Neither Peggy's salve nor the mosquito netting could protect the general from the wretched disease. Before Bouquet had time to even paint his headquarters, the fever struck him down. He died on September 2, 1765, at the age of forty-seven. One of the general's aides, Lieutenant Colonel Francis Hutchinson, assumed responsibility for disposing of Bouquet's personal property at public auction. The colonel also paid six soldiers a total of three Spanish dollars "for Carrying the Corpse to the Grave." When news of Bouquet's untimely death reached Philadelphia, the *Pennsylvania Journal* offered a brief but poignant obituary: "His superior judgement and knowledge of military matters, his experienced abilities, known humanity, remarkable politeness and constant attention to the civil rights of his Majesty's subjects, rendered him an honor to his country and a loss to mankind."[44]

When word of Henry Bouquet's death arrived in New York, General Gage was dealing with the tumultuous crisis sparked by the Stamp Act. It seemed as if the entire continent was in rebellion over the hated revenue measure. In Boston rioters sacked and destroyed the house of the lieutenant governor. A Rhode Island mob forced the stamp agents to flee to the protection of a British warship. At Annapolis, Maryland, protesters pulled down the residence of the stamp agent and burned him in effigy. In New York, right under General Gage's nose, delegates from ten of the thirteen colonies met in congress to denounce the act. Commenting on the membership of this Stamp Act Congress, Gage remarked, "They are of various Characters and opinions, but it's to be feared in general, that the Spirit of Democracy, is strong amongst them." The astute general fully comprehended the clamor over the tax measure: "The Question is not of the inexpediency of the Stamp Act, or of the inability of the Colonys to pay the Tax, but that it is unconstitutional, and contrary to their Rights, Supporting the Independency of the Provinces, and not Subject to the Legislative Power of Great Britain." Gage grew so alarmed over the escalating violence that he summoned troops from Fort Pitt to garrison the seaboard cities of Annapolis and Philadelphia. While this directive left the frontier exposed, Gage could take some comfort in knowing that peace with the Indians was finally at hand. All that was needed was for Pontiac to meet with Sir William Johnson and sign a formal peace treaty.[45]

The formal peace treaty ending Pontiac's War seemed anticlimactic when set against the backdrop of the colonists' growing resentment over British imperial policy. The meeting, which at one time had been highly anticipated, took place on July 23, 1766, at Oswego, on the shore of Lake Ontario. Substantive aspects of Sir William Johnson's negotiations with Pontiac were conducted in private, away from the prying ears of Illinois chiefs who were also present at the conference. This move may have served to heighten the growing suspicions and jealousy that many tribal leaders already felt toward Pontiac. By the time formalized negotiations began, Pontiac basked under the mantle of authority the British had bestowed on him. All of this was contrary to ancient Indian custom and a leadership system that precluded authoritarian rule of any kind. While Pontiac's influence among many Illinois tribes, and perhaps even among a few loyal Great Lakes Indians, could not be denied, to exploit such prominence was considered a serious insult and breach of protocol among tribal leaders. Despite these considerations, Pontiac opened the session by proclaiming that he spoke for "all the nations to the westward whom I command." The Ottawa chief continued his speech, informing Johnson, that "it is the will of the Great Spirit that we should meet here today, and before Him and all present I take you by the hand and never will part with it." "We shall do nothing but what is good and reject everything bad," he insisted, "not only me but all the nations of whom I am master to the northward." When the conference finally adjourned, Pontiac returned to his village on the Maumee River, where his influence among other Indian nations continued to crumble. His usurpation of authority at Oswego made more Indian leaders suspicious and resentful. One trader at Detroit predicted that "Pontiac would be killed in less than a year, if the English took so much notice of him."[46] By the spring of 1768, the commander at Fort Detroit reported rumors that Pontiac had been beaten and ostracized by members of his own tribe. The exiled leader, with only a handful of followers, moved further west into the Illinois territory, where he was frequently seen in the trading villages near Fort Chartres. Apparently, he became embroiled in some personal controversy with local Peoria Indians. When Pontiac departed the region in the fall of 1768, he vowed to return the next year and claim some sort of vengeance over that tribe.[47]

After a successful winter of hunting and trapping along the Wabash, Pontiac reemerged along the Mississippi at the small village of Cahokia in the spring of 1769. In antiquity Cahokia had been the center of one of the most developed Native American empires on the continent. As many as twenty thousand people had occupied the city, which contained a temple mound that covered sixteen acres and a fifty-acre plaza that bustled with trade and commerce. With the coming of the Europeans, the once mighty native capital declined to a collection of forty-five squalid houses, a Catholic church, and an old French trading post, now operated by the Philadelphia firm of Baynton, Wharton, and Morgan.

According to one account, on April 20 Pontiac entered the trading post accompanied by a Peoria warrior. Presumably, the chief believed that his earlier conflict with the tribe had been resolved. After conducting his business in the store, he stepped out into the street, closely followed by his Peoria companion. Suddenly, the Indian lifted his war club and smashed it into the back of Pontiac's head. While the once great Ottawa leader lay stunned in the middle of the street, the Peoria warrior finished him off with a knife. The next day, the French governor, Louis St. Ange de Bellerive, retrieved Pontiac's remains and carried them across the Mississippi River for burial in the town of Saint Louis. It is perhaps ironic, yet in many ways appropriate, that the chief met his end on ground that had once been the center of a thriving Indian empire.[48]

There were no reprisals for Pontiac's murder, and his death registered only a passing notice by British officials. The tenuous final peace that had been formalized by the chief at Oswego in 1766 continued, with only minor infractions, for a number of years. Both sides may have realized, however, that such accommodation could not last forever. As the settlers and speculators continued to press for new lands and opportunities, it became apparent that the Proclamation Line, designed to separate white and Indian worlds, could not restrain the colonists' unbridled greed. Old animosities and racial hatred, which had been kindled during the French and Indian War and fanned to a raging conflagration during Pontiac's Uprising, reignited all along the backcountry.

In January 1768 six Indians came to Frederick Stump's cabin near the Susquehanna River to beg for some food and alcohol. Presumably, Stump and another man, named John Ironcutter, got the Indians drunk and then systematically murdered them. To conceal their horrible crime, Stump and Ironcutter cut a hole through the ice in a nearby stream and submerged the bodies beneath the ice. Fearing other nearby Indians might find out about the murders, Stump visited a small Indian cabin fourteen miles away and butchered a woman and three children. He afterward set the cabin on fire to destroy any evidence. Despite all these efforts to conceal the crime, Stump and his accomplice were found out when the body of one of his victims emerged along the banks of the Susquehanna. Local authorities arrested the two men and lodged them in the jail at Carlisle to await trial. Within the week, a group of armed settlers who believed that no white man should be tried for killing Indians burst into the jail and set Stump and Ironcutter free. The two men later fled to Virginia, where they were never heard from again.[49]

Incidents such as this convinced Sir William Johnson that if peace were to be maintained, adjustments had to be made in the Proclamation Line to keep whites and Indians apart. In November 1768, therefore, the superintendent convened a treaty council at Fort Stanwix in New York in order to persuade the Iroquois to cede more land to the English. Once again, Johnson revived the old pattern of convincing the Iroquois league to sell land that they did not truly occupy. The Iroquois chiefs decided to give up a vast strip of land that extended westward from the Susquehanna to the Allegheny and Ohio and continued south into Kentucky. Neither Johnson nor the Iroquois consulted the Ohio Country people who actually occupied this land and claimed it as their hunting grounds.[50]

The Treaty of Fort Stanwix not only revived the rivalry between the Iroquois and Ohio Country people but also rekindled competition between various colonial interests. Much of the territory that the Iroquois conveyed to the British had been surveyed by various competing land speculation companies. During the negotiations at Fort Stanwix, there was general agreement that much of the land should be set aside as a form of reparations to merchants and traders who had lost considerable fortunes during Pontiac's War. One such group, led by George Croghan, was tentatively awarded more than two million acres. In addition, colonial officials desired that some of the land acquired through the treaty should be distributed among their provincial veterans. However, many veteran claims had already been bought up by speculators, such as George Washington. To further muddle the situation, the question arose as to the various boundary lines of all of these claims.[51]

The greatest rivalry arose between two groups of speculators from Pennsylvania and Virginia. The Vandalia Land Company was organized by powerful Pennsylvanians such as Benjamin Franklin, George Croghan, William Trent, and merchant Samuel Wharton. The company petitioned the crown to award it land south of the Ohio River for the creation of a new colony. The Penn family, aghast at the idea that a new colony should be carved from territory that it claimed as part of Pennsylvania, used all of its influence to block the petition. When royal officials finally balked at awarding such a substantial grant to the Vandalia speculators, the company decided to utilize an obscure interpretation of English title law that would enable them to take over the land without the crown's approbation. This simply required that the company obtain full title to the lands from the Indians.

The land the Vandalia speculators selected was also coveted by a group of Virginia speculators that appealed to their governor, John Murray, Lord Dunmore, for aid in fending off the claims of both Pennsylvania and the Vandalia Company. Eager to reassert Virginia's dormant claim to the Ohio Country and to prevent the Vandalia speculators from securing their title, Dunmore took decisive action. He sent his personal agent, Dr. John Connolly, to Pittsburgh to assert Virginia authority over the forks of the Ohio. In a bold move Connolly called out the local militia and seized Fort Pitt, which had been recently abandoned by British troops. After renaming the outpost Fort Dunmore, the Virginians then set about precipitating an Indian war to preclude the tribes from granting land to the Vandalia investors.[52]

It took very little effort to encourage the frontiersmen living in the Monongahela River Valley to lash out at the nearby Indians. In one unwarranted attack, a party of Virginia militiamen indiscriminately murdered ten members of Mingo leader John Logan's family. In retaliation Logan launched retaliatory raids throughout the Virginia backcountry. The conflict, which became known as Lord Dunmore's War, escalated throughout the summer of 1774. Fortunately for the

Virginians, the once recalcitrant Kiasutha managed to keep most of the Ohio Country tribes out of the conflict. Only the Shawnees insisted on continuing the war, and their resistance was finally broken when Dunmore's provincials defeated them at the Battle of Point Pleasant in October 1774. After the battle, the Shawnee chief Cornstalk met with Governor Dunmore and agreed to peace terms that required the Indians to cede land south and east of the Ohio River.[53]

In an attempt to preserve what they believed to be their final sanctuary, the Indians of the Ohio Country once again took up the war hatchet during the American Revolution.[54] As in all the previous conflicts, massacres of both Indians and whites, retaliatory raids, and captivity became commonplace on the frontier. At one particularly low point in the Revolution, a group of 105 settlers living near Fort Pitt petitioned the Continental Congress to send them more aid to ward off Indian attacks:

> We who have the honor of addressing you are a Number of Inhabitants of the Western Country who have been from the earliest Period of the War attached to the Cause of America and amongst whom a full proportion of Troops were raised and sent to fight the Campaigns against the British foe, yet living as it were on the Ends of the American Earth. We seem to have been to a great degree neglected by Brethren beyond the mountains who have left us exposed to the miss deeds of the Savages of the Wilderness, roused and excited by the same foe which invade from the sea.

Just as the Pennsylvania Assembly had ignored the backcountry's appeals a generation before, so the Continental Congress refused to send more troops to protect frontier families during the Revolution. The decision not to reinforce the frontier left many settlers as disgruntled with their new government as they had been with the previous one. It was far more than coincidence that in little more than a decade after the Revolution, these very same disaffected settlers would lead a compelling challenge to United States authority in the so-called Whiskey Rebellion.[55]

Like their frontier protagonists, the Indians also eventually found themselves abandoned. When British forces began to withdraw from North America following the Treaty of Paris in 1783, the tribes of the

Ohio Country lost all of the material support needed to continue the struggle to retain their homeland. Undaunted, the Indians defiantly fought on against white encroachment in the years following the Revolution. Keekyuscung's prediction that the Indians would "never come to peace again" remained true. Ohio Country and Great Lakes warriors repelled two successive military expeditions sent against them by President George Washington. It was not until General Anthony Wayne decisively defeated the confederation at the Battle of Fallen Timbers in 1794 that Indian defense of the Ohio Country collapsed. For forty years these peoples had defiantly fought the French, the British, the Pennsylvanians, the Virginians, and finally the Americans to hold on to their beloved sanctuary. The legacy of that struggle is evident in the fact that by the time of the Lewis and Clark expedition in 1803, Saint Louis was a bustling community with a population of over a thousand people, while much of the land north of Pittsburgh still remained a barren and uninhabited wilderness.

• • • •

Because it is bracketed between the Seven Years' War and the American Revolution, many scholars devoted to the history of early America have assigned little importance to the Pontiac Indian uprising. They might acknowledge that the conflict hastened into effect the hated Proclamation Line, which provided British officials with their first intimations of a revolutionary sentiment in America. For the most part, however, historians view the growth of colonial agitation from the perspective of the Atlantic seaboard communities of New York, Philadelphia, and especially Boston. While this "urban crucible" of unrest cannot be denied, historians seeking the causes of the American Revolution should also look deeper into the interior of America—to the "ends of the American earth." The first crucible was formed when wealthy land speculators and poor backcountry farmers universally condemned the Proclamation Line. The first open rebellion to challenge government authority following the French and Indian War occurred with the Paxton Boys in 1763, not among Boston's Sons of Liberty in 1770. The first time that Americans fired on British troops took place outside Fort Loudon in 1765, not at Lexington Green in 1775. A closer look at Pontiac's Uprising and its consequences reveals that the conflict galvanized the growing resentment of a backcountry population against British authority.[56]

While frontier agitation cannot compare in scope with the displays of discontent that later occurred in more settled areas, it certainly underscores the need for historians to seek a more holistic approach in identifying the causes of the American Revolution. When varying degrees of responsibility for bringing on the conflict are assigned only to economic, political, and social causes, the various colonies appear as a monolith. Nor is it sufficient to gauge the revolutionary sentiment found in one colony as compared to another. Rather, historians must look toward the regional interests and experiences *within* colonies. Doing so, we find that colonists living in the interior came to their hatred of the British as a result of neglect or mismanagement in Indian affairs. The radical sentiment of the hinterland originated in the experiences of Indian warfare during the Seven Years' War. No sooner had that conflict ended and frontier families thought themselves secure than another, more violent wave of death and destruction erupted during Pontiac's Uprising. This encounter brought the pioneers to the conclusion that the distant authority at Whitehall cared little about their lives and homes.[57]

Shaped by their experiences during the Woodland Indian conflict of 1763–1765 and by their historic disdain for British rule, it is little wonder that the Scots-Irish frontiersmen flocked to join Washington's Continental Army. Among the first troops to join the army outside Boston in 1775 was William Thompson's Cumberland County rifle battalion, which was later incorporated into the 1st Continental Regiment. One of the officers in Thompson's battalion was none other than Matthew Smith, one of the leaders in the Paxton Boys' rebellion. For these backcountry settlers, creation of revolutionary fervor had more to with hostility toward Indians and a disdain for an unresponsive and distant government than with British economic policies, parliamentary representation, or the social and class consciousness that instigated revolutionary unrest in the urban areas.[58]

The conflict that has become known as Pontiac's Uprising was more than a mere interlude between the two great global wars that engulfed North America in the second half of the eighteenth century. In fact, the struggle can be viewed as the inexorable chain that manacles together these two fateful struggles. This horrific Indian conflict provides the continuity for understanding the fissures that existed within the triumphant British Empire that, in the span of only a dozen years, led to the chaos of revolution.

The Pontiac Indian uprising should also be remembered, not as a resistance movement that failed, but as a transcendent episode in the struggle of Native Americans to retain their identity and sovereignty, a struggle that continues to this day. This war once again reminds us that the Native peoples of early America cannot be understood from a monocultural perspective. Iroquois, Delawares, Ottawas, and Shawnees faced the challenge of European domination differently. Nonetheless, they universally recognized the consequences of that domination, and they all fought in some fashion or another to resist it. In many ways this resistance, punctuating the middle of the eighteenth century, persists today. In the final paragraph of his epic history of Pontiac's war, Francis Parkman lamented that "neither mound or tablet marked the burial-place" of Chief Pontiac. Instead, Parkman self righteously proclaimed, a city had risen over his forgotten grave, filled with "the race whom he hated with such burning rancor." In a larger sense, however, for Native Americans seeking to connect with an exalted past marked by resistance, neither Pontiac nor the war that bears his name will be forgotten.

Appendix

Colonel Bouquet's Letters From Bushy Run

Camp at Edge Hill, 26 miles from Fort Pitt 5th August 1763

Sir

The Second Instant the Troops and Convoy arrived at Ligonier where I could obtain no Intelligence of the Enemy, The Expresses sent Since the beginning of July, having been either killed, or obliged to return, all the Passes being occupied by the Enemy. In this uncertainty I determined to leave all the Waggons with the Powder, and a quantity of Stores and Provisions at Ligonier, and on the 4th proceeded with the Troops & about 340 Horses loaded with Flour.

I intended to have halted to Day at Bushy Run, a mile beyond this Camp, and after having refreshed the Men and Horses, to have marched in the night over Turtle Creek, a very dangerous Defile of Several miles, commanded by high and craggy Hills; But at one o'Clock this afternoon, after a march of 17 miles, the savages suddenly attacked our advanced guard, which was immediately supported by the two light Infantry Companies of the 42nd Regiment, who drove the Enemy from their Ambuscade, & pursued them a good Way. The savages returned to the attack and the Fire being obstante on our Front and extending along our Flanks, we made a general Charge with our whole Line to dislodge the savages from the Heights, in which attempt we succeeded, without obtaining by it any decisive advantage, for as soon as they were driven from one Post, they appeared on another, till by continual Reinforcements, they were at last able to surround us, & attacked the Convoy lefft in our Rear: This obliged us to march back to protect it; The Action then became general, and though we were attacked on every Side, and the Savages exerted themselves with uncommon Resolution, they were constantly repulsed with Loss. We also suffered considerably, Capt. Lieut Graham, and Lieut James McIntosh of the 42nd are killed, & Capt. Graham wounded.

Of the R.A.R. Lieut Dow who acted as A.D.Q.M.G. is shot through the body. Of the 77th Lieut Donald Campbell, and Mr. Peebles, a Volunteer, are wounded.

Our Loss in Men including Rangers and Drivers exceeds Sixty killed or Wounded.

The action has lasted from one o'Clock till Night, and we expect to begin again at Day break.

Whatever our Fate may be, I thought it necessary to give your Excellency this early Information, that you may, at all Events, take such measures as you think proper with the Provinces for their own Safety, and the Effectual relief of Fort Pitt, as in case of another Engagement, I fear insurmontable difficulties in protecting & transporting our Provisions: being already So much weakened by the Losses of this Day in men, and Horses, besides the additional Necessity of carrying wounded, whose situation is truly deplorable.

I cannot sufficiently acknowledge the constant assistance I have received from Major Campbell during this long action, nor Express my admiration of the cool and steady behaviour of the Troops, who did not fire a Shot without orders, and drove the Enemy from their Posts with Fixed Bayonets: The Conduct of the officers is much above my Praises.

I have the honor to be with great Respect Sir

Your most obedient & most Humble Servant
Henry Bouquet

To His Excellency Sir Jeffery Amherst
Camp at Bushy Run 6th August 1763

Sir

I had the honour to inform your Excellency in my letter of yesterday of our first Engagement with the Savages.

We took Post last night on the Hill where our Convoy halted when the front was attacked/ a comodious Piece of ground, & just Spacious enough for our Purpose/ There we encircled the Whole & covered our wounded with the Flour Bags.

In the morning the Savages Surrounded our Camp, at the distance of about 500 yards, & by Shouting and yelping quite round that extensive Circumference thought to have terrified us with their numbers: They attacked us early, and under Favour of an incessant Fire, made Several bold Efforts to penetrate our Camp, and tho' they failed in the attempt, our Situation was not the less perplexing, having experienced that brisk attacks had little Effect upon an Enemy who always gave way when pressed, and appeared again immediately: Our Troops were besides extremely fatigued with the long march, and as long Action of the preceding Day, and distressed to the last Degree by a total want of water, much more intolerable than the Enemy's Fire.

Tied to our Convoy we could not lose Sight of it without exposing it & our wounded to fall a Prey to the Savages, who pressed upon us on every Side, and to move it was impracticable, having lost so many Horses, and most of the Drivers, Stupified by Fear, hid themselves in the Bushes, or were incapable of hearing or obeying any Orders.

The Savages growing every moment more audacious it was thought proper Still to increase their Confidence; by that means, if possible, to intice them to come close upon us, or to Stand their ground when attacked. With this View two Companies of Light Infantry were ordered within the Circle, & the Troops on their right and left opened their Files and filled up the Space; that it might Seem they were intended to cover the Retreat. The third Light Infantry Company, and the Grenadiers of the 42nd were ordered to Support the two first Companies. This manoeuvre Succeeded to our Wish, for the few Troops who took Possession of the ground lately occupied by the two Light

Infantry Companies, being brought in nearer to the Center of the Circle, The Barbarians mistaking these motions for a Retreat hurried headlong on, and advancing upon us with the most daring intrepidity galled us excessively with their heavy Fire; but at the very moment that certain of Success, they thought themselves Master of the Camp, Major Campbell at the head of the two first Companies Sallied out, from a Part of the Hill they could not observe, and fell upon their right Flank. They resolutely returned the Fire, but could not Stand the irresistible Shock of our Men, who rushing in among them, killed many of them, and put the rest to Flight. The Orders Sent to the other two Companies were delivered So timely by Captain Basset, & executed with such celerity and Spirit that the routed Savages, who happened to run that moment before their Front, received their full Fire, when uncovered by the Trees. The four Companies did not give them to load a Second time, nor even to look behind them, but pursued them till they were totally dispersed. The left of the Savages, which had not been attacked, were kept in awe by the Remains of our Troops posted on the Brow of the Hill for that Purpose; nor durst they attempt to support, or assist their Right, but being witness to their Defeat, followed their Example and fled.

Our brave Men disdained so much to touch the dead Body of a vanquished Enemy that scarce a Scalp was taken, except by the Rangers & Pack Horse Drivers.

The Woods being now cleared and the Pursuit over, the four Companies took Possession of a Hill in our Front, and as soon as Litters could be made for the wounded, and the Flour and every thing destroyed, which for want of Horses could not be carried, we marched without molestation to this Camp. After the Severe Correction we had given the Savages a few hours before, it was natural to Suppose we Should enjoy Some Rest; but we had hardly fixed our Camp when they fired upon us again; This was very provoking! However the Light Infantry dispersed them before they could receive Orders for that Purpose. I hope we Shall be no more disturbed, for if we have another Action, we Shall hardly be able to carry our wounded.

The behaviour of the Troops on this Occasion Speaks for itself So Strongly, that for me to attempt their Eulogium would but detract from their merit.

I have the honor to be most respectfully Sir

Your most obedient & most Humble Servant
Henry Bouquet

P.S. I have the honor to inclose the Return of the killed, Wounded, and missing in the two Engagements

H.B.
To His Excellency Sir Jeffery Amherst

Notes

PREFACE

1. Francis Parkman's place in romantic historical scholarship is discussed in Michael McConnell's superb introduction to the latest reprint of *The Conspiracy of Pontiac*, published by the University of Nebraska Press. See Parkman, *The Conspiracy of Pontiac*, vii–xv.

2. Peckham, "The Sources and Revisions of Parkman's *Pontiac*," 298–99. For an assessment of Peckham's work see John Dann's new foreward to the reprint edition of Peckham, *Pontiac and the Indian Uprising*, xiv–xix.

3. One historian who has been especially critical of Parkman's work is Francis Jennings. See Jennings, "A Vanishing Indian: Francis Parkman versus His Sources"; Jennings, "A Brahmin among Untouchables"; and Jennings, *Empire of Fortune*, 171, 438–53, 480.

4. See White, *The Middle Ground*; McConnell, *A Country Between*; Dowd, *A Spirited Resistance*; and Steele, *Warpaths*. Gregory Dowd's recent book, *War under Heaven*, does focus solely on Pontiac's Uprising. Once again, however, this volume is largely interpretive and the chronology and narrative seem to get lost in the author's masterful analysis.

5. Shy, *Toward Lexington*; Anderson, *Crucible of War*; and Brumwell, *Redcoats*.

CHAPTER 1

1. "The Journal of Christian Frederick Post, from Philadelphia to the Ohio, on a Message from the Government of Pennsylvania to the Delaware, Shawnese, and Mingo Indians, Settled There," reprinted in Thwaites, *Early Western Travels*, 185–88 (hereafter cited as Post Journal).

2. For the purposes of this study, the Ohio Country is roughly defined as the region extending from the eastern slopes of the Appalachian Mountains to the Miami River and from the Ohio River northward to the Great Lakes watershed. Helen Hornbeck Tanner, in her *Atlas of Great Lakes Indian History*, 3, includes all of this area as part of the "Great Lakes Region Principal Theatre." As the present study indicates, however, there were many important political, economic, and cultural differences that separated the Indians of the Ohio Country from those who inhabited the Great Lakes watershed.

3. For a thorough explanation of the origins and conduct of the Beaver Wars, see Richter and Merrell, *Beyond the Covenant Chain*, 20–24; Fenton, *The Great Law and the Longhouse*, 229, 244–45; and Brandão, *"Your fyre shall burn no more."* For information regarding the origins of the Mingoes see Jennings, *Empire of Fortune*, 26.

4. The word "Appalachian" means "people on the other side" in the Choctaw tongue.

5. The migration of the Delawares into the Ohio Country is discussed in McConnell, *A Country Between*, 5–20.

6. The "Walking Purchase" is discussed in Jennings, *Empire of Fortune*, 25–28.

7. Information on Shawnee migration can be found in McConnell, *A Country Between*, 14–15, 22; Sipe, *The Indian Wars of Pennsylvania*, 45–50, 749, 753; and Hanna, *The Wilderness Trail*, 1:119–60.

8. "Conrad Weiser's Journal of a Tour to the Ohio, August 11–October 2, 1748," in Thwaites, *Early Western Travels*, 31, 42.

9. Williamson's description of Native Americans, as well as that of many other observers, can be found in O'Neil II, *Their Bearing Is Noble and Proud*, 14.

10. Ibid., 16–17.

11. Ibid., 17.

12. The hypothesis that the various tribes living in the Ohio Country began to forge a common identity is well developed by Michael McConnell in his excellent study, *A Country Between*, 20, 45–46. Anthropologists refer to this process of cultural re-creation as "ethnogenesis." In his study, *The Indian Southwest, 1580–1830: Ethnogenesis and Reinvention*, 3–6, 267–68, Gary Clayton Anderson contends that ethnogenesis is especially common among "tribal societies that face advancing colonialism and are forced to change or perish."

13. Hanna, *The Wilderness Trail,* 2:302.

14. Ibid., 2:307.

15. "Minute of Instructions to Marquis Duquesne, April 1752," in Hanna, *The Wilderness Trail,* 1:20.

16. Information on the establishment and purpose of the French forts in the Great Lakes region can be found in Peckham, *Pontiac and the Indian Uprising* (1947 edition), 8–10; and Parkman, *The Conspiracy of Pontiac,* 1:55.

17. Hanna, *The Wilderness Trail,* 2:326–43. The information contained in these pages indicates that Hanna conducted a thorough search of Pennsylvania colonial records to uncover the names of traders operating on the Pennsylvania frontier. See also Hunter, "Traders on the Ohio, 1730."

18. Wainwright, *George Croghan,* 6–8. Croghan returned to Philadelphia, where he filed a deposition with the mayor, Edward Shippen, claiming that the Shawnees had taken "forty-eight horseloads of deerskins, four hundred pounds of beaver, and six hundred pounds of raccoon skins." See ibid., 8.

19. George Croghan to Richard Peters, May 26, 1747, *Pennsylvania Archives,* 1st series, 1:742.

20. Hazard, *Colonial Records of Pennsylvania,* 5:146–47 (hereafter cited as *Colonial Records).*

21. The Ohio Indians' claim of autonomy from the Onondaga council during this period is fully discussed in McConnell, *A Country Between,* 69–72; and Jennings, *Empire of Fortune,* 28–30. A description of the half-king Monacatootha, who was called Scarouady by his Shawnee charges, can be found in Alberts, *A Charming Field for an Encounter,* 6. A more complete biography of the chief is contained in Sipe, *Indian Chiefs of Pennsylvania,* 213–54.

22. Conrad Weiser to Richard Peters, June 21, 1747, *Pennsylvania Archives,* 1st series, 1:751.

23. George Croghan to Thomas Lawrence, September 18, 1747, ibid., 1:770.

24. McConnell, *A Country Between,* 72–73; Jennings, *Empire of Fortune,* 29–31.

25. Background on the Ohio Company can be found in Mulkearn, *George Mercer Papers.* Jennings provides a revealing chapter on the activities of the company in *Empire of Fortune,* 8–20. Gist's journal of his first trip to the Ohio Country can be found in Mulkearn, *George Mercer Papers,* 7–31 (the journal itself is hereafter cited as Gist's Journal).

26. Gist's Journal, 10.

27. Biographical information on Céloron de Blainville can be found in W. J. Eccles, "Céloron de Blainville," in *Dictionary of Canadian Biography,* 3:99–100.

28. Unfortunately, there is very little biographical information on Joncaire, who appears to be an important figure in relation to French and Indian

relations during this period. A brief biography exists in Malcolm MacLeod, "Chabert de Joncaire," in *Dictionary of Canadian Biography,* 3:101–2.

29. The complete record of Céloron's expedition and his conferences with the various Indian nations he encountered can be found in Darlington, *Fort Pitt and Letters from the Frontier,* 9–61. Céloron's speech to the Senecas and their reply can be found on pages 18–20.

30. Ibid., 21–24.

31. Ibid., 60–61. An insightful evaluation of Céloron's expedition can be found in McConnell, *A Country Between,* 82–88.

32. *Colonial Records,* 5:387.

33. Ibid., 5:423.

34. Ibid., 5:424.

35. Wainwright, *George Croghan,* 30.

36. Peters to Thomas Penn, October 20, 1748, Peters Letter Books, Historical Society of Pennsylvania, quoted in Wainwright, *George Croghan,* 23. For a complete discussion of Peters's plan, see pages 23–29.

37. Gist's Journal, 39.

38. Ibid., 53.

39. For a biography of Tanacharison, see Mulkearn, "Half King, Seneca Diplomat of the Ohio Valley."

40. Mulkearn, *George Mercer Papers,* 62.

41. Ibid., 63.

42. Jennings, *Empire of Fortune,* 42–43; McConnell, *A Country Between,* 96–98.

43. Hanna, *The Wilderness Trail,* 2:290.

44. Hunter, *Forts on the Pennsylvania Frontier,* 138–41.

45. Kent, *French Invasion,* 47–49.

46. Ibid., 49–50.

47. Kent, *French Invasion,* 51; McConnell, *A Country Between,* 101–2.

48. Jennings, *Empire of Fortune,* 90–92.

49. For an in-depth examination of the political controversy that engulfed Pennsylvania during this period, see Ketcham, "Conscience, War, and Politics"; Marietta, "Conscience, the Quaker Community, and the French and Indian War"; Thayer, *Pennsylvania Politics;* and Jennings, *Empire of Fortune,* 86.

50. Jennings, *Empire of Fortune,* 56.

51. Information on Washington's 1754 campaign can be found in Alberts, *A Charming Field for an Encounter.* The Walpole quote is found on page 20.

52. Kent, *Contrecoeur's Copy of George Washington's Journal for 1754,* 18.

53. For a discussion of the Great Lakes tribes that accompanied the French, see White, *The Middle Ground,* 241.

54. O'Callaghan, *Documentary History of the State of New York*, 2:338.

55. Quoted in Wallace, *Conrad Weiser*, 359.

56. The intrigues at Albany are fully discussed in Jennings, *Empire of Fortune*, 71–108. For a complete history of the Albany meeting, see Shannon, *Indians and Colonists at the Crossroads of Empire*.

57. An estimation of Braddock's character can be found in McCardell, *Ill-Starred General*, 124, 271.

58. This colorful description of the scout Montour underscores the cross-cultural exchange that had taken place on the frontier. The characterization was recorded by the Moravian missionary Count Nikolaus Ludwig von Zinzendorf and is quoted in Merrell, *Into the American Woods*, 75–76.

59. *Colonial Records*, 6:589.

60. McCardell, *Ill-Starred General*, 174–75.

61. The size of the enemy force opposing Braddock at the Battle of the Monongahela is debated by historians. These figures come from Sargent, *A History of an Expedition*, 223–24.

62. Washington's estimation of the effectiveness of British regulars against the Indians can be found in Lewis, *For King and Country*, 183.

63. McCardell, *Ill-Starred General*, 251; Sargent, *A History of an Expedition*, 229–30.

64. Hamilton, *Braddock's Defeat*, 52.

65. McCardell, *Ill-Starred General*, 260–61.

66. *Colonial Records*, 6:647–48.

67. On the Pennsylvania forts, see Hunter, *Forts on the Pennsylvania Frontier*; and Waddell and Bomberger, *The French and Indian War in Pennsylvania*, 32–35, 82–89.

68. *Colonial Records*, 7:75–76. For more on the scalp bounties, see Young, "A Note on Scalp Bounties in Pennsylvania."

69. For an overview of the British offensive of 1758 see James and Stotz, *Drums in the Forest*, 39–40.

70. Biographical information on John Forbes can be found in James, *Writings of General John Forbes*, ix–xii, 301.

71. Ibid., 205.

72. Ibid., 109.

73. Forbes's frustration with Sir William Johnson can be appreciated by reading a letter the general wrote to General James Abercromby in July 1758, which can be found in James, *Writings of General John Forbes*, 134–42. In fact, throughout the Forbes papers are numerous references to the general's exasperation with Johnson.

74. The 1757 Easton conference is covered in detail in Wallace, *Conrad Weiser*, 476–85; Wallace, *Teedyuscung*, 149–60; and Jennings, *Empire of Fortune*, 341–48.

75. James, *Writings of General John Forbes*, 83–84.
76. Quoted in Wainwright, *George Croghan*, 120, 135–36.
77. Biographical information on Post can be found in Thwaites, *Early Western Travels*, 177–84; and Thomson, *An Enquiry into the Causes of the Alienation of the Delaware and Shawanese Indians from the British Interest*, 129. Also see Heckewelder, *A Narrative of the Mission of the United Brethren among the Delaware and Mohegan*, 55.
78. All the quotations regarding Post's journey can be found in Thwaites, *Early Western Travels*, 188, 193, 195, 199.
79. Ibid., 204, 209, 212.
80. Shingas is described in Sipe, *Indian Chiefs of Pennsylvania*, 287–305. The description of Shingas's disfigured nose may be apocryphal since no contemporary portrait or description of the chief can be found.
81. Thwaites, *Early Western Travels*, 213–19.
82. James, *Writings of General John Forbes*, 255; James and Stotz, *Drums in the Forest*, 51.
83. Thwaites, *Early Western Travels*, 258, 264.
84. Ibid., 278.

CHAPTER 2

1. General Forbes's ailment, probably colon cancer, is described in James, *Writings of General John Forbes*, 169.
2. Cort, *Col. Henry Bouquet and His Campaigns*, 7.
3. Information on the creation of the Royal American Regiment can be found in Brumwell, *Redcoats*, 19, 74–75.
4. Branch, "Henry Bouquet: His Relic Possessions."
5. Considering the vast amount of his extant personal papers, it is surprising that a book-length biography has never been written about Henry Bouquet. For further biographical information, readers should consult Cort, *Col. Henry Bouquet and His Campaigns*; Fisher, "Brigadier-General Henry Bouquet"; Robbins, "Life and Services of Colonel Henry Bouquet"; Branch, "Henry Bouquet: Professional Soldier"; and Schazmann, "Henry Bouquet in Switzerland". Readers should also consult the first volume of the ambitious work Stevens and others, *The Papers of Henry Bouquet*, 1:xvi–xxvii (hereafter cited as *Bouquet Papers*, with specific references to dates and correspondents).
6. This portrait of Henry Bouquet, which was painted by John Wollaston, resides in the Historical Society of Pennsylvania. The Winterthur Museum near Wilmington, Delaware, owns two other portraits painted by Wollaston. One is of a slender lady, and the other is a likeness of a rather elderly gentleman. Both of these portraits reveal a striking resemblance to the Bouquet painting. Both subjects have the same double chin, almond-shaped eyes,

aquiline nose, and cleft in the chin. For an enlightening discussion of Wollaston's work, see Rasmussen and Tilton, *George Washington: The Man behind the Myth*, 84–86.

7. Detail of a Proposed Expedition to Fort Duquesne by Henry Bouquet, March 18, 1757, *Bouquet Papers*, 1:51–54; Forbes to Bouquet, June 27, 1758, ibid., 2:135–37.

8. Quoted in Branch, "Henry Bouquet: Professional Soldier," 45.

9. A thorough examination of Bouquet's abilities as a frontier commander can be found in Brodine, Jr., "Henry Bouquet and British Infantry Tactics," 43–61. For another assessment of Bouquet's skills, see Daudelin, "Numbers and Tactics at Bushy Run."

10. Bouquet to Young, December 15, 1756, *Bouquet Papers*, 1:37; Bouquet to Forbes, September 17, 1758, ibid., 2:521.

11. Bouquet to Anne Willing, September 17, 1759, ibid., 4:115.

12. For a discussion regarding the objectives of Grant's expedition, see James and Stotz, *Drums in the Forest*, 49; Bouquet to Forbes, September 11, 1758, *Bouquet Papers*, 2:493; Bouquet to Forbes, September 17, 1758, ibid., 2:517–21.

13. Bouquet to Forbes, September 17, 1758, *Bouquet Papers*, 2:517–21.

14. Bouquet suggested that Grant's defeat may have actually contributed to the eventual success of the campaign. He reasoned that the Indians perhaps sustained heavy casualties and were tired of the fighting. Also, with few supplies coming from their French allies, the Indians needed to return to their homes to provide for their families for the coming winter. In addition, they recognized that there was still a large British force assembling less than fifty miles away at Fort Ligonier. After making a weak attack on the British outpost in October, the Great Lakes and Ohio warriors were content to return home and let their French allies deal with Forbes's army. See James and Stotz, *Drums in the Forest*, 50.

15. *Pennsylvania Archives*, 1st series, 12:428–31; *Colonial Records*, 8:231–34.

16. Bouquet to Anne Willing, November 25, 1758, *Bouquet Papers*, 2:608.

17. For a complete discussion of the Treaty of Easton (1758), see Wallace, *Teedyuscung*, 194–207; Auth, *The Ten Years' War*, 93–108; Boyd, ed., *Indian Treaties Printed by Benjamin Franklin*, 312–18; and *Colonial Records*, 8:175–223.

18. Bouquet to the Duke of Portland, December 3, 1758, *Bouquet Papers*, 2:620–21; Forbes to Bouquet, December 4, 1758, ibid., 2:627.

19. Bouquet: Conference with the Delaware Indians, December 4, 1758, ibid., 2:621–24.

20. Thwaites, *Early Western Travels*, 283–84. Bouquet's record of the conference failed to disclose that the Indians had continued to insist that

the British withdraw back across the mountains. Post's version of events is supported by a letter from a French officer at Venango who spoke with a Delaware who had attended the meeting with Bouquet. See *Bouquet Papers*, 2: 624–26.

21. The most comprehensive biography of Hugh Mercer is Waterman, *With Sword and Lancet*. Information on Armstrong's raid on the Indian village of Kittanning can be found in Hunter, "Victory at Kittanning"; and Myers, "Pennsylvania's Awakening."

22. Mercer to Bouquet, January 19, 1759, *Bouquet Papers*, 3:58–60.

23. Mercer to Forbes, January 8, 1759, Enclosure: Indian Conference at Pittsburgh, ibid., 3:25–32.

24. A fine overview of the British offensive of 1758 can be found in Leach, *Arms for Empire*, 415–45. The quote regarding the bravery of the Highland troops can be found in Brander, *The Scottish Highlanders*, 119.

25. Waterman, *With Sword and Lancet*, 49; Invoice of Indian Stores, February 27, 1759, *Bouquet Papers*, 3:152–53; Amherst to Bouquet, March 16, 1759, ibid., 3:199–202.

26. Amherst to Governor William Denny, March 28, 1759, *Colonial Records*, 8:316–17. For a discussion of British strategy in 1759, see Leach, *Arms for Empire*, 446–47.

27. *Colonial Records*, 8:265–69, 387–92.

28. Bouquet to Mercer, May 26, 1759, *Bouquet Papers*, 3:326–27; Adam Stephen to Bouquet, July 29, 1759, ibid., 3:462–63.

29. Graydon: Journal Kept at Fort Lyttleton, ibid., 3:155–60, 222–27.

30. Bouquet to Mercer, April 13, 1759, ibid., 3:240–41; Bouquet to Mercer, May 26, 1759, ibid., 3:326–27.

31. Lt. Col. Thomas Lloyd to Bouquet, April 21, 1759, ibid., 3:246–48; Mercer to Bouquet, May 23, 1759, ibid., 3:304–6; and Lloyd to Stanwix, May 23, 1759, ibid., 3:309–11.

32. Wainwright, "George Croghan's Journal," 316–17 (hereafter cited as Croghan's Journal); *Colonial Records*, 8:389.

33. Pouchot, *Memoirs on the Late War in North America*, 183; Bouquet to James Burd, June 26, 1759, *Bouquet Papers*, 3:382–83; Croghan to Bouquet, July 11, 1759, ibid., 3:397.

34. Dunnigan, *Siege—1759*, 83–85; Croghan's Journal, 327.

35. In the pitched battle that took place between the French and the English before the ramparts of Fort Niagara, Native American allies played almost no role. This was due in part to the fact that this type of combat did not suit the Indians, as they ran the risk of sustaining too many casualties, warriors difficult to replace. In addition, Indians on both sides seemed to be content to let the Europeans fight it out and then see which one was superior. As the French began to retreat, Sir William Johnson's Mohawks did take up the pursuit, turning the orderly withdrawal into a rout. See Dunnigan, *Siege—1759*, 97–98.

36. Monckton to Bouquet, July 6, 1760, *Bouquet Papers*, 4:620–23.

37. Croghan's Journal, 378; Bouquet to Monckton, July 28, 1760, *Bouquet Papers*, 4:667–69.

38. Despite his renown, no complete biography of Robert Rogers has been written since 1959. Readers should consult Cuneo, *Robert Rogers of the Rangers*; Loescher, *The History of Rogers Rangers*; Loescher, *Genesis, The History of Rogers Rangers*; Rogers and Bouquet, *Warfare on the Colonial Frontier: The Journals of Major Robert Rogers* (hereafter cited as *Rogers's Journals*); and H. M. Jackson, *Rogers' Rangers*. Rogers's famous raid against the Abenaki village of Saint Francis has been fictionalized in the many editions of Kenneth Roberts's novel *Northwest Passage* (New York: Doubleday, 1937). Amherst's orders to Rogers can be found in Amherst to Rogers, September 12, 1760, *The Papers of Sir Jeffrey Amherst*, vol. 49, reel 1113 (hereafter cited as Amherst Papers with appropriate volume and reel numbers).

39. Rogers's expedition is described in "A Journal of the March from Montreal to Detroit performed by Robert Rogers Major of the Rangers, in pursuance of the Orders of his Excellency General Amherst," Amherst Papers, vol. 49; and *Rogers's Journals*, 183–94.

40. Croghan's Journal, 386.

41. *Rogers's Journals*, 195.

42. Croghan's Journal, 393–94; *Rogers's Journals*, 196–210.

43. An account of this conference can be found in Sullivan and others, *The Papers of Sir William Johnson*, 10:198–206 (hereafter cited as *Johnson Papers*).

44. For information on Pontiac, one needs only to consult the superlative biography by Peckham, *Pontiac and the Indian Uprising*, which contains a good description of the Ottawa's early life on pages 15–29.

45. List of Houses and Inhabitants at Fort Pitt, April 14, 1761, *Bouquet Papers*, 5:407–21; Wainwright, *George Croghan*, 192, 196, 197.

46. Bouquet to Monckton, March 20, 1761, *Bouquet Papers*, 5:352–56; Bouquet to the Several Posts, July 31, 1761, ibid., 5:675–76; and Bouquet to Captain Gavin Cochrane, July 12, 1761, ibid., 5:629–30.

47. Mulkearn, *George Mercer Papers*, 18.

48. Jordan, "James Kenny's 'Journal to Ye Westward,'" and "Journal of James Kenny," 404–5, 408, 419 (both of these journals, which appear in the same volume of *Pennsylvania Magazine of History and Biography*, are hereafter cited as *Kenny's Journals*); Wainwright, *George Croghan*, 193

49. *Kenny's Journals*, 15–16, 28, 435.

50. *Kenny's Journals*, 32–33, 35–36, 415; Bouquet to Amherst, January 12, 1762, *Bouquet Papers*, 6:36–39.

51. *Kenny's Journals*, 23, 40, 45.

52. For a comprehensive view of the British soldier in North America, see Brumwell's excellent social history, *Redcoats*.

53. For a brief discussion of the relationship between regular and provincial troops, see Leach, *Roots of Conflict*, 107–33. Information on the conditions

faced by the British army can be found throughout the Bouquet Papers. See Bouquet to Monckton, March 20, 1761, *Bouquet Papers*, 5:304; Order Halting Sales at Gun Firing, February 21, 1761, ibid., 5:352–56; and Regulations for Pittsburgh, March 28, 1761, ibid., 5:376–77. See also *Kenny's Journals*, 404, and Hunter, "Thomas Barton and the Forbes Expedition," 481–82.

54. Lieutenant Robert Stewart to Bouquet, October 31, 1760, *Bouquet Papers*, 5:91; Robert Stewart to Bouquet, November 18, 1760, ibid., 5:114; and Captain Lewis Ourry to Bouquet, January 17, 1761, ibid., 5:253–54. Biographical information on Lewis Ourry, who was a close personal friend of Henry Bouquet, can be found in Cornu, "Captain Lewis Ourry."

55. Quoted in Cornu, "Captain Lewis Ourry," 253.

56. Bouquet to Monckton, September 11, 1761, *Bouquet Papers*, 5:746–48; *Kenny's Journals*, 20.

57. Bouquet to Anne Willing, January 15, 1761, *Bouquet Papers*, 5:247–49; Ourry to Bouquet, March 10, 1762, ibid., 6:57–59; Branch, "Henry Bouquet: Professional Soldier," 46–47.

58. McDonald to Bouquet, March 29, 1761, *Bouquet Papers*, 5:379–80; Bouquet to Monckton, April 21, 1761, ibid., 5:435–39; McDonald to Bouquet, October 24, 1761, ibid., 5:840; and Bouquet: Proclamation against Settlers, October 30, 1761, ibid., 5:834.

59. Fauquier to Bouquet, January 17, 1762, ibid., 6:39–40.

60. Bouquet to Fauquier, February 8, 1762, ibid., 6:44–45.

61. Amherst to Bouquet, February 28, 1762, ibid., 6:47–48; Bouquet to Amherst, April 1, 1762, ibid., 6:71–73.

62. Evidence of Bouquet's land schemes with the wily Croghan can be found in Croghan to Bouquet, March 30, 1763, ibid., 6:169–70.

63. *Colonial Records*, 9:6–9.

64. *Johnson Papers*, 10:213–15, 231–32, 266–68.

65. Michael McConnell provides a thorough discussion of the activities along the Niagara portage in *A Country Between*, 169–71. The quotes are from *Johnson Papers*, 10:321 and 3:515.

66. Quaife, *The Siege of Detroit*, xliv, 220–21; *Johnson Papers*, 3:759.

67. Teedyuscung's warning is quoted in Auth, *The Ten Years' War*, 128.

68. *Kenny's Journals*, 152; *Johnson Papers*, 3:734.

69. *Kenny's Journals*, 19.

CHAPTER 3

1. For a biography of Jeffery Amherst, see Long, *Lord Jeffery Amherst*.

2. Ibid., 86–107. Amherst's military campaigns at Louisbourg and Ticonderoga are also well covered in Francis Parkman's classic account, *Montcalm and Wolfe*, 334–70.

3. Perhaps the best discussion of the postwar situation that Amherst faced can be found in Shy, *Toward Lexington*, 45–52.

4. *Johnson Papers*, 3:205.

5. A brief but excellent discussion of the Cherokee War can be found in Anderson, *Crucible of War*, 457–68.

6. For evidence that Amherst used the lessons of the Cherokee War to formulate his Indian policy, see Amherst to Sir William Johnson, August 11, 1761, *Johnson Papers*, 3:516–17.

7. Amherst to Sir William Johnson, February 22, 1761, ibid., 3:345.

8. There are numerous biographies of Sir William Johnson, including Flexner, *Mohawk Baronet*; Pound, *Johnson of the Mohawks*; Stone, *Life and Times of Sir William Johnson*; and Hamilton, *Sir William Johnson*. As to Johnson's sexual conquests among Mohawk women, see Wallace, *Conrad Weiser*, 247.

9. In his insightful interpretation of Pontiac's Uprising, Gregory Dowd argues that the British retrenchment in gift giving convinced the Indian nations that the English not only had little regard for them as friends and allies but also intended to ignore Indian sovereignty and dominate them. See Dowd, *War under Heaven*, 63–78.

10. Johnson to the Lords of Trade, September 25, 1763, in Alvord, *The Critical Period*, 31–32.

11. Johnson to the Earl of Egremont, May 1762, *Johnson Papers*, 10:461–62.

12. Ibid.

13. Johnson to Daniel Claus, March 10, 1761, ibid., 3:354.

14. Croghan to Sir William Johnson, December 10, 1762, ibid., 3:965.

15. Wainwright, *George Croghan*, 177, 194.

16. Campbell to Henry Bouquet, March 10, 1761, *Bouquet Papers*, 5:340–41; McDonald to Bouquet, March 10, 1761, ibid., 5:342.

17. Campbell to Henry Bouquet, December 23, 1760, ibid., 5:196; Campbell to Bouquet, May 21, 1761, ibid., 5:491.

18. John St. Clair to Henry Bouquet, August 21, 1761, ibid., 5:705; Lieutenant Elias Meyer to Henry Bouquet, September 24, 1761, ibid., 5:777–80; *Kenny's Journals*, 6, 10, 21, 40, 42, 163. The account ledger of the trading post at Fort Pitt can be found in *The Fort Pitt Waste Book*. Information regarding the council house constructed near Fort Pitt can be found in the Fort Pitt Collection, MFF 0802.

19. Cort, *Col. Henry Bouquet and His Campaigns*, 17, 23; *Bouquet Papers*, 5:505–6.

20. Wainwright, *George Croghan*, 192–93. Wainwright cites a manuscript copy of James Kenny's diary that is housed in the Historical Society of Philadelphia as the source for this information. However, none of this

material can be found in the printed version of Kenny's journal that appears in the *Pennsylvania Magazine of History and Biography*. Apparently, the editor, John W. Jordan, believing this information too shameful to include, attempted to rob scholars of a true picture of life at a frontier fort. Kenny's remarks concerning Jamey Wilson can be found in Jordan's edited version, *Kenny's Journals*, 7.

21. Thomas S. Abler, "Kayahsota," in *Dictionary of Canadian Biography*, 4:408–10; Dexter, *Diary of David McClure*, 42; Donald Campbell to Henry Bouquet, June 16, 1761, *Bouquet Papers*, 5:555–57.

22. Croghan's Journal, 409–10; Campbell to Bouquet, June 16, 1761, *Bouquet Papers*, 5:556; "Copy of the Conference sent by Capt. Campble At a Council held at the Wiandot Town near Detroit 3d July 1761 by the Deputy's of the six Nations with the Ottawas, Wiandots, Chipeweighs, & Powtewatamis," *Johnson Papers*, 3:450–53.

23. Donald Campbell to Henry Bouquet, June 21, 1761, *Bouquet Papers*, 5:569–71; Campbell to Bouquet, July 7, 1761, ibid., 5:618–21; Croghan's Journal, 410–11.

24. "Report of Indian Council Near Detroit," enclosed with Campbell to Bouquet, July 22, 1761, *Bouquet Papers*, 5:646–50.

25. Bouquet to Campbell, June 30, 1761, ibid., 5:596–97.

26. Jeffrey Amherst to Sir William Johnson, August 9, 1761, *Johnson Papers*, 3:514–16.

27. Croghan's Journal, 409–10.

28. Sir William Johnson to Jeffery Amherst, June 21, 1761, *Johnson Papers*, 10:291.

29. Amherst to Johnson, May 7, 1761, ibid., 3:387–88; Amherst to Johnson, June 11, 1761; Johnson to Amherst, June 12, 1761, ibid.,10:284–87.

30. "Amherst's Instructions to Henry Gladwin," June 22, 1761, ibid., 10:293–96. For biographical information on Gladwin, see Peter E. Russell, "Henry Gladwin," in *Dictionary of Canadian Biography*, 4:297; Peckham, *Pontiac and the Indian Uprising*, 76–77; and Quaife, *The Siege of Detroit*, 4.

31. "Niagara and Detroit Proceedings, July–September, 1761," *Johnson Papers*, 3:460–63.

32. Ibid., 464–65.

33. On the grand ball and Angelique Cuillerier, see Peckham, *Pontiac and the Indian Uprising*, 78–79.

34. Sir William Johnson to General Thomas Gage, January 12, 1764, *Johnson Papers*, 4:296; *Kenny's Journals*, 24.

35. Sir William Johnson to Sir Jeffery Amherst, November 5, 1761, *Johnson Papers*, 3:559. An evaluation of Sir William Johnson's diplomatic strategy while at Detroit can be found in Auth, *The Ten Years War*, 151–53.

36. *Kenny's Journals*, 171.

37. Loudon, *Indian Narratives*, 272–76. A similar description of the drawing can be found in the memoirs of the Moravian missionary John Hecke-welder. See Heckewelder, *History, Manners, and Customs of the Indian Nations*, 291–93.

38. For a detailed discussion of these earlier prophets and their visions, see the excellent study by Dowd, *A Spirited Resistance*, 27–33. According to one source, Neolin's name meant "Four." See Bouquet to Francis and Clayton, September 23, 1764, *Bouquet Papers*, 6:643.

39. This version of Neolin's vision comes from an anonymous journal of the siege of Detroit that has generally been credited to a French resident inside the fort named Robert Navarre. Presumably, Navarre attended an Indian council near the fort where Pontiac related Neolin's teachings to the assembled chiefs and warriors. It is also quite possible that Navarre learned of the contents of Neolin's message from some other person who attended the council. See Quaife, *The Siege of Detroit*, 8–15.

40. Ibid., 15 16.

41. Alvord, *The Critical Period*, 50–51.

42. The works of earlier scholars such as Howard Peckham, Anthony F. C. Wallace, and Charles Hunter all seem to agree that Pontiac deliberately manipulated Neolin's true message. See Peckham, *Pontiac and the Indian Uprising*, 116; Wallace, "New Religions among the Delaware Indians," 9; and Hunter, "The Delaware Nativist Revival," 46. More recent interpretations demonstrate that Pontiac accurately related the prophet's teachings. See Dowd, "The French King Wakes Up in Detroit," 259–60; and Dowd, "Thinking and Believing," 311–12. Richard White, in his masterful study *The Middle Ground*, 284, suggests that Neolin may have always directed his resentment entirely toward the English, but interpreters had difficulty translating the various Delaware words for white.

43. *Kenny's Journals*, 188; Dowd, *A Spirited Resistance*, 33–34. The Moravian missionary David Zeisberger also wrote about the practice of purging among the Ohio Country Indians. See Zeisberger, *History of the Northern American Indians*, 133–34, 173.

44. Loudon, *Indian Narratives*, 274–75.

45. *Kenny's Journals*, 170–71, 175. Seeing that his efforts to maintain peace and convert the Indians of the Ohio Country had failed, Christian Frederick Post set off for the Carolinas in September 1763 to work among the Cherokees. The following year, he sailed to Honduras and Nicaragua to establish a mission among the Indians of the Mosquito Coast. He returned to Pennsylvania in 1767 hoping to obtain additional support from the Moravian authorities but was informed that his services were no longer required. Undaunted, Post returned to Nicaragua to continue his missionary work under the supervision of the Anglican Church. He retired to Germantown,

Pennsylvania, in 1784, where he died the following year. A fine biographical sketch of Post's career can be found in *Dictionary of American Biography*, 15:113–14. Also, see Wallace, *Thirty Thousand Miles with John Heckewelder*, 42–43.

46. *Colonial Records*, 8:767.

47. Ibid., 8:648.

48. Thomas McKee to Sir William Johnson, November 1, 1762, *Johnson Papers*, 3:921. An excellent account of the Lancaster Treaty of 1762 can be found in Auth, *The Ten Years War*, 174–84.

49. Croghan to Henry Bouquet, December 10, 1762, *Bouquet Papers*, 6:137–38.

50. "Indian Intelligence from Fort Pitt," ibid., 6:155–56.

51. Amherst to Sir William Johnson, October 31, 1762, *Johnson Papers*, 3:920.

CHAPTER 4

1. Details on the Havana campaign, including casualty figures, can be found in Anderson, *Crucible of War*, 497–502. For information concerning the condition of the returning troops, see Shy, *Toward Lexington*, 106–9.

2. For a detailed discussion of frontier land issues and British policy, see Sosin, *Whitehall and the Wilderness*, 27–51.

3. Wallace, *Teedyuscung*, 254–58; Sosin, *Whitehall and the Wilderness*, 50–51.

4. For speculation on the death of Teedyuscung, see Wallace, *Teedyuscung*, 258–61.

5. Henry Gladwin to Jeffery Amherst, April 20, 1763, *Johnson Papers*, 4:95–97.

6. George Croghan to Sir William Johnson, April 24, 1763, ibid., 10:659–60; Henry Gladwin to Jeffery Amherst, April 20, 1763, ibid., 4:95.

7. For descriptions of Fort Detroit, see Peckham, *Pontiac and the Indian Uprising*, 63–65; Donald Campbell to Henry Bouquet, December 11, 1760, *Bouquet Papers*, 5:170–72; Hough, *Diary of the Siege of Detroit*, 4 (a diary attributed to a British officer inside the fort during the siege named Lieutenant Jehu Hay); and Peckham, *Detroit under Pontiac's Siege*, 7–8.

8. On the number and location of Native Americans living around Detroit, see Peckham, *Pontiac and the Indian Uprising*, 55, 86. The location of the various Indian villages can be found in an early map made by J. G. De Lery in 1752 and in another prepared during the siege of Detroit in 1763 by Lieutenant John Montresor. Remarkably, the village locations shown on both maps correspond with one another. The census of warriors made by Thomas Hutchins in the fall of 1762 is also very close to a census of warriors that

was taken by an unidentified French informant, probably Robert Navarre, and that is published in Quaife, *The Siege of Detroit*, 128. The French informant reported that "there were 250 Ottawas under Pontiac; 150 Potawatomies under Ninivois; 50 Hurons governed by Takay; 250 Chippewas under Wasson; 170 Chippewas under Sekahos; all of whom were under the authority of Pontiac, their over-chief."

9. Hough, *Diary of the Siege of Detroit*, 4; Peckham, *Pontiac and the Indian Uprising*, 127–28. An official return of the 60th Royal American Regiment made in September 1763 lists the following men present at Detroit: 3 lieutenants, 3 ensigns, 3 sergeants, 4 drummers, 86 rank and file, 10 sick or wounded, and 8 on board the vessels, for a grand total of 117. If the company of rangers is added, the total comes to 140. It is unknown, however, whether this muster was made before Lieutenant Robertson departed Detroit with his 8 men. See "Return of the Detachment of the 1st Battalion, 60th Regiment at Niagara, Detroit, etc., September 7, 1763," Amherst Papers, vol. 42, reel 1108.

10. Hatcher, *Lake Erie*, 51; Quaife, *The Siege of Detroit*, xxviii–xxix, 43–44, 219–20; and Moore, *The Gladwin Manuscripts*, 608. There seems to be considerable disagreement and speculation regarding the size and armament of the two ships. Peckham, in *Pontiac and the Indian Uprising*, 127, describes the *Huron* as a "two-masted schooner" with "six guns" and the *Michigan* as a "somewhat larger sloop." Incredibly, Francis Parkman misnames the ships altogether, calling them the *Gladwyn* and the *Beaver*!

11. Quaife, *The Siege of Detroit*, 56, 68–69; Bouquet Papers, 5:21, 44, 72, 196. Additional information concerning Hopkins's role in Rogers's Rangers can be found in Loescher, *Officers and Non-commissioned Officers*, 94.

12. Quaife, *The Siege of Detroit*, 5–17. Nevins, *Ponteach*, 225. The Moravian missionary Count Zinzendorf told the Canadian métis woman Madame Montour about his home at Bethlehem, Pennsylvania. Montour informed the missionary that she had heard of a town by that name as "The place in France where Jesus and the holy family lived." At first surprised, Zinzendorf later wrote, "I had evidence of the truth of the charge brought against the French missionaries, who are said to make it a point to teach the Indians that Jesus had been a Frenchman, and that the English had been his crucifiers." See Sipe, *Indian Chiefs of Pennsylvania*, 311.

13. Quaife, *The Siege of Detroit*, 18–20; Hough, *Diary of the Siege of Detroit*, 1. For information concerning Indian reluctance to accept high casualties in combat, see Armstrong Starkey's insightful study, *European and Native American Warfare*, 26.

14. Quaife, *The Siege of Detroit*, 21–22.

15. The author of the anonymous diary *The Siege of Detroit*, 25, states that the signal for the attack would be a war cry from Pontiac. Several other

accounts, including one by Thomas Mante, published as early as 1772, claimed that the signal would be the turning of the wampum belt. See Mante, *History of the Late War*, 486.

16. Humphrey, "The Identity of Major Gladwin's Informant," 147–62; Peckham, *Pontiac and the Indian Uprising*, 121–25; Quaife, *The Siege of Detroit*, 26–27. Further proof of Angelique Cuillerier's status as an informant to Major Gladwin can be found in a letter written by Major Henry Bassett, who served as the commandant at Detroit in 1773. In a communication to General Frederick Haldimand, Bassett wrote, "I beg to recommend Mr. James Sterling, who is the first Merchant at this place, & a gentleman of good character, during the late war, through a Lady, that he then courted, from who he had the best information, was in part a means to save this garrison, this Gentleman is now married to that Lady & is connected with the best part of this Settlement." See Humphrey, "The Identity of Major Gladwin's Informant," 152–57.

17. John Porteous Journal, Burton Historical Collections, Detroit Public Library, quoted in Peckham, *Pontiac and the Indian Uprising*, 131. According to a letter written by trader James Sterling, Gladwin refused to meet with Pontiac at this time. See *Pennsylvania Gazette*, August 18, 1763.

18. Like many other aspects of the history of Pontiac's War, the number of canoes that crossed the river that day is disputed. See the *Pennsylvania Gazette*, August 18, 1763; Peckham, *Pontiac and the Indian Uprising*, 134; and Moore, *The Gladwin Manuscripts*, 619.

19. The site of the attack in which Mrs. Turnbull and her sons were killed was latter known as Old Woman's Field. *Pennsylvania Gazette*, August 18, 1763; Quaife, *The Siege of Detroit*, 38–41; Trowbridge, "Conspiracy of Pontiac and the Siege of Detroit: Mr. Pettier's Account," 360; Moore, *The Gladwin Manuscripts*, 619.

20. *Pennsylvania Gazette*, August 18, 1763; Quaife, *The Siege of Detroit*, 38.

21. Quaife, *The Siege of Detroit*, 219–74; *Pennsylvania Gazette*, August 11, 1763. For a discussion of ritualistic cannibalism among the Woodland Indians, see Sayre, *Les Sauvages Americains*, 298.

22. *Pennsylvania Gazette*, August 18, 1763; Peckham, *Pontiac and the Indian Uprising*, 137.

23. Quaife, *The Siege of Detroit*, 50–55; Peckham, *Pontiac and the Indian Uprising*, 138; Trowbridge, "Conspiracy of Pontiac and the Siege of Detroit: Mr. Charles Gouin's Account," 346 (hereafter cited as "Gouin's Account"). In his account Peckham states that four chiefs accompanied the habitants to the fort and that the Frenchmen convinced Gladwin that it was not necessary to retain these Indians as hostages pending Campbell's safe return. In fact, Gladwin did retain two Potawatomie chiefs, Big Ears and Nokaming,

as hostages. These Indians were later traded for English captives. See Edmunds, *The Potawatomis,* 85–88; and *Pennsylvania Gazette,* July 7, 1763.

24. McDougall's account of the parley can be found in Moore, *The Gladwin Manuscripts,* 622, 640–41.

25. Hough, *Diary of the Siege of Detroit,* 6, 130–31. This portion of Hough's edited chronicle of Pontiac's War purports to be the journal of Robert Rogers. Since Rogers did not arrive at the beleaguered post until later in the siege, the information contained in this portion of the diary clearly came from someone other than the famed ranger. Indeed, Rogers's account of these events was lifted directly from a letter written by Lieutenant James McDonald to Colonel Henry Bouquet on July 12, 1763. For this account, see McDonald to Bouquet, July 12, 1763, in Henry Bouquet Papers, State Archives, Pennsylvania Historical and Museum Commission (hereafter cited as HBP). Volume 6, rather than including all the Bouquet Papers, as the previous five published volumes do, includes merely a selection of documents. The Pennsylvania Historical and Museum Commission intended to make all the remaining papers available in a microfiche supplement, but this project was never completed. Consequently, a large selection of Bouquet material remains in typescript form in the commission's state archives.

26. "Gouin's Account," 345; Quaife, *The Siege of Detroit,* 161; Hough, *Diary of the Siege of Detroit,* 34; "Speech of Pondiack to Mons de Noyon at Fort Chartres, April 15 and 17, 1764," in Major Robert Farmar to Gage, December 21, 1764, Thomas Gage Papers, vol. 28 (hereafter cited as Gage Papers).

27. Quaife, *The Siege of Detroit,* 62–64.

28. Hough, *Diary of the Siege of Detroit,* 6, 130; Quaife, *The Siege of Detroit,* 65–66.

29. Moore, *The Gladwin Manuscripts,* 645; Hough, *Diary of the Siege of Detroit,* 34. Lieutenant Jehu Hay stated in this diary that Pontiac's sign was a raccoon, while Major Robert Rogers insisted that it was an otter. The pictograph may have been a clan symbol.

30. Moore, *The Gladwin Manuscripts,* 642; Quaife, *The Siege of Detroit,* 73–75; Peckham, *Pontiac and the Indian Uprising,* 141.

31. Moore, *The Gladwin Manuscripts,* 644; Peckham, *Pontiac and the Indian Uprising,* 149.

32. DeRuvyne to Henry Bouquet, June 15, 1761, *Bouquet Papers,* 5:554; Moore, *The Gladwin Manuscripts,* 636; "Colhoon: Indian Intelligence from Tuscarawas," June 1, 1763, *Bouquet Papers,* 6:197–98; McDonald's Account, 223.

33. Moore, *The Gladwin Manuscripts,* 636; Hambach to Bouquet, October 13, 1762, *Bouquet Papers,* 6:122.

34. Morris, *Miscellanies in Prose and Verse,* 17; Moore, *The Gladwin Manuscripts,* 637; Maisons de Belestre to Henry Bouquet, December 29,

1760, *Bouquet Papers*, 5:221. For biographical information on Robert Holmes, see Loescher, *Officers and Non-commissioned Officers*, 46.

35. Alvord, *The Critical Period*, 12–13, 19; Peckham, *Pontiac and the Indian Uprising*, 161.

36. Armour, ed., *Attack at Michilimackinac*, 23–24, 45. Biographical information on Etherington can be found in *Bouquet Papers*, 5:28.

37. Armour, *Attack at Michilimackinac*, 25.

38. Ibid., 49–51.

39. Draper, "Lieut. James Gorrell's Journal," 39–47; Armour, *Attack at Michilimackinac*, 57–58.

40. Howard Peckham was mistaken in identifying the *Michigan* as the vessel sent to obtain supplies and reinforcements. Abraham Cuyler, who was aboard the ship when it returned to Detroit a month later, wrote that it was the *Huron*. See Peckham, *Pontiac and the Indian Uprising*, 149; and Moore, *The Gladwin Manuscripts*, 637. Neither of the great historians of Pontiac's War, Francis Parkman and Howard Peckham, provided Captain Newman's first name in their narratives. The able novelist Allan W. Eckert identifies the sailor as Jacob Newman in his fictionalized account of the war. See Peckham, *Pontiac and the Indian Uprising*, 149; Eckert, *The Conquerors*, 262.

41. Peckham, *Pontiac and the Indian Uprising*, 149–50; McDonald's Account, 223; Hough, *Diary of the Siege of Detroit*, 11–13.

42. Jeffrey Amherst to Thomas Gage, June 24, 1763, Amherst Papers, vol. 7, reel 1090; Peckham, *Pontiac and the Indian Uprising*, 156–57. Lieutenant McDonald informed Henry Bouquet that Cuyler's force was composed of "One Sergeant and Seventeen Soldiers of the Royal Americans, Three Sergeants and Seventy five Rank and File of the Queens Independent Company of Rangers." See McDonald's Account, 224.

43. Quaife, *The Siege of Detroit*, 108–16; McDonald to Bouquet, July 12, 1763, HBP.

44. Quaife, *The Siege of Detroit*, 121, 129. For biographical information on Wasson, see Harry Kelsey, "Wasson," in *Dictionary of Canadian Biography*, 4:761–62. Ten days after Wasson's arrival another small contingent, of forty-five Chippewa men under the leadership of Sekahos, came to Detroit. See Quaife, *The Siege of Detroit*, 128–29.

45. Hough, *Diary of the Siege of Detroit*, 19; Quaife, *The Siege of Detroit*, 123–24.

46. Hough, *Diary of the Siege of Detroit*, 22–28; Quaife, *The Siege of Detroit*, 130–32, 135–38.

47. Quaife, *The Siege of Detroit*, 143–44; Peckham, *Pontiac and the Indian Uprising*, 186–87.

48. Ibid., 144–45.

49. According to the unknown French diarist who kept a daily journal of the siege, the crew of the *Huron* fired several rounds of grapeshot into the Huron village as the schooner ascended the river. Several Indians were wounded, and the other occupants of the camp quickly dispersed. See Quaife, *The Siege of Detroit*, 150–52, 157; Hough, *Diary of the Siege of Detroit*, 37.

50. Dowd, "The French King Wakes Up in Detroit"; Moore, *The Gladwin Manuscripts*, 640; Alvord, *The Critical Period*, 51–53; Cadwallader Colden to Thomas Gage, April 14, 1764, Gage Papers, vol. 17; Gladwin to Gage, May 12, 1764, Gage Papers, vol. 18; Colonel John Bradstreet to Gage, December 5, 1764, Gage Papers, vol. 28; Major Robert Farmar to Gage, December 21, 1764, Gage Papers, vol. 28.

51. See Peckham, *Pontiac and the Indian Uprising*, 107–11; and Jacobs, "Was the Pontiac Uprising a Conspiracy?"

52. See particularly, Jennings, *Empire of Fortune*, 442–46.

53. For the text of Pontiac's speech to the habitants, see Quaife, *The Siege of Detroit*, 160–65.

54. Quaife, *The Siege of Detroit*, 171–73; Hough, *Diary of the Siege of Detroit*, 39–40. Several habitants insisted that the soldier did more than merely scalp the fallen Chippewa chief, that he "cut his body in pieces." See Trowbridge, "Conspiracy of Pontiac and the Siege of Detroit: Mrs. Meloche's Account and Mr. Gouin's Account," 342, 348.

55. Quaife, *The Siege of Detroit*, 175–76; Hough, *Diary of the Siege of Detroit*, 41. There are many different versions of Captain Campbell's unfortunate death, each more horrific than the other. For other versions, see "Mr. Gouin's Account," 348; and Henry Rutherford's account in Quaife, *The Siege of Detroit*, 248.

56. McDonald to Bouquet, July 12, 1763, HBP.

57. *Pennsylvania Journal & Weekly Advertiser*, August 11, 1763.

CHAPTER 5

1. Long, *Lord Jeffery Amherst*, 182, 188–89.

2. *Kenny's Journals*, 197–98. Alexander McKee had a long and colorful career as a frontier intermediary. See Nelson, *A Man of Distinction among Them*.

3. Heckewelder, *History, Manners, and Customs*, 270; Colhoon: Indian Intelligence from Tuscarawas, June 1, 1763, *Bouquet Papers*, 6:197–99; Loudon, *Indian Narratives*, 279–80. Colhoon's guide Daniel may very well have been Shamokin Daniel, who served as an escort for Christian Frederick Post in 1758.

4. Garrison Return of Fort Pitt, June 24, 1763, *Bouquet Papers*, 6:264; Ecuyer to Bouquet, May 29, 1763, ibid., 6:193.

5. Information on William Clapham can be found in Waddell, "Defending the Long Perimeter," 185–87; Volwiler, *George Croghan and the Western Movement*, 214; and *Bouquet Papers*, 6:194, 284–85. Concerning the Delaware warrior known as the Wolf, see *Kenny's Journals*, 173–74. For details regarding the attack on Clapham's plantation, see *Pennsylvania Gazette*, June 16, 1763.

6. *Kenny's Journals*, 198–99; Ecuyer to Bouquet, May 29, 1763, *Bouquet Papers*, 6:193. Biographical information on William Trent can be found in Slick, *William Trent and the West*.

7. Ecuyer to Bouquet, May 30, 1763, *Bouquet Papers*, 6:195–96; Ecuyer to Bouquet, June 2, 1763, ibid., 6:202–3; Ecuyer to Bouquet, June 16, 1763, ibid., 6:231–33. For a detailed description of Fort Pitt and its environs, see Stotz, *The Model of Fort Pitt*; and James and Stotz, *Drums in the Forest*, 152–85.

8. Bouquet to Amherst, June 4, 1763, *Bouquet Papers*, 6:205–6; Amherst to Bouquet, June 6, 1763, ibid., 6:209–10.

9. Amherst to Bouquet, June 12, 1763, ibid., 6:220–21.

10. According to one account, of the eight express riders sent to Fort Venango, "four were killed, two wounded, and two returned" to the safety of Fort Pitt. See Nixon, *James Burd*, 112–13.

11. Much of the details of the Byerlys' harrowing flight was passed down through family tradition and eventually recorded by Cyrus Cort, a descendent. See Cort, *Col. Henry Bouquet*, 17–18, 23–24.

12. The touching story of Maiden Foot and Mary Means is related in Sipe, *Fort Ligonier and Its Times*, 187–88.

13. John Armstrong to Henry Bouquet, June 13, 1763, *Bouquet Papers*, 6:222–23; Ecuyer to Bouquet, June 2, 1763, ibid., 6:202; Ecuyer to Bouquet, June 16, 1763, ibid., 6:231; Hunter, "Thomas Barton and the Forbes Expedition," 431–32; Nixon, *James Burd*, 118. For an excellent assessment of the martial capacity of the settlers on the Pennsylvania frontier, see Starkey, *European and Native American Warfare*, 21–22.

14. Bouquet to Amherst, June 5, 1763, *Bouquet Papers*, 6:207; Bouquet to Amherst, June 13, 1763, ibid., 6:222. On the makeup of the Pennsylvania militia, see Stephenson, "Provincial Soldiers in the Seven Years' War"; and Ward, "An Army of Servants." For evidence of Colonel Bouquet's concern for forts Ligonier and Bedford, see Bouquet to Lewis Ourry, June 23, 1763, *Bouquet Papers*, 6:253–54.

15. Archibald Blane to Bouquet, June 4, 1763, *Bouquet Papers*, 6:206–7; Blane to Bouquet, June 10, 1763, HBP. For information on the deteriorated condition of Fort Ligonier, see Stotz, *The Story of Fort Ligonier*, 14–15; and Smith, *Bouquet's Expedition against the Ohio Indians*, 13–14. For background information on Blane and his garrison see, Williams, ed., "Pay List of the Militia at Fort Ligonier."

16. A biography of Ourry can be found in Cornu, "Captain Lewis Ourry."

17. Ourry to Bouquet, June 1, 1763, HBP; Ourry to Bouquet, June 5, 1763, ibid.

18. Ourry to Bouquet, June 5, 1763, ibid.; Ourry to Bouquet, June 3, 1763, *Bouquet Papers*, 6:204–5.

19. Ourry to Bouquet, June 9, 1763, HBP.

20. Bouquet to Amherst, June 16, 1763, *Bouquet Papers*, 6:225–26; Amherst to Bouquet, June 19, 1763, ibid., 6: 239–41.

21. One of the earliest historical accounts of Pontiac's uprising, Patterson's *History of the Backwoods*, 128, refers to the conflict as "the Kiyasuta and Pontiac war." "This was the name," wrote Patterson," that "this war bore among the frontier inhabitants, and continued to bear among the settlers." The tradition continued through the early twentieth century, when C. Hale Sipe, in his volume *Indian Chiefs of Pennsylvania*, 375–76, claimed that Kiasutha was the principle leader of the Indians in the Ohio Valley during the war. More recently, the noted ethnohistorian Paul A. W. Wallace, in his influential book *Indians in Pennsylvania*, 179, insists that Kiasutha "tried to adjust peacefully the differences that arose between Indians and white men." This seems an incredible claim considering the overwhelming evidence to the contrary. Evidence of the circulation of the war belt among the Niagara Senecas can be found in Jean Baptiste de Couagne to Sir William Johnson, June 6, 1763, *Johnson Papers*, 4:137–38.

22. Concerning Fort Venango, see Montgomery, *Report of the Commission to Locate the Site of the Frontier Forts of Pennsylvania*, 2:591–94; and Rough, *The Frontier Forts of Franklin, Pennsylvania*. The only primary account of the fall of Fort Venango came from a Mohawk chief who related the particulars of the event to Sir William Johnson. See Johnson to Amherst, July 11, 1763, in O'Callaghan, *Documents Relative to the Colonial History of the State of New York*, 7:532–33.

23. For biographical information on Ensign George Price, see *Bouquet Papers*, 5:128. Accounts of the attack against Fort Le Boeuf can be found in Volwiler, ed., "William Trent's Journal at Fort Pitt," 401 (hereafter cited as Trent's Journal); and Price to Bouquet, June 26, 1763, *Bouquet Papers*, 6:266. Another dramatic account of the attack can be found in Parkman's *Conspiracy of Pontiac*, 2:16–21.

24. In a deposition given later at a court of inquiry, Cuyler simply stated that "he was not able to give them any assistance having nothing but a small Boat to land men in which would not cary above ten at a time, and being two miles from the shore." See Moore, *The Gladwin Manuscripts*, 637. Perhaps the prevailing winds would not allow the crew of the *Huron* to navigate closer to the fort. Also, the water level in the lake might have been too low to permit the schooner to approach the peninsula any closer.

25. Information concerning the siege and fall of Fort Presque Isle can be found in Trent's Journal, 402; Moore, *The Gladwin Manuscripts*, 637–39; Peckham, *Pontiac and the Indian Uprising*, 168–70; Ecuyer to Bouquet, June 26, 1763, *Bouquet Papers*, 6:259–60; Christie to Bouquet, July 10, 1763, *Bouquet Papers*, 6:301–3; and the *Pennsylvania Gazette*, July 7, 1763.

26. Ecuyer to Bouquet, June 16, 1763, *Bouquet Papers*, 6:231; Ecuyer to Bouquet, June 26, 1763, ibid., 6:259–60.

27. Trent's Journal, 400.

28. Bouquet to Ecuyer, June 26, 1763, *Bouquet Papers*, 6:261–63; Trent's Journal, 400.

29. General information on the nature of smallpox can be found in a wonderful article by Elizabeth Finn, "Biological Warfare in Eighteenth Century North America." On Croghan's bout with the disease, see Wainwright *George Croghan*, 189.

30. Amherst to Bouquet, July 7, 1763, *Bouquet Papers*, 6:301; Amherst to Bouquet, July 16, 1763, ibid., 6:315; Bouquet to Amherst, July 13, 1763, HBP; *Kenny's Journal*, 19. In his study *Empire of Fortune*, 447–48, Francis Jennings indicates that the fighting strength of the Indians during Pontiac's Uprising was greatly compromised by Ecuyer's sinister plan. The statement "we are all savages," found by La Salle, can be found in Connell, *Son of the Morning Star*, 306.

31. Journal of Indian Affairs, March 1–3, 1765, *Johnson Papers*, 11:618; Deposition of Gershom Hicks, April 14, 1764, *Bouquet Papers*, 6:514–16; Reexamination of Gershom Hicks, April 19, 1764, *Bouquet Papers*, 6:522–23.

32. For particulars concerning the July 26, 1763, Indian conference at Fort Pitt, see Ecuyer to Bouquet, August 2, 1763, *Bouquet Papers*, 6:333–35.

33. Loudon, *Indian Narratives*, 281; Sipe, *Indian Wars of Pennsylvania*, 430. For an excellent summary of smallpox during Pontiac's Uprising, see Ranlet, "The British, the Indians, and Smallpox"; and McConnell, *A Country Between*, 195–96.

34. Blane to Bouquet, June 17, 1763, HBP; Blane to Bouquet, June 28, 1763, *Bouquet Papers*, 6:268–69.

35. Ourry to Bouquet, June 17, 1763, HBP.

36. Croghan to Bouquet, June 11, 1763, *Bouquet Papers*, 6:218–19; Ourry to Bouquet, June 17, 1763, HBP; Croghan to Bouquet, June 18, 1763, HBP.

37. *Pennsylvania Gazette*, June 30, 1763; Ourry to Bouquet, June 18, 1763, HBP.

38. *Pennsylvania Gazette*, June 30, 1763.

39. Amherst to Bouquet, June 18, 1763, *Bouquet Papers*, 6:235; Amherst to Bouquet, June 19, 1763, ibid., 6:240; Bouquet to Amherst, June 22, 1763, ibid., 6:245; Allan Campbell to Bouquet, June 24, 1763, ibid., 6:255; Amherst to Bouquet, June 25, 1763, ibid., 6:257; Amherst to Bouquet, June 23, 1763,

HBP. A thorough study of the number of troops sent to Bouquet can be found in Daudelin, "Numbers and Tactics at Bushy Run."

40. The noted military historian John Shy, in his book *Toward Lexington*, 111–25, makes a gallant defense of Amherst's failure to properly reinforce the frontier garrisons. According to Shy, the general did the best he could in transferring troops from one theater to another in order to quell the disturbance. Shy maintains that Amherst was beset by orders calling for the disbandment of many battalions then serving in North America and that "by his own initiative," the commander retained two units despite directives from England that they be mustered out of service. If this is true, then Amherst had the power to retain even more troops that could have been thrown against Pontiac's warriors. Instead, he attempted to reinforce the western posts piecemeal, which proved a recipe for near disaster.

41. Bouquet to Hamilton, July 1, 1763, *Bouquet Papers*, 6:279–82; Bouquet to Amherst, July 3, 1763, ibid., 6:288–89. On July 6 the Pennsylvania Assembly finally authorized the recruitment of seven hundred men and passed a bill compelling citizens to furnish the army with transportation necessary to haul supplies. See Hamilton to Bouquet, July 6, 1763, *Bouquet Papers*, 6:299.

42. Brander, *The Scottish Highlanders*, 24, 33, 161; James, *Writings of General John Forbes*, 117. For a detailed discussion of the Highland forces in America see Brumwell, *Redcoats*, 264–89.

43. Peter Russell, in his excellent article "Redcoats in the Wilderness," makes a convincing case that many British soldiers in America were already familiar with irregular or partisan warfare, having experienced such conditions while engaged in various European conflicts. While this appears indisputable, it should be stressed that these soldiers were, nonetheless, completely unaccustomed to the particular brand of combat demonstrated by Native American adversaries. Russell does demonstrate, however, that the British army was not so rigid in its doctrine as to make it impossible to adapt to new conditions in the forests of North America. For further assessments of the British army's ability to contend with Indian warfare tactics, see Brumwell, "'A Service Truly Critical'"; and Ward, "Failure of British Military Policy in the Ohio Valley." Both Brumwell and Ward insist that, despite attempts to adapt to the Indians' irregular tactics, the British army never completely countered their Native American adversaries.

44. *Rogers's Journals*, 52–64.

45. For an account of the development of light infantry troops in North America, see Brumwell, *Redcoats*, 228–36. The formation of the 80th Regiment of Foot is discussed in Alden, *General Gage in America*, 42–43; and Cuneo, *Robert Rogers of the Rangers*, 60–61. For a description of the arms and equipment of light infantry troops, see May and Embleton, *Wolfe's Army*, 30, 46–47. Gage was not the only British officer to comprehend the

uniqueness of wilderness war and develop methods to contend with the situation. Henry Bouquet advocated and put into practice many similar innovations. See Daudelin, "Numbers and Tactics at Bushy Run," 173.

46. Exhaustive biographical treatment is given the officers of the Black Watch Regiment in Richards, *The Black Watch at Ticonderoga*, 20–25, 60–81. Information regarding the Highland officers who served with Robert Rogers can be found in *Rogers's Journals*, 53.

47. Bouquet to Amherst, June 29, 1763, *Bouquet Papers*, 6:270–71; *Pennsylvania Gazette*, July 28, 1763.

48. Bouquet to Robert Callender, June, 29, 1763, *Bouquet Papers*, 6:272. Later Colonel Bouquet hired Henry Prather to serve as the "superintendent" over the horse masters and drivers. See Bouquet: Warrant to Henry Prather, July 19, 1763, HBP.

49. Bouquet to Slough and Simon, June 29, 1763; Bouquet to Lancaster County Magistrates, June 29, 1763, *Bouquet Papers*, 6:275–76.

50. David Hay to Bouquet, July 2, 1763; Bouquet: Warrant for Powder at Carlisle, July 6, 1763, HBP.

51. Bouquet to Amherst, July 3, 1763, *Bouquet Papers*, 6:288–89.

52. Bouquet to D. Campbell and J. McIntosh, June 29, 1763, ibid., 6:273.

53. Having no wife or children, Bouquet bequeathed much of his land, including several sizable farms in Maryland and Pennsylvania, to military friends and nephews. See Will of Henry Bouquet, July 5, 1763, HBP.

54. *Pennsylvania Gazette*, July 7, 1763.

55. Ibid., July 21, 1763.

56. Loudon, *Indian Narratives*, 166–69; Egle, *An Illustrated History of the Commonwealth of Pennsylvania*, 1011–12.

57. Major James Livingston to Bouquet, July 16, 1763, *Bouquet Papers*, 6:317; *Pennsylvania Journal & Weekly Advertiser*, July 28, 1763; Ansel, *Frontier Forts along the Potomac*, 51–60.

58. Peckham, *Pontiac and the Indian Uprising*, 216–17; Doddridge, *Notes on the Settlement and Indian Wars of the Western Parts of Virginia and Pennsylvania*, 169–70.

59. Ansel, *Frontier Forts along the Potomac*, 120–21; Lucier, *Pontiac's Conspiracy and Other Indian Affairs*, 27.

60. Ourry to Bouquet, July 10, 1763, HBP; Campbell to Bouquet, July 11, 1763, ibid.

61. Robertson to Bouquet, July 13, 1763, *Bouquet Papers*, 6:311; Ourry to Bouquet, July 13, 1763, ibid, 309.

62. Court of Inquiry held at Fort Pitt, September 28, 1763, HBP. On June 26 Ecuyer reported to Bouquet that "the garrison consists of 338 men counting everyone, 104 women, 106 children, a total of 540 mouths. Of these, about 420 receive the King's provisions." See *Bouquet Papers*, 6:260.

63. Six of Major Campbell's Highlanders were too weak to accompany the command. See Return of the 42nd and 77th Regiments, Carlisle, July 13, 1763, HBP; State and Disposition of the Troops in the Southern Department, July 13, 1763, ibid; Bouquet to Amherst, July 13, 1763, ibid. The small contingent of Royal Artillery was commanded by Captain David Hay and Lieutenant Walter Mitchelson, who were ordered to join Bouquet on June 18. See Amherst to Bouquet, June 18, 1763, *Bouquet Papers*, 6:235; Bouquet to Amherst, June 22, 1763, ibid., 245; and Bouquet to Ourry, July 4, 1763, ibid., 297. There is some confusion concerning the date that Bouquet departed from Carlisle. In a letter to Henry Gladwin dated August 28, 1763, Bouquet wrote, "I marched from Carlisle the 18th of July with about 460 Rank & File." Bouquet was obviously mistaken as to this date of departure since he arrived at Fort Loudoun on July 19. It would have been impossible for his command to march that far in a single day. See Bouquet to Gladwin, August 28, 1763, HBP.

64. Bouquet to Ourry, July 4, 1763, *Bouquet Papers*, 6:297; Bouquet to Amherst, June 25, 1763, ibid, 255; and Amherst to Bouquet, June 29, 1763, ibid., 277.

65. Bouquet to Ourry, July 19, 1763, HBP; James Robertson to Bouquet, July 19, 1763, *Bouquet Papers*, 6:322; Bouquet to Amherst, July 26, 1763, ibid., 325–26.

66. Bouquet to Amherst, July 26, 1763, *Bouquet Papers*, 6:325–26; Bouquet to Robertson, July 26, 1763, HBP.

67. The other members of Barrett's ranger detachment included James Parkes, James Spencer, Henry Doring, William Spencer, Thomas Beatty, Michael Ashford, John McMillan, Nathaniel Stedman, Thomas Simpson, and perhaps a frontiersman named William Linn. See Lemuel Barrett to Bouquet, February 20, 1765, HBP; Major James Livingston to Bouquet, July 29, 1763, ibid.; Livingston to Bouquet, August 1, 1763, *Bouquet Papers*, 6:328. Evidence confirming John Jemison's relationship to Mary Jemison, the famous "White Woman of the Genesee," can be found in Seaver, ed., *Narrative of the Life of Mary Jemison*, 25; and "Minutes of the Supreme Executive Council," August 14, 1779, *Colonial Records*, 12:73–74. After Pontiac's Uprising Lemuel Barrett returned to his Cumberland County home. He served as a militia colonel during the American Revolution and later moved to Cynthiana, Kentucky, where he died in 1814. See T. Johnson to Council of Safety, January 22, 1776, in Browne and others, *Archives of Maryland*, 11:120; Council to Colonel Lemuel Barrett, May 16, 1778, ibid., 21:88–90. The Archives of Maryland can be found online at http://www.mdarchives.state.md.us. Genealogical information on Barrett can be found by consulting http://www.familysearch.com, a Web site maintained by the Church of Jesus Christ of Latter-day Saints.

68. Major James Livingston to Bouquet, July 29, 1763, HBP; Livingston to Bouquet, August 1, 1763, *Bouquet Papers*, 6:328.

69. Bouquet to Ecuyer, July 26, 1763, *Bouquet Papers*, 6:327–28.

CHAPTER 6

1. Peckham, *Pontiac and the Indian Uprising*, 171–75; Amherst to Sir William Johnson, June 16, 1763, *Johnson Papers*, 4:148–49.

2. Background information on Dalyell is sparse. See the biographical note that appears in Quaife, *The Siege of Detroit*, 200.

3. Sir William Johnson to Jeffery Amherst, June 26, 1763, *Johnson Papers*, 10:716–17.

4. Cuneo, *Robert Rogers of the Rangers*, 150–62.

5. Dalyell to Jeffery Amherst, July 3, 1763, Amherst Papers, vol. 39, reel 1106. For a discussion of the various troop movements during this time, see Shy, *Toward Lexington*, 113–15.

6. Cuneo, *Robert Rogers of the Rangers*, 162–63.

7. *Pennsylvania Journal & Weekly Advertiser*, September 8, 1763; Dalyell to Amherst, July 3, 1763, Amherst Papers, vol. 39, reel 1106; *Pennsylvania Gazette*, September 8, 1763. One of the articles printed in the *Pennsylvania Gazette* was written by Robert Rogers. Another article detailing Dalyell's expedition comes from an unidentified member of the command.

8. Quaife, *The Siege of Detroit*, 199–201; *Pennsylvania Gazette*, September 8, 1763; Hough, *Diary of the Siege of Detroit*, 53–54. Some accounts say only ten men were wounded. The anonymous author of *The Siege of Detroit* reported that two of these men later died from their wounds, while the *Pennsylvania Gazette* declared that only one soldier was killed.

9. Information concerning the progress of the siege can be found in Hough, *Diary of the Siege of Detroit*, 41–50; and Quaife, *The Siege of Detroit*, 177–99.

10. Little is known regarding the exact nature of the council that took place between Dalyell and Gladwin. Lieutenant Hay, the author of the detailed *Diary of the Siege of Detroit*, is silent on the subject, perhaps in an effort to protect Dalyell's reputation. The only information available on the conference can be found in Gladwin to Amherst, August 8, 1763, quoted in Parkman, *The Conspiracy of Pontiac*, 1:308. Sterling's assessment of the peaceful nature of the Hurons and Potawatomies can be found in Sterling to John Duncan & Company, July 25, 1763, James Sterling Letter Book, 106–7 (hereafter cited as Sterling Letter Book).

11. The following account of the Battle of Bloody Run is taken from a variety of primary sources. Readers may consult the *Pennsylvania Gazette*, September 8, 1763; Hough, *Diary of the Siege of Detroit*, 54–57; Quaife, *The*

Siege of Detroit, 203–5; 262–64; Alexander Duncan to Sir William Johnson, no date, *Johnson Papers*, 10:762–66; Jean Baptiste de Couagne to Sir William Johnson, August 24, 1763, ibid., 790–91; Trowbridge, "Conspiracy of Pontiac and the Siege of Detroit: Mrs. Meloche's Account," 342–43 (hereafter cited as "Meloche's Account"); "Gouin's Account," 348–49; Trowbridge, "Conspiracy of Pontiac and the Siege of Detroit: Mr. Gabriel St. Aubin's Account," 354–55 (hereafter cited as "St. Aubin's Account"); Trowbridge, "Conspiracy of Pontiac and the Siege of Detroit: Mr. Pettier's Account," 362–63 ("Pettier's Account" hereafter); James Sterling to John Sterling, August 7, 1763, Sterling Letter Book, 108; and James Sterling to John Duncan & Co., August 7, 1763, ibid., 110–11. Another good account of the battle, excerpted from the *Gentleman's Magazine*, October 1763, 486–87, can be found in Todish and Zaboly, eds., *The Journals of Major Robert Rogers*, 284–86.

12. Hough, *Diary of the Siege of Detroit*, 54–55; "Meloche's Account," 342; "St. Aubin's Account," 354; and "Pettier's Account," 362.

13. This account of Captain Dalyell's death is taken from "Gouin's Account," 349; and Parkman, *The Conspiracy of Pontiac*, 1:314. It may seem doubtful that in the foggy gloom of early morning, anyone could have witnessed Dalyell's death or claimed to have killed him. However, both accounts agree that the captain was in the extreme rear of the retreating command. Therefore, it is plausible that he was courageously returning to assist a fallen soldier when the warrior Geeyette spotted him.

14. Casualty figures for the Battle of Bloody Run are taken from the *Pennsylvania Gazette*, September 8, 1763. A different set of figures can be found in Hough, *Diary of the Siege of Detroit*, 56. Indian losses were reported by the captive John Rutherford. See Quaife, *The Siege of Detroit*, 263.

15. James Sterling to John Sterling, August 7, 1763, Sterling Letter Book, 108.

16. Quaife, *The Siege of Detroit*, 263–67. Amherst's reward for the death of Pontiac can be found in Amherst to Gladwin, September 9, 1763, Jeffrey Amherst Papers, vol. 2, William L. Clements Library.

17. Friend Palmer, *Early Days in Detroit*, 370–71.

18. Trent's Journal, 403–8; Darlington, *Fort Pitt and Letters from the Frontier*, 164.

19. Indian Speeches at Fort Pitt, July 26, 1763, *Bouquet Papers*, 6:333–35.

20. Ecuyer: Reply to Indians, July 27, 1763, ibid., 6:336–37.

21. Trent's Journal, 408–9; Ecuyer to Bouquet, August 2, 1763, *Bouquet Papers*, 6:332–33; *Pennsylvania Gazette*, September 1, 1763.

22. Trent's Journal, 409.

23. Ecuyer to Bouquet, August 2, 1763, *Bouquet Papers*, 6:332; Trent's Journal, 409–10; Ecuyer to Bouquet, August 3, 1763, HBP.

24. Ecuyer to Bouquet, August 3, 1763, HBP. Considerable debate has focused on the number of Indians who abandoned the siege of Fort Pitt to attack Bouquet's force at Bushy Run. A number of historians believe that the Indians met the British with little more than one hundred warriors. Their evidence for this claim comes from a single conversation between Sir William Johnson and the Delaware chief Killbuck in March 1765. In that meeting Killbuck claimed that "there were 110 Indians engaged, of whom 5 were killed on the Spot & 1 Shot thro the body who died in a little time after of his wound." Perhaps Sir William misunderstood Killbuck's statement; if not, the Delaware chief's account hardly seems credible. What Killbuck may have meant was that 110 Delawares were involved in the battle, not counting the total number of Mingoes, Shawnees, Hurons, and others present. This seems likely, considering the Delawares' determination during the war and the fact that they could easily muster over two hundred warriors themselves. If one considers Tamaqua's defection and an undetermined number of other Delawares who were still raiding elsewhere, the figure of 110 Delawares seems entirely plausible. For Killbuck's statement, see *Johnson Papers*, 11:618. For estimates of the fighting strength of the various Ohio Country tribes as late as 1765, see "Journal of the Transactions of George Croghan, Esq., Deputy Agent for Indian Affairs, with Different Tribes of Indians at Fort Pitt, from February 28 to May 12, 1765," in Rupp, *Early History of Western Pennsylvania*, appendix 17, p. 173. In this journal Croghan counted 215 Delaware warriors, 105 Shawnees, 125 Senecas, 38 Indian warriors from Sandusky (probably Ottawas, Chippewas, and so forth), and 38 more Munsee Delawares, or Minisinks.

25. It is impossible to determine the exact number of men who departed Fort Ligonier and participated in the Battle of Bushy Run. When Bouquet left Carlisle on July 13, he had roughly 456 men in his command, not including the 204 Highlanders who had already been sent forward to reinforce Bedford and Ligonier. He deposited about thirty ill men at each of those outposts and lost an undetermined number of soldiers through desertion along the way. He did, however, augment his force with Lemuel Barrett's fourteen rangers. In a letter to Henry Gladwin, Bouquet noted that he departed Carlisle with 460 rank and file. If he picked up the Highland troops that had been sent forward earlier, his entire command would have numbered over six hundred. However, this figure does not take into account losses through desertion. Considering the severity of the journey and the danger the command intended to face, that number conceivably could have approached one hundred. The *Pennsylvania Journal & Weekly Advertiser*, August 18, 1763, reported that Colonel Bouquet left his wagons "with Capt. Hay and some other Officers at Ligonier." It seems likely that all the artillerymen in the command were also left behind at the fort. Most accounts agree that the colonel had about

five hundred men under his command when he departed Ligonier. See Daudelin, "Numbers and Tactics at Bushy Run"; Cort, *Col. Henry Bouquet*, 33.

26. Despite family tradition, it is possible that the Byerlys did not accompany Bouquet's command. The militia pay list kept by Lieutenant Blane indicates that both father and son were at Fort Ligonier from August 11 through August 22. Bouquet did not reach Fort Pitt until August 10, which would not have given the Byerlys time to get back to Ligonier and enroll in the militia. On the other hand, it is just as likely that Blane continued to carry the father and son on his roster even though they were serving on detached service with Bouquet. See Williams, "Pay List of the Militia at Fort Ligonier," 256.

27. Cort, *Col. Henry Bouquet*, 33.

28. Bouquet to Amherst, August 5, 1763, *Bouquet Papers*, 6:338–40. The full contents of this letter, and another communication written by Bouquet the following day, can be found in the appendix to this book. These two letters, along with an account of the battle given by an unnamed source (quite likely Bouquet himself)—which appeared in Smith's *Bouquet's Expedition against the Ohio Indians*, 16–26—constitute the bulk of contemporary information pertaining to the Battle of Bushy Run. To this should be added reports found in the *Pennsylvania Gazette*, September 1, 1763. In recent years, another revealing letter, written by one John Dickenson to his mother and dated August 26, 1763, has come to light that provides additional information on the engagement. This letter can be found in the Logan Manuscript Collection and is hereafter cited as Dickenson Letter. Lastly, there is an eyewitness account by Robert Kirk, an enlisted man who served in the 77th Highland Regiment. Kirk later recorded his experiences in *The Memoirs and Adventures of Robert Kirk*, 75–79. Aside from these primary sources, several secondary works are also useful in reconstructing how the battle was fought. See Eid, "'A Kind of Running Fight,'" 166–71; Daudelin, "Numbers and Tactics at Bushy Run"; and Anderson, *The Battle of Bushy Run*, 8–12.

29. The area along the line of march is best described in Mochnick, *History of Penn Township*, 10–16.

30. Several years after the battle, Colonel Bouquet directed Thomas Hutchins, the army engineer, to map the battlefield. This map, later reproduced in Smith, *Bouquet's Expedition against the Ohio Indians*, clearly shows the hill to the right of the road and labels it, "the action of the 5th was here."

31. Smith, *Bouquet's Expedition against the Ohio Indians*, 17.

32. Bouquet to Amherst, August 5, 1763, *Bouquet Papers*, 6:339.

33. Kirk, *Memoirs of Robert Kirk*, 77.

34. There is no doubt that some, if not all, of Barrett's men were armed with long rifles, since Major Livingston provided the rangers with "Lead in

Proportion for the Rifles, also 2 Pounds of Powder," when they departed Fort Cumberland to join Bouquet. See Livingston to Bouquet, August 1, 1763, *Bouquet Papers*, 6:328.

35. Smith, *Bouquet's Expedition against the Ohio Indians*, 19.

36. Kirk, *Memoirs of Robert Kirk*, 78; Bouquet to Amherst, August 6, 1763, *Bouquet Papers*, 6:343. Kiasutha's participation at the Battle of Bushy Run has been debated by historians. Evidence of his presence at the engagement is bolstered by a deposition given by the noted scout and interpreter Simon Girty, who some years later testified that "he heard Hiashota acknowledge that he was in the engagement, and commanded when the attack was made on Colonel Bouquet." See Butterfield, *History of the Girtys*, 17.

37. In a letter written to Bouquet shortly after the battle, fellow officer Captain Harry Gordon, congratulated his comrade: "You have many Times talkt of the Disposition you put in practise, as preferring it,—and I made no Doubt the Consequences would shew the Justice of your Thoughts." See Harry Gordon to Bouquet, September 4, 1763, HBP.

38. Years after the battle, when anti-British sentiment was high, several writers attempted to give Lemuel Barrett credit for devising the entire ploy that won the day at Bushy Run. John Ormsby, who was a trader and commissary at Fort Pitt during the siege, claimed "that our preservation was owing to Captain Barret." Ormsby further labeled Bouquet "an artful, cowardly Swiss." See Craig, *The Olden Time*, 2:4–5. It should be noted that Ormsby may have had an ax to grind. During Pontiac's War Captain Ecuyer ordered his soldiers to burn the trader's house, which stood outside Fort Pitt, so it would not provide cover to the besieging Indians. Ormsby later threatened to have Ecuyer arrested once he returned to the "settlements." See Bouquet to Plumstead and Franks, September 30, 1763, *Bouquet Papers*, 6:418–21. Ormsby was also implicated in an attempt to defraud the crown in a shipment of flour and to illicitly sell rum to the Indians. See Fort Pitt Traders to Bouquet, February 27, 1761, ibid., 5:315; and Barnsley to Bouquet, June 10, 1762, ibid., 6:90. Lieutenant Archibald Blane, the commanding officer at Ligonier, referred to Ormsby as "an ignorant Creature." For more information on John Ormsby, see Kamprad, "John Ormsby." Another frontiersman, James Smith, also claimed that "the Generalship and bravery of Col. [*sic*] Barret, and his Virginia volunteers; were the means of saving the army and Fort Pitt. When the British made their official report to England, the Virginians or Col. Barrett were not mentioned. It was stated that the Red Coats had done it all!" See Smith, *The Mode and Manner of Indian War*, 7. Like Ormsby, James Smith had considerable contempt for the British. Bouquet's previous military career, his understanding of Indian warfare, and Harry Gordon's revealing letter, previously cited, should prove beyond doubt that it was indeed Bouquet who devised and put in motion the battle plan that was executed at Bushy Run.

39. Thomas Hutchins's map shows a company of grenadiers and a group of rangers posted with Major Campbell's light infantry. None of the contemporary accounts of the battle mentions either the grenadiers or rangers being with Campbell's men.

40. Bouquet to Amherst, August 6, 1763, *Bouquet Papers*, 6:342–44; Kirk, *Memoirs of Robert Kirk*, 79.

41. The number of Indians killed at Bushy Run has always been a source of great contention. According to the Delaware leader Killbuck, only six Indians were killed during the engagement (see note 24). This hardly seems credible in light of the ferocious nature of the charge directed at the exposed Indian flank in the final moments of the fight. The *Pennsylvania Gazette,* reporting three separate accounts of the engagement, estimated the number of Indians killed to have been between forty and sixty. Captain Basset informed John Dickenson that "the Rascals fled leaving 20 dead." Dickenson then informed his mother that "itt is imagined . . . that they have killd about 60 of them." See Dickenson Letter. Colonel Bouquet never ventured to provide a number of the enemy killed at Bushy Run. In a letter to Gladwin, Bouquet simply stated that the Indians "must have Suffered greatly by their repeated and bold Attacks in which they were constantly repuls'd." See Bouquet to Gladwin, August 28, 1763, HBP. The account of the demise of the captured Indian may be apocryphal since it comes from the recollections of Andrew Byerly (see Cort, *Col. Henry Bouquet,* 42–43). However, the *Pennsylvania Gazette,* September 1, 1763, did indeed report that the British took "only one Prisoner, and after a little Examination he received his Quietus."

42. Bouquet reported that an additional five rangers and civilians were missing. These men later turned up at Fort Ligonier, claiming that "the Enemy got between them and our People." See *Pennsylvania Journal & Weekly Advertiser*, August 18, 1763.

43. Bouquet to Lieutenant James McDonald, August 28, 1763, HBP.

44. Bouquet to Amherst, August 6, 1763, *Bouquet Papers*, 6:342–44.

45. Bouquet to Amherst, August 11, 1763, HBP.

46. "Petition of John Metcalfe," *Western Pennsylvania Historical Magazine* 16 (August 1933): 197–204; Trent's Journal, 410; *Pennsylvania Gazette,* September 1, 1763. Captain Ecuyer was perhaps more relieved than anyone to see Bouquet's column. Service on the frontier had left him a broken man. In November 1763 he begged Bouquet to allow him to retire, listing a host of ailments that underscore the consequences of harsh frontier duty. "I have a severe cold," the captain wrote, "and fever every night, stomach trouble, and a headache, with an abscess on the spot where I was wounded at Quebec, which causes me unspeakable agonies." Ecuyer was eventually retired at half pay, and he returned to England. See Ecuyer to Bouquet, November 13,

1763, *Bouquet Papers*, 6:459–60; Ecuyer to Bouquet, November 20, 1763, ibid., 6:464–65; and Bouquet to Ecuyer, February 21, 1764, ibid., 6:497.

47. Bouquet to Amherst, August 11, 1763, HBP; Bouquet to Hamilton, August 11, 1763, ibid.; Blane to Bouquet, August 18, 1763, *Bouquet Papers*, 6:365; Ourry to Bouquet, August 27, 1763, ibid., 6:371; Hamilton to Bouquet, August 29, 1763, ibid., 6:376; Nixon, *James Burd*, 116; and *Pennsylvania Journal & Weekly Advertiser*, September 1, 1763. A copy of George III's "royal approbation" can be found in Smith, *Bouquet's Expedition against the Ohio Indians*, 27. Following his service in North America, Archibald Blane was retired at half pay. His name does not resurface in military records until 1765, when he was appointed to serve as a captain in an independent company patrolling Africa's Gold Coast. He remained on duty in Africa until 1769, when his name disappears from the army officers' list. See James, "Fort Ligonier: Additional Light from Unpublished Documents," 276–77. Lewis Ourry returned to England in 1765 and settled outside London with his family. He decided not to fight against the Americans during the Revolution and resigned his commission in the 17th Regiment of Foot. He died in 1779. A fine biographical sketch of Lewis Ourry can be found in Cornu, "Captain Lewis Ourry."

48. Rupp, *Early History of Western Pennsylvania*, 163; Parkman, *Conspiracy of Pontiac*, 2:70; Peckham, *Pontiac and the Indian Uprising*, 213; and Anderson, *The Battle of Bushy Run*, 13.

49. For a discussion of the limitations of Bouquet's victory, see Flexner, *Mohawk Baronet*, 257; Jennings, *Empire of Fortune*, 448–49; Brumwell, "'A Service Truly Critical,'" 172–74; and Eid, "'A Kind of Running Fight,'" 166–71.

50. Bouquet to Amherst, August 11, 1763, *Bouquet Papers*, 6:361–62; Bouquet to Campbell, August 12, 1763, ibid., 6:363–64; and Boyd to Bouquet, August 12, 1763, ibid., 6:364.

51. Bouquet to Hamilton, August 11, 1763, HBP.

52. *Colonial Records*, 9:63–66.

53. Armstrong to Bouquet, August 26, 1763, *Bouquet Papers*, 6:370; Sipe, *Indian Wars of Pennsylvania*, 450–51; Loudon, *Indian Narratives*, 2:174.

54. *Pennsylvania Gazette*, September 1, 1763; Loudon, *Indian Narratives*, 2:191–92.

55. Loudon, *Indian Narratives*, 2:174–77. The unidentified participant in the shooting of George Allen remarked that the Indian was never able to exact his revenge.

56. *Pennsylvania Gazette*, October 13, 1763.

57. Ibid., October 27, 1763.

58. Sipe, *Indian Wars of Pennsylvania*, 459–62. Major Asher Clayton was an experienced frontier officer who first joined the Pennsylvania militia in 1756. He accompanied Forbes's campaign and was wounded during Grant's

defeat outside Fort Duquesne in 1758. For additional biographical information, see *Bouquet Papers*, 6:571.

59. Amherst to Bouquet, August 7, 1763, *Bouquet Papers*, 6:346–59; Amherst to Bouquet, August 31, 1763, ibid., 6:379–81; Amherst to Bouquet, September 7, 1763, ibid., 6:387–88.

60. Amherst to Johnson, September 30, 1763, in O'Callaghan, *Documents Relative to the Colonial History of the State of New York*, 7:568–69.

61. Croghan to Bouquet, October 11, 1763, *Bouquet Papers*, 6:430–31; Croghan to Amherst, September 26, 1763, *Johnson Papers*, 10:823–25; Croghan to John, ibid., 10:825–27; Croghan to the Lords of Trade, no date, in O'Callaghan, *Documents Relative to the Colonial History of the State of New York*, 7:602–3; William Trent: List of Indian Traders and Their Servants Killed or Captured by Indians, September 5, 1763, *Bouquet Papers*, 6:412–13. Trent later revised his estimate of goods lost during the war and submitted this revised tabulation to Sir William Johnson in February 1765. This time, Trent claimed that the Indians had confiscated more than £80,000's worth of goods. See Trent to Johnson, February 1765, *Johnson Papers*, 11:613–14.

62. Stewart's remarkable tale can be found in Loudon, *Indian Narratives*, 1:66–69.

63. Amherst to Stephen, September 30, 1763, *Bouquet Papers*, 6:421; Stephen to Bouquet, October 10, 1763, ibid., 6:427–28; Bouquet to Stephen, October 23, 1763, ibid., 6:434; and Bouquet to Gladwin, September 29, 1763, ibid., 6:402–3.

CHAPTER 7

1. Hough, *Diary of the Siege of Detroit*, 56–59.

2. Ibid., 58, 60; Peckham, *Pontiac and the Indian Uprising*, 222; "Journal of John Montresor, July–December, 1763," in Amherst Papers, vol. 50, reel 1114, p. 5 (hereafter cited as Montresor's Journal). Biographical information on John Montresor can be found in *Bouquet Papers*, 6:398–99.

3. Montresor's Journal, 6–7; Webster, *The Journal of Sir Jeffery Amherst*, 320–21; Quaife, *Siege of Detroit*, 269–70.

4. Montresor's Journal, 6–7; Peckham, *Pontiac and the Indian Uprising*, 222–23.

5. Montresor's Journal, 7–9; Collin Andrews to Sir William Johnson, *Johnson Papers*, 10:812–13.

6. Hough, *Diary of the Siege of Detroit*, 68; *Pennsylvania Gazette*, October 13, 1763; Parkman, *Conspiracy of Pontiac*, 1:318–20; Gladwin to Johnson, October 7, 1763, *Johnson Papers*, 10:873. Biographical information on Joseph Horssey can be found in *Bouquet Papers*, 5:8–9. Parkman believed that the Mohawks were responsible for revealing to Pontiac the weakness of the

Huron's crew. Gladwin's letter to Sir William Johnson, however, indicates that the two habitants provided the Ottawa chief with this intelligence.

7. Accounts of the attack on the *Huron* can be found in *Pennsylvania Gazette,* October 13, 1763; Hough, *Diary of the Siege of Detroit,* 67–68; Parkman, *Conspiracy of Pontiac,* 1:318–21; and James Sterling to Livingston and Rutherford, September 8, 1763, Sterling Letter Book, 112.

8. Hough, *Diary of the Siege of Detroit,* 68; Sterling to Livingston and Rutherford, September 8, 1763, Sterling Letter Book, 112; and Parkman, *Conspiracy of Pontiac,* 320.

9. Information concerning the disposition of fortifications along the Niagara portage can be found in Dunnigan, *Old Fort Niagara,* 54–72.

10. Amherst to Bouquet, October 3, 1763, HBP; *Pennsylvania Gazette,* October 6, 1763; Jean Baptiste de Couagne to Sir William Johnson, September 16, 1763, *Johnson Papers,* 10:815; and Van Cleve, *Reminiscences,* 62.

11. *Pennsylvania Gazette,* October 6, 1763; Van Cleve, *Reminiscences,* 62, 67; Captain George Etherington to Sir William Johnson, September 17, 1763, *Johnson Papers,* 10:817–818. For an Indian account of the Battle of Devil's Hole, see Johnson to Amherst, October 6, 1763, *Johnson Papers,* 10:867. The drummer boy, Lemuel Matthews, later lived near Queenston, Ontario Province, where he made split-cane chairs. He died in 1821.

12. Peckham, *Pontiac and the Indian Uprising,* 233; Hough, *Diary of the Siege of Detroit,* 74–75; Robert Rogers to Sir Jeffery Amherst, October 7, 1763, Gage Papers, vol. 3; and Gladwin to Sir William Johnson, October 7, 1763, *Johnson Papers,* 10:873.

13. Montresor's Journal, 22; Hough, *Diary of the Siege of Detroit,* 71.

14. Montresor's Journal, 23–26.

15. Ibid., 29–30; "Instructions of Villiers to Indian Nations," September 27, 1763, *Johnson Papers,* 10:819–821. Biographical information on Neyon de Villiers can be found in Alvord, *The Critical Period,* 224n.

16. Pontiac to Gladwin and the Reply, November 1, 1763, *Bouquet Papers,* 6:448–49.

17. Gladwin to Amherst, November 1, 1763, *Bouquet Papers,* 6:446–47.

18. Peckham, *Pontiac and the Indian Uprising,* 241–43; Montresor's Journal, 32; Gladwin to Bouquet, November 1, 1763, *Bouquet Papers,* 6:445–46. Amherst awarded Gladwin the promotion on September 17, 1763. See Moore, *The Gladwin Manuscripts,* 675. After Pontiac's Uprising the weary Gladwin received permission from General Thomas Gage to return to England in October 1764. He eventually retired to what was described as a "small paternal estate," where he kept content with "farming and rural amusements." Gladwin took no part in the American Revolution, although he was named deputy adjutant general in America until 1780. Henry Gladwin died after a long illness at his country estate in Stubbing on June 22, 1791. See Quaife, *The Siege of Detroit,* 4; Moore, *The Gladwin Manuscripts,* 606–11, 677–78.

19. Amherst's disgrace is discussed in detail in Shy, *Toward Lexington*, 122–25; Anderson, *Crucible of War*, 552–53; and Long, *Lord Jeffery Amherst*, 188–89, 195–96. On Amherst's departure, readers should also consult Gipson, *The British Empire before the American Revolution*, 9:113–14. For Croghan's assessment of Amherst's reception in England, see Croghan to Sir William Johnson, February 24, 1764, *Johnson Papers*, 4:341. Although the general never returned to America, he served a stint as an adviser to Lord Frederick North during the American Revolution. He was dismissed when the North ministry fell in 1782 but was called back to service in 1793, when war with France loomed once again. He retired two years later and died at his country estate in August 1797. Additional biographical information on Amherst can be found in Mayo, *Jeffery Amherst: A Biography*.

20. Ecuyer to Bouquet, November 20, 1764, *Bouquet Papers*, 6:464–66; Ourry to Bouquet, November 20, 1763, ibid., 6:466–69.

21. Background information on Thomas Gage can be found in Alden, *General Gage in America*, 1–88. While it appears that General Gage held no contempt for the colonial soldier, he intensely resented Major Robert Rogers. See Cuneo, *Robert Rogers of the Rangers*, 91–99.

22. An assessment of Gage's capabilities can be found in Shy, *Toward Lexington*, 125–35. The quote from Haldimand can be found in Alden, *General Gage in America*, 89.

23. Information concerning this Mississippi Company can be found in Alvord, *The Critical Period*, 19–29.

24. The significance of this diplomatic maneuver was not lost on the trader James Kenny, who recorded in his journal that Johnson's treaty with the "Delawares, Shawanas, Wyondots, Picks or Tweetwees, & others to ye Westward . . . makes those Nations a Separate Power Indcpendt of the Six Nations & that both Powers has seperately join'd in aliance now." See *Kenny's Journals*, 24.

25. An Indian Conference, March 24–April 23, 1764, *Johnson Papers*, 11:134–161.

26. Johnson's plans are outlined in a series of letters found in the *Johnson Papers*. See Johnson to Thomas Gage, January 27, 1764, *Johnson Papers*, 4:307–10; Gage to Johnson, January 31, 1764, ibid., 4:314–15; Johnson to Gage, February 19, 1764, ibid., 4:328–33; Johnson to William Eyre, January 29, 1764, ibid., 11:20–24; Journal of Indian Affairs, January 2–31, 1764, ibid., 11:24–31; Johnson to Thomas Gage, February 3, 1764, ibid., 11:36–37; and Johnson to John Stuart, March 18, 1764, ibid., 11:103–4.

27. Johnson to Thomas Gage, March 2, 1764, *Johnson Papers*, 4:351–52; Johnson to Gage, March 16, 1764, ibid., 4:367–72; Johnson to Gage, April 16, 1764, ibid., 11:131–33; and An Indian Conference, March 24–April 23, 1764, ibid., 11:159. In his book *Haughty Conquerors*, 192, William Nester asserts that one of the captives was Neolin's son. An exhaustive search of Nester's

citations, as well as other research, has failed to substantiate this claim. Andrew Montour epitomizes the enigmatic life led by mixed bloods who inhabited the eastern frontier in early America. Celebrated for his ability to slip easily from the white world into Indian culture, Montour found it problematic to exist in either. His eventful life came to an end in 1772 when he was murdered by a Seneca Indian. For a biography, see Lewin, "A Frontier Diplomat: Andrew Montour," 153–86; and Merrell, "'The Cast of His Countenance,'" 13–39.

28. Johnson to William Eyre, January 29, 1764, *Johnson Papers*, 11:23.

29. Johnson's views on making peace with the Great Lakes tribes can be found in Johnson to the Lords of Trade, January 20, 1764, in O'Callaghan, *Documents Relative to the Colonial History of the State of New York*, 7:599–602. The superintendent's estimate of Indian numbers is located in Johnson to the Lords of Trade, November 13, 1763, ibid., 7:572–84. Gage's desire to treat with the Indians can be found in Gage to Johnson, January 12, 1764, *Johnson Papers*, 4:290–93.

30. Bouquet to Gage, March 8, 1764, *Bouquet Papers*, 6:500; Lewis Ourry to Bouquet, March 24, 1764, ibid., 6:503–4; and Ourry to Bouquet, March 23, 1764, HBP.

31. Deposition of Gershom Hicks, April 14, 1763, *Bouquet Papers*, 6:514–16; W. Grant: Reexamination of Hicks, April 19, 1763, ibid., 6:522–26. It is impossible to determine now which portions of Hicks's two stories were fact and which fantasy. Perhaps the only truthful thing that the renegade reported was the death of Shingas during the winter of 1763.

32. *Pennsylvania Gazette*, June 14, 1764.

33. Franklin County (Penn.) Schools, *School Annual, 1933–34*, 11–21; Franklin County Schools, *Programme of the Fifty-ninth Annual Session Teacher's Institute*, 9–13. In 1885 a monument was erected over the common grave that held the remains of Brown and the children.

34. Sipe, *The Indian Wars of Pennsylvania*, 474; Loudon, *Indian Narratives*, 283.

35. Young, "A Note on Scalp Bounties in Pennsylvania," 210, 212–13. Information on David Owens's brutal crime can be found in John Penn to Sir William Johnson, June 9, 1764, *Johnson Papers*, 11:224–25; Johnson to Penn, June 18, 1764, ibid., 11:241; John Penn to Bouquet, April 26, 1764, *Bouquet Papers*, 6:527–28; and Sipe, *Indian Wars of Pennsylvania*, 471–72.

36. Gage to Bouquet, April 4, 1763, *Bouquet Papers*, 6:506–8; Gage to Bouquet, April 19, 1763, ibid., 6:517–19; Bouquet to Gage, May 2, 1763, ibid., 6:532–34; and Gage to Bouquet, June 5, 1764, ibid., 6:556–58.

37. Major Robert Farmar to Gage, December 21, 1764, with enclosure titled "Speech of Pondiack to Mons de Neyon at Fort Chartres, 15th & 17th of April, 1764," Gage Papers, vol. 28.

38. Peckham, *Pontiac and the Indian Uprising*, 251–52.

39. Gage to Lord Halifax, April 14, 1764, in Carter, *The Correspondence of General Thomas Gage*, 2:25–26 (hereafter cited as *Gage Correspondence*); Gage to Gladwin, April 23, 1764, Gage Papers, vol. 17.

40. Background information on John Bradstreet can be found in Godfrey, *John Bradstreet's Quest*. The historian Francis Parkman had little regard for Bradstreet, claiming that his "exploits had gained for him a reputation beyond his merits. He was a man of more activity than judgment, self-willed, vain, and eager for notoriety." See Parkman, *Conspiracy of Pontiac*, 2:162.

41. Dunnigan, *Old Fort Niagara*, 66; Mante, *History of the Late War*, 507.

42. Dunnigan, *Old Fort Niagara*, 66; Johnson to Thomas Gage, June 1, 1764, *Johnson Papers*, 11:214–16; and Heads for Colonel Bradstreet's Inspection, June 12, 1764, ibid., 11:231–33.

43. Conference with Indians, July 9–August 6, 1764, *Johnson Papers*, 11:262–328.

44. Mante, *History of the Late War*, 508.

45. Bradstreet's Negotiations with Indians at Lake Erie Camp at L'Ance aux Sevilles, August 12, 1764, Gage Papers, vol. 23. A copy of this document can be found in *Bouquet Papers*, 6:603–7.

46. Mante, *History of the Late War*, 513–14; Morris, *Journal*, 1–4.

47. Morris, *Journal*, 4–5.

48. Morris to Bradstreet, no date, excerpted in Bradstreet to Amherst, August 31, 1764, Amherst Papers, vol. 48, reel 1112 (part 2); Morris, *Journal*, 5–10.

49. Ibid., 15–25; Peckham, *Pontiac and the Indian Uprising*, 260.

50. Mante, *History of the Late War*, 514.

51. A handwritten copy of Bradstreet's Detroit conference can be found in Amherst Papers, vol. 48, reel 1112 (2). A printed excerpt of the document is in Congress with Western Indians, September 7, 1764, *Johnson Papers*, 11:349–51.

52. Gage to Bradstreet, September 2, 1764, *Bouquet Papers*, 6:637–38.

53. Bouquet to Gage, May 31, 1764, ibid., 6:549–51; Bouquet to Gage, June 21, 1764, ibid., 6:575–78; Bouquet to Gage, May 20, 1764, ibid., 6:542–44.

54. Smith, *Bouquet's Expedition against the Ohio Indians*, 33–34; Bouquet to Benjamin Franklin, August 10, 1764, *Bouquet Papers*, 6:600. The text of Governor Penn's address to the troops can be found in Williams, *Bouquet's March to the Ohio*, 23–24.

55. Bouquet to Gage, August 27, 1764, *Bouquet Papers*, 6:621; Christopher Lems to Bouquet, August 25, 1764, ibid., 6:619; Bouquet to Bradstreet, September 5, 1764, ibid., 6:629–30; Lieutenant Colonel John Reid to Bouquet, September 16, 1764, ibid., 6:640–41; Bouquet to Gage, September 26, 1764, ibid., 6:646–48.

56. Bouquet to Gage, September 26, 1764, *Bouquet Papers*, 6:648–50.

57. For the composition of Bouquet's force, see "Return of the Effectives in Colonel Bouquet's Army," November 5, 1764, HBP. For biographical information on John Reid, see *Bouquet Papers*, 6:535. Biographical information on Prevost can be found in Williams, "The Prevosts of the Royal Americans." Information concerning the lives of Asher Clayton and Turbutt Francis can be found in Williams, *The Orderly Book of Colonel Henry Bouquet's Expedition*, 57–59 (hereafter cited as Williams, *Bouquet's Orderly Book*).

58. James Smith's autobiographical account of his years of captivity and subsequent career can be found in Smith, *Life and Travels of Col. James Smith*. This narrative was later reprinted in an annotated edition edited by John J. Barsotti, *Scoouwa*. Information on Smith's Black Boys can be found in Manders, "Conococheague Rangers," 128–29.

59. Biographical information on Field can be found in Williams, *Bouquet's Orderly Book*, 56.

60. Biographical information on Alexander Lowrey can be found in Hanna, *The Wilderness Trail*, 1:177–78. Bouquet's other guides were Andrew Boggs, Samuel Brown, and Thomas Mitchell. See Guides: Receipts for Pay, December 28, 1764, HBP.

61. Bouquet: Marksmanship List, September 26, 1764, HBP; Williams, *Bouquet's Orderly Book*, 13–18. Apparently, Colonel Bouquet also favored the rifle and purchased three such weapons before embarking on his campaign to the Muskingum. See Bouquet: Order to Buy John Perry's Rifle for the Ohio Expedition; Bouquet: Order to Buy Edward Lee's Rifle; and Bouquet: Order to Buy John Long's Rifle, all September 6, 1764, HBP. Bouquet's list of Indian ringleaders can be found in Bouquet to Francis and Clayton, September 23, 1764, *Bouquet Papers*, 6:643.

62. Williams, *Bouquet's Orderly Book*, 19–32; Smith, *Bouquet's Expedition against the Ohio Indians*, 44–52; Delawares' Reply to Bouquet, October 14, 1764, *Bouquet Papers*, 6:660.

63. The various nuances of Native American diplomacy are fully discussed in James Merrell's wonderful interpretive work *Into the American Woods*.

64. There are at least four separate versions of this council, each one having subtle differences. See Conference with Seneca, Delaware, and Shawnese Chiefs, October 17–20, 1764, HBP; Speeches of Seneca and Delaware Chiefs, and Bouquet: Speech to Delaware, Shawnees, and Ohio Senecas, both October 17–20, 1764, *Bouquet Papers*, 6:669–74; "Col. Henry Bouquet's Journal and Conferences with the Western Indians, Appendix XVI," in Rupp, *Early History of Western Pennsylvania*, 150–54; and "Conference Held with the Chiefs of the Senecas living on the Ohio, the Delawares, and Shawanese," October 17, 1764, *Johnson Papers*, 439–46.

65. A great deal of literature has been generated regarding captivity in an attempt to explain why some hostages preferred to remain with their adopted Indian families. In particular, see Axtell, "The White Indians of Colonial America"; and Ward, "Redeeming the Captives." For a list of hostages released during Bouquet's Muskingum campaign, see Ewing, "Indian Captives Released by Colonel Bouquet."

66. For background information on Charlot Kaské and his influence among the Shawnee, see White, *The Middle Ground*, 300–305; and Peckham, *Pontiac and the Indian Uprising*, 267–69. Kaské's speech to the French governor can be found in Alvord, *The Critical Period*, 203–4.

67. Bouquet's negotiations with the Shawnees can be found in a series of conference minutes and letters found in *Bouquet Papers*, 6:694–707.

68. Bouquet to Gage, November 15, 1764, *Bouquet Papers*, 6:703–6.

69. An Indian Congress, May 9–11, 1765, *Johnson Papers*, 11:727–28.

70. See Sipe, *Indian Wars of Pennsylvania*, 204–9, 214–16.

CHAPTER 8

1. Smith, *Bouquet's Expedition against the Ohio Indians*, 82–83; Bouquet to John Stanwix, November 5, 1764, *Bouquet Papers*, 6:684–85; Bouquet to Gage, February 12, 1765, ibid., 6:754–56.

2. Perhaps one of the best discussions of the political machinations involved in the passage of the Proclamation Line can be found in Sosin, *Whitehall and the Wilderness*, 27–78.

3. The pitfalls of the Proclamation Line are exposed in Anderson, *Crucible of War*, 557–71; and Holton, *Forced Founders*, 3–10. The text of the proclamation can be found in *Colonial Records*, 9:80–85.

4. One of the major themes of Holton's study *Forced Founders* revolves around the debt that wealthy Virginian's faced. For Washington's situation, see Anderson, *Crucible of War*, 737–40.

5. Background on the Paxton Boys' insurrection can be found in Hindle, "The March of the Paxton Boys"; and Dunbar, *The Paxton Papers*, 3–51.

6. Dunbar, *The Paxton Papers*, 25–29; *Colonial Records*, 9:102.

7. *Colonial Records*, 9:131–34; Dunbar, *The Paxton Papers*, 38–39.

8. Dunbar, *The Paxton Papers*, 43–44.

9. The document known as "The Declaration and Remonstrance" can be found in *Colonial Records*, 9:138–42.

10. Information concerning the pamphlet war that broke out following the Paxton Boys' insurrection can be found in Olson, "The Pamphlet War over the Paxton Boys"; and Dunbar, *The Paxton Papers*, 48–51. Some historians have stressed that the Paxton Boys' rebellion was not a reflection of a growing internal revolutionary movement in which frontiersmen agitated

for more political democracy but a result of social unrest. Nonetheless, the dynamics of revolutionary sentiment must be viewed from varying perspectives that include social, economic, and political concerns. See Crowley, "The Paxton Disturbance and Ideas of Order."

11. For an overview of the Stamp Act, see Morgan and Morgan, *The Stamp Act Crisis*. Also see Nash, *The Urban Crucible*, 292–311; Anderson, *Crucible of War*, 641–708; and Jennings, *Empire of Fortune*, 463–64. On the frontier's lack of opposition to the act, see Frantz and Pencak, *Beyond Philadelphia*, xiv–xvii, 49.

12. Johnson to Gage, December 18, 1764, *Johnson Papers*, 4:623–26; Gage to Johnson, July 2, 1764, ibid., 11:249–50.

13. Gage to Halifax, December 13, 1764, *Gage Correspondence*, 1:44–47.

14. Johnson to Croghan, December 18, 1764, *Johnson Papers*, 11:509–10; Croghan to Johnson, January 1, 1765, ibid., 11:519–20; Johnson to Croghan, January 17, 1765, ibid., 11:536–38; Volwiler, *George Croghan and the Western Movement*, 176–78.

15. Gage to Johnson, April 15, 1765, *Johnson Papers*, 4:717–19; Gage to Johnson, March 31, 1765, ibid., 4:702–74; Croghan to McKee, December 6, 1764, HBP.

16. Barsotti, *Scoouwa*, 121–22; John Penn to Thomas Gage, March 21, 1765, *Johnson Papers*, 11:643–45. Perhaps the best secondary account of this incident can be found in Nye, *James Smith*, 13–15. For a wonderful fictionalized account of Smith's activities see, Swanson, *The First Rebel*. Although Swanson's is a work of historical fiction, he includes a useful appendix filled with primary-source documents.

17. Charles Grant to Bouquet, *Bouquet Papers*, 6:763–64.

18. "Deposition of Lt. Charles Grant," in Swanson, *The First Rebel*, 315–16; Barsotti, *Scoouwa*, 124.

19. Croghan to Johnson, March 12, 1765, *Johnson Papers*, 11:633–34; Nathaniel McCullough to George Croghan, March 12, 1765, ibid., 11:635–36. Gage wrote to Sir William Johnson complaining that the incident was the result of Croghan's "troubling his Head more about Trade than the Business he was employed in." See Gage to Johnson, April 15, 1765, ibid., 4:717; and Gage to Conway, May 6, 1765, *Gage Correspondence*, 1:90.

20. Lieutenant Charles Grant to Gage, August 24, 1765, in Swanson, *The First Rebel*, 363; *Pennsylvania Gazette*, March 27, 1765.

21. "Deposition of Lt. Charles Grant," in Swanson, *The First Rebel*, 316–17; "Statement of Ralph Nailer," ibid., 320; Deposition of Leonard McGlashan, ibid., 325–26.

22. Barsotti, *Scoouwa*, 124–25; "Deposition of Lt. Charles Grant," in Swanson, *The First Rebel*, 317–18.

23. Gage to Conway, May 6, 1766, *Gage Correspondence*, 91; Hawbaker, *Fort Loudon on the Frontier*, 61–63.

24. Barsotti, *Scoouwa*, 132–35; "Affidavit Concerning Fort Bedford," in Swanson, *The First Rebel*, 379–80. After the famous Black Boys' rebellion of 1765, Smith spent a great deal of time exploring Kentucky, several years in advance of Daniel Boone. When he returned to the Conococheague Valley in 1769, he resurrected his Black Boys to once again raid Indian trade convoys along the Forbes Road. At one point, Smith was arrested for murder and confined in the jail at Carlisle. Three hundred angry frontiersmen rallied near the jail to break Smith from confinement. He prevailed on the mob to allow him to stand trial according to the law, and he was later exonerated. During the American Revolution, Smith served as an assemblyman representing Westmoreland County. Later he organized a battalion of riflemen to serve as rangers. After the war, Smith moved his family to Kentucky, where he died in 1812.

25. Since the publication of Swanson's book *The First Rebel* in 1937, historians have debated the revolutionary nature of the Black Boys' rebellion. Eleanor Webster, in an article entitled "Insurrection at Fort Loudon in 1765: Rebellion or Preservation of the Peace?" downplayed the rebellious nature of the incident, claiming that the Black Boys were merely striving to uphold a law that others sought to ignore. Later historian Stephen H. Cutcliffe, in "The Sideling Hill Affair," attempted to compare the insurrection to a predisposed model established for recognizing revolutionary activity. Both works tend to be narrowly focus in that they overlook the sustained persistence of the rebellious activity by James Smith and his associates. Violence, complaints over the self-serving nature of the Indian trade, defiance to royal and provincial officials, and the willingness to rely on local control rather than distant authority, all characterized the nature of the frontier throughout the years leading up to the American Revolution. The arguments consistently advanced by backcountry inhabitants such as Smith were similar in tone to those made by revolutionary leaders like Patrick Henry and Samuel Adams. In sum, the linkage between the sentiments espoused on the frontier and those expressed by more recognizable revolutionary leaders should be apparent. For the connection between the Paxton Boys and the Black Boys, see Vaughan, "Frontier Banditti and the Indians."

26. Croghan to Johnson, March 21, 1765, *Johnson Papers*, 11:645–47; Alexander Fraser to Thomas Gage, April 27, 1765, Gage Papers, vol. 137.

27. "George Croghan's Journals, February 28, 1765–October 8, 1765," in Alvord and Carter, *The New Regime*, 4–5 (hereafter cited as Croghan's 1765 Journal).

28. Croghan to Sir William Johnson, May 13, 1765, *Johnson Papers*, 11:737–38; Croghan's 1765 Journal, 6–8. Neolin continued to be an influential holy man among the Delawares for a number of years. In 1766 two Presbyterian ministers, Charles Beatty and George Duffield, met Neolin along the Tuscarawas River at the Delaware village of Newcomer's Town (present-day

Newcomerstown, Ohio). By this time the prophet was eager to learn more about Christianity. Beatty recorded in his journal that Neolin had "been endeavouring to teach [the Delaware] Religion According to his light & attended on us privately as well as publickly in order to learn more about Religion." After Duffield "told him Some thing about the Promises of a saviour Jesus," Neolin "appeared very attentive & pleased to hear these things." Six years later another Presbyterian minister, David McClure, visited Newcomer's Town. Just prior to McClure's arrival a group of angry Delawares had banished Neolin from the village for failing to heal several ill residents. McClure had an opportunity to visit Neolin's house and confided to his diary that it was one of the best in the village. "A celler with stone wall—a stare case, a convenient stone chimney & fire place & closets & apartments, gave it the appearance of an english dwelling," McClure wrote. He also record that "between the house & the bank of the River was a regular & thrifty peach orchard. The house was for sale, but no one would purchase it. The price was fixed as low as one dollar. Such dread have they [the Indians] of the secret & invisible power of the Conjurors." It is ironic that a prophet who once vehemently preached against adopting any aspects of white culture would one day embrace such trappings of European life. No records have been found concerning Neolin following his expulsion from Newcomer's Town. See Klett, *Journals of Charles Beatty*, 65, 69–70; and Dexter, *Diary of David McClure*, 67–68.

29. Versions of this Indian conference can be found in Croghan's 1765 Journal, 10–19; and An Indian Congress, May 9–11, 1765, *Johnson Papers*, 11:723–34.

30. Croghan's 1765 Journal, 23, 38.

31. Fraser's activities at Fort Chartres are covered in a lengthy report he made to General Gage. See Fraser to Gage, April 27, 1765, Gage Papers, vol. 137.

32. Fraser to Gage, May 15, 1765, in Alvord, *The Critical Period*, 491–93; Fraser to Campbell, May 17, 1765, ibid., 493–94; Fraser to Gage, May 18, 1765, ibid., 494–95; Fraser to Campbell, May 20, 1765, ibid., 495–97.

33. Fraser to Gage, June 17, 1765, in Alvord, *The Critical Period*, 519.

34. Croghan's 1765 Journal, 29–30; Croghan to Murray, July 12, 1765, in Alvord and Carter, *The New Regime*, 58–59.

35. Croghan's 1765 Journal, 31–37.

36. Croghan to Johnson, November [?], 1765, in Alvord and Carter, *The New Regime*, 53.

37. The idea that other Indian leaders were jealous of Pontiac's undue influence is discussed in Peckham, *Pontiac and the Indian Uprising*, 287–89; and White, *The Middle Ground*, 312–13.

38. Croghan's 1765 Journal, 46–57.

39. Hutton, *Colonel Henry Bouquet, 60th Royal Americans,* 34–36; Reid to Bouquet, April 15, 1765, *Bouquet Papers,* 6:781–82.

40. For a discussion of conditions in West Florida, see Gipson, *The British Empire,* 9:200–231; Shy, *Toward Lexington,* 181–84, 282; and Howard, "Governor Johnstone in West Florida."

41. Information on Indian affairs in the Southern District can be found in Gipson, *The Triumphant Empire,* 218–24.

42. Bouquet to Benjamin Chew, July 2, 1765, *Bouquet Papers,* 6:797; Bouquet to Elizabeth Chew, July 2, 1765, ibid., 6:798; and Bouquet to Margaret Oswald, July 2, 1765, ibid., 6:799–800.

43. Branch, "Henry Bouquet: His Relic Possessions," 203–7. A map of the environs of Fort Saint George can be found in Gipson, *The Triumphant Empire,* 230.

44. Branch, "Henry Bouquet: Professional Soldier," 49–50; Branch, "Henry Bouquet: His Relic Possessions," 201–2; Cort, *Col. Henry Bouquet,* 77–78; *Pennsylvania Journal & Weekly Advertiser,* October 24, 1765.

45. Gage discussed his concern over the Stamp Act and withdrawal of troops from the frontier in Gage to Conway, September 23, 1765, *Gage Correspondence,* 65–68; and Gage to Conway, October 12, 1765, ibid., 69–70. General Gage's tenure as commander of British forces in North America ended with his withdrawal from Boston in August 1775. His only other military appointment during the American Revolution came when he was ordered to command the defense forces at Kent in 1781. He died in 1787.

46. The text of the Oswego negotiations can be found in O'Callaghan, *Documents Relative to the Colonial History of the State of New York,* 7: 854–67. Also see Peckham, *Pontiac and the Indian Uprising,* 288–97. For the prediction concerning Pontiac's death, see Norman MacLeod to Sir William Johnson, August 4, 1766, *Johnson Papers,* 12:150.

47. In his study published in 2002, *War under Heaven,* Gregory Dowd insists that Pontiac ignited a feud with the Peoria Indians when he stabbed one of their chiefs named Black Dog at Detroit in 1766. According to Dowd, Black Dog's family vowed revenge against the Ottawa chief. See Dowd, *War under Heaven,* 250, 260–62.

48. Pontiac's final years and eventual assassination are well covered in Peckham, *Pontiac and the Indian Uprising,* 298–318. Dowd offers compelling evidence that Pontiac was murdered in a Peoria Indian village near the town of Cahokia, not outside the Baynton, Wharton, and Morgan trading post. See Dowd, *War under Heaven,* 261.

49. Sipe, *Indian Wars of Pennsylvania,* 484–86.

50. For background discussion of the Treaty of Fort Stanwix, see McConnell, *A Country Between,* 238–57. Sir William Johnson continued to serve as an important figure in Indian affairs until his death in 1774. In fact,

he was in the midst of arbitrating yet another dispute between the Ohio Country Indians and the British when he collapsed and died. Johnson was succeeded as superintendent of Indian affairs by his nephew Guy Johnson, while his son, John Johnson, inherited the family estate. Both men became loyalists during the Revolution and were forced to flee to Canada.

51. For the contentious nature of boundary claims following the Treaty of Fort Stanwix, see Volwiler, *George Croghan and the Western Movement*, 261–77. George Croghan's land schemes never materialized, and he spent a great part of the remainder of his life attempting to escape debt. When he died on August 31, 1782, an inventory of his estate totaled little more than £50. He was buried in an unmarked grave at Saint Peter's Episcopal Church in Philadelphia. Two complimentary biographies have been written about Croghan's adventurous life. Readers are encouraged to consult Volwiler, *George Croghan and the Westward Movement*; and Wainwright, *George Croghan.* While Volwiler's volume was published before the discovery of a large cache of Croghan papers, it still contains valuable information not found in Wainwright's biography.

52. McConnell, *A Country Between*, 268–74; Volwiler, *George Croghan and the Western Movement* 295–96, 301–3.

53. Sipe, *Indian Wars of Pennsylvania*, 488–505. Kiasutha continued to serve as the voice of moderation during the early years of the American Revolution. The chief traveled throughout the Ohio River Valley, counseling the Mingo, Delaware, and Shawnee warriors to remain at peace. For his efforts the Continental Congress awarded him a colonel's commission and silver gorget. Younger, more vitriolic Iroquois, such as Joseph Brant, argued that the Americans desired to take Indian land and that the Iroquois should join with the British. Kiasutha eventually relented and took up the British cause. Along with Brant, he led warriors at the Battle of Oriskany. In 1782 he led a raiding party that destroyed the Pennsylvania settlement of Hannastown. After the revolution, Kiasutha's influence waned as his nephew, Cornplanter, became the leading spokesperson for the Allegheny Senecas. The chief died around 1798; the location of his grave is a matter of local legend throughout western Pennsylvania. Biographical information concerning Kiasutha can be found in Abler, "Kayahsota," *Dictionary of Canadian Biography*, 4:408–9; Sipe, *Indian Chiefs of Pennsylvania,* 371–408; and Miller, *Early Landmarks and Names.*

54. For a full discussion of Indian activities during the American Revolution, see Calloway, *The American Revolution in Indian Country.*

55. Williston, "Desperation on the Western Pennsylvania Frontier."

56. In the preface to his highly acclaimed study *The Urban Crucible*, Gary B. Nash compellingly argues that the "seaboard commercial cities were the cutting edge of economic, social, and political change" and the "crucibles

of revolutionary agitation." While it can and should not be denied that dissatisfaction among the lower classes in urban America helped to forge revolutionary sentiment, it is also important to address the "crucibles of revolutionary agitation" that took place in the interior as well. Nash himself acknowledges such ferment in his book *Red, White, and Black*, 264–66. In essence, the revolutionary experience should be understood in terms reflecting a variety of regions, ethnic groups, motivations, and perspectives.

57. The need to examine revolutionary expression from a regional perspective is discussed in Frantz and Pencak, *Beyond Philadelphia*, xviii–xxv.

58. Newland, *The Pennsylvania Militia*, 135–37. For a brilliant and engaging examination of Pennsylvania's backcountry soldier during the Revolution, see Knouff, "'An Arduous Service.'" While Knouff pays tribute to the fighting spirit of the frontier soldier, he quickly points out that many of the men in the ranks found service in the eastern theater of the war to be disquieting. For example, while the men from Thompson's battalion were among the first to report to Boston's plea for assistance, they were also among the first to mutiny in the Continental Army. This attitude seems in keeping with the fiercely independent nature that was legendary among frontier soldiers.

BIBLIOGRAPHY

PRIMARY SOURCES

Manuscript Collections

Amherst, Jeffery, Papers. William L. Clements Library. University of Michigan, Ann Arbor.

Amherst, Sir Jeffery, Papers, Great Britain, War Office 34 (148 microfilm reels). David Library of the American Revolution. Washington Crossing, Penn.

Bouquet, Henry, Papers, 1761–1765 (typescripts). State Archives. Pennsylvania Historical and Museum Commission, Harrisburg.

Fort Pitt Collection (MFF 0802). Western Pennsylvania Historical Society, Pittsburgh.

Fort Pitt Waste Book. Darlington Memorial Library. University of Pittsburgh.

Gage, Thomas, Papers. American Series, 1755–1775. William L. Clements Library. University of Michigan, Ann Arbor.

Logan Manuscript Collection. Historical Society of Pennsylvania, Philadelphia.

Porteous, John, Journal. Burton Historical Collections. Detroit Public Library.

Sterling, James, Letter Book. William L. Clements Library. University of Michigan, Ann Arbor.

Van Cleve, James. *Reminiscences of Early Steamboats and Sail Vessels on Lake Ontario with a History of the Introduction of the Propeller on the Lakes and Other Subjects with Illustrations* (1877). William L. Clements Library. University of Michigan, Ann Arbor.

Books

Alvord, Clarence W. *Collections of the Illinois State Historical Library.* Vol. 10, *The Critical Period, 1763–1765.* Springfield: Illinois State Historical Library, 1915.

Alvord, Clarence W., and Clarence Edwin Carter, eds. *The New Regime, 1765–1767.* Springfield: Illinois State Historical Library, 1916.

———, eds. *Trade and Politics, 1767–1769.* Springfield: Illinois State Historical Library, 1921.

Armour, David A., ed. *Attack at Michilimackinac: Alexander Henry's Travels and Adventures in Canada and the Indian Territories between the Years 1760 and 1764.* Mackinac Island, Mich.: Mackinac State Historical Parks, 1971.

———, ed. *Treason at Michilimackinac: The Proceedings of a General Court Martial Held at Montreal in October 1768 for the Trial of Major Robert Rogers.* Mackinac Island, Mich.: Mackinac State Historical Parks, 1972.

Barsotti, John J., ed. *Scoouwa: James Smith's Captivity Narrative.* Columbus: Ohio Historical Society, 1978.

Boyd, Julian, ed. *Indian Treaties Printed by Benjamin Franklin.* Philadelphia: Historical Society of Pennsylvania, 1938.

Browne, William Hand, and others, eds. *Archives of Maryland.* Baltimore: Maryland State Historical Society, 1883–2003. http://mdarchives.state. md.us.

Carter, Clarence Edwin, ed. *The Correspondence of General Thomas Gage with the Secretaries of State, 1763–1775.* 2 vols. New Haven: Yale University Press, 1931. Reprint, New York: Archon Books, 1969.

Dexter, Franklin B., ed. *Diary of David McClure.* New York: Knickerbocker Press, 1899. Reprint, Waterville: Rettig's Frontier Ohio, 1996.

Dunbar, John R., ed. *The Paxton Papers.* The Hague, The Netherlands: Martinus Nihoff, 1957.

Hamilton, Charles, ed. *Braddock's Defeat.* Norman: University of Oklahoma Press, 1959.

Hazard, Samuel, ed. *Colonial Records of Pennsylvania: Minutes of the Provincial Council of Pennsylvania.* 16 vols. Harrisburg, Penn.: Theodore Finn, 1851. Reprint, New York: AMS Press, 1968.

Heckewelder, John G. E. *A Narrative of the Mission of the United Brethren among the Delaware and Mohegan, from its Commencement, in the Year 1740, to the Close of the Year 1808.* Philadelphia: McCarty and Davis, 1820.

———. *History, Manners, and Customs of the Indian Nations Who Once Inhabited Pennsylvania and Neighboring States.* Philadelphia: Historical Society of Pennsylvania, 1876. Reprint, Bowie, Md.: Heritage Books, 1990.

Hough, Franklin B. *Diary of the Siege of Detroit in the War with Pontiac.* Albany: J. Munsell, 1860.

James, Alfred Proctor, ed. *Writings of General John Forbes Relating to His Service in North America.* Menasha, Wis.: Collegiate Press, 1938.

Kent, Donald H., ed. *Contrecoeur's Copy of George Washington's Journal for 1754.* Washington, D.C.: Eastern National Parks & Monument Association, 1989.

———. *The French Invasion of Western Pennsylvania, 1753.* Harrisburg: Pennsylvania Historical and Museum Commission, 1954.

Kirk, Robert. *The Memoirs and Adventures of Robert Kirk, Late of the Royal Highland Regiment.* Limerick, Ireland: J. Ferrar, [c. 1770].

Klett, Guy Soulliard, ed. *Journals of Charles Beatty, 1762–1769.* University Park: Penn State University Press, 1962.

Loudon, Archibald. *A Selection of Some of the Most Interesting Narratives of Outrages, Committed by the Indians in Their Wars with the White People.* Carlisle, Penn.: privately printed, 1808. Reprint, New York: Arno Press, 1971.

Lucier, Armand Francis, ed. *Pontiac's Conspiracy & Other Indian Affairs: Notices Abstracted from Colonial Newspapers, 1763–1765.* Bowie, Md.: Heritage Press, 2000.

Mante, Thomas. *The History of the Late War in North America.* London: W. Strahan and T. Cadell, 1772.

Moore, Charles E., ed. *The Gladwin Manuscripts.* Lansing, Mich.: Robert Smith Printing, 1897.

Morris, Thomas. *Miscellanies in Prose and Verse.* London: James Ridgway, 1791. Reprint, New Canaan, Conn.: Readex Microprint, 1966.

———. *Journal of Captain Thomas Morris.* New Canaan, Conn.: Readex Microprint Corporation, 1966.

Mulkearn, Lois, ed. *George Mercer Papers Relating to the Ohio Company of Virginia.* Pittsburgh: University of Pittsburgh Press, 1954.

O.Callaghan, Edmund B., ed.. *Documentary History of the State of New York.* 4 vols. Albany: Weed, Parsons, 1849–1851.

———, ed. *Documents Relative to the Colonial History of the State of New York,* 15 vols. Albany: Weed, Parsons, 1856–1887.

Pennsylvania Archives. 9 series. 138 vols. Philadelphia: various publishers, 1852–1949.

Pouchot, Pierre. *Memoirs on the Late War in North America between France and England.* Edited by Brian Leigh Dunnigan. Youngstown, N.Y.: Old Fort Niagara Association, 1994.

Quaife, Milo Milton, ed. *The Siege of Detroit in 1763: The Journal of Pontiac's Conspiracy and John Rutherford's Narrative of a Captivity.* Chicago: R. R. Donnelley & Sons, 1958.

Rogers, Robert, and Henry Bouquet. *Warfare on the Colonial Frontier: The Journal of Major Robert Rogers & an Historical Account of the Expedition against the Ohio Indians in the Year 1764, under the Command of Henry Bouquet, Esq.* London and Dublin, 1769. Facsimile reprint, Bargersville, Ind.: Dressler, 1997.

Seaver, James E., ed. *A Narrative of the Life of Mary Jemison.* Canandaigua, N.Y.: J. D. Bemis, 1824. Reprint, New York: American Scenic and Historic Preservation Society, 1982.

Smith, James. *An Account of the Remarkable Occurrences in the Life and Travels of Col. James Smith.* Lexington, Ky.: John Bradford, 1799.

———. *Treatise on the Mode and Manner of Indian War.* Paris, Ky.: Joel R. Lyle, 1812.

Smith, William. *An Historical Account of Bouquet's Expedition against the Ohio Indians, in 1764.* Philadelphia: 1765. Reprint, Cincinnati: Robert Clarke, 1868.

Stevens, Sylvester K., Donald H. Kent, Autumn Leonard, and Louis M. Waddell, eds. *The Papers of Henry Bouquet.* Harrisburg: Pennsylvania Historical and Museum Commission, 1951–1994.

Sullivan, James, et. al., eds. *The Papers of Sir William Johnson.* 14 vols. Albany: State University of New York Press, 1921–1963.

Thwaites, Reuben Gold, ed. *Early Western Travels, 1748–1846.* New York: AMS Press, 1966.

Thomson, Charles. *An Enquiry into the Causes of the Alienation of the Delaware and Shawanese Indians from the British Interest.* London: J. Wilkie, 1759.

Webster, J. Clarence, ed. *The Journal of Jeffery Amherst.* Chicago: University of Chicago Press, 1931.

Williams, Edward G. *Bouquet's March to the Ohio: The Forbes' Road.* Pittsburgh: Historical Society of Western Pennsylvania, 1975.

———. *The Orderly Book of Colonel Henry Bouquet's Expedition against the Ohio Indians, 1764.* Pittsburgh: Historical Society of Western Pennsylvania, 1960.

Zeisberger, David. *David Zeisberger's History of the North American Indians in 18th Century Ohio, New York & Pennsylvania.* Lewisburg, Penn.: Wennawoods, 1999.

Articles

Draper, Lyman C., ed. "Lieut. James Gorrell's Journal." *Wisconsin Historical Collections* 1 (1843): 39–47.

James, Alfred Proctor. "Fort Ligonier: Additional Light from Unpublished Documents." *Western Pennsylvania Historical Magazine* 17 (1934): 259–85.

Jordan, John W., ed. "James Kenny's 'Journal to Ye Westward,' 1758–59." *Pennsylvania Magazine of History and Biography* 37 (1913): 295–449.

———. "Journal of James Kenny, 1761–1763." *Pennsylvania Magazine of History and Biography* 37 (1913): 1–47, 152–201.

"Petition of John Metcalfe." *Western Pennsylvania Historical Magazine* 16 (August 1933): 197–204.

Trowbridge, Charles C., ed. "Conspiracy of Pontiac and the Siege of Detroit." *Michigan Pioneer and Historical Society Collections* 8 (1886): 340–69.

Volwiler, A. T., ed. "William Trent's Journal at Fort Pitt." *Mississippi Valley Historical Review* 11 (1924): 390–413.

Wainwright, Nicolas B. "George Croghan's Journal, 1759–1763." *Pennsylvania Magazine of History and Biography* 71 (October 1947): 305–444.

Williams, Edward G. "Pay List of the Militia at Fort Ligonier in 1763." *Western Pennsylvania Historical Magazine* 46 (1963): 249–57.

Newspapers

Pennsylvania Gazette, 1760–1765.
Pennsylvania Journal & Weekly Advertiser, 1760–1765.

SECONDARY SOURCES

Books

Alberts, Richard C. *A Charming Field for an Encounter: The Story of George Washington's Fort Necessity*. Washington, D.C.: Government Printing Office, 1991.

Alden, Richard. *General Gage in America*. Baton Rouge: Louisiana State University Press, 1948.

Anderson, Fred. *Crucible of War: The Seven Years' War and the Fate of Empire in British North America, 1754–1766*. New York: Knopf, 2000.

Anderson, Gary Clayton. *The Indian Southwest: Ethnogenesis and Reinvention*. Norman: University of Oklahoma Press, 1999.

Anderson, Niles. *The Battle of Bushy Run*. Harrisburg: Pennsylvania Historical and Museum Commission, 1966.

Ansel, William H., Jr. *Frontier Forts along the Potomac and Its Tributaries*. Parsons, W. Va.: McClain Printing, 1984.

Auth, Stephen F. *The Ten Years' War: Indian-White Relations in Pennsylvania, 1755–1765*. New York: Garland, 1989.

Brandão, José António. *"Your Fyre Shall Burn No More": Iroquois Policy toward New France and Its Native Allies to 1701*. Lincoln: University of Nebraska Press, 1997.

Brander, Michael. *The Scottish Highlanders and Their Regiments*. New York: Barnes & Noble Books, 1996.

Brumwell, Stephen. *Redcoats: The British Soldier and War in the Americas, 1755–1763*. Cambridge: Cambridge University Press, 2002.

Butterfield, Consul Willshire. *History of the Girtys*. Cincinnati: Robert Clarke & Company, 1890. reprint, Columbus: Long's College Books, 1950.

Calloway, Colin G. *The American Revolution in Indian Country: Crisis and Diversity in Native American Communities*. Cambridge: Cambridge University Press, 1995.

Connell, Evan S. *Son of the Morning Star*. New York: Harper Collins, 1991.

Cort, Cyrus. *Col. Henry Bouquet and His Campaigns of 1763 and 1764*. Lancaster, Penn.: Steinman & Hensel, 1883.

Craig, Neville B., ed. *The Olden Time*, 2 vols. Pittsburgh: Wright & Charlton, 1848. Reprint, Lewisburg, Penn.: Wennawoods, 2002.

Cuneo, John R. *Robert Rogers of the Rangers*. New York: Oxford University Press, 1959. Reprint, Ticonderoga, N.Y.: Fort Ticonderoga Museum, 1988.

Darlington, Mary C., ed. *Fort Pitt and Letters from the Frontier*. Pittsburgh: J. R. Weldin, 1892. Reprint, New York: Arno Press, 1971.

Dictionary of American Biography. 21 vols. New York: Charles Scribner's Sons, 1935–1943.

Dictionary of Canadian Biography. 12 vols. Toronto: University of Toronto Press. 1966–1991.

Doddridge, Joseph. *Notes on the Settlement and Indian Wars of the Western Parts of Virginia and Pennsylvania*. Pittsburgh: John S. Ritenour and William T. Lindsey, 1912.

Dowd, Gregory Evans. *A Spirited Resistance: The North American Indian Struggle for Unity, 1745–1815*. Baltimore: Johns Hopkins University Press, 1992.

———. *War under Heaven: Pontiac, the Indian Nations and the British Empire*. Baltimore: Johns Hopkins University Press, 2002.

Dunnigan, Brian Leigh. *A History and Guide to Old Fort Niagara*. Youngstown, N.Y.: Old Fort Niagara Association, 1985.

———. *Siege—1759: The Campaign against Niagara*. Youngstown, N.Y.: Old Fort Niagara Association, 1996.

Eckert, Allan W. *The Conquerors*. Boston: Little, Brown, 1970.

Edmunds, R. David. *The Potawatomis: Keepers of the Fire*. Norman: University of Oklahoma Press, 1978.

Egle, William H. *An Illustrated History of the Commonwealth of Pennsylvania*. Harrisburg, Penn.: De Witt C. Goodrich & Company, 1876.

Fenton, William. *The Great Law and the Longhouse: A Political History of the Iroquois Confederacy*. Norman: University of Oklahoma Press, 1998.

Flexner, James. *Mohawk Baronet: Sir William Johnson of New York*. New York: Harper & Brothers, 1959.

Franklin County (Penn.) Schools. *Franklin County School Annual: Programme of the Fifty-ninth Annual Session Teacher's Institute, November 17–21, 1913.* Chambersburg, Penn.: Franklin County Public Schools, 1913.

———. *Franklin County School Annual, for the School Term of 1933–34.* Chambersburg, Penn.: n.p., 1934.

Frantz, John B., and William Pencak. *Beyond Philadelphia: The American Revolution in the Pennsylvania Hinterland.* University Park: Penn State University Press, 2000.

Gipson, Lawrence Henry. *The British Empire before the American Revolution.* 15 vols. New York: Knopf, 1956.

Godfrey, William G. *Pursuit of Profit and Preferment in Colonial North America: John Bradstreet's Quest.* Waterloo, Ontario: Wilfred Laurier University Press, 1982.

Hamilton, Milton W. *Sir William Johnson: Colonial American.* Port Washington, N.Y.: Kennikat Press, 1976.

Hanna, Charles A. *The Wilderness Trail, or the Ventures and Adventures of the Pennsylvania Traders on the Allegheny Path.* 2 vols. New York: G. P. Putnam's Sons, 1911. Reprint, Lewisburg, Penn.: Wennawoods, 1995.

Hatcher, Harlan. *Lake Erie.* Indianapolis: Bobbs-Merrill, 1945.

Hawbaker, Gary. *Fort Loudon on the Frontier, 1756 1766.* York, Penn.: privately printed, 1976.

Holton, Woody. *Forced Founders: Indians, Debtors, Slaves, and the Making of the American Revolution in Virginia.* Chapel Hill: University of North Carolina Press, 1999.

Hunter, William A. *Forts on the Pennsylvania Frontier, 1753–1758.* Harrisburg: Pennsylvania Historical and Museum Commission, 1960. Reprint, Lewisburg, Penn.: Wennawoods, 1999.

Hutton, Edward. *Colonel Henry Bouquet, 60th Royal Americans, 1756–1765.* Winchester, UK: Warren & Son, 1911.

Jackson, H. M. *Rogers' Rangers.* Ottawa: privately printed, 1953.

James, Alfred Proctor, and Charles M. Stotz. *Drums in the Forest.* Pittsburgh: Historical Society of Western Pennsylvania, 1958.

Jennings, Francis. *The Ambiguous Iroquois Empire: The Covenant Chain Confederation of Indian Tribes with English Colonies from Its Beginnings to the Lancaster Treaty of 1744.* New York: W. W. Norton, 1984.

———. *Empire of Fortune: Crowns, Colonies, and Tribes in the Seven Years War in America.* New York: W. W. Norton, 1988.

Leach, Douglas E. *Arms for Empire: A Military History of the British Colonies in North America, 1607–1763.* New York: Macmillan, 1973.

———. *Roots of Conflict: The British Soldier and War in the Americas, 1755–1763.* Chapel Hill: University of North Carolina Press, 1986.

Lewis, Thomas A. *For King and Country: George Washington, The Early Years.* New York: John Wiley, 1993.

Loescher, Burt Garfield. *The History of Rogers Rangers.* Vol. 1, *The Beginnings, January 1755–April 6, 1758.* San Francisco: privately printed, 1946. Reprint, Bowie, Md.: Heritage Books, 2001.

———. *Genesis, The History of Rogers Rangers.* Vol. 2, *The First Green Berets: The Corps & the Revivals, April 6, 1758–December 24, 1783.* San Mateo, Calif.: privately printed, 1969. Reprint, Bowie, Md.: Heritage Books, 2000.

———. *The History of Rogers Ranger.* Vol. 3, *Officers and Non-commissioned Officers of Rogers' Rangers.* Burlingame, Calif.: privately printed, 1957. Reprint, Bowie, Md.: Heritage Books, 2000.

Long, J. C. *Lord Jeffery Amherst: A Soldier of the King.* New York: Macmillan, 1933.

May, Robin, and G. A. Embleton, *Wolfe's Army.* London: Osprey Books, 1995.

Mayo, L. S. *Jeffery Amherst: A Biography.* New York: Longmans, Green, and Co., 1916.

McCardell, Lee. *Ill-Starred General: Braddock of the Cold Stream Guards.* Pittsburgh: University of Pittsburgh Press, 1958.

McConnell, Michael N. *A Country Between: The Upper Ohio Valley and Its People, 1724–1774.* Lincoln: University of Nebraska Press, 1992.

Merrell, James H. *Into the American Woods: Negotiators on the Pennsylvania Frontier.* New York: W. W. Norton, 1999.

Miller, Annie Clark. *Early Landmarks and Names of Old Pittsburgh.* Pittsburgh: Daughters of the American Revolution, 1923.

Mochnick, John W. *History of Penn Township.* Greensburg, Penn.: South Greensburg Printing, 1982.

Montgomery, Thomas Lynch. *Report of the Commission to Locate the Site of the Frontier Forts of Pennsylvania.* 2 vols. Harrisburg, Penn.: William Stanley Ray, State Printer, 1916.

Morgan, Edmund S., and Helen M. Morgan. *The Stamp Act Crisis.* New York: Collier Books, 1963.

Nash, Gary B. *Red, White, and Black: The Peoples of Early North America.* 4th ed. Upper Saddle River, N.J.: Prentice Hall, 2000.

———. *The Urban Crucible: Social Change, Political Consciousness, and the Origins of the American Revolution.* Cambridge, Mass.: Harvard University Press, 1979.

Nelson, Larry L. *A Man of Distinction among Them: Alexander McKee and British-Indian Affairs along the Ohio Country Frontier, 1754–1799.* Kent, Ohio: Kent State University Press, 2001.

Nester, William. *Haughty Conquerors: Amherst and the Great Indian Uprising of 1763.* Westport, Conn.: Praeger, 2000.

Nevins, Allan, ed. *Ponteach; or the Savages of America: A Tragedy.* Chicago: Caxton Club, 1914.

Newland, Samuel J. *The Pennsylvania Militia: The Early Years, 1669–1792.* Annville: Pennsylvania National Guard Foundation, 1997.

Nixon, Lily Lee. *James Burd: Frontier Defender, 1726–1793.* Philadelphia: University of Pennsylvania Press, 1941.

Nye, Wilbur S. *James Smith: Early Cumberland County Patriot.* Carlisle, Penn.: Cumberland County Historical Society, 1960.

O'Neil, James F., II. *Their Bearing Is Noble and Proud: A Collection of Narratives Regarding the Appearance of Native Americans from 1740 to 1815.* Dayton: JTGS, 1995.

Palmer, Friend. *Early Days in Detroit.* Detroit: Hunt & June, 1906. Reprint, Detroit: Gale Research, 1979.

Parkman, Francis. *The Conspiracy of Pontiac and the Indian War after the Conquest of Canada,* 2 vols. Boston: Little, Brown & Company, 1851. Reprint, Lincoln: University of Nebraska Press, 1994.

———. *Montcalm and Wolfe: The French and Indian War.* Boston: Little, Brown & Company, 1894. Reprint, New York: Da Capo Press, 1995.

Patterson, A. W. *History of the Backwoods; or, The Region of the Ohio.* Pittsburgh: privately printed, 1843.

Peckham, Howard H. *Pontiac and the Indian Uprising.* Princeton: Princeton University Press, 1947. Reprinted with foreword by John C. Dann, Detroit: Wayne State University Press, 1994. Page references are to the 1994 edition unless otherwise noted.

———. *Life in Detroit under Pontiac's Siege.* Detroit: Wayne State University Press, 1964.

Pound, Arthur. *Johnson of the Mohawks: A Biography of Sir William Johnson, Irish Immigrant, Mohawk War Chief, American Soldier, Empire Builder.* New York: Macmillan, 1930. Reprint, Freeport, N.Y.: Books for Libraries Press, 1971.

Rasmussen, Robert M. S., and Robert S. Tilton. *George Washington: The Man behind the Myth.* Charlottesville: University Press of Virginia, 1999.

Richards, Frederick B. *The Black Watch at Ticonderoga and Major Duncan Campbell of Inverawe.* Bowie, Md.: Heritage Books, 1999.

Richter, Daniel K., and James H. Merrell, eds. *Beyond the Covenant Chain: The Iroquois and Their Neighbors in Indian North America, 1600–1800.* New York: Syracuse University Press, 1987.

Rough, Rollin S. *The Frontier Forts of Franklin, Pennsylvania: Machault, Venango, Franklin.* Franklin, Penn.: Venango County Museum Corporation, 1962.

Rupp, I. D. *Early History of Western Pennsylvania.* Harrisburg, Penn., 1846. Reprint, Lewisburg, Penn.: Wennawoods, 2001.

Sargent, Winthrop, ed. *A History of an Expedition against Fort Duquesne in 1755; Under Major General Edward Braddock.* Philadelphia: Lippincott, Grambo, & Company, 1855. Reprint, New York: Arno Press, 1971.

Sayre, G. M. *Les Sauvages Americains: Representations of Native Americans in French and English Colonial Literature.* Chapel Hill: University of North Carolina Press, 1997.

Shannon, Timothy J. *Indians and Colonists at the Crossroads of Empire: The Albany Congress of 1754.* New York: Cornell University Press, 2002.

Shy, John. *Toward Lexington: The Role of the British Army in the Coming of the American Revolution.* Princeton: Princeton University Press, 1965.

Sipe, C. Hale. *Fort Ligonier and Its Times.* Harrisburg, Penn.: Telegraph Press, 1932. Reprint, Ligonier, Penn.: Fort Ligonier Memorial Foundation, 1976.

———. *Indian Chiefs of Pennsylvania.* Butler, Penn.: privately printed, 1927. Reprint, Lewisburg, Penn.: Wennawoods, 1994.

———. *The Indian Wars of Pennsylvania.* Harrisburg, Penn.: Telegraph Press, 1931. Reprint, Lewisburg, Penn.: Wennawoods, 1995.

Sosin, Jack M. *Whitehall and the Wilderness: The Middle West in British Colonial Policy, 1760–1775.* Lincoln: University of Nebraska Press, 1961.

Starkey, Armstrong. *European and Native American Warfare, 1675–1815.* Norman: University of Oklahoma Press, 1998.

Steele, Ian. *Warpaths: Invasions of North America.* Oxford: Oxford University Press, 1994.

Stone, William L., Jr. *Life and Times of Sir William Johnson.* Albany: J. Munsell, 1865.

Stotz, Charles M. *The Model of Fort Pitt: Britain's Greatest American Stronghold.* Pittsburgh: Fort Pitt Museum, 1970.

———. *The Story of Fort Ligonier.* Ligonier, Penn.: Fort Ligonier Memorial Foundation, 1954.

Swanson, Neil. *The First Rebel.* New York: Farrar & Rinehart, 1937.

Tanner, Helen Hornbeck. *Atlas of Great Lakes Indian History.* Norman: University of Oklahoma Press, 1986.

Thayer, Theodore. *Pennsylvania Politics and the Growth of Democracy.* Harrisburg: Pennsylvania Historical and Museum Commission, 1953.

Todish, Timothy J., and Gary S. Zaboly, eds. *The Annotated and Illustrated Journals of Major Robert Rogers.* Fleischmanns, N.Y.: Purple Mountain Press, 2002.

Volwiler, Albert T. *George Croghan and the Westward Movement, 1741–1782.* Cleveland: Arthur H. Clark, 1926.

Waddell, Louis M., and Bruce D. Bomberger. *The French and Indian War in Pennsylvania, 1753–1763: Fortifications and Struggle during the War for Empire.* Harrisburg: Pennsylvania Historical and Museum Commission, 1996.

Wainwright, Nicholas B. *George Croghan: Wilderness Diplomat*. Chapel Hill: University of North Carolina Press, 1959.

Wallace, Anthony F. C. *King of the Delawares: Teedyuscung, 1700–1763*. Philadelphia: University of Pennsylvania Press, 1949. Reprint, New York: Syracuse University Press, 1990.

Wallace, Paul A. W. *Conrad Weiser: Friend of Colonist and Mohawk*. Philadelphia: University of Pennsylvania Press, 1945. Reprint, Lewisburg, Penn.: Wennawoods, 1996.

———. *Indians in Pennsylvania*. Harrisburg: Pennsylvania Historical and Museum Commission, 1961.

———. *Thirty Thousand Miles with John Heckewelder, or Travels among the Indians of Pennsylvania, New York and Ohio in the 18th Century*. Pittsburgh: University of Pittsburgh Press, 1958. Reprint, Lewisburg, Penn.: Wennawoods, 1998.

Waterman, Joseph M. *With Sword and Lancet: The Life of General Hugh Mercer*. Richmond, Va.: Garrett & Massie, 1941.

White, Richard. *The Middle Ground: Indians, Empires, and Republics in the Great Lakes Region, 1650–1815*. Cambridge: Cambridge University Press, 1991.

Articles

Axtell, James. "The White Indians of Colonial America," *William and Mary Quarterly*, 3rd series, 32 (1975): 55–88.

Branch, E. Douglas. "Henry Bouquet: His Relic Possessions." *Western Pennsylvania Historical Magazine* 22 (1939): 201–8.

———. "Henry Bouquet: Professional Soldier," *Pennsylvania Magazine of History and Biography* 62 (1938): 41–51.

Brodine, Charles E., Jr. "Henry Bouquet and British Infantry Tactics on the Ohio Frontier." In *The Sixty Years' War for the Great Lakes, 1754–1814*, edited by David Curtis Skaggs and Larry L. Nelson. East Lansing: Michigan State University Press, 2001.

Brumwell, Stephen. "'A Service Truly Critical': The British Army and Warfare with the North American Indians, 1755–1764." *War in History* 5 (1998): 146–75.

Cornu, Donald. "Captain Lewis Ourry, Royal American Regiment of Foot." *Pennsylvania History* 19 (1952): 249–61.

Crowley, James E. "The Paxton Disturbance and Ideas of Order in Pennsylvania." *Pennsylvania History* 37 (October 1970): 317–39.

Cutcliffe, Stephen H. "The Sideling Hill Affair: The Cumberland County Riots of 1765." *Western Pennsylvania Historical Magazine* 59 (1976): 39–53.

Daudelin, Don. "Numbers and Tactics at Bushy Run." *Western Pennsylvania Historical Magazine* 68 (April 1985): 153–79.

Dowd, Gregory. "The French King Wakes Up in Detroit: 'Pontiac's War' in Rumor and History." *Ethnohistory* 37 (1990): 254–78.

———. "Thinking and Believing: Nativism and Unity in the Ages of Pontiac and Tecumseh," *American Indian Quarterly* 16 (1992): 309–36.

Eid, Leroy V. "'A Kind of Running Fight': Indian Battlefield Tactics in the Late Eighteenth Century." *Western Pennsylvania Magazine of History* 71 (April 1988): 147–71.

Ewing, William S. "Indian Captives Released by Colonel Bouquet." *Western Pennsylvania Magazine of History* 39 (fall 1956): 187–203.

Finn, Elizabeth. "Biological Warfare in Eighteenth-Century North America: Beyond Jeffery Amherst." *Journal of American History* 86 (2000): 1552–80.

Fisher, George Harrison. "Brigadier-General Henry Bouquet." *Pennsylvania Magazine of History and Biography* 3 (1879): 121–43.

Hindle, Brook. "The March of the Paxton Boys." *William and Mary Quarterly*, 3rd series, 3 (1946): 461–86.

Howard, C. N. "Governor Johnstone in West Florida." *Florida Historical Quarterly* 17 (1953): 281–303.

Humphrey, Helen F. "The Identity of Major Gladwin's Informant." *Mississippi Valley Historical Review* 21 (1934): 147–62.

Hunter, Charles E. "The Delaware Nativist Revival of the Mid-eighteenth Century." *Ethnohistory* 18 (1971): 39–49.

Hunter, William A. "Thomas Barton and the Forbes' Expedition." *Pennsylvania Magazine of History and Biography* 95 (October 1971): 431–83.

———. "Traders on the Ohio, 1730." *Western Pennsylvania Historical Magazine* 35 (June 1952): 85–92.

———. "Victory at Kittanning." *Pennsylvania History* 23 (July 1956): 376–407.

Jacobs, Wilbur. "Was the Pontiac Uprising a Conspiracy?" *Ohio Archaeological and Historical Quarterly* 51 (1950): 26–37.

Jennings, Francis. "A Brahmin among Untouchables." *William and Mary Quarterly*, 3rd series, 42 (1985): 305–28.

———. "A Vanishing Indian: Francis Parkman versus His Sources." *Pennsylvania Magazine of History and Biography* 87 (July 1963): 306–23.

Kamprad, Walter. "John Ormsby, Pittsburgh's Original Citizen." *Western Pennsylvania Historical Magazine* 23 (1940): 203–22.

Ketcham, Ralph L. "Conscience, War, and Politics in Pennsylvania, 1755–1757." *William and Mary Quarterly*, 3rd series, 20 (1963): 416–39.

Knouff, Gregory T. "'An Arduous Service': The Pennsylvania Backcountry Soldiers' Revolution." *Pennsylvania History* 61 (January 1994): 45–74.

Lewin, Howard. "A Frontier Diplomat: Andrew Montour." *Pennsylvania History* 33 (1966): 153–86.

Manders, Eric I. "Conococheague Rangers, Cumberland County, Pennsylvania, 1763" *Military Collector and Historian* 46 (fall 1994): 128–29.

Marietta, Jack D. "Conscience, the Quaker Community, and the French and Indian War." *Pennsylvania Magazine of History and Biography* 95 (January 1971): 3–27.

Merrell, James. "'The Cast of His Countenance': Reading Andrew Montour." In *Through a Glass Darkly: Reflections on Personal Identity in Early America,* edited by Ronald Hoffman, Mechal Sobol, and Fredrika J. Teute. Chapel Hill: University of North Carolina Press, 1997.

Mulkearn, Lois. "Half King, Seneca Diplomat of the Ohio Valley." *Western Pennsylvania Historical Magazine* 37 (summer 1954): 64–81.

Myers, James P., Jr. "Pennsylvania's Awakening: The Kittanning Raid of 1756." *Pennsylvania History* 66 (summer 1999): 399–420.

Olson, Alison. "The Pamphlet War over the Paxton Boys." *Pennsylvania Magazine of History and Biography* 123 (January–April 1999): 31–55.

Peckham, Howard H. "The Sources and Revisions of Parkman's *Pontiac.*" *Papers of the Bibliographic Society of America* 37 (1943): 298–99.

Ranlet, Philip. "The British, the Indians, and Smallpox: What Actually Happened at Fort Pitt in 1763?" *Pennsylvania History* 67 (summer 2000): 427–41.

Robbins, Edward E. "Life and Services of Colonel Henry Bouquet." *Western Pennsylvania Historical Magazine* 3 (1920): 120–39.

Russell, Peter. "Redcoats in the Wilderness: British Officers and Irregular Warfare in Europe and America, 1740–1760." *William and Mary Quarterly,* 3rd series, 35 (October 1978): 629–52.

Schazmann, Paul-Emile. "Henry Bouquet in Switzerland." *Pennsylvania History* 19 (July 1952): 237–48.

Stephenson, R. Scott. "Provincial Soldiers in the Seven Years' War." *Pennsylvania History* 62 (spring 1995): 196–212.

Vaughan, Alden T. "Frontier Banditti and the Indians: The Paxton Boys' Legacy, 1763–1775." *Pennsylvania History* 51 (January 1984): 1–29.

Waddell, Louis M. "Defending the Long Perimeter: Forts on the Pennsylvania, Maryland, and Virginia Frontier, 1755–1765." *Pennsylvania History* 62 (spring 1995): 171–95.

Wallace, Anthony F. C. "New Religions among the Delaware Indians." *Southwest Journal of Anthropology* 12 (1956): 1–21.

Ward, Matthew C. "An Army of Servants: The Pennsylvania Regiment during the Seven Years' War." *Pennsylvania Magazine of History and Biography* 119 (January–April 1995): 75–93.

———. "'The European Method of Warring Is Not Practiced Here': The Failure of British Military Policy in the Ohio Valley, 1755–1759." *War in History* 4 (1997): 247–63.

———. "Redeeming the Captives: Pennsylvania Captives among the Ohio Indians, 1755–1765." *Pennsylvania Magazine of History and Biography* 125 (July 2001): 161–89.

Webster, Eleanor. "Insurrection at Fort Loudon in 1765: Rebellion or Preservation of the Peace." *Western Pennsylvania Historical Magazine* 47 (1964): 125–39.

Williston, George C. "Desperation on the Western Pennsylvania Frontier: A 1781 Petition to Congress for More Effective Defense." *Pennsylvania History* 67 (spring 2000): 298–311.

Williams, Edward G. "The Prevosts of the Royal Americans." *Western Pennsylvania Historical Magazine* 56 (1973): 1–38.

Young, Henry J. "A Note on Scalp Bounties in Pennsylvania." *Pennsylvania History* 24 (1957): 207–18.

INDEX

Relying on extensive research, including
sources unavailable to earlier historians,
Never Come to Peace Again broadens understanding of the social and political climate
that led to the American Revolution.

VOLUME 7 IN THE CAMPAIGNS AND COMMANDERS SERIES

DAVID DIXON is Professor of History at
Slippery Rock University, Pennsylvania. He
is the author of the award-winning book
*Hero of Beecher Island: The Life and Military
Career of George A. Forsyth.*

On the jacket: The Conspiracy-Fort Michilimackinac, by
Robert Griffing. On June 2, 1763, a group of Chippewa
and Sauk Indians attacked the British garrison during a
lacrosse game. This painting depicts the Indians discussing their plan of attack. Courtesy Paramount Press.